Sanctuary Practices in International Perspectives

Sanctuary Practices in International Perspectives examines the diverse, complex, and mutating practice of providing sanctuary to asylum-seekers. The ancient tradition of church sanctuary underwent a revival in the late 1970s. Immigrants living without legal status and their supporters, first in the United Kingdom, and then in the US, Canada, and elsewhere in Europe, have resorted to sanctuary practices to avoid and resist arrest and deportation by state authorities. Sanctuary appeared amidst a dramatic rise in asylum-seekers arriving in Western countries and a simultaneous escalation in national and international efforts to discourage and control their arrival and presence through myriad means, including deportation. This collection of chapters by prominent US, European, Canadian, and Japanese scholars is the first to place contemporary sanctuary practices in international, theoretical, and historical perspective. Moving beyond isolated case studies of sanctuary activities and movements, it reveals sanctuary as a far more complex, varied, theoretically rich, and institutionally adaptable set of practices.

Randy K. Lippert is Professor at the University of Windsor, Canada. He specializes in socio-legal studies and is the author of *Sanctuary, Sovereignty, Sacrifice: Canadian Sanctuary Incidents, Power, and Law* (UBC Press, 2006), co-editor (with Aaron Doyle and David Lyon) of *Eyes Everywhere: the Global Growth of Camera Surveillance* (Routledge, 2011) and (with Kevin Walby) of *Policing Cities* (Routledge, 2013).

Sean Rehaag (SJD, University of Toronto) is Associate Professor at Osgoode Hall Law School, York University, where he specializes in immigration and refugee law.

Sanctuary Practices in International Perspectives

Migration, citizenship and social movements

Edited by
Randy K. Lippert and Sean Rehaag

First published 2013
by Routledge
2 Park Square, Milton Park, Abingdon, Oxfordshire OX14 4RN

Simultaneously published in the USA and Canada
by Routledge
711 Third Avenue, New York, NY 10017

A GlassHouse Book

First issued in paperback 2014

Routledge is an imprint of the Taylor & Francis Group, an informa business

© 2013 Randy K. Lippert and Sean Rehaag

The right of Randy K. Lippert and Sean Rehaag to be identified as the editors of this work, and the contributors of their individual chapters, has been asserted by them in accordance with sections 77 and 78 of the Copyright, Designs and Patents Act 1988.

All rights reserved. No part of this book may be reprinted or reproduced or utilised in any form or by any electronic, mechanical, or other means, now known or hereafter invented, including photocopying and recording, or in any information storage or retrieval system, without permission in writing from the publishers.

Trademark notice: Product or corporate names may be trademarks or registered trademarks, and are used only for identification and explanation without intent to infringe.

British Library Cataloguing in Publication Data
A catalogue record for this book is available from the British Library

Library of Congress Cataloging in Publication Data
A catalog record for this book has been requested

ISBN 978-0-415-67346-4 (hbk)
ISBN 978-1-138-78914-2 (pbk)
ISBN 978-0-203-12894-7 (ebk)

Typeset in Baskerville
by Taylor & Francis Books

Contents

Notes on contributors   viii
Foreword: *The Ambiguity of Migration*   xii
Acknowledgements   xv
List of abbreviations   xvi

Introduction: sanctuary across countries, institutions, and disciplines   1
RANDY K. LIPPERT AND SEAN REHAAG

PART I
Sanctuary perspectives: historical, theological, legal, theoretical   13

1   Sanctuary for crime in the early common law   15
KARL SHOEMAKER

2   'I took up the case of the stranger': arguments from faith, history and law   28
DAVID H. MICHELS AND DAVID BLAIKIE

3   The potential of sanctuary: acts of sanctuary through the lens of camp   43
AGNES CZAJKA

4   Sanctuary *sans frontières*: social movements and solidarity in post-war Northern France   57
NAOMI MILLNER

PART II
Sanctuary movements and practices in the United States: old and new 71

5 Legacies and origins of the 1980s US–Central American sanctuary movement 73
HECTOR PERLA JR. AND SUSAN BIBLER COUTIN

6 The voice of the voiceless: religious rhetoric, undocumented immigrants, and the New Sanctuary Movement in the United States 92
MARTA CAMINERO-SANTANGELO

7 'I didn't know if this was sanctuary': strategic adaptation in the US New Sanctuary Movement 106
GRACE YUKICH

PART III
Sanctuary movements and practices in Europe and Canada: international comparative and case studies 119

8 Holy territories and hospitality: Nordic exceptionality and national differences of sanctuary incidents 121
JILL LOGA, MIIKKA PYYKKÖNEN AND HANNE STENVAAG

9 The rise and features of church asylum in Germany: 'I will take refuge in the shadow of thy wings until the storms are past' 135
WOLF-DIETER JUST

10 Ethnography of relationships among church sanctuary actors in Germany 148
HIROSHI ODA

11 The emergence of the Ontario Sanctuary Coalition: from humanitarian and compassionate review to civil initiative 162
HILARY CUNNINGHAM

12 Religious sanctuary in France and Canada 175
CAROLINE PATSIAS AND NASTASSIA WILLIAMS

PART IV
Emergent realms: Cities of Sanctuary and military sanctuaries 189

13 Everyday enactments of sanctuary: the UK *City of Sanctuary* movement 191
JONATHAN DARLING AND VICKI SQUIRE

14 The birth of a *sanctuary-city*: a history of governmental sanctuary in San Francisco 205
PETER MANCINA

15 The city as a sanctuary in the United States 219
JENNIFER RIDGLEY

16 Seeking sanctuary in a border city: sanctuary movement(s) across the Canada–US border 232
JULIE E.E. YOUNG

17 Framing militant sanctuary practices in Afghanistan and Iraq, 2001–11 245
MICHAEL A. INNES

Index 258

Notes on contributors

Susan Bibler Coutin is Professor in the departments of Criminology, Law and Society and Anthropology at the University of California, Irvine, where she is also Associate Dean of the Graduate Division. She is the author of *The Culture of Protest: Religious Activism and the US Sanctuary Movement* (Westview, 1993), *Legalizing Moves: Salvadoran Immigrants' Struggle for US Residency* (University of Michigan Press, 2000), and *Nations of Emigrants: Shifting Boundaries of Citizenship in El Salvador and the United States* (Cornell University Press, 2007).

David Blaikie is a faculty member of the Schulich School of Law at Dalhousie University, Halifax, Nova Scotia.

Marta Caminero-Santangelo is Professor in the English Department at the University of Kansas. She is the author of *On Latinidad: US Latino Literature and the Construction of Ethnicity* and *The Madwoman Can't Speak: Or Why Insanity Is Not Subversive*, and is working on a new book, *Documenting the Undocumented*.

Hilary Cunningham is Associate Professor of Cultural Anthropology at the University of Toronto. Her ethnography of the U.S. Sanctuary Movement, *God and Caesar at the Rio Grade* (University of Minnesota Press, 1995) won a Choice Outstanding Academic Book award. Her current research is based in northern Ontario and explores what she terms 'gated ecologies', especially those pertaining to wildlife sanctuaries, nature reserves and wilderness areas.

Agnes Czajka is Lecturer in the Department of Sociology at the University College Cork, Ireland. Her research interests include contemporary social and political thought, continental political philosophy, critical citizenship studies, nationalism, and refugee and minority politics in Europe and the Mediterranean region.

Jonathan Darling is Lecturer in Human Geography at the University of Manchester. His research focuses on the spatial politics of asylum, geographical ethics, and the politics of everyday urban life. He has published articles on hospitality, responsibility, and asylum in *Environment and Planning*

D: Society and Space, *Transactions of the Institute of British Geographers*, and *Political Geography*.

Michael A. Innes has published widely in both scholarly and popular media outlets. He is Director of Thesiger & Company (www.thesigers.com), an emerging markets research and advisory firm based in London, and is affiliated with the universities of Leeds, London (SOAS), and Syracuse. From 2003 to 2009, he served in Belgium, Bosnia-Herzegovina, Kosovo, and Afghanistan as a civilian staff officer with NATO.

Wolf-Dieter Just PhD theology (University of Heidelberg), is retired Professor of Social Ethics and Social Philosophy at the Protestant University of Applied Sciences, Bochum (Germany), where he still teaches. He was Chairman of the German Ecumenical Committee on Church Asylum from 1994 to 2004 (and has been honorary chairman since 2004). He has published many books and articles on issues of migration, asylum, and church asylum.

Randy K. Lippert is Professor of Sociology and Criminology at the University of Windsor, Canada, where he specializes in governance and socio-legal studies. He is the author of *Sanctuary, Sovereignty, Sacrifice: Canadian Sanctuary Incidents, Power, and Law* (UBC Press, 2006), co-editor (with David Lyon and Aaron Doyle) of *Eyes Everywhere: The Global Growth of Camera Surveillance* (Routledge, 2011) and (with Kevin Walby) of *Policing Cities* (Routledge, 2013). He is currently researching the securitization of Canadian cities.

Jill Loga, DrPolit (1972), works at the Uni Rokkan Centre in Norway. Her fields of research include immigration policy, projects on integration in local communities, the Nordic model, and policy of health and quality of life. She was a member of the government-appointed commission to outline a holistic, Norwegian integration policy in 2011.

Peter Mancina is a PhD candidate in the Department of Anthropology at Vanderbilt University. He has authored articles focusing on transnational migration and the formation of power in Chiapas, Mexico, and San Francisco, California. His current ethnographic research focuses on municipal governance and immigrant political power in sanctuary-cities.

David H. Michels, BTh (Tyndale), MA (Providence Seminary), MLIS and PhD (candidate) (Dalhousie), is Public Services Librarian and a faculty member of the Schulich School of Law, Dalhousie University, Halifax, Nova Scotia. Michels' research has focused on church leaders' information seeking, faith and technology, and religion in the public sphere. Prior to entering librarianship, he was a Baptist minister.

Naomi Millner is a political geographer and geography lecturer at the University of Bristol. Her research focuses on community responses to asylum, the politics of security and immigration, and land rights struggles. She volunteers with a local drop-in centre for asylum-seekers and refugees and is part of a working group that offers accommodation to asylum-seekers experiencing destitution.

Hiroshi Oda, Dr.sc.hum. (University of Heidelberg), is Associate Professor of Cultural Anthropology in the Graduate School of Letters at Hokkaido University, Sapporo. His recent research centres on church sanctuary as well as post-war and post-colonial reconciliation initiatives in Germany. He has published *Spontanremissionen bei Krebserkrankungen aus der Sicht des Erlebenden* (Beltz, 2001) and *Doing Ethnography* (in Japanese, Shunjusha, 2010).

Caroline Patsias is an Assistant Professor of Political Science at the Université du Québec à Montréal. Her research focuses on the transformation of governance and political participation of citizens. Through the study of citizen committees, social movements, and community groups, she questions the boundaries of the political, the process of politicization, and avoidance of politics.

Hector Perla Jr., PhD (UCLA, 2005), is Assistant Professor of Latin American and Latino Studies at University of California Santa Cruz. He earned his BA in International Relations from San Francisco State University and his MA in Latin American Studies from Stanford University.

Miikka Pyykkönen, PhD (sociology and cultural policy), is a Senior Lecturer in the Master's Program in Cultural Policy at the University of Jyväskylä. He specializes in politics of cultural diversity and multiculturalism, civil society, and Foucauldian methodology and analytics of power. He has recently published on transformations of cultural policy, theoretical conceptions of civil society, immigrant associations and 'sanctuary politics' in Finland, and historical governance of the Roma and Sami in Finland.

Sean Rehaag, (SJD, University of Toronto) is Associate Professor at Osgoode Hall Law School, York University, where he specializes in immigration and refugee law. His doctoral dissertation used a legal pluralist approach to assess the competing legal claims that arise when faith-based communities offer sanctuary to unsuccessful refugee claimants. He was co-guest editor (with Randy Lippert) of a special issue of *Refuge: Canada's Periodical on Refugees* (2009) dealing with sanctuary.

Jennifer Ridgley is a geographer and a postdoctoral fellow at the Center for Place, Culture and Politics, City University of New York (CUNY). Her first book manuscript, *Cities of Refuge*, documents the evolution of city sanctuary policies in the United States, highlighting the significance of the city as a site through which to understand the bordering practices of state institutions.

Karl Shoemaker is Associate Professor of History and Law at the University of Wisconsin, Madison, and a former member of the Institute for Advanced

Studies, Princeton. He is the author of *Sanctuary and Crime in the Middle Ages, 400–1500* (2011), and a dozen scholarly articles, as well as co-editor of *Who Deserves to Die?: Constructing the Executable Subject* (2011).

Vicki Squire is Associate Professor of International Security at the Department of Politics and International Studies (PAIS), University of Warwick, UK. Her research crosses the fields of critical citizenship, migration and security studies, reflecting her interest in the materialization, development and transformation of socio-political formations and subjectivities under conditions of intensified mobility. She is author of *The Exclusionary Politics of Asylum* (2009), editor of *The Contested Politics of Mobility* (2011), and Assistant Editor of the journal, *Citizenship Studies*.

Hanne Stenvaag is a doctoral student in religious studies at the University of Tromsø. She wrote her Master's thesis on church sanctuaries in Norway, and has been involved in sanctuary work since 1993.

William Walters is a Professor in the departments of Political Science and Sociology and Anthropology at Carleton University in Ottawa. His recent research examines migration from the perspective of its minor politics, figures, and spaces. He is also interested in the history of government and has a forthcoming publication, *Governmentality: Critical Encounters* (Routledge, 2012).

Nastassia Williams is currently completing a Master's degree in political science at the Université du Québec à Montréal. Her Master's thesis explores how the political culture of indigenous communities in India is affecting their strategic choices for mobilization. Williams' field of interest is social contestation and transnational mobilization, especially of marginalized groups.

Julie E.E. Young is a doctoral candidate in the Department of Geography at York University in Toronto. She has worked as a researcher in academic, public sector, and non-profit settings. Her dissertation focuses on refugee policy, politics, and advocacy across the Windsor–Detroit border between Canada and the United States.

Grace Yukich is Assistant Professor of Sociology at Quinnipiac University. From 2010 to 11, she was Religion and Public Life Fellow at Princeton University's Center for the Study of Religion, where she worked on a book on the US New Sanctuary Movement. Her research on religion and politics has appeared in scholarly journals such as *Mobilization* and *Sociology of Religion*.

Foreword: The Ambiguity of Migration

There is a moment quite early in *The Grapes of Wrath* when the young Tom Joad learns an important lesson from Muley. Along with the ex-preacher Casy, Joad and Muley are taking shelter at the Joad family's semi-derelict farmhouse. Joad's entire family has abandoned the farm while he was in prison, joining thousands of other impoverished ex-homesteaders on the road to California. Banks and large agribusinesses have seized control of the cotton fields. While Joad and his fellow itinerants are planning their next move, distant headlights are spotted. Figuring it is the Sheriff's Deputy, Joad resolves to face him down. He's doing no harm and has nothing to fear. After all, this is – or was – his father's farm. But Muley, who's been living rough for some time, insists that they are in fact 'tresspassin''. Better to hide out in the cotton field in the dark than get arrested or even kill a man. At first, Joad is reluctant to hide. But as the headlights draw nearer he manages to overcome his urge to confront and fight. Pride and aggression are channeled into other emotions. An instinct for survival takes new shapes. As Muley predicted, they thwart the Deputy's efforts and he soon departs. Joad confesses he never thought he would be hiding out at his old man's place. 'You'll be hidin' from lots of stuff,' replies Muley. It is a remark that will hang over Joad and his family as their westward odyssey unfolds. Learning when to hide, when to stand, when to fight: this will be part of Joad's re-making, his becoming migrant.

Springsteen is right in his tribute to Steinbeck: 'The highway *is* alive tonight.' If Steinbeck's roadscape is as relevant to our own time as it was to the Great Depression that he chronicled, this is not just because many of its themes and social questions are now being revisited. It is not just because we are once again facing great migrations set in motion by the depletion of farmland, the enclosure of commons, and the dispossession of whole communities. If the *Grapes of Wrath* speaks so powerfully to us today, it is because Steinbeck is able to capture the depth of human complexity and profound ambiguity that marks any experience of mass migration in a way that has rarely (if ever) been rivaled. The public face of migration is one of dualisms: dirty/clean, bona fide/bogus, resident/vagrant, us/them, legal/illegal, haves/have-not. Time and again, Steinbeck shows the instability of these lines, how inadequate they are as tools of comprehension, how the flux of migration confounds such oppositions. For instance, any sentimentality we might feel about the dispossession of the Joad's farmland is tempered by the knowledge it was perhaps founded upon a not dissimilar act of dispossession: 'Grampa took up the land, and he had to kill the Indians and drive them away.'

To say that the kind of understanding of migration that Steinbeck strives for in his novel has typically eluded the social sciences is to offer too harsh a judgment, and to make a statement that risks generalizing about diverse literatures. But such a claim does carry more than a grain of truth. Frequently, political scientists, economists, and sociologists have conducted their investigations within frames that leave unquestioned the very ground on which migrations unfold. Just witness the extent to which so much scientific analysis continues to accept at face value terms like 'immigrant' and 'immigration', embedding the political normativity of a world divided into states into its methodology and epistemology.

Fortunately, this is far from true of all scholarly writing on migration. For some years there has existed a significant, interdisciplinary body of work that is increasingly sensitive to the molecularities as much as the molarities of global migration, that regards migration as a locus of social struggle, a factor in the transformation of subjectivity as much as spatiality, and a domain fraught with dilemmas and ambiguities. It is as a vital and timely contribution to this counter-movement that I would place Randy Lippert's and Sean Rehaag's excellent book on sanctuary, *Sanctuary Practices in International Perspectives*. This collection represents, to my knowledge, one of the first attempts to explore the phenomenon of sanctuary in both historical and international perspective. As such, *Sanctuary Practices in International Perspectives* promises to expand our understanding of the complexity of human migration. By challenging the idea that it is only states that can offer asylum, by revealing the significantly diverse forms and rationalizations that sanctuary can take, and by disclosing situations where resilience might be a more appropriate analytic than resistance, this book cautions against making hasty generalizations about the practices it investigates.

Many features make *Sanctuary Practices in International Perspectives* an important contribution that will be read and debated for many years to come. In the cramped space that is the lot of any Foreword I will highlight just one.

The chapters in this book underscore sanctuary as an ambiguous, contradictory, and indeterminate phenomenon. Does the practice of sanctuary contest the sovereign power of the nation-state or does it function as a supplement, shoring it up? Does the provision of sanctuary unsettle the exclusionary logics that underwrite the state's policing of migrants and refugees, or do such logics get reproduced every time the offer of sanctuary is made conditional upon an assessment of the truth of its subject? Are the subjects of sanctuary guests to be hosted, a flock to be tended, victims to be protected, fugitives to be hidden, or political subjects to be engaged? As with those very contemporary experiments in humanitarianism that are becoming ever more central both to the machinery of migration control and its contestation, and with which sanctuary overlaps significantly, it seems we are dealing with a blurry, ill-defined landscape of power for which critical analysis still lacks adequate maps and orientation. The essays collected here mark a major step towards a better understanding. They do not answer these questions or resolve these dilemmas. We shouldn't expect them to, for sanctuary is a multiplicity. Instead, they pose the problem of sanctuary in the first place. For the moment, this is the best we can ask for. Steinbeck portrays migration as a maelstrom of fear and hope, desperation and transformation. He registers the ambiguity of migration. By casting the ambiguity of sanctuary at the center of our attention, *Sanctuary Practices in International Perspectives* is destined to significantly advance our understanding of the new territories carved out by contemporary migrations.

William Walters
January 2012

Acknowledgements

Randy K. Lippert is grateful, as always, to Francine C. Lippert for loving support and patience during the long course of co-editing this volume.

Sean Rehaag would like to thank his tireless research assistants at Osgoode Hall Law School who helped with the volume: Umair Abdul, Anastasia Mandziuk and Ian McKellar.

We also wish to acknowledge financial support from the University of Windsor's Vice-President of Research Ranjana Bird, from Dean Lorne Sossin and Associate Dean Poonam Puri (Research, Graduate Studies and Institutional Relations) at Osgoode Hall Law School, and from York University.

Special thanks are due, of course, to each contributor for believing in the project from the outset, and for following through with timely, insightful, and often fascinating chapters. We feel fortunate to have been able to exchange ideas with every one of them.

Finally, this book owes its existence to the talented, supportive, and professional people at Taylor & Francis, and especially to the efforts of Colin Perrin, the acquisition editor, and to Melanie Fortmann-Brown, the editorial assistant. We knew we were in very capable hands from the moment we contacted Colin about the project. Melanie's gentle nudges about deadlines and quick responses to questions helped us to stay on schedule.

List of abbreviations

ABC	*American Baptist Churches v. Thornburgh*
AHCSD	Ad Hoc Committee to Stop the Deportations
ARENA	Alianza Republicana Nacionalista
CAFOD	Catholic Overseas Development Agency
CARECEN	Central American Resource Center
CAROP	Central American Refugee Organising Project
CCCB	Canadian Conference of Catholic Bishops
CIS	Centro de Intercambio and Solidaridad, Center for Exchange and Solidarity
CISPES	Committee in Solidarity with the People of El Salvador
CLUE	Clergy and Laity United for Economic Justice
CO	Conscientious Objector
CRECE	Comité de Refugiados Centroamericanos/the Central American Refugee Committee
CRECEN	Centro de Refugiados Centroamericanos
CRS	French riot police
CSQ	*Certificat de sélection du Québec*
CSS-SF	Catholic Archdiocese's Catholic Social Service
DSC	Detroit Sanctuary Coalition
DWRC	Detroit/Windsor Refugee Coalition
EBSC	East Bay Sanctuary Covenant
ECHR	European Court of Human Rights
ELCA	Evangelical Lutheran Church in America
ELCC	Evangelical Lutheran Church in Canada
EVD	Extended Voluntary Departure
FEC	Finnish Ecumenical Council
FMLN	Frente Farabundo Marti para la Liberación Nacional
GDP	gross domestic product
GECCA	German Ecumenical Committee on Church Asylum
HCR	Humanitarian and Compassionate Review
HRC	Human Rights Commission

HRIFA	*Haitian Refugee Immigration Fairness Act*
ICE	U.S. Immigration and Customs Enforcement
IIRIRA	*Illegal Immigration Reform and Immigrant Responsibility Act*
INA	Immigration and National Act
INS	Immigration and Naturalization Services
IRB	Immigration and Refugee Board
IRCA	Immigration Reform and Control Act
IISS	International Institute of Strategic Studies
LATF	Latin American Task Force
MASPS	Movimiento Amplio en Solidaridad con El Pueblo Salvadoreño
MDM	*Médecins du Monde*
MSF	*Médécins Sans Frontières*
NACARA	*Nicaraguan Adjustment and Central American Relief Act*
NCSC	Northern California Sanctuary Churches
NGO	non-governmental organisation
NSM	New Sanctuary Movement
OCAP	Ontario Coalition Against Poverty
PAF	French border police
PCC	Presbyterian Church in Canada
PIFWCs	Persons Indicted for War Crimes
SCITCA	Southern California Interfaith Task Force on Central America
SFSC	San Francisco Sanctuary Covenant
SI/PLC	Social Issues/Police Liaison Committee
SM	Sanctuary Movement
SMOs	social movement organizations
SOS	Stop Our Ship
STCA	*Safe Third Country Agreement*
TPS	Temporary Protected Status
TWRC	Third World Resource Centre
UCC	United Church of Canada
UNO	National Opposition Union
WCARSN	Windsor Central American Refugee Sponsorship Network

Introduction

Sanctuary across countries, institutions, and disciplines

Randy K. Lippert and Sean Rehaag

Beginning in the late 1970s, sanctuary practices underwent a revival. Immigrants living without legal status and their supporters, first in the United Kingdom, and then in the United States, Canada, and elsewhere in Europe, have resorted to sanctuary practices to avoid and resist arrest and deportation by state authorities. Sanctuary appeared amidst a dramatic rise in the number of asylum-seekers arriving in Western countries and a simultaneous escalation in national and international efforts to discourage and control their arrival and presence through myriad means, including arrest and deportation.

This volume explores sanctuary in its multiple iterations and examines the conceptual and theoretical issues into which they provide insight in new national and institutional contexts. Assembled are 17 chapters written by scholars from eight countries. Each chapter either explores key issues that sanctuary practices raise or details the development and trajectory of a particular sanctuary movement. Most do both. In so doing, this volume showcases the multi-disciplinary character of sanctuary scholarship, with chapters authored by scholars writing from the disciplines of anthropology, geography, political science, sociology, law, theology, and English. Among these scholars are also several sanctuary movement participants. The chapters are geographically diverse, exploring sanctuary in the US, Canada, the UK, Germany, Finland, Norway, Sweden, Denmark, France, Iraq and Afghanistan.

The volume is organized as follows. This Introduction highlights key themes and overviews the chapters. The volume is then divided into four Parts: Part I on historical, theological and theoretical perspectives on sanctuary that reveal its justifications and rationales; Part II on the US context, including the 1980s US Sanctuary Movement's effects and the recent inter-faith New Sanctuary Movement (NSM); Part III, an international section, primarily focused on traditional faith-based sanctuary practices and movements in Europe and Canada; and Part IV on emergent forms of sanctuary, which also has an international flavour in covering developments in the US, Canada, and the UK, as well as Iraq and Afghanistan. There is inevitably some overlap of purpose among the four Parts, but Part I is broadly focused on ways of seeing and justifying sanctuary; Parts II and III expose details of neglected contemporary sanctuary movements and practices internationally; and, finally, Part IV encompasses chapters that explore the broadening of sanctuary beyond Christian churches and its emergence in other institutional realms such as municipal governments and in international/military relations.

In the English-speaking world, most people associate contemporary sanctuary practices with a faith-based social movement commencing in the early 1980s in the US. This movement spawned an extensive multi-disciplinary body of scholarship, ranging from ethnographies informed by social movement theory, to sociological studies of so-called 'deviant behaviour', to consideration of legal questions surrounding constitutional freedom-of-religion claims, especially in the wake of US state authorities charging and convicting several sanctuary activists. However, by the early 1990s, this self-defined social movement had all but expired in the US.

The existing scholarship on sanctuary, drawing mostly on this US experience, has exposed sanctuary as a set of practices, including spatial practices, as a fertile site to unearth and examine theoretical and conceptual questions from across several disciplines. Scholars have theorized sanctuary in relation not only to migration and citizenship processes but also gender, race, church–state relations, social movements, civil disobedience, freedom of religion, and political identity. Activists and scholars have wrestled with several vital questions about contemporary sanctuary practices. Do these practices constitute a social movement or a string of unrelated events that merely share similar tactics? Are these practices faith-based or an assemblage of disparate elements, some secular, some sacred? How do these practices relate to law; are they 'illegal' as state agents often argue or are they a means to actuate higher forms of law, including international law?

The collection's aim is to surpass isolated accounts and case studies of sanctuary practices and movements in one country, from one perspective, and one historical period that characterize sanctuary scholarship to date. Rarely noted in existing scholarship is that sanctuary practices have had a presence outside the US, continue to persist, and have undergone a recent US resurgence. Thus, neglected are sanctuary activities outside the US before (as in the UK), and after the early 1980s (as in Canada, Germany, France and the Nordic countries). That said, the US remains a key site of sanctuary, especially with the rise of the NSM, which culminated in a national sanctuary meeting in New York City in 2009 and which helped inspire in continental Europe an international conference on sanctuary in Germany in 2010. Sanctuary, therefore, would seem to be garnering popular and scholarly attention in the US once again. Two chapters in this collection focus exclusively on the NSM and its significant conceptual and theoretical implications. Moreover, the US has been the source or location of several of sanctuary's other forms that are explored in Part IV.

This volume also seeks to reveal sanctuary as a more international, institutionally-flexible, and perhaps above all, theoretically-rich set of practices. The collection's multi-disciplinary and international character raises new questions about sanctuary movements and practices. Among the principal issues that require such consideration and debate include: What is the critical potential of sanctuary practices? Are these acts of consequence beyond the relatively small spaces and the few lives positioned at their centre? Are they the symbolic tip of an iceberg of resistant acts waiting to surface if conditions present themselves? Alternatively, are they merely another appendage of the state systems of inclusion and exclusion involving refugee determination and immigrant selection, merely a temporary corrective for flaws in these systems, despite their accompanying rhetoric of resistance and sovereignty? Are these practices representative of asymmetrical power relations at their core?

At the centre of contemporary sanctuary activities has been – almost exclusively – immigrants (often asylum-seekers) living without legal status in Western countries. All but two of the 17 chapters in this volume focus on sanctuary in relation to migration and to a lesser extent citizenship processes or on the role of immigrants without legal status in sanctuary practices. These two chapters, the first and last in this volume, situate sanctuary in an even broader perspective. They reveal that sanctuary's terrain in the past was not always migration and citizenship and that it may not be so in the future. Sanctuary was once about protecting persons alleged to have committed criminal acts, rather than immigrants facing expulsion, as Karl Shoemaker's Chapter 1 on medieval sanctuary documents. Nor is it clear this link will continue in the future, because sanctuary has quickly begun acquiring new forms and meanings during its revival in the 1980s and during the post-9/11 context since. As Michael Innes shows in Chapter 17, 'sanctuary' has been increasingly invoked in military and/or international relations discourse to refer to 'terrorist and militant' havens and spaces of terrorism in Iraq and Afghanistan.

Other themes that emerge in the volume are equally significant. These concern visibility, asymmetry, agency, sovereignty, legality, mutability and transformative potential. Reflected in the earliest scholarly accounts of contemporary sanctuary practices, the division between visibility and non-visibility is seen in the analytical distinction between sanctuary as 'exposure' and sanctuary as 'concealment'. The former – exposure – is a strategy to provide protection to immigrants in a church or religious building and to gain the attention of mass media, the public and state authorities. The latter – concealment – is the antithesis of this effort whereby sanctuary provision is purposely concealed from state authorities. Whether sanctuary practices are invisible or visible has much to do with the shifting rationales and purposes of sanctuary practices that are well-documented in this volume. In Hector Perla and Susan Bibler Coutin's Chapter 5, for example, the issue manifests in relation to questions of whether Central American activists needed to remain quiet and become invisible to foster North Americans' involvement in the 1980s sanctuary movement. In other words, invisibility was maintained to hide practices, not only from US authorities, but also from other movement activists or would-be participants.

As Perla and Bibler Coutin's contribution suggests too, there is a certain asymmetry at work in at least some sanctuary practices. While sanctuary may appear at first glance as obviously a form of resistance to state power, a transparent counter-stroke to state processes of exclusion, or at least its arbitrary exercise, several chapters question this assumption by looking more closely at these practices. Thus chapters by Naomi Millner, Hiroshi Oda, and Jonathan Darling and Vicki Squire (chapters 4, 10 and 13) problematize the sanctuary relationship as asymmetrical, each calling it into question in a different way. This raises the spectre that these practices may reproduce some dominant discourses that sanctuary practices overtly seek to counter. The question of asymmetry of power relations swirling about sanctuary practices emerges as a consequence.

The issues of visibility and asymmetry are directly related to another: agency. To what extent are those persons at the centre of sanctuary practices the agents, rather than merely the recipients, of sanctuary's protection and aligned 'hospitality'? Put simply, are these people takers or receivers of sanctuary? This question looms in the background of most chapters such that there is little doubt immigrants aid the genesis, production, and cessation of sanctuary activity. These immigrants faced with immediate deportation sometimes defy sanctuary's paternalistic currents, whether by deciding to exit sanctuary, by challenging sanctuary's restrictions and conventions, or by playing a key role in enacting sanctuary practices in the first place. Yet, it is also true that immigrants without legal status often – even if only temporarily – adopt passive, obedient roles to flow with these paternalistic currents or otherwise deem it necessary to 'stay quiet'. Furthermore, close study of efforts to mobilize the significant legal and financial resources required to gain legal status through sanctuary plainly reveal that undocumented immigrants are often not positioned to move to the visible forefront of the resistance effort. To state otherwise risks denying the grim, precarious reality in which many people receiving or taking sanctuary find themselves due to organized state efforts to control them. There is an accompanying risk of overstating opportunities for effective resistance, regardless of the extent of immigrants' involvement in initiating sanctuary practices or escaping its conceptual and physical confines. Thus, while questions of agency are crucial to understanding sanctuary practices, in our view, the extent of agency is best left as an empirical question in each site. Indeed, it would seem there is a danger of throwing the potentially resistant baby out with the bathwater where asymmetry is discerned.

A related question concerns sovereignty. Sovereignty is considered in this volume by Karl Shoemaker who shows, in his account of medieval sanctuary, how kings wielded sanctuary, before the emergence of the modern state, to shore up their sovereignty. However, Agnes Czajka, Hilary Cunningham, Hiroshi Oda, and Caroline Patsias and Natassia Williams in their chapters (3, 10, 11 and 12) also each raise the possibility that sanctuary challenges the modern state's monopoly on sovereignty.

Tied to the issue of sovereignty is the matter of legality. Several chapters engage the question of whether sanctuary is lawful, and if so, according to what legal order (e.g. state law, international law, religious law, higher law, natural law). David Michels and David Blaikie, for example, in Chapter 2, contend that sanctuary providers in the UK, the US and Canada on occasion resort to natural law and international law arguments to justify sanctuary practices, while nonetheless typically conceding that sanctuary is unlawful according to domestic state law. Along similar lines, a number of chapters raise the question of the legitimacy of civil disobedience. When is it appropriate to violate domestic state laws on the grounds that these laws are unjust? But of course, debates over whether sanctuary is a legitimate form of civil disobedience presume sanctuary is in fact unlawful – a point, as Patsias and Williams note in Chapter 12, on which not all sanctuary supporters concur. Indeed, as Cunningham suggests in Chapter 11, an unwillingness to concede the illegality of sanctuary, even as a matter of domestic state law, leads some sanctuary supporters to argue that sanctuary is a 'civil initiative' (a practice whereby individuals act to uphold the law in face of unlawful state actions) rather than civil disobedience.

This brings us to mutability and transformative potential. That sanctuary practices mutate over time is well documented in this volume, even across two traditional sanctuary movements in the US, as described in chapters by Marta Caminero-Santangelo and Grace Yukich (Chapters 6 and 7). Similarly, Naomi Millner's account in Chapter 4 of sanctuary in Northern France details a shift towards sanctuary as solidarity. Investigating transformative or critical potential is more difficult. Agnes Czajka, for example, in Chapter 3, argues that a self-limitation of social movement goals to advocacy for policy reform, such as a merit-based appeal for asylum-seekers in Canada, as important as this may be for asylum-seekers' well-being, nonetheless casts doubt on sanctuary's transformative potential. Similarly, when sanctuary is cast as civil initiative, this implies sanctuary may be merely a new arm of the state system, rather than possessive of a transformative capacity. Jonathan Darling and Vicki Squire's account of the *City of Sanctuary* in Chapter 13 also identifies tactics of resistance in the formal practices of this movement that may imply the potential for the movement's wider political effects.

Until this volume, a rarely stated or documented fact is that since the late 1970s sanctuary has not limited itself to spaces of Christian churches and their members' beliefs and practices. To be sure, the link between Christian churches and sanctuary remains tight. However, sanctuary practices have been present beyond Christian churches in other faith-based communities (e.g., a Mosque in London in the 1970s and a Sikh temple in Vancouver in the 2000s) and also in relation to secular institutions. Sanctuary has adopted other institutional forms and affiliations and is acquiring new meanings in the process. This is evident, for example, in 'sanctuary cities' in the UK, US, Canada discussed in the chapters by Jonathan Darling and Vicki Squire, Peter Mancina, Jennifer Ridgley and

Julie Young (chapters 13, 14, 15, and 16). While at first glance sanctuary would seem necessarily sacred, city governments in the US such as San Francisco's and New York's have embraced this symbolism of safety in political engagements with the US federal government, as early as the 1980s, but devoid of its religious trappings. That urban space can be a space of sanctuary is, of course, not historically new. Rather, it suggests a return to sanctuary's early history: the Cities of Refuge in the Bible.

We suggest these varied themes above are not mutually exclusive, but are instead interrelated and overlapping. For example, it would seem that acts of sanctuary must be visible to be conceived as demonstrable instances of sovereignty. Similarly, asymmetry would appear to be consonant with seeing sanctuary practices devoid of immigrants' agency, and is a quality that is worthwhile identifying for modification if sanctuary practices are mutable, and so on. In the end, the volume, which draws together scholars from various disciplinary traditions, and looks at sanctuary practices through multiple historical, theoretical and comparative lenses, confirms the need for further multi-disciplinary and comparative inquiry and dialogue in this particularly fertile field. The themes that emerge in the volume, especially of asymmetry, agency, sovereignty, legality, and transformative potential, represent, in our view, merely seeds from which further inquiry and dialogue can grow. Sanctuary's significance extends far beyond any one country, institution, discipline, or, indeed, epoch; the multiple questions these practices raise and which are represented in these themes are as relevant to understanding human survival and protection in our globalized, conflict-ridden twenty-first-century world as they are to the practices of medieval Europe.

Part I Sanctuary perspectives: historical, theological, theoretical

In Part I, four chapters investigate sanctuary from several key perspectives. Many scholars and supporters discuss sanctuary as though the nature of these early practices is well known, that there is a 'tradition' that informs closely aligned contemporary practices. Very few scholars, though, have actually researched these early practices, which is why Karl Shoemaker's Chapter 1 on medieval sanctuary is essential to commence this volume. His chapter shows continuity between early and contemporary sanctuary practices is doubtful. He notes that in the mid-sixteenth century criminals who were able to reach a church's sacred spaces could anticipate protection from prosecution. However, he argues sanctuary practices were not due primarily to weak forms of medieval authority or to flaws in existing criminal law processes. Rather, kings might have defended existing sanctuary laws as a way to demonstrate their strength. Sanctuary's later abolition across Europe resulted from a significant shift whereby deterrence began to be viewed as a quality of sovereignty, and in which long-standing legal practices linked to penitential discipline and dispute resolution became viewed as nuisances. In so doing, Shoemaker provides an understanding of medieval sanctuary as a lawful and celebrated practice – one that may be deployed to reinforce, rather than challenge, sovereignty.

Examining further the justifications for sanctuary is Chapter 2 by David Michels and David Blaikie. These authors empirically and comparatively investigate three types of contemporary public justifications for acts of sanctuary directed at undocumented immigrants and asylum-seekers in the UK, the US and Canada, which, they argue, share similar legal, faith and cultural histories. They seek to discern how these distinct political and geographic contexts, however, might influence sanctuary practices, which they find vary significantly. Furthermore they discovered that while strong religious arguments were not deployed to justify these practices, there was a common motivation and, from self-avowed Christians, a broad theological commitment that encompassed sanctuary's various expressions.

In Chapter 3, Agnes Czajka asks a vital and largely overlooked question about contemporary sanctuary practices: do they reproduce state discourses and technologies or do they possess critical, transformative potential? To do this, Czajka turns to intersections between the spaces and subjectivities found in the social theory of Giorgio Agamben, in particular, camp and bare life, on the one hand, and the refugee and sanctuary's spaces and subjectivities, on the other. Through this, she argues that while what she calls 'acts of sanctuary' must be challenged, they nonetheless possess a potential to disrupt the state's attempt to monopolize territorial sovereignty and ways of being political.

Echoing similar themes but using different theoretical tools in an understudied context, Naomi Millner explores sanctuary practices in Northern France in the post-war period in Chapter 4. In particular, she examines how existing notions of citizenship are reinforced through compassionate assistance and the creation of safe havens within international humanitarianism. Yet, underscoring the multiple influences on ethical subjectivity, Millner shows how sanctuary is being renegotiated due to immigrants' activities. By focusing on migration via the shelter Sangatte and *sans-papiers* movements, she reveals how ideas of collective belonging that move beyond and problematize citizenship are changing ethical responses to migrants. Significantly, sanctuary is replaced with a philosophy of solidarity whereby equality becomes shared by various social movements that embrace the existence of a universal community of migrants that precedes those categories that are closely tethered to the nation-state.

Part II Sanctuary movements and practices in the United States: old and new

Given that the US sanctuary movement is by far the most studied and well-known example of sanctuary activity, and because of the nascent NSM, a separate section on the US is appropriate. The chapters in Part II are not the only ones in this volume about sanctuary in the US. Part IV includes three chapters that focus on sanctuary activity in a US city context, those by Peter Mancina, Jennifer Ridgley, and Julie Young. However, the chapters here in Part II focus more closely on US church sanctuary movements and practices as they traditionally have been understood.

Chapter 5 recasts an understanding of the nature and significance of the original US movement many years after its cessation. Hector Perla and Susan Bibler Coutin provide a retrospective exploration of this movement, arguing that the movement's structure and effects were transnational rather than national in character. The sanctuary movement arose consonant with broader activities of Central Americans who sought to encourage North American support for social justice activists. This rethinking of the movement's origins also reveals unintended consequences of sanctuary that include legal and policy changes in the US, increased remittances to Central America, and the Central American community's growth in the US. These consequences cast doubt on the efficacy of social movement theories that centre on instrumental (i.e., intentional) action. Moreover, as exemplified recently in sanctuary incidents in Canada, which are more closely linked to refugee determination and immigration processes, these unanticipated consequences suggest the particularity of sanctuary activity. This attention to social movements and how far this particularity should be considered is pertinent to other chapters that describe sanctuary movements and practices in specific countries.

A key point made by Perla and Bibler Coutin is that the first US sanctuary movement has important legacies that reach beyond participants' stated goals. One such legacy, albeit one still being negotiated, is the New Sanctuary Movement (NSM). Marta Caminero-Santangelo authors the first of two chapters centred on the NSM. She argues in Chapter 6 that, compared to the first sanctuary movement, the NSM has been less about offering physical protection to undocumented immigrants and more about offering a new way to tell the story of the effects of US deportation policies. Like the earlier chapter by Blaikie and Michels, this chapter analyzes public justifications for sanctuary used both by US-citizen movement participants and undocumented immigrants. She asks how the narratives of the NSM differ from justifications for the earlier movement and how the former sought to constitute a new form of intervention in debates over immigrant rights in the US. In the NSM, she argues, sanctuary became reconfigured as a public and performative practice that provides a counter-discourse to the dominant rhetoric on immigration and that constructs an activist faith community.

Grace Yukich, in Chapter 7, considers the NSM in relation to how a social movement adapts older tactics to a new political environment and in this way complements Chapter 6 and other chapters that show how sanctuary practices can change over time. She argues that the political terrain of the 2000s required activists to attempt to create and disseminate a new version of sanctuary: a strategy of 'radical accompaniment' rather than a primary tactic of church-based physical sanctuary. She asserts that sanctuary's history, and in particular the earlier US sanctuary movement, is an obstacle to strategic adaptation, since activists already assume what sanctuary entails. Uncertainty resulted from the movement's adaptation of sanctuary, harming its ability to recruit members and create a collective identity and commitment. The NSM highlights both sanctuary's power as a symbol and practice, but also the difficulties inherent in altering its meaning.

Part III Sanctuary movements and practices in Europe and Canada: international comparative and case studies

Following Part II on US sanctuary practices is a section that deals with various case studies of sanctuary movements in Europe and Canada. In the first English language scholarly account of its kind, Jill Loga, Miikka Pyykkönen and Hanne Stenvaag illuminate church sanctuary practices in four Nordic countries: Denmark, Finland, Norway and Sweden. Echoing other chapters, they argue that while there are many similarities, there are also significant differences among these countries that stem from, among other things, distinct state–church relations, migration histories, and networks. Nordic church sanctuary practices are rooted in the official legal position of sanctuary during the pre-Reformation era. Two justifications for sanctuary practices in Lutheran and various other Christian churches remain: the obligation to respond to everyone within the holy territory of churches, and the priests' ethical duty to help the distressed. They argue that sanctuary providers have increasingly deployed these justifications as asylum-seeker migration to the Nordic countries has increased beginning in the 1980s.

In Chapter 9, Wolf-Dieter Just provides an overview of the long-standing German sanctuary movement. In the early 1980s, this movement emerged as a reaction to restrictive German asylum policies and poor living conditions for refugees. By 1994, a nationwide network of individuals and parishes prepared to provide church sanctuary had developed. Just argues that this network offered opportunities to provide mutual support, for theological reflection and for political protest against German asylum policies. Parishes offering sanctuary attempted to serve immigrants facing social hardship and physical harm and to fight for the right to human dignity as set out in the German Constitution. As in Canada, Just suggests that sanctuary is provided only as a last resort when legal means to prevent deportation have failed – and has proven surprisingly successful in preventing deportation. Just asserts that this practice has also had a positive impact on congregations involved in giving members' Christian faith a practical expression.

Still focusing on Germany, Hiroshi Oda investigates, in Chapter 10, the relationship among actors in Germany's sanctuary movement. He recounts the story of a Kurdish refugee who took sanctuary. In his first refugee determination hearing, chronological inaccuracies in his story were overemphasized in judging his credibility. In the second hearing and in taking sanctuary, his credibility was constructed instead based on face-to-face relationships and compassion.

Although compassion is referred to in the German Constitution, Oda argues the rights of foreigners have been restricted by state sovereignty. As a result, a confrontation emerged in which sanctuary became necessary. In this respect, sanctuary can be understood as a manifestation of local communities' potential for hospitality.

Moving from Europe back to North America, in Chapter 11, Hilary Cunningham documents the rise of the Ontario Sanctuary Coalition (OSC), which is one of the first Canadian sanctuary movements, from 1993 onward. Like other faith-based groups, such as those in Germany described above, the OSC adopted church sanctuary to respond to Canada's restrictive immigration and refugee process. However, she argues, it adopted a unique coalition culture and has continued to underscore the role of a 'civil initiative' and reform of Canada's refugee determination process.

Caroline Patsias and Nastassia Williams, in Chapter 12, explore sanctuary by comparing two contexts that are discussed separately in previous chapters: Canada and France. The authors argue that how one understands sanctuary's legitimacy depends in part on whether one adopts a liberal or republican view of democracy. The authors illustrate how different visions of political obligation, liberal and republican, highlight certain aspects of sanctuary. To do this, they compare two sanctuary incidents in Catholic parishes in Montreal and Paris. Beyond cultural and political differences between Canada and France, they show that the supporters of sanctuary practices help redefine new 'pockets' of sovereignty, where citizens assert their vision of justice and contest the state when it drifts too far from social realities.

Part IV Emergent realms: Cities of Sanctuary and military sanctuaries

The final Part in this volume is about sanctuary's emergent realms, including cities of sanctuary and military sanctuaries. Jonathan Darling and Vicki Squire commence Part IV by interrogating the politics of the *City of Sanctuary* network in Sheffield, in the UK. This network forms part of a national association that attempts to create a 'culture of hospitality' for immigrants. Resonating with Czajka's argument, but again using different theoretical tools, the authors assert that many activities of this network create possibilities for disruptive acts of sanctuary which are discussed via attention to everyday activities such as volunteering. The authors identify a series of tensions between the formal articulation of the movement and everyday enactments. They suggest the latter problematize the uneven relations of privilege that surround practices of hospitality. They show too how the *City of Sanctuary* actively propagates exclusions by permitting the supporting groups and city councilors to become part of the network without politicizing its status. The chapter draws upon Henri Lefebvre's well-known idea of the 'right to the city' as a means by which to understand the disruptive potential of everyday enactments of sanctuary.

Next, in Chapter 14, Peter Mancina describes the history of a grassroots sanctuary movement in San Francisco, and how municipal officials enforced governmental sanctuary practice. Activists' efforts led to the incorporation of the sanctuary movement ethics, such as providing 'support, protection, and advocacy' for undocumented refugees, into the municipal government's culture. The municipal government then deployed sanctuary as a means to govern the city's mixed-status population. What emerged was a sanctuary city governance apparatus, a network of departments, commissions, agencies, officials, and front-line employees, to manage and improve the precarious situation of undocumented immigrants. By forbidding city employees from conducting intrusive surveillance and information gathering and sharing details of immigrants' legal status, the municipal government provided life-sustaining municipal services as sanctuary city services to undocumented immigrants and advocated on their behalf. Such sanctuary practices encouraged undocumented residents to remain healthy, law-abiding, and cooperative with municipal agents, and were therefore used as techniques of governance and welfare promotion.

Broadening and complementing Mancina's chapter, Jennifer Ridgley in Chapter 15 describes the history and politics of city sanctuary in the US. She begins with events leading to Berkeley declaring itself a sanctuary for soldiers refusing to fight in the Vietnam War. Tracing the changing practices and meaning of sanctuary as it was enveloped in the legal and institutional spaces of city governments, she describes how sanctuary shifted from faith-based origins toward policies of limiting local enforcement of federal immigration law. She also discusses city sanctuary in San Francisco and New York City during the major immigration reforms of the 1980s and 1990s, and how city sanctuary re-emerged after 2001 during new security initiatives.

While much is written about sanctuary movements and activities within US cities, little is known about the Canada–US borderlands. Julie Young rectifies this via a case study of responses to the Central American refugee 'crisis' of the late 1980s in Detroit (USA)–Windsor (Canada), with particular attention on the Detroit–Windsor Refugee Coalition. Young argues in Chapter 16 that coalition members re-conceptualized the international boundary line that divides and joins this border city. Advocates focused on 'overground' methods, strategically mobilizing Canada's less restrictive refugee policies to enable undocumented immigrants to leave the US to secure legal status as refugees in Canada. Local sanctuary activities created a space of refuge that spanned the boundary line, relying on cooperation between organizations and individuals on the two sides of the Detroit River, thereby highlighting the value of working as though these two cities were one.

The final chapter also explores sanctuary practices beyond those located in churches, but in a very dissimilar emergent realm. Michael A. Innes focuses on militant sanctuaries in the context of international relations. He asserts that sanctuary is many things: the most important form of support a state can provide to armed surrogates, a humanitarian shelter to civilians, and a protected base area from which guerrilla movements can operate. He argues that if states are the immutable facts of international politics, then sanctuaries are their illegitimate offspring. He explores the limitations of recent research, policy, and framing efforts, arguing for greater epistemological self-questioning among analysts and for a dynamic, constructivist view in which sanctuaries are defined by ideas, beliefs and actions rather than material features. Innes concludes by discussing the importance of practices in understanding places, the complexities of units and levels of analysis, and challenges of social distance in war.

Part I

Sanctuary perspectives
Historical, theological, legal, theoretical

Chapter 1

Sanctuary for crime in the early common law

Karl Shoemaker

Introduction

Around the year 1086, speaking through a royal charter attributed to him, William the Conqueror reminisced about his military victory over the English at the Battle of Hastings twenty years earlier and recalled, 'I made a vow then that if by God's grace we would be able to obtain victory I would construct a church to the honour of God.' Making good on this battlefield vow, William ordered the endowment of a church on the site and named it Battle Abbey in honour of the decisive battle by which he secured the English crown. As was customary in such charters, the king then proceeded to enumerate a list of liberties that the abbey could claim against royal justice. Last in the list was the following: 'If any thief or homicide or other guilty person flee from fear of death to this church, let him not be harmed, but let him be released wholly free' (Davis 1913: charter no. 62). With these words King William conferred upon the church at Battle Abbey the right to serve as a sanctuary for criminals who might take refuge within it.

Three points should be noted immediately. First, the specific articulation of sanctuary rights in the charter was superfluous because any consecrated church in England, and indeed throughout medieval Christendom, was understood to provide sanctuary to fugitive criminals, regardless of whether or not the right had been granted by a specific royal act. Second, and much more important for our present purposes, the royal charter is spurious. It was forged nearly a century after William's death, probably in the 1170s, by monks at Battle Abbey who sought to secure a raft of privileges against the crown by resting them upon William's imagined grant (Searle 1980: 17–23). But like all forgeries produced with any hope of success, the charter put assertions into William's mouth that rang with plausibility to contemporaries. The image of a heroic king, flush with victory and Christian piety, announcing that a criminal would be free from harm if he fled to the church provided the monks with an effective vehicle by which to authenticate the privileges they hoped the crown would honour. The monks were not merely attempting to secure sanctuary protections through a forged charter. Rather, they invoked a royal grant of sanctuary in their charter in order to create a more convincing forgery. Seen in this light, the forged Battle Abbey charter prompts an important observation: the expectation that a murderer or thief could find escape from punishment by fleeing to a church and claiming sanctuary was so replete within twelfth-century England that royal recognition of it could be used to manufacture authenticity in a forged charter. Nor was medieval English law exceptional in its regard for sanctuary. At the time the monks at Battle Abbey forged this charter in the late twelfth century, they might have noted that sanctuary for criminals had been attested not only in centuries of ecclesiastical legislation, but also in centuries of Anglo-Saxon and Frankish royal legislation, as well as in late imperial Roman law. To these legislative examples one might add the myriad instances of sanctuary for crimes that had been described in patristic letters, chronicles, and saints' lives. The monks at Battle Abbey had good reason to pin their forgery to the image of a sanctuary-granting king (Shoemaker 2011: 8–37). The forged charter evoked a pleasing confluence of royal and ecclesiastical power, reminding its audience that good Christian kings looked favorably on sanctuary protections for fugitive criminals. Finally, a third point requires emphasis. The sanctuary contemplated by the Battle Abbey charter, and indeed by medieval sanctuary law as a whole, was specifically aimed at protecting avowed criminals, even (or perhaps especially) murderers and thieves. It was not intended to protect innocent fugitives, though it may on occasion have accomplished this. Sanctuary was for the guilty.

The Battle Abbey charter serves as a useful introduction to medieval sanctuary law because it appeared at a crucial juncture in the life of sanctuary, particularly in England. For while sanctuary had been recognized in Anglo-Saxon law for centuries, procedural reforms instituted (or perhaps reinstituted) by Henry II in the 1170s were about to bring sanctuary more squarely within the ambit of royal administration, domesticating sanctuary within the processes of the English common law (Shoemaker 2011: 112–51). Once integrated into the common law procedures governing felonies, sanctuary survived for nearly four more centuries until it was all but abolished by legal reforms instituted under Henry VIII. The virtual abolition of sanctuary in the sixteenth century was a pan-European phenomenon, accomplished in Protestant and Catholic countries alike by a combination of royal, parliamentary, and papal decrees. Before examining the fate of sanctuary in sixteenth-century Europe, however, it will be instructive to explore the attempts by which early modern and modern historians have attempted to understand the development and eventual decline of medieval sanctuary laws.

Historians and sanctuary

How did the notion that criminals who fled to churches should receive impunity come to occupy such a central place in medieval European law? Why, in other words, would those who had committed the worst sorts of violence and depredation be singled out for special protections which were announced and enforced by Church and Crown alike? Since its abolition in the sixteenth century, sanctuary has attracted the attention of historians who sought to explain its ubiquitous presence in medieval legal traditions. Sometimes, but certainly not always, these explanations could be mapped onto confessional differences. Some early modern Protestant scholars accused the medieval Church of smuggling pagan sanctuary practices into Christian law (Mattheas 1684, 1987–94: 4, 632). Samuel Pegge, for example, denounced ancient 'Christian leaders, from whom we might expect the best' for recklessly 'transferring all of the privileges and immunities of the Heathen temples … onto the Christian churches'. Sanctuary laws consecrated in the ancient sources, Pegge continued scathingly, were born from a pagan propensity for 'blind reverence and devotion' and rested upon 'a mistaken and ill-judged veneration for fabrics, and altars, and the saints' (Pegge 1787: 1).

Such arguments were often a response to attempts by some early modern canon lawyers to ground sanctuary in reason or divine law, as opposed to ancient pagan superstitions. For example, sixteenth-century Italian canon lawyer Jacobus Menochius acknowledged that sanctuary privileges could be found among pagan peoples, but then asked rhetorically: 'If even the *ius gentium*' recognized sanctuary, 'how much more should these immunities be bestowed upon the churches of God?' (Menochius 1695: 298). Despite such attempts to ground sanctuary in divine law, however, by the late sixteenth century even the papacy was working to restrict the scope of sanctuary law by drastically limiting the sorts of crimes for which one could claim sanctuary (Shoemaker 2011: 172).

Interestingly, whatever they thought of its origins, jurists and historians of all stripes largely held the end of sanctuary to be a good thing. Scholarly descriptions of medieval sanctuary law often veered into litanies of the evils it visited upon society. On account of sanctuary, 'the strong, the swift, the premeditating murderer cheated the gallows' (Maitland and Montague 1915: 71). In sum, sanctuary was an 'error … costly to the civilized community, in that wrongdoing was protected' (Trenholme 1903: 96). From its infancy, criminology agreed. Beccaria concluded that 'places of asylum invite to crime more than punishments influence against it' (Beccaria 1986: 92). By the early modern period, not only had sanctuary come to be identified with injustice, but it was also credited with encouraging more crimes.

Just as detrimental was sanctuary's infringement upon the province of the sovereign and its laws. 'Within the borders of a country there should be no place independent of its laws', and 'to multiply such places of asylum is to create so many small sovereignties … where laws have no say' (ibid.: 92). With the end of sanctuary, 'we may see more clearly from what a fruitful source of outrages we are freed by the laws obtaining in all cases their natural and uninterrupted course' (Pegge 1787: 2).

The abolition of sanctuary, then, was heralded as a hallmark of progress. In the modern age, 'under a due administration of Justice', sanctuary can only be 'simply and constantly mischievous' (Hallam 1818: 2, 449). One nineteenth-century writer asserted that 'the more the administration of laws improved, and the less imperfect was the system of laws which they had to administer, the fewer the instances of resort to sanctuary' (de Mazzinghi 1887: 101). Indeed, if due process and a fair trial were guaranteed, 'sanctuary was a public nuisance' (Maitland and Montague 1915: 70). Its 'abolition was a measure calculated to advance the interests of justice and morality in the land' (Trenholme 1903: 98). For 'with the advent of a well-organized judiciary and even-handed justice, sanctuaries and asylums became places of escape rather than refuge' (ibid.: 1). The triumph of the rule of law was thought to have rendered sanctuary detrimental to the public good.

The uniform judgment of nineteenth- and early twentieth-century historians confirmed these opinions. For historians, sanctuary laws thrived in the Middle Ages because structures of law enforcement were weak and unorganized, leaving the field to violent bloodfeuds or, on occasions where wrongdoers were actually apprehended, to the overwhelming cruelty of royal punishments. In this lawless welter, historians saw sanctuary laws providing 'some green spots in the wilderness, where the feeble and the persecuted could find refuge' (Hallam 1818: 2, 449). 'The sanctuaries of medieval Christendom' were a stopgap measure – 'necessary remedies for a barbarous state of society' (Stanley 1861: 414). Indicative of 'all rude ages', sanctuary was thought to have 'substituted impartiality for prejudice' and 'mitigated the ferocious punishment' (de Mazzinghi 1887: 102). Examples could be multiplied, but the gist is clear. Without 'a universally competent public justice, where neither the general peace nor protection of the individual was well assured, and where common respect for sacred things preserved certain edifices and certain districts from acts of violence', sanctuaries flourished (Le Bras 1930: 1035). On the other hand, 'strong political power assured the order and restraint of asylum' (Timbal 1939: 454).

Recent scholarship has moved beyond assessing the utility of sanctuary for weak states. For example, Gervase Rosser has noticed that medieval sanctuary flourished not only in periods of relative disorder and violence but also in periods of relative stability and strong governance (Rosser 1996: 61). In addition, William Jordan has recently cautioned against 'reading the medieval history of sanctuary from the early modern assault on it', helpfully recognizing the extent to which early modern juridical accounts of sanctuary established the parameters of the historical accounts (Jordan 2008: 17). An essay by Richard Helmholz sets sanctuary law within its internal juridical context, showing how medieval sanctuary provides fertile ground for exploring how medieval canon lawyers developed rules to administer it (Helmholz 2001: 22). If we recall for a moment the creative forgers at Battle Abbey, it is clear that they considered sanctuary to be both an expression of strong, pious kingship and an integral feature of a just legal order.

Sanctuary and good kingship

Therefore, it is worth considering in more detail the historical conditions under which our forgers thought it significant to have William the Conqueror pronounce sanctuary protections for their church. For one thing, by the late twelfth century, William, despite being a conqueror, represented legal continuity with Anglo-Saxon rule. William had, after all, claimed the English throne by right of succession, not sheer conquest. The policies articulated in William's authentic post-Conquest charters and often repeated in twelfth-century Anglo-Norman legal collections favoured confirmation of the old laws and customs of England. William the Conqueror himself oversaw an ecclesiastical council in Normandy in 1080 which gave attention to the preservation of sanctuary law (Vitalis 1968–80: 5.5). The image of sanctuary-respecting kings was sufficiently powerful that William I's son, King Henry I, explained to Pope Calixtus II that he had invaded Normandy in 1106 because he had heard reports of frequent sanctuary breaches there. He thought he could justify his actions to the Pope by reference to his desire to protect sanctuary rights (ibid.: 6.12).

Twelfth-century English legal collections consistently credited old kings with promulgating laws that protected criminals who fled to churches. The so-called *Leis Willelme* affirmed sanctuary in its very first chapter, immediately following the prologue: 'Concerning some misdeed that a man has done, if he is able to come to a holy church, he shall have peace of his life and his limbs' (Liebermann 1903–16: 1, 498). The *Leis* were not promulgated by William. They were compiled (and created) by twelfth-century scribes who knew, or guessed, what the laws of William should have looked like (Wormald 1999: 410). Such collections, which proliferated in the twelfth century, consistently emphasized sanctuary to be chief among the legislative acts that gave old kings their proper kingly attributes.

The early twelfth-century *Laws of Edward the Confessor* provide similar evidence. Their fifth chapter provided that only a bishop or his ministers could remove one guilty or accused of a crime who had fled to a church (Liebermann 1903–16: 1, 630). The sanctuary articles in the *Laws of Edward*, consistent with twelfth-century canon laws, also extended sanctuary protection to the house of priests, not just the church itself (ibid.). At the same time, the *Laws of Edward* commanded thieves who fled to sanctuary to return what they had stolen or to make restitution from out of their own goods (ibid.). They also provided that those we might today call recidivists, those who took frequent recourse to sanctuary, were to 'foreswear the province and never return' (ibid.). If such a repeat offender did return from exile, the laws declared: 'let no one presume to receive him' except by consent of the king (ibid.). It has been observed that the sanctuary provisions in Edward's laws bore more similarity to the canons of Frankish church councils than to pre-Conquest Anglo-Saxon sanctuary laws, but the important point conveyed by the text to the twelfth-century reader was that King Edward stood firmly in favor of sanctuary (O'Brien 1999: 65–70). In fact, although the *Laws of Edward* sometimes betrayed considerable ignorance of Anglo-Saxon law in the time of Edward, portions of them have been considered to 'derive from [twelfth-century] experience' (Wormald 1999: 410).

Such developments were not peculiar to England. Traditions of sanctuary-granting kings circulated on the Continent as well. Some were factual, such as when Charlemagne introduced sanctuary legislation to the Saxons shortly after finally subduing them and forcing their conversion to Christianity in the 770s (Shoemaker 2011: 73–4). Others were apocryphal (though no less important on that account), such as the sanctuary legislation Roman Emperor Constantine was reputed to have issued in honour of his conversion and baptism (ibid.: 33). Whether they were aware of these precedents or not, twelfth-century English monks and legal compilers continually reminded English kings of how attentive their predecessors had been to sanctuary law. In this way, they emphasized to English kings that giving homicides and thieves a place to claim sanctuary was a pious and noble act, an expression of a particular form of kingly power that proved to be incredibly persistent. Far from a concession in the face of inept governance, sanctuary was understood in the twelfth century as an attribute of good kingship.

Sanctuary and the English common law

It was perhaps partly because of these reminders that when Henry II implemented his sweeping reforms of English criminal procedure in the 1160s and 1170s, sanctuary was brought securely within the ambit of royally defined legal process, at the same moment when other jurisdictional privileges were targeted for restriction (Shoemaker 2011: 102–3). Under policies which were solidified in the late twelfth century, sanctuary-seekers were required to identify themselves to royal officials and acknowledge the felony for which they had fled as a condition of receiving sanctuary. This was accomplished by charging the coroner, a royal office instituted in 1194, with the task of enrolling the name and the possessions of each sanctuary-seeker. After enrolling the offender and his felony, the coroner was required to administer an abjuration oath to the sanctuary-seeker. The abjuration oath was a solemn vow to leave England, with no hope of return without explicit royal permission. Abjuration oaths had been used occasionally for malefactors in early twelfth-century English law, but by the 1190s they were an integral feature of English sanctuary law. Typically, each sanctuary-seeker was required to choose a seaport from which to leave England within the space of 40 days. Although the documentary records of Henry's reforms at Clarendon and Northampton say nothing about sanctuary explicitly, thirteenth-century treatises paint a detailed picture of the sanctuary and abjuration process that had emerged in the common law. The early common law treatise *Britton*, for example, offers an oath that combined the confession of felony with the promise to abjure the realm:

> Hear this, coroner and other good people, that I, for such act that I did feloniously or assented to do, will go out of the realm of England … and

never will I return unless by consent of the king or his heirs, so help me God and the Saints.

(Nichols 1865: c. 17)

Rather than always being freely chosen, the plea rolls occasionally show coroners or others assigning the port from which the sanctuary-seeker was to depart (Hunnisett 1958: 41–2). According to *Britton*, abjurers then were required to don the garb of a penitent exile or crusader and travel 'with a wooden cross in their hands, unshod, ungirt, head uncovered and in their tunic only' (ibid.). Abjurers were to keep to the main highways until they reached the port and sailed away from England, never to return without royal permission.

A case that came before royal justices sitting in Berkshire in 1241 nicely illustrates how sanctuary had come to operate within the common law in the thirteenth century. Some time before 1241, and for reasons that are not stated in the record, Richard le Vacher and John Dobyn had come to the home of Matilda la Daye and killed her. Afterwards, they fled to the Church of St. Laurence in Reading. There, they claimed sanctuary, acknowledged their felony before two of the king's coroners, and, in exchange for safe passage and immunity from prosecution, abjured the realm of England. John and Richard appear to have left the church separately, for as John travelled out of Reading, Matilda's two daughters pursued him raising the hue and cry so that John was soon captured by villagers and taken to nearby Charlton. After being tried by the bailiff and men from Charlton and the surrounding hundreds, John was hanged.[1]

When the eyre came to Berkshire in 1241, the royal justices were informed of these events by twelve jurors from the nearby hundreds of Charlton. The first matter the justices inquired about was why a man who had claimed sanctuary and abjured the realm before two of the king's coroners had been captured, tried for felony by a hundred court, and hanged. The jurors attempted to explain the events by claiming that John had only 'abjured the fee of the abbot' of the Church of St. Laurence, not the realm of England, implying thereby that the abjuring felon was not protected once he left the abbot's jurisdiction. It appears that the eyre court was suspicious of this explanation, because the plea roll contains an interlinear addition in which one of the justices' scribes remarked that this account was 'according to what is testified by the jurors'. The coroners who administered the abjuration oaths offered a different account, claiming that John had 'abjured the realm of England', and was therefore illegally seized and executed. Because the jurors had misrepresented the facts of John's abjuration in their testimony, they were fined, as were the bailiffs and hundreds that had illicitly hanged John. Richard le Vacher avoided the summary justice that John had received. Although he was apparently also captured after abjuring from the church, he was still alive and in custody when the eyre justices arrived. He was brought before the eyre justices where he elected to stand trial and was acquitted of the felony and allowed to go free (NA, JUST 1/37/33r).

As the records of the thirteenth-century common law show, men and women of all stations and trades, nameless wanderers, and occasionally clerics took sanctuary for all sorts of felonies. At any given eyre visitation, scores of suspected or accused homicides, thieves, and other malefactors were entered in the rolls as having 'fled to the church, acknowledged the felony, and abjured the realm'. For example: 'Two malefactors fled to the church at Haliwell. It is not known where they were from, nor are their names noted. At the church they acknowledged thefts and abjured the realm' (NA, JUST/1/951A/3r). Or, 'a certain William and Radbert, under suspicion of wrongdoing, fled to the church, acknowledged thefts, and abjured the realm. They were strangers' (NA, JUST/1/951A/5d). Or again: 'two men and two women stole bread in the village of Ballingsbury, fled to the church, acknowledged the theft, and abjured the realm' (NA, JUST/1/229/14r).

Husbands and wives sometimes took sanctuary and abjured the realm together. On the other hand, Edith fled to the church, confessed to killing her husband, and abjured alone (NA, JUST/1/4/30d). Gernasius, who had assisted Edith in the killing, fled as well, but not to a church, so he was outlawed (ibid.). Infrequently, women abjured alone; more often, they did so with company (Shoemaker 2011: 124). When 'Greta who was the wife of Walter Russel put herself in the church' and abjured, 'the jurors testified that Angus of London, Alicia his consort, William Potter, and Henry of Winton' abjured as well (NA, JUST/1/60/29r). It may be that coroners consolidated abjurers when they arrived at a church to take acknowledgement of felony, assigning a single port to all the sanctuary-seekers who had arrived at a church since the last batch had been dispatched. Fathers and sons sometimes fled to sanctuary together, as did brothers, and occasionally entire bands of marauders (Shoemaker 2011: 123–5). This system of sanctuary and abjuration worked fairly smoothly for several centuries.

Sanctuary and the new criminal jurisprudence

Medieval English law, unlike its early modern and modern critics, seemed relatively untroubled by the fact that sanctuary-seekers avoided the penalties otherwise specified for felons, namely execution. However, as early as the thirteenth century such concerns were beginning to trouble canon lawyers. Gratian's *Decretum*, a twelfth-century legal text which formed one half of the foundation of the medieval *Corpus Iuris Canonici*, specifically asked whether someone who claimed sanctuary should be prosecuted anyway.

> Some say if no one is able [to bring an accusation] crimes would remain unpunished: but this ought not be. For in this manner the privilege of the Church would be an occasion for much delinquency. On account of this some say that [the sanctuary-seeker] is able to be accused by anyone, lest in this way [sanctuary] permit impunity.[2]

Such comments reveal a theoretical tension that medieval canon law was never able to resolve. Canonists were simultaneously developing doctrines of deterrence that would eventually clash with the underlying logic of sanctuary and at the same time striving to protect ecclesiastical liberties like sanctuary. The tension was neatly evident when the King of Scotland wrote to Pope Innocent III asking 'what should be done in regard to those who, perpetrating wrongs, flee to church so that, on account of reverence for the sacred place, they might succeed in evading due punishment?'[3] Innocent's answer first harkened to ancient principles, 'According to the sacred canons and the civil law … it must be distinguished whether the fugitive is a freeman or a *servus*.' Regarding *servi*, Innocent followed the rules that had survived from ancient Roman law: 'If a slave has fled to church, after his master has given an oath of impunity before the churchmen, let the slave be compelled to return to the service of his master, even unwillingly.' As to freemen, Innocent also began with the ancient principle:

> If free, no matter how grave a wrong he has committed, he is not to be violently dragged from the church, nor should he be condemned to death or punishment; but rectors of churches ought to strive to save the fugitive's life and members.

Then, partially following the *Decretum*, Innocent added: 'Above this, however, what he has done iniquitously should be punished in some other legitimate way.' The text of the *Decretum* had actually said that, once the fugitive's life and members were secure, 'he should *make composition* for what he did iniquitously'. Innocent replaced composition with punishment. But the truly remarkable change Innocent worked came next, when Innocent added: 'That is, unless the fugitive was a public thief or destroyer of fields by night, who often had insidiously and aggressively beset public highways', explaining that 'for wrongdoing of this magnitude, which both impedes public utility and noxiously molests everyone, the fugitive can be extracted' so that he does not succeed in gaining impunity.[4]

This was the direction the papacy continued to move in the fourteenth century. Noting the dangers that emerged in an age where the 'rod failed to correct', Pope Clement V ordered a bishop to remove a criminal from sanctuary in 1310 (Shoemaker 2011: 166). That the criminal had been complicit in a homicide may have sufficed under Roman law to remove him from the privilege, but Clement never invoked a rule excluding homicides from sanctuary and the papal court seems not to have applied a consistent policy in such cases. Instead, Clement stated that even though the sanctuary to which the killer fled was approved 'from ancient times', he was unwilling that crimes 'might remain unpunished' (ibid.). A decade later, Pope John XXII absolved Oddo, the duke of Burgundy, for seizing a cleric from an ecclesiastical immunity at Cluny. The duke had humbly explained that he had acted, not from 'contempt of the

Church, but from zeal for justice' and made sure to catalogue the cleric's considerable misdeeds (ibid.: 166). It was now, in the fourteenth century, possible to justify breaching sanctuary, and to oppose sanctuary laws in general, by claiming a laudable 'zeal for justice'.

Criticism of sanctuary consonant with the canonical critique began appearing in English sources by the end of the fourteenth century and with increasing frequency in the fifteenth century. In 1465, a complaint was lodged by the Commons to Edward IV that:

> Persons of diverse estates, resident both in the city of London and in its suburbs, as also from other parts of the kingdom ... flee with their masters' goods to the college of St. Martin le Grand in London with the intent of living there.
>
> (Shoemaker 2011: 168)

Almost two decades later, and again to Edward IV, the Commons complained anew of the permanent character acquired by the chartered sanctuaries so that felons in them:

> daily depart and go out of the said sanctuaries doing treasons and robberies and felonies ... despoiling [people] of their goods ... [And then] they resort again to the said sanctuaries ... there living by the goods ... [and by this] many of your people [are] undone.
>
> (NA, C 49/40/10)

Although Edward rejected the bill, the characterization of sanctuary as a cause for criminality, and the concomitant claim that reducing the scope of sanctuary would deter crime, stuck.

A petition made to Parliament in 1483 furthered the critique, which had been initiated within canon law, that sanctuary-seekers 'be not sorry of their outrageous treasons, felonies, and other offences'. Instead, 'by occasion of the said sanctuaries they ... commit great or greater treasons, felonies, and other offences [than] ever they did before time' (NA, C/49/40/10). Not only were sanctuary-seekers perceived not to regret their crimes, the existence of sanctuaries appeared to encourage ever more audacious crimes. The petition linked this lack of regret to an insufficient 'dread for the sovereign's laws' (ibid.). The rhetoric of the petition was rife with anxieties about the capacity of the penal law to prevent law-breaking and firm convictions that sanctuary laws only hindered good order. As such late fifteenth-century complaints against sanctuary grew more vociferous, chartered sanctuaries, like Westminster, became the foil for sanctuary's opponents. But restricting these perceived abuses was not simply a matter of royal fiat. Because liberties once granted to the Church could prove difficult to take back, the last half of the fifteenth century featured several abortive attempts to undo the chartered liberties and the sanctuary privileges they offered (Kaufman 1984: 465–76).

No longer understood as an appropriate response to serious crime, sanctuary had come to be seen as a nuisance. Some wrongs were perceived to pose such a threat to public interest that their perpetrators could not be protected by sanctuary. Rather than a way for wrongdoers to make satisfaction for their wrongs, sanctuary was simply a way to evade punishment. Worse yet, because some wrongdoers might commit wrongs in anticipation of claiming sanctuary, sanctuary was recast as an invitation to commit crime. Canon law could now routinely express a tension between sanctuary and the new conception of punishment. As Pope Euginius IV wrote to the Bishop of Lincoln in 1442, by virtue of sanctuary, wrongdoers 'escape the punishment of their evil deeds and the satisfaction of their debts' and effect 'the supplanting of justice', providing a 'detestable example to others'. Many 'live [in sanctuary] for a long time, even with dishonest women', to the 'scandal and corruption of the religious and other honest men who dwell therein' (Tremlow 1912: 9.282).

With a frontal attack, Henry VIII accomplished what his predecessors had half begun, restricting sanctuary privileges almost completely. Given Henry VIII's break with the papacy, the classic view was that the fate of English sanctuary law was entirely determined by a struggle between royal prerogative and ecclesiastical privilege (Thornley 1924: 182). Henry did remove 'willful murder, rape, burglary, robbery in the highway or any house' as well as arson from the sanctuary privilege.[5] As a result, churches could only serve as sanctuaries for lesser offences, while the most serious felonies, which had made up the majority of sanctuary cases in the earlier centuries, were excluded from the privilege. By 1540, Henry had designated eight towns in England as permanent sanctuaries, though there were limits on how many fugitives could reside in a sanctuary town at one time. These alternative sanctuaries were intended, in part, to curtail abjuration because Henry feared that abjuring Englishmen were teaching archery and other martial skills to the French. Meanwhile, a significant effort by royal justices steadily narrowed the scope of the sanctuary privilege (Thornley 1924: 200–1).

As Isobel Thornley (ibid.: 204) noted, 'Sanctuary was a very tough privilege which survived more than one legal abolition.' It is clear that sanctuary men were part of an abbot's procession in 1556, so apparently the practice continued in some form through the middle of the sixteenth century (Cox 1911: 75). Under James I, there were several attempts to draft legislation that abolished the privilege entirely, and the legislation passed in 1623 seems to have accomplished this aim. At that point in seventeenth-century England, the promiscuous availability of sanctuary for murder and theft was all but gone.

Tempting as it is to read this as a strand of confessional conflict, sanctuary was also undergoing important restrictions at this time in Catholic countries as well. In France, large-scale restrictions on sanctuary were issued in 1539, 1547 and 1555. The frequency of legislation prohibiting sanctuary is in part a testament to the endurance of the practice in regions of France, but also a result of the decentralized legislative power in sixteenth-century France (Timbal 1939:

430–1). In 1591, a papal bull from Gregory XIV all but abolished sanctuary within the canon law, but the groundwork had already been laid in the previous centuries.

The *Codex Juris Canonici* of 1917 offered a distilled, but recognizable version of the rule: 'A Church enjoys the right of sanctuary … Wrongdoers who have fled to church should not be dragged out without the consent of the ordinary or rector. An exception is allowed only in extreme necessity' (CIC 1917: c. 1179). In the most recent edition no rule concerning sanctuary even appears (Landau 1994: 47). But in truth, this was only the quiet disappearance of a law whose claim had long ago fallen silent and whose faint echoes we perhaps are no longer able to hear.

Notes

1. The archival records of itinerate justices in medieval England are housed in the National Archive (hereinafter NA) in Kew, England. The convention for citing to these unpublished manuscripts is to refer to them by the file name and number under which they are archived. In the case mentioned here, the citation is JUST/1/37/33r.1
2. *Glos.ord.* to C. 17. q. 4. c. 9. The translation is mine.
3. *Liber Extra* 3.49.6.
4. Ibid.
5. 22 Henry VIII, c. 14; 27 Henry VIII, c. 19; 32 Henry VIII, c. 12, in *Statutes of the Realm*, (1810).

References

Beccaria, C. (1986) *On Crimes and Punishments*, ed. R. Bellamy, trans. R. Davies, New York: Cambridge University Press.

[CIC] *Codex Iuris Canonici* (1917) Vatican City: Typis Polyglottis Vaticanis, available in English translation in: Peters, E. (2001) *The 1917 or Pio-Beredictive Code of Canon Law: In English Translation with Extensive Scholarly Apparatus*. San Francisco: Ignatius Press.

Cox, J.C. (1911) *Sanctuaries and Sanctuary Seekers*, London: G. Allen and Sons.

Davis, H.W.C. (ed.) (1913) *Regesta Regum Anglo-Normannorum, 1066–1154*, Oxford: Oxford University Press.

de Mazzinghi, T. (1887) *Sanctuaries*, Stafford: Halden and Sons.

Hallam, H. (1818) *A View of the State of Europe During the Middle Ages*, 2 vols, London: John Murray.

Helmholz, R. (2001) *The Ius Commune in England: Four Studies*, Oxford: Oxford University Press.

Hunnisett, R.F. (1958) 'The Origins of the Office of Coroner', *Transactions of the Royal Historical Society* 8: 86.

Jordan, W.C. (2008) 'A Fresh Look at Medieval Sanctuary', in R.M. Karras, J. Kaye and E.A. Matter (eds) *Law and the Illicit in Medieval Europe*, Philadelphia, PA: University of Pennsylvania.

Kaufman, P. (1984) 'Henry VII and Sanctuary', *Church History*, 53: 465–76.

Landau, P. (1994) 'Traditionen des Kirchenasyl', in K. Barwig and D.R. Bauer (eds) *Asyl am Heiligen Ort: Sanctuary und Kirchenasylvom Rechtsanspruchzurethischen Verpflichtung*, Ostfildern: Schwabenverlag.

Le Bras, G. (1930) 'Asile', in A. Baudrillart (ed.) *Dictionnaire d'histoire et de géographie ecclésiastiques*, Paris: Institut Catholique de Paris de l'Académie Française, Col. 1035–47.

Liebermann, F. (1903–16) *Gesetze der Angelsachsen*, ed. F. Liebermann, Halle: M. Niemeyer, reprinted (1960) Aalen:Scientia.

Maitland, F. and Montague, F. (1915) *A Sketch of English Legal History*, New York: G.P. Putnam and Sons.

Mattheas, A. (1987–94) *On Crimes: A Commentary on Books XLVII and XLVIII of the Digest*, ed. and trans. M.L. Hewett, Cape Town: Juta.

Menochius, J. (1695) *De ivrisdictione, imperio et potestate ecclesiastica ac secvlari libritres. Accessit liber quartus De immunitate ecclesiae, pro ad eamconfugientibus*, Geneva: J.A. Cramer & P. Perachon.

Nichols, F.M. (ed. and trans.) (1865) *Britton*, Oxford: Clarendon Press.

O'Brien, Jr. B.R. (1999) *God's Peace and King's Peace: The Laws of Edward the Confessor*, Philadelphia, PA: The University of Pennsylvania Press.

Pegge, S. (1787) 'A Sketch of the History of Asylum, or Sanctuary', *Archaeologia*, 8: 1.

Rosser, G. (1996) 'Sanctuary and Social Negotiation in Medieval England', in J. Blair and B. Golding (eds) *The Cloister and the World: Essay in Honour of Barbara Harvey*, Oxford: Clarendon Press.

Searle, E. (ed. and trans) (1980) *The Chronicle of Battle Abbey*, New York: Oxford University Press.

Shoemaker, K. (2011) *Sanctuary and Crime in the Middle Ages, 400–1500*, New York: Fordham University Press.

Stanley, A.P. (1861) *Memorials of Westminster*, London: John Murray.

Thornley, I.D. (1924) 'The Destruction of Sanctuary', in *Tudor Studies Presented to A.F. Pollard*, London: The University of London Board of Studies in History.

Timbal, P. (1939) *Le droit d'asile*, Paris: Sirey.

Tremlow, A. (1912) *Calendar of Entries in the Papal Registers Relating to Great Britain and Ireland, Papal Letters, 1431–1447*, London.

Trenholme, N. (1903) *The Right of Sanctuary in England: A Study in Institutional History*, Columbia, MO: The University of Missouri Press.

Vitalis, O. (1968–80) *The Ecclesiastical History of Orderic Vitalis*, ed. and trans. M. Chibnall, Oxford: Oxford Medieval Texts.

Wormald, P. (1999) *The Making of English Law: King Alfred to the Twelfth Century*, vol. 1, Oxford: Blackwell.

Chapter 2

'I took up the case of the stranger'
Arguments from faith, history and law

David H. Michels and David Blaikie

Introduction

It may seem surprising that faith groups would offer sanctuary to refused refugees, or material support to undocumented migrants. These acts of resistance and compassion require normally law-abiding moral people to make a conscious choice to defy government and perhaps, if necessary, even break the law. The success of sanctuary movements (defined broadly here) relies on broad public support both to attract willing collaborators and to forestall government intervention. Previous studies have examined the discourse around sanctuary practice, and the ensuing public debates. This chapter adds to this body of work by offering an empirical study of how individuals and groups publicly justified acts of sanctuary. We offer a comparative analysis of these claims in Canada, the United States and the United Kingdom, and finally we attempt to respond, in a limited way, to the challenges raised by these voices. The jurisdictions considered share similar legal, faith and cultural histories, but we seek to understand how their distinct political and geographic contexts shaped their movements. We find that sanctuary practice, and even its very definition, vary widely across these jurisdictions, from shelter in a church – our traditional conception – to rescue in the wilderness. We also discover that sanctuary supporters we heard share a common motivation, and perhaps for those from a Christian worldview, a theological commitment broad enough to encircle all these expressions.

Note on method

In order to capture a snapshot of the public discourse on sanctuary, we conducted a thematic analysis of English language newspaper articles accessible through the *Factiva News* database published since 1980 in the three jurisdictions. *Factiva* archives major new sources, and included 26 UK, 39 US and 6 leading Canadian sources at the time of the search. The periodicals included would have the widest circulation. We chose print media stories, as they appeared to be the primary means to access the general public. We used search terms 'asylum' or 'sanctuary' and 'church' or 'mosque' or 'temple' and 'refugee'. We removed irrelevant/duplicate articles from these results, and then identified direct quotations by sanctuary supporters that offered some justification for their actions. We analyzed these justifications to identify reoccurring themes. The use of print news sources raises concern over journalistic bias and misrepresentation of religious issues (see Haskell 2009; Marshall *et al.* 2008; but contra Buddenbaum 2010; Underwood 2002). Are these the justifications of the sanctuary supporters or merely the media's construction? That question is beyond the scope of this work, but to balance potential news media bias we listened for 'echoes' of identified themes in other media such as articles published in church publications since 1980, accessed through the *ATLA Religion Index*, web documents published by sanctuary advocate groups, and finally, court/legislative documents accessed through the *Lexis-Nexis* legal database. For each jurisdiction we included a section called 'Echoes' where we briefly described instances where we heard these themes mirrored outside the news media.

Hearing their voices

The United Kingdom

The newspaper accounts we gathered spanned 31 years, from 1987 to 2008. There was an even distribution across that span except for a spike of seven stories in 1989. We identified 29 stories that contained specific justifications for the practice of sanctuary and coded 105 quotations. The stories contained voices of clergy and laypeople, Catholics, Protestants, Muslims, and those un-religious. The beneficiaries of sanctuary in these accounts all appeared to be refugee claimants who had been through the refugee process, and who were now under deportation orders without further state assistance. Often, they had developed relationships within the community during the lengthy period when their cases were being adjudicated. Notable at the outset was that these sanctuary practitioners in the UK understood their acts were illegal, and that any sanctuary right had been long abolished. Although several allusions were made to international human rights standards, there were no attempts to suggest these sanctuary acts were in any way legal. However, natural justice concepts permeated their discourse; 'when we are faced with laws that we believe are unfair laws, then changing those laws has to be the top priority in a democracy' (Paterson 1997) and 'I will keep fighting until I win, because justice is on our side' (Sharratt 1988).

Moral outrage

In most stories, compassion was a justification. Practitioners saw their acts as basic human kindness. A prevalent sub-theme was moral outrage: outrage at what was deemed a broken refugee system, and outrage at how their government handled deportees. The system was often portrayed as unhearing, uncaring, and unaccountable, in the face of what practitioners viewed as very real threats to human life and safety. Several accounts alleged systemic discrimination and racism. The argument being built through many news accounts was that these are broken and vulnerable people in need of protection. Where the state was perceived to have failed to provide that protection, communities and frequently churches were portrayed as having stepped into this role, and, in doing so, claimed the higher moral ground.

The conception of the broken system also invoked both puzzlement and anger. In more recent articles, many refugees were also described as positive contributors to society, and consequently their removal was baffling: 'Britain's going to be a better place for them, not a worse place, so I just don't know what the problem is' (Stevenson and Grant 2008). There were frequent accounts of positive experiences with refugee claimants clearly intended to rebut negative stereotypes that practitioners felt were often portrayed in the media. In these accounts, the UK needed the refugee claimants' contributions as much as the claimants needed protection.

There was acceptance in many stories that some claimants' refugee applications will fail, and they will be deported. The frequent argument here was that the process needed to be more humane. This is significant because how the state dealt with failed refugee claimants was perhaps the most galvanizing element for these practitioners. 'It was like watching the Gestapo – men with armour, going in to flats with battering rams ... I am not going to stand by and watch this happen again' (ibid.). There were frequent accounts of alleged inhumane treatment against deportees and strong-arm tactics by police. The strong language, alluding to Anne Frank, jackboots, and the Gestapo, might create a visceral reaction with readers.

Faith

Faith was also a theme, though usually articulated by clergy, not lay supporters. One clergy practitioner alluded to the liberation activists of Central America (Vulliamy 2006) but voices were more pragmatic than theological. Christian faith was often portrayed as the source of morality in these accounts: 'the 69 year old is a committed Christian and believes the choice of "leave or starve" is inhumane' (Stevenson and Grant 2008). Curiously, the biblical practice of sanctuary was not invoked in these stories, but rather responsibility to the stranger:

> The most important place to find the beginnings of our idea is not in any political action but in the Bible. There is a constant emphasis in the Bible that the stranger, the alien, the friendless is a special responsibility of God's people.
>
> (Scott 1996)

This idea figured strongly, and was usually portrayed as intrinsic to the calling of the Church: 'They are doing what any church should do – giving help to those who need it' (Paterson 1997). Heroes of the faith were held up as exemplars, like St Francis of Assisi, St Thomas à Beckett, and Jesus Christ: 'where else are we to find Jesus if not with the outcast and oppressed?' (Vulliamy 2006). Antitypes such as the Kings Henry II and VIII were also noted.

Faith arguments often placed Christian duty at odds with duty to the state, and in those situations Christian duty usually took precedence. This conflict was often framed as merely 'fulfilling the law of Christ', but in several articles it was very explicit:

> Christians ought to observe the law and support the state. But ever since New Testament times, Christians have also felt that they also have an obligation to God and that may occasionally come into conflict with the state. When that happens, Christians have found that what, in prayer and conscience, they take to be the will of God, takes precedence over the laws of the state.
>
> (Paterson 1996)

This conscious choice rarely brought the church and state into direct conflict. The reference to English martyr Thomas à Beckett compared Manchester police's forcible removal of failed refugee Viraj Mendis in 1989 to King Henry's slaughter of Beckett in Canterbury Cathedral (Miller 1989). By invoking inflammatory imagery, the state's violation of sanctuary was paralleled with historical attacks against the English Church. Interestingly, the 2002 forcible removal of the Ahmadi family from a mosque raised questions whether police would have acted similarly in a Christian church (Coyish 2002).

Echoes

When we considered online documents posted by sanctuary supporters, we found, not surprisingly, more developed and nuanced positions. The plight of refused asylum seekers was addressed in documents from sites such as the *General Synods of the Church of England* (Church of England 2011), the *Methodist Church* (Harvey 2009a), and *Churches Together in Britain and Ireland* (Harvey 2009b). In these documents we saw an emphasis on the principles of natural justice, the experiences of individual asylum seekers, and the Church's obligation to assist. These emphases were similar to the expressions in the news stories. A briefing document from the 2009 *Church of England Synod* reminded delegates 'to take Deuteronomy 10:19 seriously: "You shall also love the stranger, for you were strangers in the land of Egypt"' (Church of England 2009). These texts offered a fuller articulation of Christian theology around asylum, but also explored human rights obligations in international law. This latter theme was rarely seen in the news stories, but this is not surprising because most sanctuary supporters interviewed were involved at the local church level, and would not be expected to possess an understanding of international humanitarian law.

The United States

We identified 30 news stories falling between 1991 and 2009 containing 84 justifications for sanctuary. It appeared that all speakers were of the Christian faith. The distribution of the news stories reflects the two sanctuary movements of recent US history. Newspaper accounts from 1991 to 1996 are about 'The Sanctuary Movement' (SM) of the 1980s. The primary concern of this social movement was the plight of Central American refugees, mainly from El Salvador and Guatemala. One scholar explained the political and social context of the time:

> The 1980s mass movement formed in response to the Refugee Act of 1980. During this time, violent wars raged in El Salvador and Guatemala; El Salvador had been engulfed by civil war since 1979, while in Guatemala, 11,000 people were killed in just 1983 alone. Thousands of refugees from these countries fled to the United States seeking political asylum, only to be routinely rejected and deported. The main problem lay with the 1980 *Refugee Act*, which was supposed to be a fairer version of the refugee policy already existing in the United States, but proved to be quite the opposite. The Act intended to establish a non-ideological standard for refugee and asylum determination, stating that a refugee was 'any person' who was 'unable or unwilling to return to … that country because of persecution or a well-founded fear of persecution.' In reality, someone fleeing a country friendly to the United States was less likely to gain asylum than someone fleeing an unfriendly country, such as one from the Soviet bloc, even if the harms suffered were the same.
>
> (Wild 2009: 3; see also Chinchilla *et al.* 2009)

Newspaper accounts from 2001 to 2009 described practices that developed into what is now called the 'New Sanctuary Movement' (NSM) (see Yukich, Chapter 7, and Caminero-Santangelo, Chapter 6, in this volume). This movement arose in response to the treatment of migrant workers and undocumented migrations from Mexico and South and Central America. A 2007 newspaper story covering the formal launch of the new movement, explained:

> Churches in a handful of U.S. cities are preparing to launch a 'sanctuary movement' to help illegal immigrants stave off deportation, hoping to unite faith-based groups in a push for immigration reform …
>
> The movement 'will enable congregations to publicly provide hospitality and protection to a limited number of migrant families whose legal cases clearly reveal the contradictions and moral injustice of our current immigration system,' according to the New Sanctuary Movement's Web site …
>
> The new sanctuary plans come as immigration reform legislation has been stalled since last summer, with Congress split over whether to first

strengthen border security and immigration laws or extend a path to citizenship to illegal immigrants.

(Prengaman 2007)

Some stories appearing between 2001 and 2009 were retrospective accounts of the SM. Still others focused on and quoted individuals involved in both movements; from individuals in the first movement commenting on the second; or from individuals in the second movement who look to the history and perceived success of the first as a source of inspiration and direction. The newspaper stories revealed an overlap between the two movements in membership, strategy, and justifications, a fact commented on by some scholars (see e.g. Wild 2009; but see Yukich, Chapter 7, in this volume).

Saving lives

Many justifications articulated by supporters in both movements underscore the life-saving goal of their actions. The justification is presented in clear and stark terms, a moral imperative: people are dying and someone must do something. Newspaper accounts in 2003 are about individuals and groups providing assistance to illegal immigrants crossing the Arizona desert. The number of immigrants who had died trying to cross the desert galvanized them. 'Too many people were dying,' said the Rev. Robin Hoover, pastor of the First Christian Church in Tucson. 'Death in the desert has called on many of us—former players and new ones—to coordinate our efforts to again address this situation' (Ellingwood 2001). 'It's a pretty, upsetting situation, and frankly, we are in a humanitarian crisis,' said another (Innes 2002). To save lives, supporters searched border areas for people in distress and also started a programme of setting up water stations in the desert. To the charge that their actions were illegal, one leader of the nascent movement stated: 'We are doing nothing more than giving humanitarian aid to people in the desert who may be dying or in failing health' (ibid.).

Asked to sum up the SM, one person responded simply: 'It's the work of saving lives' (Tai 1993). Reflecting on the movement's success, another asserted that it 'saved a great deal of people who might otherwise have been killed in their own countries' (Pence 1996). 'These people were in a life-or-death situation. It was a matter of saving lives. If they were caught by Border Patrol and sent back to their country in handcuffs, they were delivered to the death squads,' explained one person in a 2009 retrospective account (Matas 2009). A response to the charge by authorities and opponents that the immigrants were simply migrant workers entering the US to find work was that 'We were able to counter their argument with evidence of why the refugees were really coming here—because they were trying to save their lives, not make money' (Pence 1996).

Challenging and changing unjust laws

Participants in the SM believed that the US government – their own government – was involved in some way in the torture and killing of people in Central America (see Hector Perla and Susan Bibler Coutin, Chapter 5, in this volume). They further contended that the government was breaching international law or the domestic *Refugee Act* by refusing entry to or deporting persons from Central America. In 1991, Sister Kathleen Healy, head of the San Francisco Covenant, stated that: 'The Justice Department today implicitly acknowledges that it has been in gross violation of the law of the land for 10 years' (Egelko 1991). Movement leaders accused the US of war crimes and acting in contravention of the 1949 Geneva Convention (Innes 2002).

Participants in the latter part of the SM contended, in justification of their actions, that American immigration laws were unjust.

> As an organization, we do not encourage people to break the law. We, do, though, advocate quite strongly that unjust laws be changed. In fact, we don't think it's right that honest people should have to die in the desert to try to find a job.
> (Seigel 2001)

Some participants argued that the domestic laws are unjust and appeal to a higher law, whether international laws protecting human rights or a superior and superseding moral law. As one person stated in justifying the actions of the NSM: 'Our function is to help the weakest. Sometimes that means going against the rules, but God's laws are superior' (Trevizo 2007). Facing a choice between competing laws, many in the NSM saw themselves in a situation where they had to make a decisive choice and take practical steps to counter unjust laws.

Echoes

When we reviewed online documents produced and disseminated by sanctuary groups, we noted parallels to justifications identified in newspaper accounts. For example, a 1984 study paper published by the Evangelical Lutheran Church in America (ELCA) asserted that justifications for the movement were not to be found in the ancient theological traditions of hospitality or the Old Testament tradition of cities of refuge. Rather, the paper contended, the sanctuary movement is more properly understood in the tradition of civil disobedience (see also Cunningham, Chapter 11, in this volume). This pronouncement by the ELCA is consonant with the prominent justifications identified above: saving lives and countering unjust laws (ELCA 1984). In a similar vein, online material posted by NSM supporters focused on concerns that appeared prominently in the newspaper accounts: unjust laws that cause human suffering. In a blog called

'God's Politics: A Blog by Jim Wallis and Friends', a story appears by Rev. Alexia Salvatierra, the Executive Director of CLUE (Clergy and Laity United for Economic Justice) (Salvatierra 2007). Rev. Salvatierra writes:

> Sanctuary is an act of compassion, an expression of mercy. It is, however, not mercy at the expense of justice. Participants in the New Sanctuary Movement believe that our current immigration system is profoundly unjust – so unjust that we believe that we are facing one of those unique moments throughout history when divine law and human law are in conflict and God's justice demands that we stand with those who break unjust laws even at the risk of sharing their punishment.

It is noteworthy that not all NSM advocates would agree that these actions are in fact illegal under US law (e.g. Center for Human Rights and Constitutional Law 2011).

Canada

We identified 98 unique news stories in the Canadian media press, and coded 253 quotations that contained justifications for sanctuary. These stories were drawn from the period 1987 to 2011 but were not evenly distributed across that time period. There were several very significant spikes in occurrences around 1987 (n = 5), 2004 (n = 8), 2006–7 (n = 37) and 2010 (n = 10). The 1987 spike reflects Canada's involvement in the US Sanctuary Movement, the 2004 spike coincides with the Canadian government's first violation of sanctuary, and the latter two spikes appear to coincide with changes in government refugee and immigration policy (see Lippert 2006).

Caring for neighbours and friends

Moral arguments were the most common justification, occurring in 134 quotations. Rarely did we find grand arguments about the role of sanctuary in Canadian society, and when they were made, they were usually articulated by clergy: 'We're also called to be a kind of conscience of the nation and raise questions when we feel things are unjust' (Mayeda 2006). The earliest news story on Central American refugees in 1987 contained the justification: 'We're doing it because we believe they have a right to come to Canada … we're not going to change that just because of a law.' Most moral arguments were rather personal concerns for the safety of the refused refugee and their families: 'These people are established. They are our neighbours and friends. Why the hell are they being treated like this?' (Sanders 2007). The majority of cases were claimants who had been in the community during their lengthy process, developed deep ties, and were now perceived differently. Not all refugees in sanctuary were Christian or in churches, but there was a perception expressed in several stories that the government would be less inclined to violate sanctuary of a Christian church rather than of a mosque or temple. Canadian sanctuary supporters appear willing to ignore past illegal behaviour in offering sanctuary. Those sheltered have included former spies and convicts who later changed their lives. Undergirding some justifications were particular ideas about Canada and Canadians, 'I believe my country of Canada behaves with compassion and decency' (Schultz 2007), perhaps suggesting that sanctuary supporters rather than the government represented the 'true Canada'. Although many speakers expressed strong emotions, few resorted to inflammatory language, though one supporter invoked the memory of French citizens who hid Jews from Nazis (Petricevic 2006).

Two subsets of cases at both ends of this period were noteworthy. One presented a unique Canadian problem: US deserters during the Iraq War, and the second regarding Central American refugees, and the US Sanctuary Movement. During the Vietnam War, Canada welcomed large numbers of war resisters from the United States, and churches, notably the United Church of Canada supported these new arrivals (Maxwell 2006: 807). Though not supporting the Iraq War, this time the Canadian government did not automatically extend refugee status to American deserters. In response, some churches sheltered resisters from deportation, and justified this action both on moral and historical grounds: 'To embrace those resisting war is part of our heritage ... the strong Canadian tradition as a haven from militarism' (Petricevic 2006). The second unique group was Central American refugee claimants particularly discussed in news stories from 1987 to 92. These sanctuary supporters appeared to identify with their American counterparts, and were more likely to speak in strong moral terms: 'I'm sorry, but we have a wicked government' (Cleroux and Wilson 1987).

Bridging the gap

The second most dominant theme was the 'broken system', expressed in 73 quotations. General complaints described systemic problems: 'clearly, he was lost in the shuffle and that's not his fault, it's the fault of the system' (Egan 2007). These complaints included unreasonably slow processes, lost documentation, and rigid policies – problems endemic to many bureaucracies. Supporters countered that the consequences of a breakdown of this system might be catastrophic: 'when genuine refugees fall between the cracks in a system, they can die there' (Kapica 1993). Supporters had specific issues with the system, particularly the lack of an appeal process for refused refugees. This was a contentious issue in the later years when supporters' alleged promised reforms were not implemented (see also Lippert 2009; Czajka, Chapter 3, in this volume). Consequently, supporters proposed the gap justification: 'Churches engage in this act of civil disobedience largely because of inadequate appeal procedures' (Parker 2006) and 'many people feel they are conscience-bound to fill the gap that the government has created' (Logan 2004). This justification was often paired with an expressed reluctance to be involved: 'Fix the system,' said one supporter, 'and sanctuary would not be needed' (Read 2007). In several narratives, supporters argued they offered sanctuary only rarely and after careful consideration. The information sources supporters used in their determinations were described as superior to that used by the government.

Faith and tradition

We identified justifications invoking faith or tradition in 64 quotations. Some were framed as expressions of a church mission to take counter-cultural positions or simply to express compassion: 'This was a really positive time in our church life: what the church is for, what is the church's mission' (Suderman 2006). There were other descriptions of positive impacts on the supporting church. Supporters justified sanctuary as part of every major faith tradition, premised on the sacredness of life. Explicit biblical citations were few, focusing on care of the poor and strangers, and, in only three occurrences, the biblical concept of sanctuary. Sacred figures were also invoked in several accounts, such as the Holy Family fleeing to Egypt as refugees, the Good Samaritan, and Sir Thomas More as an archetype of God's servant before the King. Perhaps the boldest affirmations were those that juxtaposed God and King: 'No Christian needs reminding that we owe obligations to both God and Caesar' (Hunter 2000) and, 'there's a higher law, the law of God. We cannot take a decision against someone's life' (Bongers 1992). The sanctuary tradition could be either 'respected' or 'violated' by authorities. Thus, the meaning of tradition varied and was invoked as a tradition of humanitarian aid, war resistance, biblical sanctuary, refugee support or shelter in the House of God.

Echoes

We identified documents created by the United Church of Canada (UCC), the Canadian Conference of Catholic Bishops (CCCB), the Presbyterian Church in Canada (PCC), and the Evangelical Lutheran Church in Canada (ELCC). Several of these documents were created to give guidance to local congregations considering offering sanctuary. When we considered these documents, we noted that none of these supporters argued these practices were legal, only morally necessary. We found that appeals to historical and Biblical sanctuary practice were present (e.g. 'cities of refuge', United Church of Canada 2004: 3) but not emphasized. The more common appeal was to moral religious obligations to 'offer hospitality to the stranger ... ' (Presbyterian Church in Canada 2006: 2), and to act on conscience when laws violate the moral order (Canadian Conference of Catholic Bishops 2005: s. 12). Each document noted the absence of an appeal process based on merit, echoing concerns raised by supporters as noted above.

Two important themes

In our review we were faced with the question, 'What is sanctuary for these supporters?' For some, it entwined ideas of hospitality and compassion, while it was civil disobedience for others. In all jurisdictions grassroots sanctuary supporters described being motivated by real concern for human suffering. In the UK, Canada, and the SM in the US, supporters appear to sincerely believe the threat to refugees' lives if they were returned home. The UK supporters also addressed the immediate deprivation of basic necessities for refugees, while the later US movements addressed an immediate danger of death by exposure. Sanctuary supporters appeared to be acting in good faith as Good Samaritans. In all jurisdictions there were general concerns about the fairness of their respective refugee systems, but supporters in the UK and Canada sought to address specific problems by their actions. Supporters found it impossible to ignore the withdrawal of state support in the UK for failed refugees and the alleged heavy-handed removal tactics. The lack of an appeal process in the Canadian system provided both the opportunity and perceived necessity for intervention. Where many factors behind refugee migrations are beyond individual state control, supporters identified issues that governments were able to address. The US supporters appeared far more critical about the viability of their nation's immigration system.

Turning briefly to religious arguments, supporters were quick to note that concepts of sanctuary exist in most faith traditions. 'Abd al-Rahim, for instance, has argued for an Islamic understanding of sanctuary founded on the dignity of humans ('Abd al-Rahim 2008). Most religious justifications in these news stories were rooted in a Christian worldview. We have addressed elsewhere the applicability of the biblical practice of sanctuary like the 'Cities of Refuge' to contemporary practices (Michels and Blaikie 2009). It is sufficient here to note that this biblical and the modern practice addressed different issues, and were not analogous. Sobrino has offered perhaps the earliest modern theological justification of sanctuary:

> The sanctuary movement is justified theologically because it is a way of defending the lives of the poor and thus of believing and acting out biblical faith. The central theological thesis is as follows: God is the defender of the lives of the poor and that defense is absolute and unconditional.
> (Sobrino 1988: 169)

Acknowledging later theological justifications, we felt Sobrino's thesis remains wide enough to include all the expressions of sanctuary we identified. We recognized that many supporters wrestled with a theological tension. We heard expressed the two New Testament maxims: 'we must obey God rather than human beings' (Acts 5:19) and 'give to Caesar what is Caesar's and to God what is God's' (Mark 12:17). Against these is the further obligation of respect and obedience to temporal authorities (Romans 13:1). The interpretative history of these texts is considerable, (see Pervo 2009: 144; also Evans 1982: 245; Marcus 2000: 826) and points to the challenges that Christians have had in being faithful to these obligations, and the difficult choices they have made when they cannot.

Conclusion

Given the considerable involvement by churches in sanctuary provision, we had anticipated more complex religious arguments. There was some evidence of these in the documents of religious groups. More often, supporters argued from a moral ground, and invoked the role of conscience, frequently using religious terminology. We are inclined to believe that the religious justifications were in some respects after-thoughts, though supporters were frequently motivated by the strong moral traditions of these communities. Rather, many supporters presented their acts in the traditions of civil disobedience, rooted in the social history of Western democratic states. This potentially situates these actions within the ethos of our times with the 'Arab Spring' and the 'Occupy Wall Street' movements. Theologians like Jim Wallis are already making these connections:

> Offering that sanctuary to the Occupiers – at our tables, on our property, in our parish halls and church basements, and in our sanctuaries for the quiet prayer and reflection that every movement needs to sustain itself – could be the beginning of a powerful relationship between the faith community and the leaders of an emerging generation that is so clearly and passionately committed to creating a better world.
>
> (Wallis 2011)

We are uncertain how to interpret the choice of moral rather than religious arguments. Certainly, the failures to address clergy abuse in Canada, the UK, and the US have undermined public confidence in the churches' moral leadership. Justifications built on conscience rather than faith may be perceived as more readily accepted. Yet it appears to us that there may be room for a religious argument as well that draws on these strong moral traditions of compassion, justice and care giving. Perhaps it will be the impetus for other civil movements such as Wallis described above that will inspire religious groups to develop and more clearly articulate a theology of sanctuary and civil action rooted in their own understandings of human dignity.

References

'Abd al-Rahim, M. (2008) 'Asylum: a Moral and Legal Right in Islam', *Refugee Survey Quarterly* 27: 15–23.

Bongers, A. (1992) 'Church Groups Hide Rejected Refugees "Matter of Conscience" Nun Says', *The Hamilton Spectator*, 11 July, p. A1.

Buddenbaum, J.M. (2010) 'Blind Spot: When Journalists Don't Get Religion', *Journal of Media and Religion*, 9: 47–51.

Canadian Conference of Catholic Bishops (2005) *A Briefing Note for the Bishops of Canada Concerning Sanctuary for Refugees in Catholic Churches*. Available at: http://www.cccb.ca.

Center for Human Rights and Constitutional Law (2011) *Legal Justification for the Legal Status of Sanctuary Communities*. Available at: http://www.newsanctuarymovement.org/legal.htm.

Chinchilla, N.S., Hamilton, N. and Loucky, J. (2009) 'The Sanctuary Movement and Central American Activism in Los Angeles', *Latin American Perspectives* 36: 101.

Church of England (2009) *Special Agenda: IV Diocesan Synod Motions, Justice and Asylum Seekers, a Background Paper from the Diocese of Southwell and Nottingham*, GS Misc. 908A, Asylum and Immigration Synod, Church of England. Available at: http://www.churchofengland.org.

—— (2011) 'The Christian Responsibility', Asylum and Immigration Synod, Church of England, Available at: http://www.churchofengland.org.

Cleroux, R. and Wilson, D. (1987) 'Planned Law on Refugee Smuggling Would Jail "Samaritans," Critics Say', *The Globe and Mail*, 17 August, p. A5.

Coyish, D. (2002) 'Refugee Groups Attack Mosque Raid', *Morning Star*, 26 July, p. 5.

Egan, K. (2007) 'He Paints Seagulls and Longs to Be Free', *Ottawa Citizen*, 16 September, p. A7.

Egelko, B. (1991) 'Judge Approves Settlement Blocking Central America Deportations', *Los Angeles Daily News*, 2 February, p. N3.

Ellingwood, K. (2001) 'Humanitarians Work Together to Assist Migrants', *Los Angeles Times*, 14 January, p. A23.

Evangelical Lutheran Church in America (1984) *Sanctuary: A Question for the Church, a Study Paper of the Lutheran Church in America*. Available at: http://www.elca.org/What-We-Believe/Social-Issues.

Evans, C. (1982) 'Mark 8:27–16:20', in Ralph P. Martin (ed.) *Word Biblical Commentary*, Nashville, TN: Thomas Nelson.

Harvey, A. (2009a) *Asylum in Britain: A Question of Conscience*, Asylum and Immigration, Methodist Church of England. Available at: http://www.methodist.org.uk.

—— (2009b) *Asylum in Britain: Bible Study*, Churches Together in Britain and Ireland. Available at: http://www.ctbi.org.uk.

Haskell, D. (2009) *Through a Lens Darkly: How the News Media Perceive and Portray Evangelicals*, Toronto: Clements Academic.

Hunter, I. (2000) 'Lucy Lu Invokes an Ancient Privilege', *National Post*, 27 December.

Innes, S. (2002) 'Entrant Aid: From Covert to Overt', *Arizona Daily Star*, 17 July, p. A1.

Kapica, J. (1993) 'Church Groups Sanctuary to 23 Refugee Claimants', *The Globe and Mail*, 1 June, p. A5.

Lippert, R.K. (2006) *Sanctuary, Sovereignty, Sacrifice: Canadian Sanctuary Incidents, Power and Law*, Vancouver: University of British Columbia Press.

—— (2009) 'Whither Sanctuary?', *Refuge* 26(1): 57–67.

Logan, M. (2004) 'Rights: Canadian Police Seize Algerian Asylum-Seeker in Church', 10 March, n.p.

Marcus, J. (2000) 'Mark 8–16', in John Collins (ed.) *Anchor Bible Commentary*, New Haven, CT: Yale University Press.

Marshall, P., Gilbert, L. and Green-Ahmanson, R. (2008) *Blind Spot: When Journalists Don't Get Religion*, Oxford: Oxford University Press.

Matas, K. (2009) 'Living Up to One's Faith in Sanctuary Movement', *Arizona Daily Star*, 2 January, p. B1.

Maxwell, D. (2006) 'Religion and Politics at the Border: Canadian Church Support for American Vietnam War Resisters', *Journal of Church and State*, 48(4): 807–29.

Mayeda, A. (2006) 'Iranian in 31st Month Living in City Church', *Vancouver Sun*, 23 December, p. A3.

Michels, D. and Blaikie, D. (2009) 'Religious Justification for the Practice of Ecclesiastical Sanctuary', in *Giving Sanctuary to Illegal Immigrants: Between Civil Disobedience and Legal Obligation*, Sherbrooke, QC: Les Editions Revue de Droit de l'Université de Sherbrooke.

Miller, N. (1989) 'Viraj Mendis and Asylum', *The Independent*, Letters, 20 January, p. 19.

Parker, S. (2006) 'Ask the Religion Experts', *Ottawa Citizen*, 28 January, p. E14.

Paterson, M. (1996) 'Christians "Right to Break Law"', *The Scotsman*, 23 May, p. 4.

——(1997) 'Kirk Ready to Defy "Unfair" Asylum Law', *The Scotsman*, 9 May, p. 3.

Pence, A. (1996) 'Sanctuary Force Regroups to Preserve Refugees' Rights', *The Arizona Daily Star*, 28 April, p. 1B.

Pervo, R. (2009) *Acts: A Commentary, Hermeneia*, ed. H.W. Attridge, Minneapolis: Fortress Press.

Petricevic, M. (2006) 'Bringing Refugee Plight to Light', *Kitchener-Waterloo Record*, 15 March, p. B1.

Prengaman, P. (2007) 'Clergy to Offer Sanctuary to Illegal Immigrants', *The Oakland Tribune*, 16 March, n.p.

Presbyterian Church in Canada (2006) *Sanctuary: A Statement and Guidelines for Congregation: A Report Presented to the 132nd General Assembly (2006)*. Ottawa: The Presbyterian Church in Canada.

Read, B. (2007) 'Time to Fix the Refugee System', *Ottawa Citizen*, 19 July, p. A13.

Salvatierra, A. (2007) 'Alexia Salvatierra: Sanctuary Breaks an Unjust Law', God's Politics: A Blog by Jim Wallis and Friends, Tuesday, July 10, 2007. Available at: http://blog.beliefnet.com/godspolitics/.

Sanders, C. (2007) 'Family Marks Anniversary in "Guantanamo North"', *Winnipeg Free Press*, 2 August, p. B1.

Schultz, H. (2007) 'Couple Fear Returning Alone to Troubled Land; It's Offensive to Force Them to Leave: Minister', *Edmonton Journal*, 19 June, p. B1.

Scott, K. (1996) 'Making a Stand for the Oppressed', *The Herald* (Glasgow), 5 April, p. 13.

Seigel, R. (2001) 'Analysis: Movement Under Way to Help Illegal Immigrants Make It Safely from Mexico to the U.S.', *NPR: All Things Considered*, 14 June.

Sharratt, T. (1988) 'Sri Lankan Loses Appeal for Refugee', *The Guardian* (London), 18 June, n.p.

Sobrino, J. (1988) 'Sanctuary: A Theological Analysis', *Cross Currents* 38: 164.

Stevenson, R. and Grant, H. (2008) 'The Land of No Return', *The Guardian*, Features, 13 June, p. 4.

Suderman, B. (2006) '"Holy Detention" Church Offers Safe Haven for Refugee Family Facing Deportation', *Winnipeg Free Press*, 5 November.

Tai, W.S. (1993) 'Minnesota Law Project Is Helping Immigrants Get Asylum', *Star-Tribune Newspaper of the Twin Cities*, 4 July, p. 1b.

Trevizo, P. (2007) 'Offering Sanctuary is Duty in Some Churches', *Chattanooga Times/Free Press*, 10 September, n.p.

Underwood, D. (2002) *From Yahweh to Yahoo! The Religious Roots of the Secular Press*. Urbana, IL: University of Illinois Press.

United Church of Canada (2004) *Sanctuary for Refugees?: A Guide for Congregations*, Toronto: United Church of Canada.

Vulliamy, E. (2006) 'Welcome to the New Holy Land', *The Observer*, Features, 17 December, p. 4.
Wallis, J. (2011) 'A Church Sanctuary for the Occupy Movement', *Sojourners*, November 17. Available at: http://sojo.net.
Wild, K.L. (2009) 'The New Sanctuary Movement: When Moral Mission Means Breaking the Law, and the Consequences for Churches and Illegal Immigrants', August. Available at: http://works.bepress.com/kara_wild/1.

Chapter 3

The potential of sanctuary
Acts of sanctuary through the lens of camp

Agnes Czajka

Introduction

The provision of sanctuary to those deemed deportable by the state where they sought refuge has inspired much debate since its arrival in the 1980s, and its subsequent North American and European revivals. The most salient debates have emerged as sanctuary providers, advocates, and scholars have grappled with a series of questions about contemporary sanctuary practices. How can these be characterized? Do they comprise a movement, or a series of disparate events? Have they retained their theological underpinnings, or have they become secularized? Do they exist within the realm of the law, or outside of it? And finally, do contemporary sanctuary practices reproduce the discourses and technologies of the state, or do they contain critical, transformative potential?

This chapter focuses on the final question. Those who have previously confronted it have argued that sanctuary practices often replicate the dominant discourse on refugees – which manufactures a distinction between legitimate and illegitimate asylum seekers, constituting the former as vulnerable, apolitical supplicants – and the practices and technologies through which this discourse is reproduced (see, for instance, Lippert 2005a, 2005b, 2009; Perla and Coutin 2009: 13; Pyykkönen 2009). While these critiques have been incisive and apt, I suggest that a critical, transformative potential underlies sanctuary practices. This potential is rooted in the challenge sanctuary practices present to the state's attempt to monopolize territorial sovereignty and govern the political; it is linked to, and can be uncovered if sanctuary practices are considered through the conceptual framework offered by Giorgio Agamben (1998, 2005).

As the question of sanctuary's potential is linked to the other questions that have structured the debate on sanctuary practices, the chapter first examines how these questions have influenced interpretations of contemporary sanctuary. In contrast to much of the existing literature, my engagement with sanctuary cuts across the latitudinal divide often drawn between sanctuary's emergence in the 1980s and its more recent appearances (for examples, see the chapters by Caminero-Santangelo, Chapter 6, and Yukich, Chapter 7 in this volume). The chapter then attends to the intersections between the spaces and subjectivities that populate Agamben's thought – camp, bare life, and the refugee – and the spaces and subjectivities of sanctuary. The chapter suggests that while certain practices of sanctuary providers and advocates must be challenged, sanctuary's promise lies in its potential to disrupt the state's attempt to monopolize territorial sovereignty and ways of being political.

Contemporary sanctuary practices

Over the past three decades, scholars, practitioners, supporters, and critics of sanctuary have contributed to the emergence of an extensive literature on sanctuary practices (see Lippert 2005a, 2005b, 2009; Irazábal and Dyrness 2010; also Perla and Bibler Coutin, Chapter 5 in this volume). Practices of sanctuary have also garnered attention in the religious and secular press (see, for instance, Slimp 1985; Brazao 1987; Kennel-Shank 2007; Markey 2007; Moloshok 2007), and have served as case studies for scholars of social movements (Hildreth 1994; Wiltfang and Cochran 1994).

As previously mentioned, most have grappled with five central questions about sanctuary practices. While the bulk of this chapter is dedicated to the question of whether sanctuary practices reproduce the discourses and technologies of the state or contain critical, transformative potential, it is imperative to situate this discussion within the other debates permeating the sanctuary literature.

The first three questions – regarding the characteristics of sanctuary practices – are best answered in tandem. Much of the literature narrates US sanctuary practices of the 1980s as a relatively cohesive, faith-based sanctuary movement. At its height, the Central American Sanctuary Movement is said to have involved over 400 sanctuary spaces that, together with 2000 supporting congregations, provided sanctuary to at least 3000 Central American refugees (Brazao 1987: A14; Gibson 1991: 624). A United Methodist church in Chicago is said to have been the first to offer sanctuary as part of the New Sanctuary Movement (NSM) (Kennel-Shank 2007: 15), named during a January 2007 meeting of faith-based groups in Washington, DC (Irazábal and Dyrness 2010: 368). As of 2007, more than 50 churches, synagogues and temples had joined the movement (ibid.).

The NSM, as the moniker implies, is generally interpreted as a revival of the 1980s Central American Sanctuary Movement. While some have argued that the goals of the NSM differ from those of its predecessor (see Yukich, Chapter 7 in this volume), it continues to be interpreted as a relatively cohesive, faith-based social movement. Interpretations of sanctuary outside the US are often set against the narrative that constructs the Central American and New Sanctuary movements as cohesive, faith-based social movements. Offering the most sustained analysis of sanctuary practices in Canada, Randy Lippert (2005a, 2009) has argued that sanctuary practices in Canada differ from those of sanctuary movements in the US in at least two ways. First, sanctuary practices in Canada do not constitute a national social movement, and are more aptly characterized as a collection of socially and geographically detached and temporally limited incidents (Lippert 2005a: 383). Second, although the provision of sanctuary often involves the use of sacred spaces, Canadian sanctuary practices are less closely associated with the theological imperative of sanctuary than US sanctuary movements, and less exemplary of religious activism positioned against the state (ibid.: 385).

Disrupting the dichotomy

The typology distinguishing US sanctuary from other sanctuary practices has had considerable analytical and heuristic value. The comparative framework that it lent itself to has enabled the emergence of a coherent narrative about the historical and geographical transformations of sanctuary. However, the framework is less useful if the critical potential of sanctuary is to be addressed. It makes it more difficult, for instance, to interpret sanctuary practices as offering a sustained (although not uninterrupted and undifferentiated) challenge to the state's monopoly on territorial sovereignty or ways of being political. It can also conceal the diversity of practices and struggles over the meaning and purpose of sanctuary among providers and advocates. The comparative perspective can thus risk glossing over minor (in the Deleuzian sense) practices, trajectories, and contests that might contain the greatest critical potential. Alternately, it may hinder an appreciation of recurring practices and technologies that need to be rethought for sanctuary's potential to be actualized. For these reasons, this chapter interprets sanctuary as distinct yet interconnected sanctuary practices – or as acts of sanctuary[1] – that vary across space and time, but whose characteristics cannot be read off from the spatial–temporal nexus in which they emerge.

Setting aside the comparative perspective and interpreting contemporary sanctuary through the framework of acts of sanctuary enables us to interpret sanctuary practices as heterogeneous, as enacted by an array of actors with differing interests and objectives, and as often fiercely contested. It also reveals that sanctuary cannot be easily sorted into contrasting and mutually exclusive practices such as religious and secular. Instead, acts of sanctuary often straddle or vacillate between the categories into which they have been traditionally placed.

As previously mentioned, the comparative perspective lent itself to narrations of US sanctuary practices as comprising relatively cohesive, faith-based national movements, in contrast to sanctuary practices outside of the US. It is certainly true that the theological imperative to sanctuary underlined many of the practices in the US, and that attempts were made – with some success – to construct national sanctuary networks that would anchor a national movement. It is also true that sanctuary practices beyond the US tended to be disconnected (with the possible exception of Germany, see Just, Chapter 9 in this volume), and did not capture the national imagination like the Central American Sanctuary Movement did in the mid-1980s. Yet, if the comparative framework is set aside, and if sanctuary is interpreted through the framework of acts of sanctuary, it becomes possible to view contemporary sanctuary as comprising distinct acts of sanctuary with more or less critical and transformative potential, and greater or lesser capacity to challenge the state's attempt to monopolize territorial sovereignty and ways of being political.

As Stoltz Chinchilla *et al.* (2009) show, for instance, in addition to advocacy and provision of sanctuary by religious congregations, the Central American Sanctuary Movement also comprised various other efforts undertaken by diverse actors with differing ideologies and motivations. By 1987, 24 cities, 15 universities, and 13 secular groups were engaged in sanctuary activism (ibid.: 107). In California, several universities and colleges declared campus spaces safe havens for Central American refugees, and grouped into the Inter-Campus Sanctuary Network, which opened a safe house for undocumented Salvadorans and Guatemalans (ibid.: 117). Berkeley, California, proclaimed itself a city of refuge in February 1985, declaring that city employees would not cooperate with Immigration and Naturalization Services (INS) in investigations or arrests of Salvadoran and Guatemalan refugees (ibid.: 118); Los Angeles followed in November, arguing that the tragedy of denying entry to Jewish refugees in the 1930s and 1940s must not be repeated in the case of Central American refugees (ibid.) (on the emergence of New York City and San Francisco as sanctuary cities, see Mancina, Chapter 14, and Ridgley, Chapter 15 in this volume).

Various acts of sanctuary – many of which remain vigorously contested by both advocates and critics – likewise comprise the NSM. Initiatives like No More Deaths – with groups such as the Border Action Networks, Border Links, Samaritans, Human Borders and Christian Peacemaker Teams – engage in activities as diverse as the maintenance of desert water stations and migrant welcome centres and efforts to break the Israeli blockade of Gaza. The heterogeneity of the movement complicates the dominant narrative, and speaks to the utility of assessing sanctuary through the framework of acts of sanctuary.[2] Moreover, while nation-wide networks developed for certain activities linked to sanctuary movements, there is also a regional, geographically-limited dimension to many US sanctuary practices. Disagreement also exists among supporters and within affected communities over the efficacy and legitimacy of various practices and strategies. These include disagreement over the 'political' or 'humanitarian' nature of sanctuary (see Nelson 1986); the discourses of philanthropy, and constructs of refugee-hood that many practitioners continue to rely on (see Perla and Bibler Coutin, Chapter 5 in this volume); the question of what count as legitimate sanctuary practices; and, perhaps more importantly, whether sanctuary practices ought to remain within the confines of law.

The framework of acts of sanctuary enables us to similarly complicate sanctuary outside the US, and highlight its heterogeneity. While sanctuary practices outside the US are often characterized as less dependent on the theological imperative to sanctuary (see also Millner, Chapter 4 in this volume), it remains a motivating factor for many sanctuary advocates. Its echoes can be discerned in discussions and practices of sanctuary in Canada (Creal 2009) and Europe (see Loughlin 1997; Mittermaier 2009; Pyykkönen 2009). At the same time, the theological imperative to sanctuary and its provision in sacred spaces do not characterize all sanctuary practices, which also include efforts to enact and network cities of sanctuary (see Darling and Squire, Chapter 13, Mancina, Chapter 14 and Ridgley, Chapter 15 in this volume; Derrida 2001), or implement Don't Ask, Don't Tell campaigns.[3]

At the limits of the law

Discussions of sanctuary have also been anchored by the debate over the legality of various sanctuary practices. Constructions of sanctuary practices as legal or illegal have generally hinged on whether those to whom sanctuary is offered are perceived as *bona fide* refugees; on whether state laws are perceived to be legitimate; and on whether actions of the government or judiciary are perceived to be in line with the state's legal and moral obligations. While sanctuary practices have been characterized as acts of civil disobedience at times, more often than not participants and advocates interpret them as acts of civil initiative (see, for example, Cunningham, Chapter 11 in this volume), on the grounds that acts of sanctuary ensure the government is not contravening the national and international laws to which it is subject (for versions of this argument, see Gibson 1991; Wiltfang and Cochran 1994; Rehaag 2009). In this way, sanctuary practices have been interpreted as upholding laws to which the state is bound, but which it is breaking. Advocates of sanctuary in the US, for instance, have argued that the US government was 'illegally and immorally disregarding international and domestic law concerning refugees', and as such, sanctuary providers should not be perceived as breaking the law, but as acting on their legal and moral obligation to uphold it (Gibson 1991: 645). As Pyykkönen (2009) argues in relation to the Finnish case, and Rehaag (2009) shows regarding the Canadian case, the argument that sanctuary practices uphold the law is often buttressed by sanctuary providers' deployment of technologies akin to those deployed by the state in the refugee determination process. As Rehaag notes, sanctuary providers rigorously screen applications for sanctuary, turning away most applicants and providing sanctuary only to those with strong cases for refugee protection (ibid.: 44).

Sanctuary practitioners and advocates also generally situate contemporary sanctuary practices within the context of modern state and international law, rarely drawing loose parallels between contemporary and medieval sanctuary practices.[4] The link between contemporary and medieval sanctuary is more often drawn by critics, who use the comparative framework to delegitimize contemporary sanctuary. While some argue the illegality and illegitimacy of contemporary sanctuary practices arise from their violation of state laws against aiding in the commission of a criminal offence or harbouring those who have committed one (see Rehaag 2009), others do so on the grounds of its distinction from medieval sanctuary practices (see Shoemaker, Chapter 1 in this volume). As one critic has argued, 'the current sanctuary movement aligns itself in carefree historical abandon with the sanctuary theologies of the High Middle Ages', disregarding the fact that they have little in common, as the medieval right to sanctuary was 'a limited doctrine not a wide-open invitation to shelter any and all comers' (Slimp 1985: 25). As Fred Slimp proceeds to argue, sanctuary was always only extended to a limited class of individuals and in no case did the right to sanctuary extend beyond 40 days, at which time the refugee had the option of settling the score with those whom he had wronged, or 'abjuring the realm' with a vow to never return; 'no open-ended period of time that resulted in defiance of the secular authority was tolerated' (ibid.). One could counter with evidence that contemporary sanctuary practices are as, or more, selective than their medieval predecessors. Yet, as the Christian principle of sanctuary was abolished in England in 1623, and its civil version in 1723, critics argue that all of the above is a moot point (ibid.: 26). As Alan Nelson, speaking on behalf of the INS said in reference to US sanctuary practices, the sanctuary movement is involved in the organized and deliberate violation of law (Nelson 1986: 483).

The potential of sanctuary

If we are to appreciate the potential of sanctuary, it is essential to set aside both the comparative framework and the dichotomies through which it is structured. The potential of sanctuary practices does not depend on their categorization as a collection of disparate events or as part of a cohesive social movement; it does not depend on their interpretation as legal or illegal, or as religiously or secularly motivated. Rather, the potential of sanctuary derives at least in part from the heterogeneity, multiplicity, fluidity, and indeterminateness of acts of sanctuary, and their related capacity to challenge the state's attempt to monopolize territorial sovereignty and govern the political. While not all acts of sanctuary offer the same critical potential, the potential of sanctuary is linked to, and can be uncovered if, acts of sanctuary are considered through the conceptual framework offered by Agamben's camp and its attendant subjectivities.

Agamben's interpretation of camp as the hidden matrix and *nomos* of the political space we inhabit (Agamben 1998: 166) and as the space that is opened when the state of exception begins to constitute the rule (ibid.: 169) has captured the imagination of scholars of migration and refugee studies. The camp and its attendant subjectivity – bare life – have been frequently deployed to describe or denounce the spaces to which asylum-seekers are increasingly confined, and the subject positions to which they are reduced. The camp, as the material expression of state sovereignty, i.e. its ability to delineate the state of exception and demarcate exceptional spaces and subject positions, seemed to offer an apt description or suitable analytical tool for understanding spaces such as refugee camps, detention, and offshore processing centres, as well as spaces and procedures of extraordinary rendition through which states engage in various degrees of excision of territory and legal responsibility (see, for example, Davidson 2003; Diken 2004; Rajaram and Grundy-Warr 2004).

While the applicability of the concept of camp to such spaces and processes did not go unquestioned (see, for instance, Isin and Rygiel 2007; Walters 2008), the concept of bare life generated even more controversy. Many scholars, interested in the resonances between Agamben's bare life and Hannah Arendt's discussion of the plight of the human being following the Declaration of the Rights of Man and Citizen, interpreted bare life exclusively in the context of Arendt's critique. As the document with which human rights were effectively effaced through the absorption of the human being into the citizen, and human rights into citizens' rights, the declaration was, for Arendt, a harbinger of the plight of refugees in inter-war Europe who, insofar as they remained unrecognized as citizens of any state, lost not only all rights, but also the right to have rights (Arendt, 1951: 126–8, 295–6). Reduced to the status of bare or mere life, they became those to whom anything could be done, often consigned to (camp) spaces where anything was possible.

The controversy surrounding the interpretation of the refugee as bare life hinges on an interpretation of bare life as undifferentiated, aberrant, abject, apolitical, and devoid of agency. Representative of this critique is the argument of William Walters, who suggests that Agamben's conceptual schema 'seems to offer little space for registering the political and social agency of its subjects', as:

> In Agamben's account, and even more so in much of the research that has explored his themes in the context of migration studies, refugees and migrants are depicted as *cast* into spaces at the limit of the law, contained outside the system of legal protection, *trapped* in zones of indistinction … they are subjects to whom all manner of things are done … but rarely agents in their own right.
>
> (Walters 2008: 188)

As deployed in migration and refugee studies, Agamben's schema thus ironically reproduces a flattened conception of migrants as passive, helpless supplicants (ibid.).

Two things can be said about such arguments that are of relevance to understanding the potential of sanctuary. First, while it may be true that the deployment of the concepts of camp and bare life in migration and refugee studies has highlighted the vulnerability of refugees at the expense of their political and social agency, it is also true that the national order of things and spaces of exception not only work to limit the agency of non-citizen subjects, but also make all manner of things done to non-citizen subjects acceptable. Second, as I have argued elsewhere (Czajka 2008: 219–25), little in Agamben's work suggests that that camp and its attendant subjectivities need to be interpreted in this 'apocalyptic' fashion (Walters 2008: 187). In fact, when read in tandem with Agamben's other work – particularly *The Coming Community* (1993) – and interventions by scholars like Jean-Luc Nancy and Jacques Derrida into debates on sovereignty, community, and the political, the critical and transformative potential of camp and bare life is revealed (Czajka 2008: 259–70). The criticisms levelled against Agamben are perhaps more fitting of Arendt, whose understanding of being political (and hence also of being human) remains institutionally, spatially, and performatively tied to the state. Although Agamben's interpretations of camp and bare life certainly resonate with those of Arendt, their distinct interpretations of the political, and of being political, produce distinct interpretations of the possibilities of the space of camp and the subjectivity of bare life.

Agamben's suggestion that 'camp inhabitants are stripped of every political status' (Agamben 1998: 171) and that in the camp 'power confronts nothing but pure life, without any mediation' (ibid.: 183), need not be interpreted as implying that camp is an apolitical space and that its inhabitants are non-political beings. That the discourses and technologies through which the nation-state claims monopoly over the contours and ways of being political, and the sovereign prerogative to control entry into the political community depoliticize and pacify the spaces and subjectivities of camp, does not mean that the spaces and subjectivities become depoliticized and pacified – only that they are deemed as such by the state. If this is taken into account, it is possible to interpret both the space of the camp and the subjectivity of bare life as having the potential to disrupt the state's attempt to monopolize territorial sovereignty and ways of being political.

What, then, is the potential of camp (as embodied in practices of sanctuary) and bare life (as embodied in the figure of the refugee) to disrupt the state's monopoly on territorial sovereignty and ways of being political? For Agamben, the camp as the space of exception is created by the sovereign through a juridical process. As such, it remains within the realm of law at least in the sense that the law structures its parameters, even if it then effectively withdraws from the space it has delineated. Yet the exception created by the sovereign with the intent of capturing within it what disturbs and disrupts fictions of sovereign right and organic community is always already pregnant with the potential to disrupt, and reveal the contingency of the order that it attempts to preserve. Time and again, spaces of camp are transformed into spaces of resistance and challenge to precisely the order they are configured to preserve. Riots, hunger strikes, acts of self-mutilation, and other forms of resistance by asylum-seekers and deportable subjects confined to spaces of exception, or transformations of refugee camps into spaces over which the state is only conditionally sovereign, reveal the potentiality inherent in the most seemingly forlorn circumstances.

Spaces of sanctuary are not, of course, spaces excised by the state. As critics of sanctuary practices have noted, the right to sanctuary was abolished centuries ago, and 'public relations, not law, keeps the idea of sanctuary alive' (Olsen 2006: 35). Spaces of sanctuary are usurped from the state, if only precariously,[5] by sanctuary providers and advocates who attempt to create spaces of refuge to which state sovereignty does not extend. Once usurped, sanctuary providers and advocates often attempt, through previously discussed arguments about sanctuary's effective legality, to creatively reinscribe sanctuary practices into the law. In this manner, spaces and practices of sanctuary, as spaces and practices of exception, disrupt the state's attempt to monopolize sovereignty through a monopoly on deciding the exception.

Acts of sanctuary can also be interpreted as challenging state sovereignty in another, related way. They can be interpreted as a challenge to the state's monopolization of decisions on the right of residence and citizenship. Next to exclusive dominion over territory, the right to determine criteria for inclusion in the political community therein – and thus the right to determine who has the right to have rights – constitutes a fundamental prerogative of sovereignty. In attempting to both excise territory and challenge the state's monopoly on deciding the criteria for belonging, acts of sanctuary pose a fundamental challenge to the state's claim to sovereign right. They can thus also be interpreted as calling into question the equation of state and people. The modern state legitimates its sovereignty with the claim that its sovereignty is the sovereignty of the people.[6] By unsettling the equation – which sanctuary providers do by enacting themselves as sovereign against and in contradistinction to the state – acts of sanctuary call into question the legitimacy of state sovereignty.

The potential of acts of sanctuary derives also from the refugee's enactment as a rights-bearing subject against the discourse of the state that deprives her of the right to have rights and be political. For the state, to be political, one must be recognized as such through the technology of citizenship. Thus, from the perspective of the state, responsibility toward the refugee – the ultimate non-citizen subject who, by virtue of being a citizen of nowhere, loses the right to be political anywhere – does not extend beyond an ethical or moral responsibility that lies outside of the realm of the political. The refugee is likewise expected to, at most, enact herself as deserving of a moral or ethical response, but not as a political being. It is for this reason that the political nature of the demands of sanctuary recipients and advocates is so disruptive. The refugee, by refusing to be deported and enacting herself as belonging to the territory and political community in contradiction to the determination of the state, challenges not only state sovereignty, but also the state's monopoly on the political. This disruptive potential is discernible in the apprehension generated by refugees and sanctuary recipients who are perceived to be, or enact themselves as, political beings. It is also discernible in the anxiety generated when sanctuary practices unsettle or are perceived to unsettle the political–humanitarian dichotomy on which the state's monopoly of the political partially depends. As one critic of sanctuary practices argued, the Central American Sanctuary Movement is dangerous precisely because it is a '*political* protest movement, involving lawlessness which takes advantage of the *humanitarian* instincts of many well-intentioned people' (Nelson 1986: 484, emphasis added).

While sanctuary has the potential to undermine state sovereignty and call its legitimacy into question, not all sanctuary practices have harnessed this critical potential. As previously argued, the setting aside of the comparative framework enables us to more clearly scrutinize three decades of sanctuary practices and distinguish between those that challenge, and those that reproduce state discourses and practices.

Among the most promising acts of sanctuary are those that not only usurp state sovereignty, but also challenge the state's definitions of who and what counts as political, and who deserves or has the right to have rights. Over the past three decades sanctuary practices have undermined or usurped sovereign power in various ways. Cities of Sanctuary, Don't Ask, Don't Tell campaigns, the provision of refuge in sacred and secular spaces, as well as less visible and more localized practices such as the provision of 'resident' ID cards by parishes and cities to undocumented migrants (Markey 2007: 5a), or sanctuary providers' use of guidelines and technologies akin to those of the state's refugee determination system, have challenged the state's monopoly on territorial sovereignty and the political. Yet, if sanctuary practices are to fulfill their transformative potential, they must do more than usurp sovereign power. They must also include a re-valuation of state values, and must undermine the discourses through which the state governs. Otherwise, they risk reproducing the discourses and practices of the state.

Many, if not most, sanctuary providers are concerned with selecting a 'suitable' sanctuary recipient from among many applicants. The suitable sanctuary recipient is often one with a valid refugee claim, and one 'sympathetic' enough for the public to support.[7] Concern over the validity of a potential sanctuary recipient's refugee claim has often led to the reproduction by sanctuary providers of the technologies deployed by the state to determine the worthiness of the asylum-seeker – technologies designed to teach seekers of sanctuary to be truthful and free subjects, and expose themselves through interviews, discussions and document checks (Pyykkönen 2009: 27). It has also led to the monitoring, surveillance, and discipline of sanctuary recipients by providers (ibid.: 29), and to the reproduction of the refugee determination system by sanctuary providers. As Rehaag notes, 'Screening mechanisms mimic the official refugee determination system: lawyers get involved, alleged fears of persecution are scrutinized, supporting country condition documentation is considered, and various interpretations of refugee law are propounded' (2009: 43–4). Reproducing state discourse regarding who qualifies as a refugee, one sanctuary provider even argued that most sanctuary seekers are in fact 'economic refugees who can't prove they face physical danger' (ibid.: 44).

For acts of sanctuary to be truly transformative, sanctuary providers must challenge rather than reproduce the values of the state. The expropriation of sovereign power through, for instance, the reproduction of the refugee determination systems outside the institutions of the state is an important achievement. However, for sanctuary practices to fulfil their critical potential, to be true acts of resistance that create micro-alternatives through which living out a different logic becomes possible (Creal 2009: 72), they must both expropriate sovereign power and overturn the values and discourses reflected in state practices.

Concern over the need to evoke sympathy has likewise resulted in the replication of discourses that produce the deserving or *bona fide* refugee as a vulnerable, apolitical supplicant. As noted by Perla and Coutin, tension over the 'limitations imposed by the refugee identity' existed as early as the 1980s, when Central American refugees were often presented – to the chagrin of many of the refugees themselves – as 'innocent victims' in need of support, and 'representatives of the poor and oppressed, on whose behalf religious communities were compelled to advocate' (2009: 13). Dominant perceptions of vulnerability and merit – often related to gender, age and perceived politicalness of the refugee – continue to be reflected in the choice of sanctuary recipients. Women, women with children, and families – portrayed as vulnerable and apolitical – are often considered more suitable than single, young men. The latter, it is argued, are less likely to evoke public sympathy, as they are more likely to be seen as capable of caring for themselves, and perhaps even as having somehow directly contributed to their own predicament (Lippert 2009: 61).

A related and equally concerning development is the increasing support by some sanctuary advocates for a merit-based appeal system for rejected asylum applicants (Lippert 2009: 58; see also Cunningham, Chapter 11 in this volume). Like the above-mentioned practices of screening for, and selecting only suitable and sympathetic sanctuary recipients, a merit-based appeal process reproduces dominant state discourses and practices of distinguishing between deserving and undeserving applicants, and state constructions of what a worthy applicant looks and behaves like. It likewise reproduces the state discourse that separates the political from the humanitarian, and the political being from bare life, thus reproducing the state's designation of what and who counts as, and has the right to be, political.

Conclusion

Do contemporary sanctuary practices reproduce the discourses and technologies of the state, or do they contain critical, transformative potential? The chapter suggested that the potential of sanctuary is more readily discernible if we set aside the comparative framework that has structured discussions of contemporary sanctuary, and consider sanctuary through the lens of acts of sanctuary. Such reorientation highlights the sanctuary practices that contain the greatest critical potential, and present a sustained challenge to the state's monopoly on sovereignty and ways of being political. Likewise, it enables us to discern which acts of sanctuary need to be rethought in order for sanctuary's potential to be realized.

The chapter then situated the question of the potential of sanctuary within the context of salient debates over contemporary sanctuary practices. It suggested, first, that the typologies through which sanctuary has been generally interpreted – as theologically or secularly motivated, legal or illegal, political or humanitarian – have tended to oversimplify sanctuary practices, and in doing so, have obfuscated the potential that derives from the fact that acts of sanctuary often straddle or undermine these dichotomies. It suggested, second, that the critical potential of sanctuary can also be highlighted if sanctuary practices are considered through the conceptual framework offered by Agamben's interpretation of camp and its attendant subjectivities. The conceptual framework offered by Agamben, the chapter suggested, enables us to interpret the spaces and subjectivities produced through acts of sanctuary as having the potential to challenge the state's monopoly on territorial sovereignty, and its capacity to delineate the parameters and ways of being political.

Yet, the chapter concluded on a more cautious note, arguing that while sanctuary practices do have critical potential, this potential is not always actualized because sanctuary advocates often inadvertently – but at times consciously or strategically – reproduce state discourses and practices. The chapter suggested that the most promising practices of sanctuary are those that not only usurp the technologies through which the state exercises its sovereignty, but also revalue its values, and contest its definitions of who and what counts as political and who has the right to have rights.

Notes

1 For more on the conceptual framework of 'act', see Isin and Nielsen (2008).
2 For more on the No More Deaths initiative, see http://www.nomoredeaths.org/.
3 For more on Don't Ask, Don't Tell campaigns, see The Ontario Coalition Against Poverty (OCAP 2004), available at: http://www.ocap.ca/node/604.
4 It seems more common for those motivated by the theological imperative to legitimate sanctuary practices through medieval church practice or the 'biblical imperative' to hospitality (Markey 2007: 5a).
5 As Lippert (2009) and others (for instance, Loughlin 1997) have noted, the excision of spaces of sanctuary from the sovereign power of the state is becoming increasingly precarious, as the state seems increasingly willing to breach, and reassert its sovereignty over these spaces.
6 The modern state – the nation-state – conflates the people with the nation. On the consequences of this, see Arendt (1951) and Foucault (1997).
7 As Lippert (2005a) shows, this has varied in Canada. Those with weak refugee claims are at times granted sanctuary on the grounds that the state should have accepted them as immigrants. In these cases, their merit as immigrants is highlighted.

References

Agamben, G. (1993) *The Coming Community*, Minneapolis: University of Minnesota Press.
—— (1998) *Homo Sacer: Sovereign Power and Bare Life*, Stanford, CA: Stanford University Press.

——(2005) *State of Exception*, Chicago: University of Chicago Press.
Arendt, H. (1951) *The Origins of Totalitarianism*, New York: Harcourt Press.
Brazao, D. (1987) 'Church Groups Guide Refugees to Canada', *Toronto Star*, March 17, A14.
Creal, M. (2009) 'What is Entailed in Offering Sanctuary? Findings from a Consultation Held at Romero House Toronto, November 2007', *Refuge*, 26(1): 71–2.
Czajka, A. (2008) 'The Camp and the Political: Palestinian Refugee Camps in Lebanon', unpublished dissertation, York University, Toronto, Canada.
Davidson, R. (2003) 'Spaces of Immigration "Prevention": Interdiction and the Nonplace', *Diacritics*, 33(3–4): 3–18.
Derrida, J. (2001) *On Cosmopolitanism and Forgiveness*, London: Routledge.
Diken, B. (2004) 'From Refugee Camps to Gated Communities: Biopolitics and the End of the City', *Citizenship Studies*, 8(1): 83–106.
Foucault, M. (1997) *Society Must Be Defended: Lectures at the Collège de France, 1975–1976*, New York: Picador.
Gibson, M.L. (1991) 'Public Goods, Alienation, and Political Protest: The Sanctuary Movement as a Test of the Public Goods Model of Collective Rebellious Behavior', *Political Psychology*, 12(4): 623–51.
Hildreth, A. (1994) 'The Importance of Purposes in "Purposive" Groups: Incentives and Participation in the Sanctuary Movement', *American Journal of Political Science*, 38(2): 447–63.
Ontario Coalition Against Poverty (2004) 'Immigration Status: Don't Ask, Don't Tell', Available at: http://www.ocap.ca/node/604.
Irazábal, C. and Dyrness, G.R. (2010) 'Promised Land? Immigration, Religiosity, and Space in Southern California', *Space and Culture*, 13(4): 356–75.
Isin, E.F. and Nielsen, G. (eds) (2008) *Acts of Citizenship*, London: Zed Books.
Isin, E.F. and Rygiel, K. (2007) 'Abject Spaces: Frontiers, Zones, Camps', in E. Dauphinee and C. Masters (eds) *Logics of Biopower and the War on Terror*, Basingstoke: Palgrave, pp. 181–203.
Kennel-Shank, C. (2007) 'Living in God's House: Finding Sanctuary in a Chicago Storefront Church', *Sojourners Magazine*, September–October: 15.
Lippert, R.K. (2005a) 'Rethinking Sanctuary: The Canadian Context, 1983–2000', *International Migration Review*, 39(2): 381–406.
——(2005b) *Sanctuary, Sovereignty, Sacrifice: Canadian Sanctuary Incidents, Power, and Law*, Vancouver: University of British Columbia Press.
——(2009) 'Whither Sanctuary?', *Refuge*, 26(1): 57–67.
Lippert, R.K. and Rehaag, S. (2009) 'Introduction: Sanctuary in Context', *Refuge*, 26(1): 3–6.
Loughlin, K.L. (1997) 'Sanctuary Churches', *Christian Century*, 114(7): 212.
Markey, E. (2007) 'The Church's Children', *National Catholic Reporter*, September 14: 3–5.
Mittermaier, V. (2009) 'Refuge in Europe? Church Asylum as Human Rights Work in Fortress Europe', *Refuge*, 26(1): 68–70.
Moloshok, D. (2007) 'Dilemma on Sheltering Immigrants', *Christian Century*, July 10: 12–13.
Nelson, A. (1986) 'The Sanctuary Movement: Humanitarian Action, Political Opposition or Lawlessness?', *Vital Speeches of the Day*, 52(16): 482–5.
Olsen, T. (2006) 'Asylum vs. Assistance: Offering Sanctuary Isn't About Political Protest', *Christianity Today*, October 31, 50: 35.
Perla, H. and Coutin, S. (2009) 'Legacies and Origins of the 1980s US-Central American Sanctuary Movement', *Refuge*, 26(1): 7–19.

Pyykkönen, M. (2009) 'Deportation Versus Sanctuary: The Rationalities, Technologies, and Subjects of Finnish Sanctuary Practices', *Refuge*, 26(1): 20–32.

Rajaram, P. and Grundy-Warr, C. (2004) 'The Irregular Migrant as Homo Sacer: Migration and Detention in Australia, Malaysia and Thailand', *International Migration*, 42(1): 33–64.

Rehaag, S. (2009) 'Bordering on Legality: Canadian Church Sanctuary and the Rule of Law', *Refuge*, 26(1): 43–56.

Slimp, F.A. (1985) 'Gimme Sanctuary: The Right of Asylum', *National Review*, May 17: 24–8.

Stoltz Chinchilla, N., Hamilton, N., and Loucky, J. (2009) 'The Sanctuary Movement and Central American Activism in Los Angeles', *Latin American Perspectives*, 36: 101–26.

Walters, W. (2008) 'Acts of Demonstration: Mapping the Territory of (Non-)Citizenship', in E.F. Isin and G. Nielsen (eds) *Acts of Citizenship*, London: Zed Books, pp. 182–206.

Wiltfang, G.L. and Cochran, J.K. (1994) 'The Sanctuary Movement and the Smuggling of Undocumented Central Americans into the United States: Crime, Deviance, or Defiance?', *Sociological Spectrum*, 14: 101–28.

Chapter 4

Sanctuary *sans frontières*

Social movements and solidarity in post-war Northern France

Naomi Millner

Introduction

Calais has long been known as a 'bottleneck' within Europe, and as a site of conflicting conceptions of citizenship rights and claims. As the geographically most proximal point to the UK in mainland Europe, it had been the site of past migrations and anti-immigrant riots for centuries (Derville 1985). But as changing EU laws had made clandestine movement an almost necessary part of seeking asylum in Europe (Bolten 1991; Schuster 2005; Huysmans 2006), the presence of hundreds of migrants in the town, trying to cross the Channel, brought it to a new level of symbolic significance. This significance was amplified when the Red Cross built a humanitarian shelter, Sangatte, although it was closed in 2002 only eighteen months later (Laacher 2002; Fassin 2005). This materialisation of a literal 'sanctuary' in Northern France reflected the increasing displacement of religious, mission-based forms of sanctuary by secular, transnational associations, upholding internationally-sanctioned notions of human rights. Some argue this emergent production of spaces is part of a broader project of the extension of state sovereignty, which depends on the ability to 'ban' others from belonging for its very existence, and reproduces hierarchies of citizenship belonging (Agamben 1997; Fassin 2005; Darling 2009).

However, this is not the only story that can be told of Sangatte, or of Calais and Northern France in the post-war period. The collaborations which formed to assert the rights of *sans-papiers* in the remaking of the French Republic, distinctive articulations of immigrants' rights in the 1960s and 1970s, and new forms of organising that emerged as migrant squatter camps, or 'jungles', were destroyed in 2009, also reflect the influence of other social movements, newly linked within and across nation-states (Freedman 2008). While in Paris and in Calais, protesters frequently took refuge in churches and sacred social spaces, such acts also drew on other histories, including European Leftist, post-colonial, and migrant-led forms of organising. This chapter explores sanctuary practices enacted in Northern France as one form of ethical response to irregular migrants in the post-war period. However, highlighting the multiple influences on ethical subjectivity besides a history of state-making, I demonstrate how this notion has been transformed, and is being displaced, by notions of collective belonging that exceed and problematise citizenship.

Most importantly in this context is the emergence of an ethos of 'solidarity': a platform of equality shared by different social movements, asserting the existence of a universal community of migrants prior to categories linked with the nation-state. As such, solidarity is a remaking of the idea of sanctuary, *sans frontières*. My analysis draws on my ethnographic work with social movements and humanitarian organisations in the Nord-Pas-de-Calais region, and on my archival work on social movements in Northern France in the post-war period. This work focused on non-governmental organising in Calais after the destruction of the jungles, specifically the construction and transformation of ethical responses to undocumented migrants in six humanitarian associations and the solidarity network 'No Borders'.

In pointing to the new kinds of ethical subjectification emerging among social movements we move from a negativist, to a positive style of critique (Foucault 1997: 315), problematising a narrative in recent scholarship which has construed sanctuary spaces in the EU as sites of biopolitical abjection. In recent years the 'autonomy of migration' perspective has sought to address a passive reading of space and subjectivity by phrasing migration as an active constitution of citizenship – an 'act' of citizenship (Isin and Nielson 2008; Isin 2009; see also Czajka, Chapter 3 in this volume). This chapter builds on this research, focusing on how the social movements, including migrants' movements, have inflected particular conceptions of sanctuary, as part of an ongoing redefinition of ethical subjectivity.

Sanctuary and humanitarianism in Northern France

Between 1945 and 2009, new forms of political organising responded to the 'impossible condition' of the refugee between these universal and specific articulations of asylum, including international humanitarianism, and new transnational non-governmental advocacy organisations (Tyler 2006; Darling 2009). The post-war period saw the concept of the 'asylum-seeker' acquire currency, first, in international instruments (including the Universal Declaration of Human Rights in 1948, and the Convention Relating to the Status of Refugees in 1951), and later in national asylum systems and regional conventions (Huysmans 2006; Dikeç 2009). Meanwhile, the development of air travel and media technologies supported the emergence of new geographies of movement and connectivity (Isin 2009). While it might not be true that the European Union has a deliberate policy of excluding poor migrants, it is possible to trace the emergence of a regime of 'fuzzy' borders (Christiansen *et al.* 2000) – intermediate spaces both inside and outside polities, which operate selectively in relation to migrant populations (Sparke 2006). In this context, humanitarian activists have challenged, with increasing vocality, the representation of asylum in EU security policies, as well as the growing confusion between economically-motivated 'migrants' and legitimate 'asylum-seekers', seeking to rehabilitate those counted out of the political community by appealing to the 1951 Refugee Convention.

In France, the involvement of humanitarian groups in asylum issues followed two main waves. The first began as a form of medical accompaniment for military missions with a religious nuance, aiming to respond to human suffering from a 'neutral' political ambition (Redfield 2006). Associated in particular with the development of the International Red Cross and Red Crescent movement, along with Catholic organisations, such as the Catholic Overseas Development Agency (CAFOD) and Caritas, these organisations were *inter*national rather than transnational, maintaining strongly national bases. The Red Cross movement evolved from a private humanitarian institution founded in 1863 in Switzerland, and developed its international dimension in particular between the two World Wars, grounding its involvement in concern for the effects of crisis on civilian populations. It derived its authority to intervene from international humanitarian law, especially as expressed in the Geneva Conventions formulated after World War II and aimed to respond to human suffering from a 'neutral' political ambition.

The second wave, associated with *Médécins Sans Frontières* (MSF) and *Médecins du Monde* (MDM) developed as a partial critique of Red Cross neutrality. MSF was established in France by former Red Cross doctors, frustrated by delays in obtaining permission to provide aid during the Nigerian Civil War (1967–70). It was conceived as a new kind of organisation *sans frontières*: without borders. As it would not mediate its interpretation of international law through the bureaucracies of states, it could provide an outspoken critique of particular regimes (Terry 2002: 20–1). As such, MSF was characterised by political frankness in its interventions both overseas and in France. Situated by new efforts to think through ethical responses to crisis in secular and transnational terms, this second wave is also associated with the search for new bases of knowledge and authority from which to lobby for change – especially after the failed revolution of 1968 revealed the limits to political forms of organisation grounded in national categories. MSF and MDM worked to develop a 'testimonial' discourse comprising technical and scientific claims to truth (including statistics and the results of independent investigations) as opposed to moral injunctions (Redfield 2006).

The proliferation of transnational non-governmental associations in France in the 1980s and 1990s was therefore marked by new definitions of ethical responses to irregular migrants in the context of supranational agreements and transnational movements. The religious roots of many non-governmental aid organisations had previously defined humanitarianism as the temporary construction of sanctuary places, where basic needs could be met and hospitality offered (Lauren 2011: 228–30). Transcending the nation-state, this community would supplement the state with moral vision and the care of body and soul. Such a project helped found an international community of human rights to replace declining forms of traditional authority like the church and state (Arendt 1951). Meanwhile, mobilised increasingly according to the networks and resources of social movements across states, transnational associations of political and social movements increasingly redefined this international vision as humanistic. Secular and immanent, this notion of universalism – and the universal declarations of rights which formed its 'scripture' – re-inflected Judaeo-Christian ideas of sanctuary, newly defining hospitality to stateless persons as a means to transform state legislation *from within* (Dillon 1999).

In Northern France, religious organisations have offered sanctuary to refugees since the late 1700s, with Paris forming a key destination for Jewish refugees before and during World War II. The international Red Cross was most visibly involved in the asylum issues in France through their establishment of Sangatte. Meanwhile, MSF has worked in France since 1987, especially in Paris, and became involved in Calais after Sangatte's closure, providing vaccinations, cold weather support and food distribution through a mobile clinic. In Sangatte's wake, the provision of sanctuary has been mainly led by transnational organisations that maintain an uneasy or ambivalent relation to state intervention. In Calais, a diversity of charitable bodies were formed to continue providing informal shelter, as well as food and legal advocacy. The most vocal of these, 'SALAM', was set up as a specific response to the closure of Sangatte, while others have formed from the regional expressions of international religious and care charities, such as the Catholic charity CAFOD (*Secours Catholique*) and *France Terre d'Asile*.

In 2002, the six main associations in Calais created the 'C-SUR' agreement – a commitment to recognise the *sans-papiers* who remained in the Nord-Pas-de-Calais region as legitimate potential refugees. This agreement helped establish a precarious system of assistance for the squatter camps which had expanded around the port during the subsequent decade to support nearly a thousand people. Here 'sanctuary' spaces were established in sanctioned compounds where food was served, basic medical facilities were provided, and sometimes music and dancing were organised. In September 2009, this system of organisation was drastically altered by the Sarkozy administration's attempt to eradicate the Calais squatter camps. The destruction of the largest jungles was preceded by the dismantling of other camps, including Loon-Plage and Teteghem near Dunkerque on 17 June 2009 (Rygiel 2011), although only Calais received significant media attention. At the time of writing, the site remains a point of passage for hundreds of migrants at a time, despite the French Immigration Minister Eric Besson's declaration that Calais was now to be a 'migrant-free zone' (Calais Migrant Solidarity 2009). As such, it also remains a conflicted site for contrasting notions of 'responsibility'.

Towards a positive critique of sanctuary practices

While sanctuary practices, such as those enacted by charities and local citizens in Calais, are articulated as a means of supplementing, even resisting, state and inter-state forms of governing migration, the humanitarian vocabulary of advocacy has been linked with a conception of ethical responsibility which figures the nation as a sanctuary space (Tyler 2006). For several scholars, this discourse reflects a remaking of state power as the power over *life* – what Agamben and Foucault refer to as the emergence of 'biopolitics' as a rationality for governing. Evidenced by a governmental language of care for the management of life, the beginning of biopolitics is also marked by the conditions of possibility for the refugee camp (Agamben 1995, 1997; Perera 2002; see also Czajka, Chapter 3 in this volume). The camp becomes a space for a population excluded from the political community, whose exceptionality is required for the sovereign order to exist.

Fassin (2005) calls the 'humanitarian' treatment of stateless persons a form of 'compassionate repression', characterising sanctuary practices as a biopolitical form of abjectification. For him, turning asylum into an issue of moral sympathy is to extend a zone of indiscernibility: it draws attention away from the political construction of citizenship, focusing instead on the nation's benevolent role (see also Darling 2009). Likewise, Ticktin (2006) argues that humanitarianism forces the refugee to compromise biological integrity to secure state assistance, describing how pressure from advocacy groups led to the introduction of the 'humanitarian clause' in French law. She links this clause with an increasing depoliticisation of asylum-seeking bodies, citing an ensuing spate of medical cases where those at risk of deportation infected themselves with the AIDS virus or refused treatments, to guarantee care. Both scholars see humanitarianism preventing existing regimes of citizenship from challenge.

But the analytical tropes underpinning these claims need to be problematised. A key issue with this version of ethical subjectification is how it renders passive the acts and spatialities of non-citizenship (see also Darling and Squire, Chapter 13 in this volume). In part, this can be linked with Agamben's particular reading of Arendtian and Foucauldian biopolitics. After Foucault, the emergence of 'biopolitics' as a rationality of power marks a shift in the question of government toward the problem of governing biological life, and hence the emergence of a form of power *over* life – in contrast with a formerly prevalent 'sovereign' form of power; the power to ordain death. For Foucault (1978: 143), the emergence of 'biopolitics' also marks the threshold of political modernity, placing transformations of bodily life at the centre of political order as disciplining the individual body, and regulating the body of the population (see Lemke 2005). But Agamben does not follow Foucault in tracing this same decline of sovereign power within these transformations to governmentalities. For Agamben, 'biopolitics' refers to the state's assumption of responsibility for the care of the nation, and a highly particular production of subjects and spaces of exception from the political community. This he regards as an intensification of sovereignty, not its displacement: a new work on what remains when life is stripped of all social locations (De Genova 2011). According to Agamben, therefore, and, against Foucault, 'politics is always already biopolitics' (Lemke 2005: 4), in contrast to Foucault's insistence on the perpetual production of ever-new forms of power, and radically different ways of being a subject of biopolitics.

Through an 'autonomy of migration' perspective, scholars have already begun to theorise the importance of exploring the way social movements, especially migrants' movements, are perpetually transforming the material ideas of citizenship (Moulier Boutang 1998; Walters 2008; De Genova 2011; Mezzadra 2011). This theoretical and empirical approach foregrounds acts of 'taking' citizenship, and acts of demonstration over strategies of containment, and highlights the primacy of movement within histories of capitalism or the nation-state. The 'autonomy of migration' here prioritises the movements of the people to the organisation of capital, the regulation of the states, and static or structural points of view. In this approach, acts of migration are reconstrued as political and creative acts; first, as the generative forces which security and political-economic rationalities are ever-striving to keep up with (Mezzadra and Neilson 2008; Papadopoulos et al. 2008), and, second, as the embodiment of *experiential* forms of knowledge with their own authority to speak to ongoing political practices (Isin 2009). This is a lens through which to see that, besides being subjects of proliferating forms of mobility control, refugees and migrants are emerging as major protagonists in political struggles (Isin and Neilson 2008), and are actively engaged in constituting new forms of citizenship (see Nyers 2003). By emphasising migration as a constitutive political and aesthetic act, the autonomy of migration literature encourages further exploration of the autonomies of embodied experience, which, I claim are also critical in remaking ethical practices such as sanctuary.

Foucault's (e.g. Foucault 1998) work on Bataille, Blanchot and other writers shares this nuance, as he aligns himself with their efforts to move beyond existing conceptual structures and historical limits *on* experience. Experience in my reading is relational and collective, and is closely connected to existing forms of government. It is also local and experimental (Foucault 1997: 316) and aims toward that critical work on ourselves through which new historical experiences might become possible. The theorisation of an ethos of 'positive critique' relates, in this reading, to the conviction that experience is a matter of engaging the processuality, connectedness and openness of relationships and forces in the world, rather than reintroducing the embedding, continuity, stability or security of a subject (ibid.: 315). This is still an approach that seeks to denaturalise the 'universals' underpinning moral conduct (Foucault 1998: 441), but which aims, moreover, to engage the limits of the normative and institutional system it relies upon.

A positive critique of sanctuary practices from this perspective consists of working toward the constitution of *new* subjectivities and a multiplication of norms which can offer more space for autonomy and for ethical self-transformation. Such a re-reading of ethical subjectivity demands an interrogation of the social movements' ethos toward irregular migrants that is attentive both to the value it gives to experience, and to how habitual navigations of experience disturb fields *of* that experience, for example, definitions of citizenship. The following sections build on the autonomy of migration perspective to demonstrate how the idea of sanctuary is being pushed beyond borders, and incorporated within new definitions of political belonging. We focus on the Red Cross shelter Sangatte and the *sans-papiers* protests of Paris in the 1990s.

Remaking sanctuary

Routes through Sangatte

The Red Cross shelter known as 'Sangatte' opened in September 1999, when increased numbers of Kosovan refugees attempted to travel via Calais to the UK (Laacher 2002; Liagre and Dumont 2005). From the beginning, its establishment was hotly contested and highly mediatised (Laacher 2002: 13). For large sections of the British public, Sangatte stood for a French government 'bent on offloading its unwanted population upon the United Kingdom', while for others it stood for testimony to 'over-generous' UK asylum provisions (Walters 2008: 183). Between 1999 and 2001, approximately 76,000 people passed through Sangatte, many of whom eventually made asylum claims in the UK. During this time the shelter housed up to 1900 people – although it had been provisioned for 600 (Coureau 2011). The centre was closed after opening largely due to political pressure from both sides of the Channel. The UK blamed Sangatte, and France's lax approach to security, for supporting illicit border activity, while French ministers complained about the UK's liberal policies, claiming this as a key motivation for the UK's appeal as a destination.

The humanitarian interventions at Sangatte reframed Calais as a place of sanctuary responding to the plight of refugees. Inside migrants lived in tents, mobile cabins, or slept on the floor, remaining segregated according to nationality and ethnicity, as if in refugee camps (Coureau 2011). Meanwhile, outside the French riot police (CRS) were a passive presence 24 hours a day, manifesting growing fears about the risk migrants posed. Around the entrance the border police (PAF) conducted controls and collected declarations of individuals' nationality, identity and route taken into France, providing a 'conditional' welcome to the centre; '*un acceuil sous conditions*' (Laacher 2002: 17). The centre's establishment – through the secularised vision of international rights embodied by the Red Cross – played a role in further shaping asylum as an issue of moral sympathies, while reinforcing moves to securitise the French state.

However, there is another dimension to Sangatte. Calais was a way-marker on a route through Europe for those trying to flee war, persecution or economic poverty before the current geographic borders of the European Union became established. Although the specific routes taken are entangled in Western governmental histories, such routes must be understood as creative adaptations, and not productions of emerging EU regimes of movement (Liagre and Dumont 2005). And, importantly, other techniques and forms of knowledge have evolved in keeping with the transformations of sites like Calais into border zones and sanctuary spaces. As the fast-moving communication networks of expatriates communicated home the tiny success rates and harsh policing at entry-points like Italy and Greece,[1] clandestine travel rapidly adapted to keep old routes open, and forge new passages across Europe. Meanwhile, as old borders dismantled within a project of economic integration, highly coordinated networks of 'agents' became a vital resource to those seeking asylum in the EU (Coureau 2011). Using technological devices on a par with new border technologies, networks of *'les passeurs'* (people-smugglers) have flourished in Europe, making businesses out of expert knowledge about important crossings (Laacher 2002).

The routes through Sangatte thus reveal not only how EU regulations reshape movement, but also the new knowledge developing in relation to new definitions of the border (Walters 2008). Laacher (2002) records the textures of experience and arduous decisions made along a voyage which entailed living in a state of illegality for several months. Offering a counterbalance to portrayals of sanctuary spaces as sites of abjection, he details Sangatte as a site of exchange and resourcefulness, within difficult journeys forged to establish lifelines for families at home, or escape routes from intolerable living situations. Coureau (2011: 376) emphasises the new relations between places established by such movements, providing ethnographic detail of migrants' dealings with the smuggling networks at Calais, whom he describes as experts who 'know how to flee'. His portrayal of Sangatte as a site of resilience, danger and resourceful negotiation also problematises conventional understandings of sanctuary: the centre run by humanitarian agencies formed a point of encounter between those attempting to move, new entrepreneurs, and situated efforts to incarnate ideas of international rights.

Sangatte was a temporary place within a broader geography of movement, and the physical space of refuge it offered has since been replaced by camp-like spaces of the jungles, and squatted buildings in Calais, defended in various ways by humanitarian and activist groups. But we can rethink the site as a locus of experimental movements, knowledge production, and particular claims to presence. The basis of our citizenship is at stake, while the ethos of critique itself is under renegotiation. In the following section we move to consider how other forms of organising across this same period were accompanied by an attempt to conceive of ethical responses to irregular migrants as 'solidarity' – an ethos I suggest is progressively displacing sanctuary as an ethical response.

Sans-papiers *and solidarity*

Let us turn to the expressions of solidarity with *sans-papiers* at Calais and in Paris. The mobilisation of immigrants and their allies in occupied buildings (especially churches); hunger strikes, and demonstrations were not new phenomena in France in the 1990s. Indeed, as early as December 1972, nineteen Tunisians facing expulsion had occupied a church in Valence and then went on a hunger strike (Freedman 2008: 82). Their success and the favourable response they received from the French government (all nineteen were granted legal residence papers) helped catalyse about twenty other occupations the following year.[2] What is critical for an account of ethical subjectification in Northern France is that the conditions for enacting sanctuary were not a blank canvas, but a thick background of material ideas, built up over time. In France, the growth and spread of 'sanctuary' campaigns were effective partly due to their coincidence with other problematisations of citizenship through issues of race and colonialism (Germain 2008). Moreover, as different social movements came together in particular struggles, enduring articulations of a politics of irregular migration were altered. In the well-known protests of the 1990s, the figure of the *sans-papiers* took on a new resonance across diverse campaigns, fostering a new language of '*solidarité*', and gradually displacing the idea of offering sanctuary as citizens.

Although the movements had begun earlier,[3] the Parisian *sans-papiers* caught the worldwide media attention on the 22nd March 1996 when the French government ordered special police forces to break down the doors of Saint-Ambroise Church in the 11th *arrondissement* of Paris, to expel the 300 Africans, mainly from Mali and Senegal, staging a hunger strike inside (Freedman 2008). Mamady Sané (1996: 45), one of those involved, records in his journal how they were violently removed from the scene:

> Sixty-two adults were arrested and the others who had escaped were surrounded by policemen. They told them that they should know that blacks had no place here in France, and asked whether they thought they were in Africa.

The police did not recognise the legitimacy of the migrants' claims to sanctuary and the gathering was quickly disbanded. Such claims challenged French definitions of citizenship, and posed more of a threat than humanitarian provisions of shelter and assistance. However, this expulsion and its spectacular media coverage quickly rallied other immigrants and parts of the French population, who joined demonstrations and petitioned for the migrants' regularisation. In the weeks that followed, many who had previously occupied Saint-Ambroise moved to multiple locations in Paris, initially taking refuge in the Cartoucherie Theatre in Vincennes under the theatre director Arianne Mnouchkine's direction, and, between March 22nd and June 28th, they occupied a second church, a 'leftist' bookstore, and an unused railway site (Siméant 1998; Rassiguer 2010: 19). The original *sans-papiers* collaborated with a group of mediators, including academics, lawyers, and blue-collar French workers on ten criteria for a status change, and ultimately convinced the French government to look at the three hundred files (see also Lippert 2006: 189–90, for a remarkably similar sequence in the Canadian context, involving Chilean asylum-seekers).

In France, this campaign drew many supporters through its resonance with the longer-standing 'race' issue in France, highlighted by postcolonial writers, and post-war testimonial literatures. Advocates suggested the way the protests were disbanded exposed the racially discriminatory nature of the policing of migration in France. For example, in August 1996, when over a thousand police forcibly entered the St Bernard church, Madjiguène Cissé (1999), points out how 'whites' and 'blacks' were separated using tear gas. This resulted in a situation where several white *sans-papiers* avoided arrest, while many blacks with residence papers *were* arrested, and the former were able to offer support. Immigrant struggles had been associated with the more 'radical' or 'heretical' end of Leftist politics for some time, but how French communities mobilised around the hunger strikes and *sans-papiers* occupations evidenced a new level of public identification with their claims (Siméant 1998). Although the legal ground taken as a result of the actions was often patchy, internally conflicted, and sometimes reversible, the *sans-papiers* movement and the responses of Parisians also caught a wider European imagination, finding resonance across political and social movements (Pojman 2008). The immigration issue might not have been new, but new linkages across left-leaning, anarchist, and post-colonial forms of organising seized on the trope of the *sans-papiers* as a means of creating new platforms of commonality not based on gender, sexuality, or race identity (Freedman 2008). What is distinctive about the forms of shelter and support offered in comparison with 'sanctuary' movements, is how the spaces occupied were linked with claims *among equals* (see also Darling and Squire, Chapter 13 in this volume). Importantly, the claims of those without papers became the mobilising force within the campaigns, while those offering their churches, houses, and theatres increasingly questioned the idea of French citizenship in its dominant form. The solidaristic forms of organising which emerged between these differently situated groups led new strategies for critiquing and transforming existing regimes of citizenship.

The figure of the *sans-papiers* became a new point of intersection between social movements which had previously organised separately – trade unions, feminist and anti-racist movements, migrant-led and humanitarian campaigns – partly because it foregrounded the migrants' claim to presence as a claim we all share. Rassiguer (2010: xiv) asserts that, rather than presenting something new, these struggles highlighted within disparate social movements the paradox of the French idea of the 'exception', exported in the form of international humanitarianism: the notion of an abstract universal equality that founds ideas of unconditional rights, yet which also functions to veil the mechanisms required to maintain a national identity which upholds such a value (ibid.: 1). Rather than being articulated through universal rights claims, asserting particular obligations on states and citizenship regimes, the act of solidarity with irregular migrants' claims to presence problematises the partiality of state citizenship categories.

Conclusion

Acknowledging migration as a creative and political act enables us to consider how social movements' conceptions of citizenship and political ethos are being reframed by new forms of movement. Attending to sites of sanctuary as experimentation and interaction rather than as spaces of abjection reveals that sanctuary practices are being increasingly displaced, or remodelled, in Northern France based around the concept of the irregular migrant as political actor, rather than the citizen. This led to the development of partnerships, and the establishment of autonomous spaces of dwelling as part of a new wave of political protests.

This shift was particularly evident at the end of 1996 when Juppé's government introduced two new bills on illegal residence and work in France, including the Debré law, adopted at a first reading in the National Assembly in December 1996, along with stringent amendments. The upshot of the bills was to end the automatic renewals of ten-year residence permits, meaning that long-standing immigrants could be deported. In addition, French nationals who received any non-EU citizens in their house were required to inform local authorities of their arrival and departure (Rassiguer 2010). This was widely perceived as an infringement of the freedoms of nationals *and* immigrants, and a significant race issue (Freedman 2008: 83–4). Reaction to the clause was, in this case, led by a group of filmmakers, who published a petition in *Le Monde* and *Libération* declaring they were all themselves guilty of receiving illegal foreign residents in their own houses and calling for a campaign of civil disobedience against the new Debré Law (*Le Monde, Libération,* February 12, 1997). More than 100,000 demonstrators gathered for a demonstration in Paris on the 22nd of February, 1997, and, under pressure, the *Conseil d'Etat* issued a statement that the law might have been 'unconstitutional' anyway, and the bill was reworded (Rassiguer 2010). Although the success of this lobbying seems to evidence the audibility of citizens' voices compared to an apparently silent migrant population, it was the actions and claims of the *sans-papiers* which had led to the new tactics used in these protests. The declarations staged by French residents saw citizens referring to themselves as 'migrants', and framing their sanctuary practices as acts of 'solidarity' with other migrants denied the rights to remain – this ultimately reflects a refusal of the difference between migrants and citizens implied by the new law.

Moreover, the broad momentum of critical organising was fuelled in this moment, and – faced with anti-immigrant sentiment from both Left and Right incumbent governments – it grew. And, in the wake of the destruction of the Calais jungles, a new generation of 'solidarity activists' continue to work experimentally alongside migrants to establish temporary dwellings, while local village residents assert the rights for common spaces to be used for transitory refugee communities. This is a notion of sanctuary which challenges the borders which are the conditions of its own possibility, in particular, the boundaries and conditions of who or what counts as a citizen. We can observe, then, the emergence of an ethos of sanctuary *sans frontières*, or as it is newly articulated, of 'solidarity' among those who move, and those who do not have to.

Notes

1 In 2008, Greece gave asylum to only 379 out of 20,000 applicants (*Guardian*, September 27, 2009). In 2009, 16,076 applications were filed and 11,144 asylum appeals heard, yet only 6 applicants (0.02 per cent) received refugee status at the initial claim, and 344 at the stage of appeal (11.3 per cent). This process appears to be designed to force asylum claimants to become illegal (Bolten 1991).
2 For example, in February 1980, seventeen Turks illegally employed in workshops in Paris began a hunger strike to gain regularisation and better working conditions. The CFDT union active in this sector supported the campaign and around 3000 Turkish textile workers were regularised (Freedman 2008). As French government policies have become more restrictive on immigration and work, these movements have grown. While the *sans-papiers* movements have represented the largest of these movements, work-related immigration protests have also been widespread.
3 Migrant-led activism in Europe was not a new phenomenon in the 1990s.

References

Agamben, G. (1995) 'We Refugees', *Symposium*, 29: 114–16.
——(1997) 'The Camp as *Nomos* of the Modern', in H. de Vries and S. Weber (eds) *Violence, Identity and Self-Determination*, Stanford, CA: Stanford University Press, pp. 106–18.
Arendt, H. (1951) *The Origins of Totalitarianism*, New York: Harcourt Brace Jovanovich.
Bolten, L. (1991) 'From Schengen to Dublin: The New Frontiers of Refugee Law', in H. Meijers *et al.* (eds) *Schengen: Internationalization of Central Chapters of the Law on Aliens, Refugees, Privacy, Security and the Police*, Utrecht: W.E.J. Tjeenk Wilink-Kluwer, pp. 8–36.
Calais Migrant Solidarity (2009) 'Demo at Sous-Prefecture', available at: http://calais migrantsolidarity.wordpress.com/2009/09/ (accessed 30 April 2012).
Christiansen, T., Petito, F. and Tonra, B. (2000) 'Fuzzy Politics around Fuzzy Borders: The European Union's "Near Abroad"', *Cooperation and Conflict*, 35: 389–415.
Cissé, M. (1999) *Parole de sans-papiers*, Paris: La Dispute.
Coureau, H. (2011) '"Tomorrow Inch Allah, Chance!" People Smuggler Networks in Sangatte', *Immigrants and Minorities*, 22(2): 374–87.
Darling, J. (2009) 'Becoming Bare Life: Asylum, Hospitality, and the Politics of Encampment', *Environment and Planning D: Society and Space*, 27(4): 649–65.
De Genova, N. (2011) 'The Deportation Regime: Sovereignty, Space, and the Freedom of Movement', in V. Squires (ed.) *The Contested Politics of Mobility: Borderzones and Irregularity*, London: Routledge.
Derville, A. (1985) *Histoire de Calais*, Dunkerque: Les Editions des Beffrois.
Dikeç, M. (2009) 'Guest Editorial: The "Where" of Asylum', *Environment and Planning D: Society and Space*, 27(2): 183–9.
Dillon, M. (1999) 'The Scandal of the Refugee', in D. Campbell and M. J. Shapiro (eds) *Moral Spaces: Rethinking Ethics and World Politics*, Minneapolis: Minnesota University Press, pp. 92–124.
Fassin, D. (2005) 'Compassion and Repression: The Moral Economy of Immigration Policies in France', *Cultural Anthropology*, 20: 362–87.
Foucault, M. (1978) *The History of Sexuality: An Introduction*, vol. 1, New York: Vintage Books.

——(1997) *Ethics: The Essential Works 1*, London: Penguin.
——(1998) 'Afterword to the Temptation of Saint Anthony', in J. Faubion (ed.) *Michel Foucault: Aesthetics, The Essential Works*, vol. 2, London: Allen Lane, pp. 103–22.
Freedman, J. (2008) 'The French "Sans-Papiers" Movement: An Unfinished Struggle', in W. Pojman (ed.) *Migration and Activism in Europe since 1945*, New York: Palgrave Macmillan.
Germain, F. (2008) 'For the Nation and for Work: Black Activism in Paris of the 1960s', in W. Pojman (ed.) *Migration and Activism in Europe since 1945*, New York: Palgrave Macmillan.
Huysmans, J. (2006) *The Politics of Insecurity: Fear, Migration and Asylum in the EU*, London: Routledge.
Isin, E.F. (2009) 'Citizenship in Flux: The Figure of the Activist Citizen', *Subjectivity*, 29: 367–88.
Isin, E.F. and Nielsen, G.M. (2008) 'Introduction: Acts of Citizenship', in E. Isin and G. Nielsen (eds) *Acts of Citizenship*, London: Zed Books.
Laacher, S. (2002) *Après Sangatte: Nouvelles Immigrations, Nouveaux Enjeux*, Paris: La Dispute.
Lauren, P.G. (2011) *The Evolution of International Human Rights: Visions Seen*, Philadelphia, PA: University of Pennysylvania Press.
Lemke, T. (2005) 'A Zone of Indistinction: A Critique of Giorgio Agamben's Concept of Biopolitics', *Outlines: Critical Social Studies*, 7(1): 3–13.
Liagre, R. and Dumont, F. (2005) 'Sangatte: vie et mort d'un centre de "réfugiés"', *Annales de Géographie*, 641(1): 93–112.
Lippert, R. (2006) *Sanctuary, Sovereignty, Sacrifice: Canadian Sanctuary Incidents, Power and Law*, Vancouver: UBC Press.
Mezzadra, S. (2011) 'The Gaze of Autonomy, Capitalism, Migration and Social Struggles', in V. Squires (ed.) *The Contested Politics of Mobility: Borderzones and Irregularity*, London: Routledge.
Mezzadra, S. and Neilson, B. (2008) 'Border as Method, or, the Multiplication of Labor', *Transversal* 06–08, available at: http://eipcp.net/transversal/0608/mezzadraneilson/en (accessed 20 May 2011).
Moulier Boutang, Y. (1998) *De l'esclavage au salariat. Économie historique du salariat bride*, Paris: Puf.
Nyers, P. (2003) 'Abject Cosmopolitanism: The Politics of Protection in the Anti-Deportation Movement', *Third World Quarterly*, 24(6): 1069–93.
Papadopolous, D., Stephenson, N. and Tsianos, V. (2008) *Escape Routes: Control and Subversion in the 21st Century*, London: Pluto Press.
Perera, S. (2002) 'What is a Camp … ?' *Borderlands*, 1(1), available at: http://www.borderlandsjournal.adelaide.edu.au/issues/vol3no1.html (accessed 5 May 2011).
Pojman, W. (ed.) (2008) *Migration and Activism in Europe since 1945*, New York: Palgrave Macmillan.
Rassiguer, C. (2010) *Reinventing the Republic: Gender, Migration, and Citizenship in France*, Stanford, CA: Stanford University Press.
Redfield, P. (2006) 'A Less Modest Witness: Collective Advocacy and Motivated Truth in a Medical Humanitarian Movement', *American Ethnologist*, 33(1): 3–26.
Rygiel, K. (2011) 'Bordering Solidarities: Migrant Activism and the Politics of Movement and Camps at Calais', *Citizenship Studies*, 15(1): 1–19.
Sané, M. (1996) *Sorti de l'ombre: Journal d'un sans-papiers*, Paris: Le Temps des Cerises.
Schuster, L. (2005) 'A Sledgehammer to Crack a Nut: Deportation, Detention and Dispersal in Europe', *Social Policy and Administration*, 39(6): 606–21.

Siméant, J. (1998) *La Cause des Sans-Papiers*, Paris: Presses de Sciences Politiques.
Sparke, M. (2006) 'A Neoliberal Nexus: Economy, Security and the Biopolitics of Citizenship on the Border', *Political Geography*, 25: 151–80.
Terry, F. (2002) *Condemned to Repeat? The Paradox of Humanitarian Action*, Ithaca, NY: Cornell University Press.
Ticktin, M. (2006) 'Where Ethics and Politics Meet: The Violence of Humanitarianism in France', *American Ethnologist*, 33: 33–49.
Tyler, I. (2006) '"Welcome to Britain": The Cultural Politics of Asylum', *European Journal of Cultural Studies*, 9(2): 185–202.
Walters, W. (2008) 'Acts of Demonstration: Mapping the Territory of (Non-)Citizenship', in E. Isin and G. Nielsen (eds) *Acts of Citizenship*, London: Zed Books.

Part II

Sanctuary movements and practices in the United States

Old and new

Chapter 5

Legacies and origins of the 1980s US–Central American sanctuary movement

Hector Perla Jr. and Susan Bibler Coutin

Given the proliferation of sanctuary activities internationally and the emergence of the new sanctuary movement in the US (see Millner, Chapter 4, Just, Chapter 9, Yukich, Chapter 7 and Cunningham, Chapter 11 in this volume), it is worthwhile re-examining what may be the best-known instance of sanctuary practices: the US–Central American sanctuary movement of the 1980s. Our re-examination of this movement is motivated by two factors. The first is our sense that, with the passage of time, it is possible to discern movement that could not be fully articulated (even by its protagonists) while it was ongoing, and also that, with hindsight, the legacies of the sanctuary movement may now be more apparent. In particular, we seek to draw attention to the *transnational* nature of the US–Central American sanctuary movement. It is perhaps obvious that a movement that was dedicated to securing political asylum for Central American asylum-seekers and that (in at least some quarters) opposed US military intervention in Central American was transnational. What may be less obvious, however, is the degree to which sanctuary activities emerged as part of Central Americans' broader effort to mobilize North Americans in support of organized civil society actors working for social justice in El Salvador. Furthermore, although it is beyond the scope of this chapter to discuss those particular connections, Mexican and Canadian organizers and colleagues were part of the underground and above ground 'railroad' along which Central Americans travelled, and Mexican movement participants were among those prosecuted in the 1985–86 Tucson sanctuary trial (Lippert 2005). This transnational, political, and organizational focus presents a clear difference between the 1980s US–Central American sanctuary movement, which was one part of a broader Central America peace and solidarity movement, and current sanctuary practices in Canada, the US, and elsewhere, in which local communities seek immigration remedies for individuals who are at immediate risk of deportation (ibid.).

Second, we believe that revisiting the US–Central American sanctuary movement can give us powerful insight into future understandings of sanctuary as a concept and practice. The legacies of the US–Central American sanctuary movement extend beyond movement participants' stated goals of securing refuge, condemning human rights abuses, and preventing US military intervention abroad. Unintended consequences of sanctuary practices include complex legal changes in the US, increased remittance flows to Central America, and the development of new networks of civil society organizations in both countries. Though not the sole cause, sanctuary activities were a necessary precondition for these developments. Thus, re-examining the movement's origins and legacies suggests that apparent resemblances in the form of sanctuary incidents may hide underlying differences. It also allows us to note that shifts in the bases for legitimacy lead some transnational connections and movement objectives to be celebrated while others are obscured, and suggests that current sanctuary practices may eventually have unanticipated consequences as well.

In re-examining the US–Central American sanctuary movement, we bring together two different sorts of expertise. Hector Perla is a political scientist, specializing in US–Latin American relations, social and revolutionary movements, and Central American political engagement in the US. Perla's work highlights the formal and contentious strategies that Central American activists, in their home countries and in the diaspora, use to challenge US foreign policy toward the region. The bulk of his interviews have been with Salvadoran solidarity activists and revolutionary militants in San Francisco and Los Angeles (Perla 2005, 2008, 2009). Susan Bibler Coutin, an anthropologist, did fieldwork within the San Francisco East Bay and Tucson, Arizona segments of the US–Central American sanctuary movement during the 1980s. As part of this fieldwork, she participated in sanctuary activities, interviewed 100 movement participants, and collected documents produced by, and about, the movement (Coutin 1993). During the 1990s and the 2000s, she followed Central Americans' efforts to secure permanent legal status for their undocumented or only temporarily documented compatriots (Coutin 2000, 2007). It is important to note that because our fieldwork focused on sanctuary communities in California and Arizona, there may be differences between the accounts derived from this research and the origins and advocacy work in other key movement sites, such as Chicago.

Bringing our expertise together allows us to focus on the agency of Central American collective actors in the context of a strategic interaction, without sacrificing a deep understanding of the on-the-ground dynamics of the sanctuary movement. Moreover, we contextualize our analysis in a transnational framework that does not force a dichotomous definition of sanctuary as either a purely foreign or completely domestic movement. Specifically, we are now able to show how certain relationships between North and Central American activists were celebrated, while others were hidden, due either to fear for Salvadoran immigrant activists' safety or to concern about inadvertently undermining the movement's legitimacy. Part of what made the US–Central American sanctuary movement so powerful was that it emerged as part of a broader effort by Central American revolutionaries to mobilize opposition to US support for the Salvadoran government. But to do so, Salvadoran immigrants had to be willing to strategically stay quiet, become invisible, or abstain from taking on certain leadership roles, while, for the sake of achieving their and the movement's objectives, embracing identities, such as 'refugees' or 'victims' that, to some, implied weakness or passivity. In this way, Salvadoran immigrant activists used their strategic invisibility as a form of power, along the lines of what political scientists Keck and Sikkink (1998: 16) have called leverage and accountability politics. Analyzing the movement's framing of Central Americans as refugees makes it possible to identify legacies that may not have been intended or anticipated by the movement's organizers. In particular, the success of the 'refugee' framing created legal benefits that, in the post-war context, allowed the many years that Central Americans had lived in the US to be recognized as grounds for granting legal permanent residency, a recognition that had implications for Central American economies and non-governmental organizations.

First, we describe the origins of the sanctuary movement in the US. Second, we document the transnational nature of the movement. Third, we explore the unintended positive and negative consequences that the sanctuary movement engendered. Finally, we discuss how the movement has come full circle, in that unjust economic and political conditions in El Salvador, conditions to which US foreign policy contributed and that originally gave rise to the sanctuary movement, are still present in the country today. Consequently, we document ways that organizations and activists that are in El Salvador and that have roots in, or links to, sanctuary are now fighting for Salvadoran citizens' right *not* to become migrants.

Historical context of the US–Central American sanctuary movement

From 1932 until the late 1970s, El Salvador was ruled by a series of military dictators who came into office through either uncompetitive elections or coups. Starting in the late 1960s this system of governance began to be challenged by a growing collection of social movements. By 1972, this challenge had evolved to include a coalition of political parties of the centre and left (National Opposition Union, or UNO) with the support of many important civil society actors, which fielded a strong presidential candidate, José Napoleón Duarte. While it is widely believed that the UNO coalition won these elections, its candidates were not allowed to take office. In fact, its presidential candidate was arrested and tortured, and had to go into exile. This electoral challenge was repeated in 1977 with similar results, anointing another high-ranking military officer, Carlos Romero, winner of the presidential race.

As a result of government intransigence, these institutional political challenges were accompanied by an upswing in social movement mobilization among unions and student, peasant, and religious organizations. The Salvadoran government responded to this contentious political challenge in much the same way that it met formal political challenges to its authority – with even greater and ever-increasing levels of brutality. This brutality fed support for the incipient but rapidly growing armed revolutionary organizations that began forming in the early 1970s and would come together in 1980 to form the FMLN (Frente Farabundo Marti para la Liberación Nacional) Farabundo Marti National Liberation Front, a coalition of five guerrilla organizations and its supporters (Montgomery 1995; Brockett 2005). Violence also caused many students, union members, and other activists to migrate to the US.

The rise of the US–Central American sanctuary movement was directly related to this dramatic increase in migration. Today, Salvadorans are the fourth-largest Latino-origin group in the US, behind only Mexicans, Puerto Ricans, and Cubans, numbering over two million and making up between 3 and 5 per cent of the total Latino population of the US (Jones-Correa *et al.* 2006). While Salvadorans have resided in the US since at least the end of World War II, they did not come in large numbers until the late 1970s and early 1980s (Menjívar 2000). As the violence escalated, particularly from government security forces and allied clandestine death squads, Salvadorans began moving from the Salvadoran countryside to the cities and eventually abroad, especially to the US. By 1984, according to Byrne (1996: 115):

> Within El Salvador there were 468,000 displaced people (9.75 percent of the population), 244,000 in Mexico and elsewhere in Central America, and 50,000 more in the US, for a total of more than 1.2 million displaced and refugees (25 percent of the population).

While the US census estimated that in 1970 there were only 15,717 Salvadorans in the country, by 1980 that figure had grown to 94,447 and by 1990 had skyrocketed to 465,433 (Andrade-Eekhoff 2003). Other estimates during the mid and late 1980s put the number significantly higher. Whatever the true number, the reality is that the massive influx of Salvadoran refugees arriving daily throughout the decade, some with papers but most without, quickly overburdened the capacity of established kinship and friendship social networks to provide adequate assistance to the new arrivals (Menjívar 2000).

Meanwhile it was becoming clear that US foreign policy toward the country would play a crucial role in determining the outcome of El Salvador's future governance. Despite its rhetorical commitment to human rights, the Carter administration largely supported the Salvadoran regime. When the Reagan administration took up office, this support increased exponentially. Throughout the 1980s, US military and economic support for the Salvadoran government would exceed US $6 billion. This support not only included extensive counter-insurgency training and provision of vast quantities of sophisticated armaments but also active combat engagement against the FMLN by US military personnel (Graham 1996: A1).

Transnational nature of the Central American sanctuary movement

It was in this context of increased repression, immigration, and US involvement that the US–Central American sanctuary movement was born. The earliest organizational precursors to what would become the Central American solidarity movement, of which the US–Central American sanctuary movement was a key component, were several Salvadoran immigrant-based organizations (Coutin 1993). These organizations were made up primarily of already established Salvadoran immigrant and US-born Salvadoran activists, who initially came together to denounce the lack of democratic freedoms in their home country, the Salvadoran military's human rights violations, and US aid to the Salvadoran government under these conditions. The first of these organizations was the Comité de Salvadoreños Progresistas (Committee of Progressive Salvadorans), which was founded in San Francisco in 1975 in response to the massacre of students from the University of El Salvador. The organization grew quickly, and soon had the capacity to publish a weekly newspaper and even occupy the Salvadoran consulate. Shortly thereafter, other Salvadoran immigrant-based organizations sprouted in others cities around the US with large Salvadoran communities. Among the most prominent of these organizations were Casa El Salvador (several cities), the Comité Farabundo Martí (also known as Casa El Salvador – Farabundo Martí), and the Movimiento Amplio en Solidaridad con El Pueblo Salvadoreño (MASPS). These immigrant-based groups often had ties to social movement organizations in El Salvador, which in turn were connected to different FMLN factions. These linkages usually originated in kinship or friendship ties, although some originated from immigrants' own previous activism in El Salvador. While these organizations primarily sought to reach out to the Salvadoran and Latin American populations in the US, almost immediately progressive North Americans began gravitating toward their efforts (Perla 2008). In many instances, the North Americans brought with them prior experiences, such as involvement in anti-war activism during the Vietnam War, the freedom rides of the civil rights movement, and church-based refugee resettlement work. Therefore, sanctuary practices built on both North and Central Americans' rich experiences of social justice work.

During a 2000 interview, Don White, a Los Angeles-based organizer with the Committee in Solidarity with the People of El Salvador (CISPES), recalled how North Americans were brought into Central American solidarity work:

> Very early in the 80s, the different tendencies from El Salvador then began to develop their projects. And this is nothing that people were critical about. It was very natural for the political entities in El Salvador to come here and organize among their own compañeros, compañeras, their comrades they felt comfortable with. So certain agencies grew up [that were] identified with one of the five armies of the FMLN. We collaborated over ending U.S. military intervention, to end all military aid to El Salvador. All groups agreed on that point of unity. So it was easy to collaborate with all. The second [point] was direct political support to the FMLN and political and economic material support to the popular movement. And sending delegations and mobilizing U.S. citizens to oppose intervention, and those

who were able to make the next step to declare their solidarity with the struggle in El Salvador. But many CISPES activists, many North Americans, were anti-interventionists, but never took the step toward solidarity. If we once took them to El Salvador and got them in El Salvador to meet the Salvadorans, to see the struggle, especially during the war, when it was a very dramatic experience, often they would become solidarity activists, raise money for the popular movement.

In addition, these immigrant-based organizations' missions were originally focused on changing US foreign policy. However, it quickly became apparent to immigrant activists that they needed to do something to respond not only to the plight of their compatriots in their home country, but, with growing urgency, to the plight of an ever-increasing number of Salvadorans who were seeking refuge in the US. They also realized that these new arrivals' testimonies were compelling educational tools for North American audiences. As the then-director of the San Francisco Comité Farabundo Martí, Jose Artiga, in an interview with Hector Perla in February 2007, explains:

> This is where I feel that the Salvadorans' role is very important, sometimes making the invitation, sometimes giving their blessing [through their testimonies]. The invitation was really important because people after a presentation or after becoming aware of the situation would have a really bad feeling and you'd say it's your tax dollars that are financing these human rights violations and the question they would ask, is what can I do? And here is where with lots of creativity we had a menu of things that people could do ... join CISPES, sanctuary, support refugees.

To meet the immediate survival needs of their community and to advocate for their legal needs, both Salvadoreños Progresistas and Casa El Salvador Farabundo Martí created new organizations, which began providing housing and social as well as legal services for refugees in the late 1970s at Most Holy Redeemer's Catholic Church in San Francisco. The first organization, started by Salvadoreños Progresistas, was called Amigos de El Salvador (Friends of El Salvador) (interview with F. Kury, by Hector Perla, February 19, 2007). Casa Farabundo Martí soon followed suit, creating two organizations: the Centro de Refugiados Centroamericanos (CRECEN) and the Central American Resource Center (CARECEN) (according to Artiga, interview). This redundancy is illustrative of the infighting that became prevalent among Salvadoran immigrant-based organizations throughout the 1980s and mirrored divisions among social movements and the FMLN in El Salvador. To again quote Don White:

> Certain agencies grew up [that were] identified with one of the five armies of the FMLN ... In the early days, they often did not visit each other's agencies, because they saw them as I suppose both competitive, but also to

some degree a different line of the Salvadoran struggle, which they might not have agreed with.

As a result of these fratricidal conflicts, organizations such as Salvadoreños Progresistas and Amigos de El Salvador, despite their early accomplishments, were effectively red-baited and evicted from their offices (interview, Kury 2007). While neither of these organizations would play a direct role in the creation of the US–Central American sanctuary movement, it is important to note that Salvadoreños Progresistas pioneered the strategy of immigrants approaching members of religious organizations to collaborate with them in an effort to mobilize the religious community. In 1981, following this strategy, members of the Santana Chirino Amaya Refugee Committee and the Southern California Ecumenical Council came together in Los Angeles to create El Rescate. The organization's stated mission was 'to respond with free legal and social services to the mass influx of refugees fleeing the war in El Salvador' (El Rescate 2007).

CARECEN, CRECEN, and El Rescate would each go on to play a key role in the development of the national sanctuary movement. Through these organizations, Central American activists mobilized pastors and congregants by educating them about events in Central America, US foreign policy, and the imminent danger that persecution victims would be deported back to their place of persecution. In Los Angeles, these groups worked closely with the Southern California Interfaith Task Force on Central America (SCITCA) to offer sanctuary to Central American refugees (Hamilton and Chinchilla 2001). In the San Francisco East Bay, where Susan Coutin did fieldwork in the late 1980s, a member of the Comité de Refugiados Centroamericanos (CRECE) sent a representative to monthly steering committee meetings of the East Bay Sanctuary Covenant (EBSC). CRECE also arranged for Central Americans to speak to US audiences about their experiences (Coutin 1993). Central Americans were also an active force in sanctuary communities in Tucson, Washington, D.C., Houston, New York, Milwaukee, and elsewhere. As Jose Artiga, the former director of the San Francisco Comité Farabundo Martí, recounts in interview:

> Our goal was to create more organizations, to create more chapters (contacts)…not among the Salvadorans, if they were there we'd organize them, but more than anything the larger focus was the North Americans … so that they would be part of something [solidarity or peace organizations]. Then parallel to that was formed the sanctuary churches. That was a different group of people … who took that and gave it its own life … This menu of activities also included a range of political pressure, which included participating in a vigil to participating in civil disobedience … I remember that in Philadelphia, we asked the sanctuary churches to go to the house of Senator Specter after Sunday services … they would hold vigils directly in front of his house and even if they were not large, but with 10 people in front of his home they made him uncomfortable.

Early on, solidarity activists recognized the strategic framing of the 'refugee identity'. This framing was a particular way of talking about and presenting Salvadoran immigrants to North American audiences, especially to those with no previous knowledge of the conflict and without any political, ideological, or epistemic connection to the plight of the Salvadoran people. Salvadoran immigrant activists realized that it was not enough to educate North Americans about what was happening in El Salvador and about US government complicity. It was also essential to create empathy, to spark a sense of urgency and obligation or responsibility that would motivate North Americans to take a stand against their own government on behalf of an 'other' with whom they were largely unfamiliar (Coutin 1993). Central Americans' organizing practices also had to be adapted to dominant US norms, values, and perceptions of how North Americans saw themselves and saw Third World 'others'. The narrative construct of the 'refugee' met these needs by simultaneously drawing on shared Judeo-Christian traditions regarding exile, oppression, and refuge while also directing political attention to human rights abuses in Central America and to Salvadoran and Guatemalan immigrants' need for safe haven. Sanctuary also had a spatial dimension in that declarations of sanctuary attempted to 'bound' US law by creating 'safe spaces', even as participants argued that the US territory ought to serve as a refuge for victims of persecution in Central America. Furthermore, the term 'refugee' has a legal dimension that countered accusations of lawlessness and therefore was central to the movement's claim to legitimacy. In other words, activists suggested that since the US government was failing to live up to its moral and legal obligations to grant political asylum, then it was the obligation of congregations to do so, in the process using their moral credibility to openly defy what they considered unjust legal practices. Yet, while this identity allowed Salvadorans to reach out to broad US audiences, it also constrained their ability to act in those settings and, by reifying the asymmetric power relations between North and Central Americans, limited the relationships that could be developed. Such constraints were often fully overcome only by sanctuary activists who came to experience Salvadoran immigrants acting as empowered and strategic activists outside of the 'refugee' identity.

The limitations imposed by the 'refugee' identity are clear in two practices that were central to the US–Central American sanctuary movement: granting sanctuary and publicizing refugee testimonies. Sanctuary activists granted sanctuary by housing undocumented Central Americans in the churches, synagogues, or homes of congregation members. This arrangement provided Central Americans with material assistance, such as housing, food, access to medical care, job assistance, and other social services. At the same time, sanctuary was designed to bring congregation members into close contact with victims of persecution in Central America, and thus to raise congregants' and others' consciousnesses and spur them to action. As one Salvadoran who was living in sanctuary in Tucson during the 1980s explained, 'The moral and spiritual support that they gave us was great. In return, we collaborate in the various churches, telling about the terrible experiences that we've had in El Salvador' (Coutin 1993: 18). Refugee testimonies – public accounts of personal experiences of violence and persecution – were central to these consciousness-raising efforts, and were often accompanied by fundraising appeals or information about how to get involved. Sanctuary thus often exposed Central Americans to intensive scrutiny, and to well-meaning but nonetheless culturally laden offers to 'help' (Lippert 2005). While they often wanted to educate the North American public about conditions in their home countries, Central Americans also sometimes chafed at the refugee role. One Salvadoran living in sanctuary in the San Francisco East Bay in the 1980s commented that he preferred relationships that were 'person to person instead of person to refugee'. He added, 'I left my country due to the violence and due to the fear and danger of disappearing, not in order to become a refugee. To me, the word "refugee" implies inferiority and superiority' (Coutin 1993: 120). Such criticisms did not go unheard, and in fact, there were tensions between different segments of the sanctuary movement (in particular, between Tucson and Chicago participants) over the necessity of coupling sanctuary with testimonies and over which sorts of 'stories' ought to be publicized. The visibility, invisibility, and politicization of Central Americans were major issues within these debates.

The 'refugee' frame therefore largely presented Central Americans to sanctuary workers and to the broader US public as 'innocent victims' in need of support and as representatives of the poor and the oppressed, on whose behalf religious communities were compelled to advocate. While refugee testimonies frequently described Central Americans' actions (such as leading a labour union or becoming a catechist) in pursuit of social justice in their homelands, the 'refugee' frame also made it difficult to convey the organizational role that Central Americans played in mobilizing religious workers and the solidarity movement more generally. Thus, sanctuary activists spoke of hearing the Central Americans' call for solidarity and accompaniment, or of listening to the Central Americans and following their lead. However, the refugee framing necessarily positioned such responses as instances of materially better off North Americans acting strategically on behalf of the ostensibly innocent, authentic, or genuine (as opposed to strategic) Central Americans. As a result, this framing prevented Central American immigrant activists from publicly identifying as political protagonists able to take credit for devising joint strategies for social and political change, although of course there was local and regional variation in the degree to which Central and North Americans achieved or were presented as equal partners within sanctuary practices. Such framings were themselves, at times unconsciously, strategic, in that because the US government accused sanctuary workers of serving political rather than humanitarian and religious goals, the revelation that members of FMLN groups were involved in or behind the movement in some capacity, or behind the Central American organizations with which sanctuary workers collaborated, would have undermined sanctuary's legitimacy.

Legacies and unintended consequences

Just as the nature of transnational linkages becomes more clear with the passage of time, so too do the unintended consequences of US–Central American sanctuary practices. Significantly, the rights that Central Americans achieved through sanctuary and solidarity activities created grounds in the post-war period for claiming US residency, despite a changed political context. Furthermore, participants' organizing experiences created a basis for establishing a transnational network of immigrant rights NGOs. Although the US–Central American sanctuary movement was not the only cause of these developments, it was an important precursor whose long-term impact is felt in both the US and El Salvador. Sanctuary workers' stated goals included securing safe haven for Central American refugees, convincing US authorities to apply asylum law without regard for the politics of the regime from which refugees fled, drawing attention to human rights abuses in Central America, providing protection to Central Americans who were at risk of persecution, and preventing further US military intervention in Central American nations. To some degree, these objectives were achieved, though not solely due to sanctuary activities. In the wake of FMLN's final offensive and the assassination of six Jesuit priests in 1989, the US government began to pursue a negotiated settlement to the civil conflict; the 1990 *Immigration Act* created Temporary Protected Status and named Salvadorans as the first recipients; asylum procedures were reformed in the early 1990s; and in 1997, Salvadorans and Guatemalans who had immigrated during the civil war were given the right to apply for legal permanent residency. Sanctuary practices thus helped to set in motion a complex set of legal developments in the US. At the same time, the movement contributed indirectly to the rise in remittances to El Salvador, the creation of new civil society organizations in El Salvador and the US, and the continued circulation of US activists, students, scholars, and religious workers in Central America. These indirect effects of the movement have helped to maintain attention on social justice issues and on the needs of refugees and migrants.

In the US, a key but not always acknowledged legacy of the sanctuary movement is the development of new law to address the needs of asylum-seekers. Throughout the 1980s, sanctuary activists sought legislation, known as 'Moakley–Deconcini' after its sponsors Joe Moakley and Dennis Deconcini, that would have granted Extended Voluntary Departure (EVD) status to Salvadorans and Guatemalans. This bill faced stiff opposition from the Reagan and Bush administrations, which argued that Salvadorans and Guatemalans were economic immigrants who had fled poverty rather than violence. While efforts to pass Moakley–Deconcini were under way, sanctuary workers launched their own legal case against the US government. In 1985, eleven sanctuary activists were indicted on charges of conspiracy and alien-smuggling (Coutin 1995). In response, sanctuary communities and refugee service organizations filed a civil suit, known as *American Baptist Churches v. Thornburgh* or *ABC*, seeking a halt to sanctuary prosecutions, the granting of safe haven to Salvadorans and Guatemalans, and reforms that would prevent US foreign policy considerations from influencing the outcome of asylum cases. The first two of these claims were dismissed on the grounds that US immigration law had changed since the earlier sanctuary prosecutions and that immigration laws were not self-executing. Litigation on the third claim went forward, and the *ABC* case ceased to be *directly* about sanctuary *per se*. Then, in 1990, following the devastating events of the 1989 final offensive, in which six Jesuit priests, their housekeeper, and her daughter were murdered by the Salvadoran army, legislation creating a new legal form – Temporary Protected Status (TPS) – was approved, and Salvadorans were designated as the first recipients (Rubin 1991). During the same year, the US government agreed to settle the *ABC* case out of court, and in 1991, the settlement agreement gave some 300,000 Salvadorans and Guatemalans the right to apply or reapply for political asylum under rules designed to ensure fair consideration of their claims. It would seem that sanctuary activists' goal of at least gaining a fair hearing for Salvadoran and Guatemalan asylum-seekers had been achieved, while at the same time, TPS put a halt to deportations. Sanctuary and Central American activists had cause to celebrate.

Despite these victories, in the 1990s, events conspired to thwart the promise that TPS and the *ABC* settlement held out. First, the US Immigration and Naturalization Service (INS) put *ABC* asylum applications on the back burner in order to focus on quickly deciding new asylum petitions. Peace accords were signed in El Salvador in 1992 and in Guatemala in 1996, but interviews on *ABC* class members' asylum claims were not scheduled until 1997. By then, it was more difficult for applicants to demonstrate a well-founded fear of persecution, given that the wars in their homelands were officially over. Second, in 1996, the US Congress approved the *Illegal Immigration Reform and Immigrant Responsibility Act* (*IIRIRA*), which made many forms of legalization more difficult. In particular, *ABC* applicants had hoped that if their asylum claims were denied, they could then apply for Suspension of Deportation, a form of legalization available to individuals who could demonstrate good moral character, seven years of continuous presence in the US, and that deportation would be an extreme hardship. *IIRIRA* replaced Suspension of Deportation with Cancellation of Removal, for which applicants had to prove good moral character, ten years of continuous presence, and that deportation would pose extreme and exceptional hardship for the applicant's US citizen or legal permanent resident spouse, parent, or child. The heightened hardship standard, increased number of years of continuous presence, and introduction of the requirement of a qualifying relative meant that fewer *ABC* class members were likely to qualify. Furthermore, *IIRIRA* capped cancellation cases at 4000 annually, making this an unlikely solution for the approximately 300,000 *ABC* class members with pending asylum claims.

In this changed legal scenario, Central American organizations and immigrant rights activists sought new legislation that would enable *ABC* class members to become legal permanent residents. By allying with Nicaraguans and with the support of the Clinton administration and the Central American governments, advocates obtained the passage of the *Nicaraguan Adjustment and Central American Relief Act* (*NACARA*) in 1997. *NACARA* basically restored *ABC* class members' suspension eligibility (renaming this 'special rule cancellation') and exempted these cases from the 4000 cap. The regulations that implemented *NACARA* also granted applicants a rebuttable presumption of hardship, virtually guaranteeing a grant in most cases, and took the unprecedented step of codifying the factors that went into the assessment of hardship. Through *NACARA*, some 83,340 Salvadorans and Guatemalans were able to become legal permanent residents (B. P. Christian. Program Manager, *ABC-NACARA*, Asylum Division, Office of Refugee, Asylum and International Operations, U.S. Citizenship and Immigration Servicespers. comm., March 1 2004). These legal developments benefited not only Central Americans, but also nationals from other countries (including Burundi, Honduras, Nicaragua, Somalia, Sudan, Liberia, Sierra Leone, Bosnia, and Herzegovina) who have received TPS due to emergencies in their home countries, as well as establishing a precedent for other groups, such as Haitians, who benefited from the passage of the *Haitian Refugee Immigration Fairness Act* (*HRIFA*) in 1998. Sanctuary and Central American advocates' original focus on asylum, El Salvador, and Guatemala changed the US legal landscape in ways that could not have been anticipated.

While not solely attributable to sanctuary activities, increased remittances to El Salvador are an indirect effect of these legal changes. As legal developments have increased the stability and job security of Salvadorans living in the US, they may also have improved these migrants' ability to remit to family members in El Salvador (Abrego 2008). Specifically, remittances increased gradually throughout the 1980s, but grew more rapidly after 1990, when TPS was awarded. While in 1990 the country received less than US$500 million, by 2007, Salvadorans living abroad sent almost $3.7 billion in remittances to family members living in El Salvador (Banco Central de Reserva 2008). The quantity and importance of remittances to the country have not only risen in absolute terms; even more tellingly, they have risen as a share of the country's total gross domestic product (GDP). Between 1990 and 2004, remittances more than doubled as a share of the country's overall economy, going from about 6 per cent to over 15 per cent of El Salvador's GDP (PNUD 2005). At the same time, migrant remittances have had a huge impact on the economy of El Salvador, permitting the economy to stay afloat through economic readjustment programmes of the post-war period (ibid.). This development in turn has made the legal status of Salvadorans in the US a matter of concern in El Salvador. Indeed, extending TPS, which was re-awarded to Salvadorans following the 2001 earthquakes and which, as of January 2011, was scheduled to expire in September 2013, has been a high priority of the Salvadoran government (Weiner 2004). In fact, during the 2004 presidential election in El Salvador, some US politicians suggested that the US could cut off remittance flows by rescinding TPS, were the FMLN candidate to be elected (Coutin 2007: 93–4).

Networks of civil society organizations in both El Salvador and the US were another legacy of the US–Central American sanctuary movement. During a 2001 interview, an attorney who represented one of the first successful Salvadoran asylum seekers at the beginning of the 1980s described how his work provided a model for other groups dedicated to immigrants' rights:

> I organized networks of lawyers in big law firms to provide assistance in political asylum cases, or *pro bono* cases. That's sort of the Lawyers Committee's mode of operation. They organize big law firms and their lawyers to do free work on big civil rights matters. Or small civil rights matters. It's a way of organizing networks ... And I, in addition to organizing legal work and volunteer representation also organized teams of policy people from different organizations to look at big policy questions ... Now, that work in the Lawyers Committee, in my own mind at least, accomplished a couple of things. In addition to the work we actually did, it became the model for lawyers committees and the rights offices around the country. So, Robert Rubin's operation in San Francisco, Public Counsel's immigration work in LA, the Immigrant Rights Projects of the Lawyers' Committees in Boston and Chicago all were kind of modeled on what I started here in Washington...[And,] this political work I was doing at the Lawyers Committee, as opposed to the legal work, was the foundation for the National Immigration Forum.

In addition to these networks of immigrant rights organizations, many of the Central American groups that mobilized sanctuary workers have become established institutions, providing much-needed social services and advocacy work in their communities. For example, in Los Angeles, CARECEN purchased its own building during the 1990s, and, in September 2008, celebrated its 25th anniversary. Most recently, in Los Angeles, networks of attorneys and civil society organizations have been mobilized in response to workplace raids conducted by Immigration and Customs Enforcement. According to a recent *Los Angeles Times* article, 'The effort has parallels to the sanctuary movement of the 1980s, when churches brought Central American refugees to the US to protect them from political violence' (Gaouette 2008: A18).

Likewise, in El Salvador, groups that focused on refugee rights during the 1980s have given rise to coalitions that now advocate for migrants' rights more generally. During the 1980s, the El Salvador offices of the United Nations High Commission for Refugees, the International Organization for Migration, Catholic Charities, and Catholic Relief Services provided support for refugees who were attempting to flee persecution, while groups such as Comité Cristiano pro-Desplazados de El Salvador (Christian Committee for the Displaced of El Salvador) and Tutela Legal denounced and publicized human rights violations. During this period, sanctuary congregations in the US sometimes also became sister parishes of congregations in El Salvador, through the SHARE Foundation, which also organized delegations of visitors to war-torn communities. During the post-war period, as border enforcement in Mexico and the US became more stringent and as deportations from the US mounted, Maria Victoria de Áviles, the human rights ombudsperson in El Salvador, founded the Mesa Permanente sobre Migrantes y Población Desarraigada (Permanent Board on Migrants and Uprooted Populations), which in turn developed into the Foro del Migrante (Migrant Forum), and most recently, the Mesa Permanente de la Procuraduría para la Defensa de los Derechos Humanos para las Personas Migrantes (Permanent Board of the Ombudsry for the Defense of Human Rights for Migrant Peoples). The composition of these coalitions has varied, but generally has included government, academic, religious, and community groups concerned about human rights and immigration. In addition, some solidarity organizations that were formed in the US have founded their own counterparts in El Salvador. An example is CARECEN Internacional, located in San Salvador, which grew out of the network of CARECEN organizations in the US. The opposite has also occurred, with the San Salvador office of the gang violence prevention group Homies Unidos giving rise to a Los Angeles office of the same group (Zilberg 2011).

These networks of civil society organizations in the US and El Salvador have fostered the continued circulation of activists, scholars, students, and religious workers in El Salvador. Conferences, events, meetings and workshops regularly bring together scholars, students, and NGO members who work on or in El Salvador. NGOs in El Salvador collaborate with US students and researchers to collect data and issue reports, and with other US and Salvadoran NGOs to exchange information and develop strategies. CIS (Centro de Intercambio and Solidaridad/Center for Exchange and Solidarity), SHARE, and other groups continue to organize delegations to El Salvador. Hometown associations in the US are also key components of this continued circulation, as they direct resources and knowledge from the US to El Salvador and *vice versa* (Pederson 2002). This continued circulation has given rise to a transnational civil society circuit, not unlike the transnational linkages that mobilized solidarity and sanctuary work in the US during the 1980s. By directing resources, knowledge, labour, and particular products (including reports, testimonies, and expertise) to organizations and individuals, this circuit is critical to the continued mobilization of social justice work in El Salvador and in the US. Moreover, political parties on both the left and right have taken notice of these thick social networks and the resources to which they have access, and have sought to work with these organizations while setting up their own support networks in the US. For instance, during the buildup to the 2009 Salvadoran presidential campaign, both the FMLN and ARENA (Alianza Republicana Nacionalista) candidates visited several major US cities where Salvadorans are most concentrated, vying for the community's political and financial support (Rodrigo Presidente Webpage 2008; FMLN 2008).

Conclusion: coming full circle

The US–Central American sanctuary movement originally began as an attempt to draw attention to the unjust conditions in El Salvador, conditions that US foreign policy greatly exacerbated. The movement has now come full circle as campaigns by immigrant rights organizations in El Salvador have gone from advocating for the rights of refugees, to immigrants' rights, to the right not to migrate. This most recent focus is designed to call attention to unjust conditions within El Salvador, the dangerous nature of the trek to the US, and the lack of rights accorded to unauthorized immigrants upon arrival. In El Salvador, immigrants' rights organizations, such as CARECEN Internacional, publicize the risks of migration, such as losing limbs while attempting to board a moving train or dying of thirst or suffocation while crossing a desert or hiding in a locked compartment of a vehicle. These groups also present forums to Salvadoran youth, warning them of the dangers of the journey and urging them to develop their own leadership, entrepreneurial, and job skills in El Salvador. Finally, such groups urge Salvadoran authorities to address the root causes of emigration. For example, the opening section of the Mesa Permanente's 2007 minimum platform on migrants' rights states:

> Salvadoran migration, like that of so many other Latin American countries, is the ultimate choice of thousands of compatriots faced with a context of serious violations of their human rights, especially their economic, social, and cultural rights...
>
> The current reality of the Salvadoran state, characterized by economic inequalities, lack of work, low salaries, constant increases in the cost of living, and the lack of educational opportunities, leads thousands of Salvadoran men and women to choose to migrate to a country that will allow them to find and satisfy those living conditions that El Salvador neither afforded them nor permitted them to achieve.
>
> (Mesa Permanente de la Procuraduría para la Defensa de los Derechos Humanos para las Personas Migrantes 2007: 17)

In other words, the focus on the right not to migrate is intended to motivate individuals, communities, NGOs, and Salvadoran authorities to address the unjust underlying social, economic, and political conditions that give rise to emigration, and thus prevent it, rather than focusing only on the human rights of migrants in transit or on migrants' legal rights in the US. Such a move builds on earlier movement debates over the validity of the distinction between economic migrants and political refugees, debates that were muted by asylum law that focused on political persecution rather than economic need. The current refocusing, like solidarity and sanctuary work of the 1980s, is designed to promote peace and justice within El Salvador.

By revisiting the US–Central American sanctuary movement, we have sought to draw attention to the transnational nature of this movement and to the movement's long-term impact. Central Americans who were members of popular movements in El Salvador have played key roles in mobilizing religious workers to develop sanctuary activities, yet, for strategic and cultural reasons, their role was not fully acknowledged during the 1980s. That is, Central Americans were publicly recognized as inspirations and examples to follow, but were not openly treated as political organizers of sanctuary activities within the US. These framings of Central Americans as inspirations and examples emphasized the religious and humanitarian nature of the movement in contrast to US authorities' attempts to discredit sanctuary as a purely political activity. The framing of Central Americans as refugees, as innocent victims in need of aid, furthered the notion that Central Americans were beneficiaries rather than protagonists in the movement. In noting how Central American activists mobilized sanctuary and solidarity work as part of a broader effort to oppose the Salvadoran government during the civil conflict, we do not mean to suggest that movement members deliberately misled anyone, or that Central Americans themselves concealed their roles from North Americans. Rather, we draw attention to the ways that historical, political, and social contexts shape what can be said and known, and the fact that with hindsight, additional relationships and actions become apparent.

Hindsight also makes it possible to assess the unintended consequences of social movements. Social movement theory draws attention to the strategic goals that movements pursue, and to the factors, such as political opportunities, resources, and successful framing, that permit movement members to achieve these goals. As we have shown in this chapter, Salvadoran activists were precluded from fully claiming credit for their roles in the sanctuary movement by the very refugee identity that the movement used to effectively frame the issue. Unfortunately, some of the scholarly work on the Central American sanctuary movement has also been analytically constrained by this refugee frame and thus inadvertently reinforced Central American immigrant activists' inability to claim credit for their roles in the movement (Coutin 1993; Perla 2008).

We have also sought to identify the unintended consequences of pursuing strategic goals. Sanctuary workers and Central American activists set out to oppose human rights abuses in El Salvador and Guatemala, curtail US intervention in Central America, obtain asylum for persecution victims who had fled to the US, promote the legitimacy of the popular struggle and provide protection to Salvadoran and Guatemalan communities that were at risk of military violence. Movement actors did not, at the time, envision that Central Americans would be filing suspension or cancellation claims (as provided by *NACARA*), that Congress would create TPS, that their work would contribute to remittance flows, that they would play a key role in creating a transnational network of civil society organizations, or that such organizations would foster the continued circulation of activists and others between the US and El Salvador. Such outcomes were by-products of the movement, perhaps a means to an end, rather than explicit goals and, of course, are not wholly attributable to the movement itself. Nonetheless, theory that treats social movements primarily as instrumental action, even while acknowledging the symbolic components (such as 'framing') of such action, has a difficult time explaining movements' unintended consequences.

Finally, we hope to stress the particularity of sanctuary activities. In some ways, in California and Arizona at least, the US–Central American sanctuary movement of the 1980s was not about immigration at all, but rather sought to address social injustice in Central American nations, US intervention in Central America, and the effects of political violence on individuals and communities. Although sanctuary, as currently carried out in Canada, Europe, and the US, may bear formal similarity to US–Central American sanctuary practices of the 1980s, it might be wise to pay attention to the specificity of the particular immigration flows that give rise to sanctuary in particular social and historical contexts, whether these be local, national, or regional. Why are some individuals granted sanctuary while others are not? What particular laws or policies are sanctuary practices designed to address? And are sanctuary practices geared primarily toward a local or national context or do they also seek to intervene in transnational relationships and conditions? Addressing these questions will enrich scholarship on sanctuary in its many manifestations.

Acknowledgements

An earlier version of this article appeared in *Refuge: Canada's Periodical on Refugees* (26(1), 2009). The authors thank Sean Rehaag and Randy Lippert, the participants in the sanctuary panel at the US and the Canadian Law and Society Associations' joint meeting in Montreal in 2008, and the many organizations and individuals that provided us with information and assistance. Susan Coutin acknowledges the following funding agencies: American Association of University Women, the National Science Foundation's Law and Social Science Program (SBR-9423023, SES-0001890 and SES-0296050, and SES-0518011), and the John D. and Catherine T. MacArthur Foundation.

Hector Perla Jr. acknowledges the support of the Ohio University Baker Fund Award, and the University of California President's Postdoctoral Fellowship Program, as well as the Committee on Research's Faculty Research Grant, and the Chicano Latino Research Center's Individual Faculty Grant from the University of California, Santa Cruz.

References

Abrego, L.J. (2008) 'Barely Subsisting, Surviving, or Thriving: How Parents' Legal Status and Gender Shape the Economic and Emotional Well-Being of Salvadoran Transnational Families', doctoral thesis, University of California, Los Angeles.

Andrade-Eekhoff, K. (2003) *Mitos y realidades: el impacto económico de la migración en los hogares rurales*, San Salvador: FLACSO Programa El Salvador.

Banco Central de Reserva (2008) 'Ingresos mensuales en concepto de remesas familiares', *BCR Homepage*. Available at: http://www.bcr.gob.sv/estadisticas/se_remesas.html (accessed 10 September 2008).

Brockett, C. (2005) *Political Movements and Violence in Central America*, New York: Cambridge University Press.

Byrne, H. (1996) *El Salvador's Civil War: A Study of Revolution*, Boulder, CO: Lynne Rienner.

Coutin, S.B. (1993) *The Culture of Protest: Religious Activism and the U.S. Sanctuary Movement*, Boulder, CO: Westview Press.

——(1995) 'Smugglers or Samaritans in Tucson, Arizona: Producing and Contesting Legal Truth', *American Ethnologist*, 22(3): 549–71.

——(2000) *Legalizing Moves: Salvadoran Immigrants' Struggle for U.S. Residency*, Ann Arbor, MI: University of Michigan Press.

——(2007) *Nations of Emigrants: Shifting Boundaries of Citizenship in El Salvador and the United States*, Ithaca, NY: Cornell University Press.

El Rescate (2007) 'El Rescate's 20 Years of Aid and Advocacy', *El Rescate Homepage*. Available at: http://www.elrescate.org/main.asp?sec=about (accessed 6 February 2007).

FMLN (2008) 'Empresarios Salvadoreños en Estados Unidos apoyan a Mauricio Funes', *FMLN Homepage*. Available at: http://www.fmln.org.sv/detalle.php?action=fullnews&id=36 (accessed 17 September 2008).

Gaouette, N. (2008) 'Tip-offs Dilute Surprise of ICE Raids', *Los Angeles Times*, 14 Sept. A18.

Graham, B. (1996) 'Public Honors for Secret Combat; Medals Granted after Acknowledgment of US Role in El Salvador', *Washington Post*, 6 May, A1.

Hamilton, N. and Chinchilla, N.S. (2001) *Seeking Community in a Global City: Guatemalans and Salvadorans in Los Angeles*, Philadelphia, PA: Temple University Press.

Jones-Correa, M., Fraga, L.R., Garcia, J.A., Hero, R.E., Martinez-Ebers, V. and Segura, G.M. (2006) *Redefining America: Findings from the 2006 Latino National Survey*. Available at: www.wilsoncenter.org/index.cfm?event_id=201793&fuseaction=events.event_summary (accessed 17 September 2008).

Keck, M. and Sikkink, K. (1998) *Activists Beyond Borders*, Ithaca, NY: Cornell University Press.

Lippert, R. (2005) *Sanctuary, Sovereignty and Sacrifice: Canadian Sanctuary Incidents, Power and Law*, Vancouver: UBC Press.

Menjívar, C. (2000) *Fragmented Ties: Salvadoran Immigrant Networks in America*, Berkeley, CA: University of California Press.

Mesa Permanente de la Procuraduría para la Defensa de los Derechos Humanos para las Personas Migrantes (2007) *Plataforma Mínima de los Derechos de las Personas Migrantes*, San Salvador: Procuraduría para la Defensa de los Derechos Humanos.

Montgomery, T.S. (1995) *Revolution in El Salvador: From Civil Strife to Civil Peace*, Boulder, CO: Westview Press.

Pederson, D. (2002) 'The Storm We Call Dollars: Determining Value and Belief in El Salvador and the United States', *Cultural Anthropology*, 17(3): 431–59.

Perla, H. (2005) 'Revolutionary Deterrence: The Sandinista Response to Reagan's Coercive Policy against Nicaragua, Lessons toward a Theory of Asymmetric Conflict', doctoral thesis, University of California Los Angeles.

——(2008) 'Si Nicaragua Venció, El Salvador Vencerá: Central American Agency in the Creation of the U.S.-Central American Peace & Solidarity Movement', *Latin American Research Review*, 43(2): 136–58.

——(2009) 'Heirs of Sandino: The Nicaraguan Revolution and the U.S.-Nicaragua Solidarity Movement', *Latin American Perspectives*, 36(6): 80–100.

Programa de las Naciones Unidas para el Desarrollo (2005) *Informe sobre Desarrollo Humano, El Salvador: Una Mirada al Nuevo Nosotros*, San Salvador: PNUD.

Rodrigo Presidente Webpage (2008) 'Ávila Agradece al 8° Sector por Apoyo Recibido', available at: http://www.rodrigopresidente.com/octavo.php (accessed 17 September 2008).

Rubin, R. (1991) 'Ten Years After: Vindication for Salvadorans and New Promises for Safe Haven and Refugee Protection', *Interpreter Releases*, 68(4): 97–109.

Weiner, T. (2004) 'U.S.-Backed Rightist Claims Victory in Salvador Election', *New York Times*, 22 March. Available at: http://www.nytimes.com (accessed 22 March 2004).

Zilberg, E. (2011) *Space of Detention: The Making of a Transnational Gang Crisis between Los Angeles and San Salvador*, Durham, NC: Duke University Press.

Chapter 6

The voice of the voiceless

Religious rhetoric, undocumented immigrants, and the New Sanctuary Movement in the United States

Marta Caminero-Santangelo

The New Sanctuary Movement (NSM), in which churches and congregations in the United States gave 'sanctuary' to undocumented immigrants at risk of deportation, was launched publicly in May 2007 in major cities including Chicago, Los Angeles, San Diego, New York, and Seattle. By year's end, congregations in approximately 50 cities were involved or expressing interest (Bazar 2007; Serjeant 2007; New Sanctuary Movement 2011). The movement was modeled on the Sanctuary Movement of the 1980s, in which over 400 religious congregations had offered sanctuary – as well as other kinds of assistance – to Central American refugees fleeing repressive regimes but unable to obtain political asylum in the United States (see Perla and Coutin, Chapter 5 in this volume). The NSM, however, has been less about physical sanctuary than about providing a new means of telling the story of the human costs of current US deportation policy. In the NSM, undocumented immigrants, who have generally tried to stay 'under the radar' to avoid attention to their status, have been encouraged to speak publicly about their stories. Thus 'sanctuary' – typically associated with offering refuge to fugitives, a form of 'symbolic salvation from coercion' through hiding and concealment (Lippert 2005: 8, 25) – in the NSM became reconfigured as a public and performative practice, meant to offer a potential counter-discourse to dominant rhetoric on immigration and to constitute an activist community of faith.

Pierrette Hondagneu-Sotelo has argued that religious faith can be instrumental in immigrant rights advocacy at multiple levels, both inspiring advocacy as citizens come to feel that their faith calls them to act on behalf of the oppressed, and providing a framework for the *presentation* of immigrant justice claims by foregrounding 'faith' over 'politics' (2008: 7, 156–9). The use of faith frameworks for immigrant-rights claims in the NSM is a powerful illustration of this point. This chapter will analyze the kinds of discourse used publicly both by US-citizen participants in the movement (in media interviews, statements, and the like), and by undocumented sanctuary recipients themselves (including the prominent figure Elvira Arellano, who served in large part as the movement's inspiration). While US citizen NSM participants have deployed a religious rhetoric, more often associated with the Christian Right in public debates, to explain their own involvement, sanctuary recipients also have been expected to become public spokespeople for immigration rights by telling their personal stories in a compelling way. In this chapter, I consider the questions: How have the narratives of the NSM differed from the justifications offered for the Sanctuary Movement of the 1980s? And how have NSM narratives (by citizen-participants and undocumented immigrants) attempted to constitute a new form of intervention in the immigrant rights debates?

Surely there is no category of persons in contemporary US society *more* publicly 'voiceless' than the undocumented. As Amalia Pallares writes, 'The undocumented have always faced the fundamental question of whether they can be represented, much less represent themselves, given their lack of legal standing' (2010: 222). Much recent scholarship on activism and human rights, however, has emphasized the power of personal stories to give concrete meaning and reality to abstract and complex struggles. Yet the issue of the power of public storytelling within immigrant activism comes with its own set of questions:

> Who represents those in need of protection? Can the endangered speak for themselves? What are the possibilities and constraints that (dis)allow political activism by non- or quasi citizens? For their agency to be recognized as legitimate and heard as political, does it require mediation from other citizen groups?
>
> (Nyers 2010: 415)

The NSM might be understood as one effort to challenge the exclusion of the undocumented from the nation-state, in part by insisting that 'endangered' non-citizens represent themselves through individual first-person accounts that narrate the trauma of unauthorized existence, familial separations, and living in fear of deportation. In an era of rapidly escalating deportations, some undocumented activists have begun to insist on the legitimacy – indeed, the moral primacy – of their own voices within debates on immigration policy. Elvira Arellano, a Mexican immigrant who sought sanctuary in Adalberto United Methodist Church in Chicago in 2006 with her young son Saul (a US citizen), and who became the most prominent spokesperson for the emerging immigrant rights movement, insisted on the importance of offering a counter-narrative from the unauthorized immigrant's point of view: 'I wanted to talk about what was happening in my case in particular and to call attention … to what is going on … and ask what we want to do about it. I wanted to give us a voice' (Terry 2007: 43). Flor Crisóstomo, who took sanctuary in Adalberto Church during 2008–9 after Arellano's departure,[1] likewise insisted on the imperative of 'the leadership that emerges out of our own families and out of our own communities'. She noted that: 'We, who are directly affected by this system's repressive immigration policies', were not included in congressional discussions about immigration reform (Crisóstomo, 2010). Rev. Walter Coleman of Adalberto Church also underscored this point: 'This is a movement where people most affected were not speaking for themselves. Sanctuary has let them be their own voice' (Terry 2007: 44).

Yet the NSM has also been a heavily 'mediated' practice in Nyers' terms: undocumented immigrants have become 'spokespeople' on these issues by being 'accepted' into sanctuary by citizen-participants, who also see themselves as spokespeople. Indeed, the voices of US-citizen participants have often overshadowed immigrant voices in media reporting on the movement.[2] Further, media coverage of the platform provided by the NSM so far has been apparently short-lived; most coverage dates to 2007 when the movement was unveiled, with very little media reporting on continuing NSM activities since then. Despite these limitations, however, the NSM, like its predecessor, has attempted to maximize the potential power of personal testimonies to move people and change politics.

Background: the 1980s sanctuary movement

Between 1982 and 1987, hundreds of Central American refugees came forward to tell their stories publicly, primarily through the vehicle of the Sanctuary Movement. The personal 'testimonies' (*testimonios*) of Central American refugees were crucial in recruiting movement participants, which in turn brought media attention to the plight of Central American refugees and to the US role in supporting repressive regimes, especially in El Salvador and Guatemala (Westerman 1998: 226). These testimonies detailed the disappearances, rapes, kidnappings, tortures, and mass murders that the refugees and their families and communities experienced at the hands of the military or death squads in their home countries (Golden and McConnell 1986: 9–10, 40, 159–60; Coutin 1993: 68; see also Perla and Coutin, Chapter 5 in this volume). They were thus filled with what were, for US audiences, unimaginable horrors.

The refugees used their stories to implore US citizens to exert pressure on the US government to cease its support of these repressive regimes (Westerman 1998: 225–6; Golden and McConnell 1986: 29). 'Pedro', for instance, observed,

> Every bullet that travels from the United States ends up in a dead peasant. We don't need that kind of aid. North Americans think they are fighting communists. They are being lied to by their government. I believe there is still time for the people to uncover the truth.
>
> (Golden and McConnell 1986: 11)

A sanctuary worker pleaded, 'Go out and spread the word about what's happening here. Tell people about the human consequences of the war. Publish the refugees' stories. Include pictures of their bullet scars and photos of the mutilated bodies' (Coutin 1993: 70). Clearly, Sanctuary participants understood how the refugees' stories could be used for 'political' purposes – to affect public opinion about foreign policy.

Nonetheless, US citizen-participants described their involvement in the 1980s Sanctuary Movement primarily in religious terms that seemed to transcend earthly politics. They frequently framed participation in terms of Jesus' own identification with the poor and oppressed. For example, one minister described his involvement by explaining that 'accompaniment, for me, is a way of saying, "We will be with you." ... Which is what Jesus did with the poor.' Another participant elaborated: 'For me, by helping a refugee, it's my way of helping the church ... It's where I see the Lord crucified' (Coutin 2001: 69–70). Sanctuary workers also made reference to Moses freeing the Israelites from their oppression by the Egyptians and to Herod's massacre of innocent babes, which Joseph and Mary fled when giving birth to Jesus (Coutin 1993: 77, 79, 206). Indeed, some citizen-participants went so far as to suggest that the movement, to be truly 'religious', ought to be politically 'neutral' insofar as whether sanctuary recipients were fleeing governments on the Left or Right (Coutin and Hirsch 1998: 10–11).

Other participants and movement leaders acknowledged the political implications of sanctuary practices, constructing a faith-based critique of the actions of the US government (both in supporting oppressive regimes and in denying asylum). Jim Corbett, a Quaker in Arizona and a founder of the Sanctuary Movement, justified his own actions – which included the radical step of actually transporting refugees into the United States – by saying:

> When the government itself sponsors the torture of entire peoples and then makes it a felony to shelter those seeking refuge, law-abiding protest merely trains us to live with atrocity ... Where oppression rules, the way of peace is necessarily insurgent.
>
> (Golden and McConnell 1986: 37)

Rev. John Fife, the Presbyterian minister who co-founded the movement with Corbett, declared that: 'When the law of the land is in conflict with the law of God, a Christian's first duty is clear' (Crittenden 1988: 71). Sanctuary participants also repeatedly made analogies with the Underground Railroad of the abolitionist movement – clearly underscoring how they saw their own arguably 'illegal' practices as opposing laws that, like those of slavery, were immoral at their core (Crittenden 1988: 73; Coutin 1993: 207; Golden and McConnell 1986).

The New Sanctuary Movement (NSM)

The unveiling of the NSM in May 2007, widely covered in media across the country, suggests the degree to which the new movement looked to its 1980s predecessor – which had expired by the early 1990s (Cunningham 1998: 384) – for inspiration and for models of effective rhetoric. Once again, the movement cited problems with US 'law' and the overarching religious imperatives of movement participants; once again, those taken into sanctuary were asked to tell their stories to raise public awareness of the problems with the 'law' and to put a human face on the immigrants who had suffered under it. But behind these apparent similarities, there were some significant shifts. For one thing, deportation no longer meant being sent 'home' to face risks of persecution or even death; government-sponsored torture and murder had ceased to be the looming context. One participant in the 1980s movement had argued that: 'Sanctuary is giving aid and succor to someone who is escaping persecution and death. What else is the church called to do but that? How can you not do that and still be in the church?' (Coutin 1993: 206). But the argument for Sanctuary in 2007, as one scholar noted, was no longer about a 'terrified, perhaps bleeding ... person at one's door' but rather about immigrants 'whose motivations are not life and death' (Van Biema 2007a; see also Yukich, Chapter 7 in this volume).

Further, while 'sanctuary' for some NSM immigrants has meant literal refuge – ICE (US Immigration and Customs Enforcement) has been reluctant to enter churches to execute deportation orders while insisting on its right to do so [Anon, 2007a: 13] – for others, it has meant far less radical forms of 'sanctuary'. The pledge that allied faith communities of the NSM are asked to take includes several options for participation, only one of which involves actually hosting an immigrant family (New Sanctuary Movement). For Rosa Ramirez (a pseudonym) and her family in the Kansas City area, sanctuary was an actual safe haven: 'I would feel safe in the church, but when I went out to drop off [my son] at work, I can't describe the fear I felt' (Gross 2008; my translation). But the Ramirez family was also understood to be receiving sanctuary – in the form of accompaniment, support, and aid – even when they had left the Quaker meeting house where they were briefly housed. For Marco Castillo, who came with his mother from Mexico when he was 4 years old, the form of sanctuary he described receiving from San Diego Quakers was 'spiritual sanctuary', rather than physical shelter (Bazar 2007).

Because the NSM focuses its attention not on newly-arrived refugees but on long-standing US residents, the personal stories told by sanctuary recipients differ significantly from those recounted by Central American refugees in the earlier Sanctuary Movement. For one thing, NSM immigrants tend to stress life in the receiving country, rather than the situation in the sending country. Their stories are less about violence and terror than about the quotidian, ordinary life they have built – less about 'bearing witness' than about narratives of *national belonging*: we have been here for years; we have contributed to society, our communities, and the national economy; and we have raised our children here. The public face of the NSM is not the individual refugee fleeing persecution, but the 'mixed-status' family with both undocumented and US-citizen members.

Nonetheless, the NSM seeks to draw a direct line to its predecessor. The language of humanitarian crisis and human rights violations that circulated during the earlier Sanctuary Movement was redeployed and modified for its new context, focusing especially on the issue of family separation. Rev. John Fife, co-founder of the original Sanctuary Movement, used strikingly similar language in describing the new crisis: 'Nursing moms are being deported, people are being picked up on the street and immediate family members are disappearing ... The church needs to stand up and say this is a gross violation of human rights' (Innes 2007). Indeed, rhetoric such as Fife's drew a parallel between current actions of the US government in deporting parents and separating them from their children and the infamous Central American 'disappeared' – those who were kidnapped or killed without an official record – in the 1970s and 1980s. Belinda Passafaro (2007) wrote about her own introduction to the NSM:

> I knew that silence during this poignant time in our nation's history would be betrayal of our fellow brothers and sisters. How could we, rooted in a faith tradition that compels us to act on behalf of the most vulnerable members of our society, not respond to this grave humanitarian crisis?

Such framing presented the NSM as an heir of the first movement – both were responses to human rights violations.

The emphasis on family separation, as the core of the new humanitarian crisis, featured prominently in media coverage of the NSM at its 2007 launch. NSM co-founder Rev. Alexia Salvatierra of the Evangelical Lutheran Church in Los Angeles explained that the immigrants the movement helps are 'decent folks who have been working hard and contributing and have citizen children and are coming up against this irrational system that is tearing families apart' (Serjeant 2007). Rev. Rick Behrens of Grandview Park Presbyterian Church in Kansas City, and one of the co-founders of the NSM coalition in that area, said: 'It is the very soul of the nation that is at stake ... We are losing our soul as we separate children from parents' (Anon 2007b). The statement on the website of the NSM, 'When we see families in need or danger, we are called by our faith to respond', foregrounds the imperative of family preservation, thus tapping into the 'family values' rhetoric that has featured as a conservative slogan (see Pallares 2010: 230–1).

The same issue was prominent in the accounts of the undocumented immigrants themselves. Juan, a Guatemalan immigrant with two US-citizen daughters who had lived in the US for fifteen years when he sought sanctuary in 2007, echoed the language emphasizing the primacy of family bonds and US contributions: 'I can't bear to be separated from my family. We work hard, we take care of our families. We pay taxes' (Serjeant 2007). Jean, an undocumented immigrant from Haiti who received 'sanctuary' in the form of support and legal assistance from a New York church, explained, 'I have no one in Haiti. This is my country now. I have been here 22 years. It is not right for the government to separate my family. How can they take away a father?' (Markey 2007: 5a). Other undocumented immigrants likewise emphasized their concern for their children as motivating them to seek sanctuary; one said, 'I'm a mother, not a criminal', while another noted that 'my obligation to my kids was bigger' than her responsibility to report as ordered for deportation (Bazar 2007; Griggs 2007).

Generally, however, the impassioned arguments heard in the 1980s Sanctuary Movement about how the US was violating its own laws and international human rights law gave way to more measured commentary about a 'broken' system or 'unjust immigration laws' that tear families apart (see, for example, Markey 2007: 5a; Bazar 2007; New Sanctuary Movement 2011). Indeed, sometimes the phrase 'broken law' was used as a play on the notion of 'breaking the law', in an effort to dramatically shift responsibility for *who* 'broke' immigration laws to begin with (Arellano 2007b; Coleman 2006). At the same time, participants' emphasis on being willing to *violate* immigration law for the sake of a higher law all but disappeared. Rabbi Laurie Coskey, a movement spokesperson in San Diego, insisted that: 'There is no illegal activity going on … In our country, it is not illegal to take care of a human being' (Sifuentes 2007). Julie Wakelee-Lynch, an associate pastor of St. Luke's Episcopal Church in Long Beach, California, concurred: 'This is not hiding, this is public hospitality' (Anon 2007a: 12). As citizen-participants made sure to explain, 'Participating churches believe that providing humanitarian assistance does not violate the law as long as it is done openly and they do not hide illegal immigrants' (ibid.: 12). 'It isn't a matter of hiding families', Rabbi Coskey said: 'It's a matter of providing spiritual, emotional, and physical sanctuary' (Olivo 2007).

While the 'Underground Railroad' had been a frequently used metaphor in the 1980s Sanctuary Movement, NSM participants did not take up this particular rhetorical legacy; in the new political climate, to do so would surely be a highly inflammatory rhetorical move, suggesting the willful and deliberate 'transport' to the US of unauthorized immigrants (see also Yukich, Chapter 7 in this volume). The heated discourse on illegal immigration, backed by laws proposed or passed at state and federal levels,[3] has placed increasing opprobrium on those who 'aid and abet' the illegal presence of aliens within US borders (see, for instance, Griggs 2007). In the new context, comparisons to an Underground Railroad were replaced with a general insistence that participants were not breaking laws, because they were not 'hiding' undocumented immigrants from authorities but were openly and publicly announcing their sanctuary activities.

Despite apparent differences between sanctuary movements 'old' and 'new', however, the NSM inherits from the earlier movement an insistence on faith-based and scriptural justification, though this rhetoric tends to come primarily from citizen-participants, rather than from the immigrants themselves. The use of religious rhetoric can be understood in part as a strategic response towards strong and pervasive anti-immigration rhetoric insisting on the cultural unassimilability of the current influx of immigrants. Samuel Huntington, for instance, has argued that recent immigrants threaten American culture, including its core 'Protestant values', thus aligning those values with anti-immigrant sentiment (2004: 40).

Conversely, the NSM has relied heavily on these same 'values' to make its case for a more humane and hospitable treatment of undocumented immigrants. Arguments based on scripture vividly counter Huntington's proposition that 'we' are fundamentally different from 'them', using precisely the Christian moral ethos Huntington invokes. Rev. Salvatierra, for instance, declared of the movement's inspiration that when undocumented families 'are ripped apart by raids and deportations, they become the suffering "strangers within your gates" that the Bible tells us to aid.' Reverend Frank Alton, of Immanuel Presbyterian Church in Los Angeles, cited Leviticus 19: 33: 'The stranger who dwells among you shall be to you as one born among you, and you shall love him as yourself; for you were strangers in the land of Egypt' (Van Biema 2007b). Passafaro explained that: 'Sanctuary congregations and allied partners span the theological and political spectrum but are united in a common tradition of welcoming the stranger and of loving neighbors as ourselves' (2007: 21). In Kansas City, the launch of the regional NSM coalition was marked with a highway billboard that rendered the Scripture more topically as, 'Love the Immigrant as Yourself.' Such scriptural passages, deployed in this context, redrew the lines around 'we' and 'they' so that the circle of moral obligation includes both groups; 'neighbors' and 'strangers' must be morally understood 'as one born among us – as ourselves'. Another text frequently invoked to underscore the sense of a specifically Christian, faith-based mandate to care for immigrants was Matthew 25:35: 'For I was hungry and you gave me food, I was thirsty and you gave me drink, I was a stranger and you welcomed me' (Van Biema 2007a).

While the political Right in the US tends to be associated with both the most vocal 'faith' voice and the most strident positions in favor of 'cracking down' on illegal immigration and 'securing the border', a faith-based movement advocating for more humane immigration laws disrupts this polarized binary in which 'conservative' and 'religious' are automatically perceived as aligned (Hondagneu-Sotelo 2008: 6). Although Catholics are often conservative when it comes to social issues such as abortion and gay rights, it was a Catholic Cardinal, Roger Mahony of Los Angeles, who served as one catalyst for the NSM in 2006, when he announced that he intended to instruct priests in his Archdiocese to ignore certain provisions of a major bill (HR 4437, also known as the 'Sensenbrenner Bill', which had passed the US House of Representatives in December 2005, but subsequently failed to pass the Senate) that would arguably have imposed criminal penalties on workers in humanitarian and social-aid organizations that provided services to undocumented immigrants (O'Rourke 2006: 201–3).[4] The high visibility of the 'faith' voice in immigrant rights, as this example illustrates, is a rather dramatic turning of the tables, underscoring the point that the NSM has made use of the political power of the religious voice by putting that voice at the forefront of immigration debates.

The public commentary of sanctuary recipients themselves, however, has focused much less on scriptural authorization and more on the threat of separation from their families through deportation. Indeed, the issue of forced family separation has allowed the NSM to make a different sort of analogy to slavery than that of the Underground Railroad. One sanctuary recipient, for example, described seeing coverage of a raid on television, shortly after receiving final deportation orders: 'I saw how people were being tied like animals ... and I thought. When it happens to me, my daughter will watch as the agents carry me off like a slave' (Van Biema 2007b). The metaphorical comparison of the treatment of undocumented immigrants to animals and slaves highlights movement participants' sense that immigration law enforcement, as well as dominant US rhetoric on immigration, robs immigrants of their humanity – their status as human beings whose lives are of equal value and importance with those of American citizens. (They become the essential 'Other', a 'Them' without recognizable commonality with 'Us'.) Crisóstomo similarly deployed metaphors of slavery to describe the struggles of the undocumented. In a statement made in Washington, DC, Crisóstomo declared:

> Politicians have not taken into account our families' pain during the years we have waited to be free from bondage, that time which has maintained us as slaves within this system, as fugitives within a reality that lawmakers and the privileged have not had to face.
>
> (Crisóstomo 2010)

Slavery metaphors are a particular kind of rhetorical appeal; in comparing family separations caused by raids and deportations to family separations under slavery, undocumented activists suggest an equivalent grievous moral violation. Arellano, too, portrayed the situation of undocumented families in terms reminiscent of rhetorical strategies of slave narratives; commenting on the detention of a pregnant woman, she said, 'They speak of family values but when they shackled her and chained her pregnant stomach, where were their family values? Are not our families worth as much as theirs?' (Pallares 2010: 230). She also employed images of physical and violent separation of parents from children: 'Out of fear and hatred ... you have set out to destroy our lives and our families. As you knocked on my door, you are knocking on thousands of doors, ripping mothers and fathers away from their terrified children' (Arellano 2007b). Such rhetoric highlights the issue of family unity as a fundamental tenet of human rights law (see Golash-Boza 2012: 111–12).[5]

When faith has been invoked by NSM immigrants, it tends to be as a part of their daily praxis rather than as scriptural justification. Arellano emphasized the passing of her religious practices to her son in her statement upon leaving sanctuary: 'I will read to him from the Holy Scriptures as I do everyday [sic] ... I will accept whatever God gives me to accept' (2007b). Everyday practice can, of course, involve church attendance and participation in church activities; in this sense, faith is also constitutive of social support networks for immigrants. Scholarship on religion in immigrant life has suggested an important connection between faith communities and immigrant incorporation into a larger US society and public sphere (Palacios 2007). As Rev. Salvatierra insisted: 'So many of us in our congregations know these families' (Serjeant 2007). Yolanda, a Guatemalan woman who received sanctuary at a Lutheran church in Los Angeles, had been a Deacon in her church (Van Biema 2007b). Liliana, who took sanctuary in a Simi Valley, California church, married her husband (who later became a US citizen) in 1999, in a church wedding with over 300 guests in attendance. She noted that 'keeping her family together would be impossible without the help of her parents ... and volunteers from the church and affiliated congregations who support the movement' (Griggs 2007). Frameworks which position undocumented immigrants as 'illegal aliens' who do not belong in and are not part of 'our' communities are challenged by the insistence that immigrants are full members of specific, local faith communities in the United States – communities for which membership, by common understanding, cannot be regulated by the government.

Perhaps even more radically, appeals made to faith communities and religious associations – to 'people of faith' themselves – can be understood as a form of speech-act which attempted to construct a nationwide activist 'community', thus serving as an illustration of the 'performative role of discourse' in sanctuary practices (Lippert 2005: 11). Yolanda said, 'I have faith that this will touch the heart of the people so they can help us with this situation we are having' (Van Biema 2007b), a comment that intertwined 'faith' with both community and activism. In a more definitive mode, Arellano insisted: 'Sanctuary is a form of solidarity among our people, in which we refuse to permit that they divide us and disrespect us ... instead we unite together in our faith' (2007a). Sanctuary, in Arellano's sense, becomes constitutive of new forms of community, as the demarcating lines around 'our people' are redrawn to include citizen-participants, immigrants documented and undocumented, and all those of faith.

The public statement Arellano made upon leaving sanctuary to engage in more public forms of immigration activism demonstrates particularly powerfully the rhetorical construction of an activist community through the language of faith:

> I believe ... that we must come forward in the witness of faith to bring a resolution to this crisis ... On September 12th, I will go to Washington D.C. I will go to pray and fast in front of the Congress ... But I ask my community, the families facing separation, to join me ... I ask all people of conscience and good will to join me ... Together in faith and prayer I hope that we can join together to heal the will that is broken in Congress.
> (Arellano 2007b)

For Arellano, faith and prayer became a call to action, a way of imagining a collective political and performative response to the immigration crisis in which the faith community and the activist community become indistinguishable. The statement is itself a *call* – a solicitation or hailing to a nationwide 'imagined community' (see Anderson 1983) that offers an alternative to dominant paradigms for imagining the 'nation', and that becomes 'real' through the persuasiveness and effectiveness of its own rhetorical imagining.

American religious communities can facilitate the imagining of immigrants as *part* of an American community; religious associations 'can serve both as a bridge to American public life and a haven for one's already established social life … [Faith communities] can help the immigrant move private concerns … to public solutions' (Palacios 2007: 74–5). As we have seen, for at least some NSM immigrants, sanctuary was indeed a 'haven', a refuge from the fear of imminent deportation. However, it was also by its very conception a 'bridge … to public solutions', allowing undocumented immigrants one of the few venues available to them for public speech, even if that speech was heavily mediated by citizen-participant allies. Steven Camarota, director of research at the Center for Immigration Studies (which advocates for decreased immigration) called the NSM a 'publicity stunt' at its unveiling (Serjeant 2007); if by this he meant that it was a calculated effort to gain publicity – a public hearing – for the undocumented, he was surely right. Arellano came to redefine sanctuary itself not as a protected haven but as a public platform: 'I learned that sanctuary is not a place where you hide … [It is] a space in which you speak the truth to the powerful, as Jesus did' (2007a). For Arellano and other undocumented immigrants, 'sanctuary' was indeed about 'publicity'; it was a way of speaking, as the subaltern, that for once could be heard by the American public.

The NSM has sought to maximize the potential of faith-based support networks, providing simultaneously both a 'haven' from, and a 'bridge' to, the larger public. It is by *seeking sanctuary* (by becoming 'refugees', in the most literal and fundamental sense of *taking refuge*) that undocumented immigrants gained access to a media voice. If that speech, in the case of the NSM, was rather limited in scope and volume, if it was heavily mediated by the more-often heard voices of the citizen-participants, and if it was relatively short-lived in terms of public exposure, it can still be regarded as an attempt to intervene in public discourse and to change the direction of that discourse, by appealing to, and in the process at times constructing, an activist community of faith. The question of whether the NSM, like the first Sanctuary Movement, will ultimately be regarded as having had any identifiable effect on law and policy has yet to be answered.

Notes

1 Arellano was arrested in Los Angeles and deported shortly after leaving sanctuary in 2007, but continued to speak and write for immigrant rights from Mexico.
2 A sampling of ten mainstream media articles (both national and local) covering the emergence of the NSM in 2007 reveals that direct quotations of citizen-participants and movement supporters amounted to a total of 811 words, while quotations of undocumented immigrants themselves totaled only 257 words. (This tally does not include opposing perspectives, ICE representatives, or scholars commenting on the movement, which would further increase the 'citizen' voice.)

3 The 'Sensenbrenner Bill' (HR 4437) offered what appeared to be a more restrictive version of the existing Immigration and National Act (INA), by proposing to make it illegal to transport an undocumented migrant when such an action 'will aid or further in any manner' that immigrant's *presence in the U.S.* (rather than, more specifically, the immigrant's *violation of the law*). The new wording potentially covered a much wider range of actions than the wording of the INA, since humanitarian assistance efforts could conceivably be construed as 'amount[ing] to assistance and doubtless increase that person's ability and desire to remain in the United States' (O'Rourke 2006: 202–3, 207–8). Likewise, Arizona's state law SB 1070, passed in 2010,

> adds a separate criminal offense under state law for any person, 'who is in violation of a criminal offense,' to transport or harbor unauthorized aliens, or encourage or induce such aliens to come to or reside in the state, when such activities are done in knowing or reckless disregard of the alien's unauthorized status.
> (Garcia *et al.* 2010: 13)

The 'offense' under the new law would presumably occur regardless of whether or not the transportation or harboring itself is considered to be in 'furtherance' of illegal presence. Note that, on June 25, 2012, the U.S. Supreme Court ruling on SB 1070 struck down several key provisions of the law.
4 Legal scholar Allen O'Rourke noted that: 'Nothing would prevent the government from interpreting section 202 broadly'—that is, as also applying to humanitarian aid efforts—'once House Bill 4437 became law' (2006: 204).
5 On the potential problems with the reliance on 'family values' rhetoric in immigrant rights discourse, however, see Pallares (2010: 231).

References

Anderson, B.R. (1983) *Imagined Communities: Reflections on the Origin and Spread of Nationalism*, London: Verso.
Anon (2007a) 'Dilemma on Sheltering Immigrants', *Christian Century*, 10 July: 12–13.
——(2007b) 'KC Churches Offer Sanctuary to Illegals with American Kids', *Columbia Daily Tribune* (MO), 26 September. Available at: http://infoweb.newsbank.com/iw-search/we/InfoWeb?p_product=NewsBank&p_theme=aggregated5&p_action=doc&p_docid=11BEB39A2895FFD8&p_docnum=1&p_queryname=9 (accessed 6 October 2011).
Arellano, E. (2007a) 'El significado de los santuarios', *El Diaro / La Prensa*, 39(1319295): 23 [Translation mine]. Available at: http://proquest.umi.com.www2.lib.ku.edu:2048/pqdweb?index=8&did=1409105721&SrchMode=3&sid=1&Fmt=3&VInst=PROD&VType=PQD&RQT=309&VName=PQD&TS=1317741194&clientId=42567&aid=3 (accessed 21 September 2011).
——(2007b) 'Statement of Elvira Arellano on August 15, 2007', *Los Angeles Independent Media Center*, 20 August. Available at: http://la.indymedia.org/news/2007/08/205070.php (accessed 20 September 2011).
Bazar, E. (2007) 'Illegal Immigrants Find Refuge in Holy Places; Churches, Citing "Broken Law," Revive the Ancient Tradition of Sanctuary', *USA Today*, 9 July. Available at: http://proquest.umi.com.www2.lib.ku.edu:2048/pqdweb?index=3&did=1301585001&SrchMode=1&sid=2&Fmt=3&VInst=PROD&VType=PQD&RQT=309&VName=PQD&TS=1316525809&clientId=42567 (accessed 20 September 2011).
Coleman, W. (2006) 'Latino Mother Defies Deportation Order', *FinalCall.com News*, 29 August. Available at: http://www.finalcall.com/artman/publish/article_2884.shtml (accessed 21 September 2011).

Coutin, S.B. (2001) 'The Oppressed, the Suspect, and the Citizen: Subjectivity in Competing Accounts of Political Violence', *Law and Social Inquiry*, 26(1): 63–94.

—— (1993) *The Culture of Protest: Religious Activism and the US Sanctuary Movement*, Boulder, CO: Westview.

Coutin, S.B. and Hirsch, S.F. (1998) 'Naming Resistance: Ethnographers, Dissidents, and States', *Anthropological Quarterly*, 71(1): 1–17.

Crisóstomo, F. (2010) *Statement by Flor Crisóstomo*, 21 March. Available at: http://floresiste.wordpress.com/2010/03/23/statement-by-flor-crisostomo-washington-d-c-march-21-2010/ (accessed 13 October 2011).

Crittenden, A. (1988) *Sanctuary: A Story of American Conscience and the Law in Collision*, New York: Weidenfeld & Nicolson.

Cunningham, H. (1998) 'Sanctuary and Sovereignty: Church and State Along the US-Mexico Border', *Journal of Church and State*, 40(2): 370–86.

Garcia, M.J., Eig, L.M., and Kim, Y. (2010) 'State Efforts to Deter Unauthorized Aliens: Legal Analysis of Arizona's S.B. 1070', *Congressional Research Service*, May 3. Available at: http://graphics8.nytimes.com/packages/pdf/topics/science/immigcrs.pdf (accessed 10 November 2011).

Golash-Boza, T.M. (2012) *Immigration Nation: Raids, Detentions, and Deportations in Post-9/11 America*, Boulder, CO: Paradigm.

Golden, R. and McConnell, M. (1986) *Sanctuary: The New Underground Railroad*, Maryknoll, NY: Orbis Books.

Griggs, G.W. (2007) 'Sanctuary Sharpens the Divide on Immigration', *The Cincinnati Post*, 29 November. Available at: http://infoweb.newsbank.com/iw-search/we/InfoWeb?p_product=NewsBank&p_theme=aggregated5&p_action=doc&p_docid=11D410D16EC92858&p_docnum=1&p_queryname=6 (accessed 14 September 2011).

Gross, S.M. (2008) 'Church Leaders House Undocumented Immigrants', *KC Currents* [Kansas City], 8 September. Available at: http://www.publicbroadcasting.net/kcur/news.newsmain?action=article&ARTICLE_ID=1360315&sectionID=1 (accessed 5 October 2011).

Hondagneu-Sotelo, P. (2008) *God's Heart Has No Borders: How Religious Activists Are Working for Immigrant Rights*, Berkeley, CA: University of California Press.

Huntington, S. (2004) *Who Are We? The Challenges to America's Identity*, New York: Simon & Schuster.

Innes, S. (2007) ''80s Sanctuary Leader Calls for New Local Role', *Arizona Daily Star*, 11 May: B1. Available at: http://infoweb.newsbank.com/iw-search/we/InfoWeb?p_product=NewsBank&p_theme=aggregated5&p_action=doc&p_docid=1198685D562D4AB8&p_docnum=1&p_queryname=8 (accessed 23 September 2011).

Lippert, R.K. (2005) *Sanctuary, Sovereignty, Sacrifice: Canadian Sanctuary Incidents, Power, and Law*, Vancouver: UBC Press.

Markey, E. (2007) 'Ecumenical Sanctuary Movement Responds to "Humanitarian and Ethical Crisis"', *National Catholic Reporter*, 14 September: 4a–5a.

New Sanctuary Movement (2011) Available at: http://www.newsanctuarymovement.org/index.html (accessed 8 September 2011).

Nyers, P. (2010) 'Abject Cosmopolitanism: The Politics of Protection in the Anti-Deportation Movement', in N. De Genova and N. Peutz (eds) *The Deportation Regime: Sovereignty, Space, and the Freedom of Movement*, Durham, NC: Duke University Press.

Olivo, A. (2007) 'Illegal Immigrant Sanctuaries Set; Religious Groups in 5 Cities Back Plan to Win Sympathy', *Chicago Tribune*, 9 May. Available at: http://www.

newsanctuarymovement.org/graphics/press/ChicagoTribuneOlivoMay92007.pdf (accessed 23 September 2011).
O'Rourke, A.T. (2006) 'Good Samaritans, Beware: The Sensenbrenner-King Bill and Assistance to Undocumented Migrants', *Harvard Latino Law Review*, 9: 195–208.
Palacios, J.M. (2007) 'Bringing Mexican Immigrants into American Faith-Based Social Justice and Civic Cultures', in P. Hondagneu-Sotelo (ed.) *Religion and Social Justice for Immigrants*, New Brunswick, NJ: Rutgers University Press.
Pallares, A. (2010) 'Representing "La Familia": Family Separation and Immigrant Activism', in A. Pallares and N. Flores-González (eds) *¡Marcha! Latino Chicago and the Immigrant Rights Movement*, Chicago: University of Illinois Press.
Passafaro, B. (2007) 'Standing Up for Sanctuary', *Sojourners*, 36(9): 21.
Serjeant, J. (2007) 'Immigrants Take Sanctuary in US Churches', *Reuters*, 9 May. Available at: http://www.reuters.com/article/2007/05/10/us-immigration-sanctuary-idUSN0924974520070510 (accessed 23 September 2011).
Sifuentes, E. (2007) 'Religious Leaders Offer Sanctuary to Illegal Immigrants', *North County Times*, 10 May. Available at: http://www.nctimes.com/news/local/article_19a52a64-54ce-5934-b7d7-9016975ec886.html (accessed 20 September 2011).
Terry, D. (2007) 'The New Sanctuary Movement', *Hispanic*, August: 42–5.
Van Biema, D. (2007a) 'Does the Bible Support Sanctuary?', *Time*, 20 July. Available at: http://www.time.com/time/printout/0,8816,1645646,00.html (accessed 14 September 2010).
——(2007b) 'Sweet Sanctuary', *Time*, 30 July: 45–7. Available at: http://search.ebscohost.com.www2.lib.ku.edu:2048/login.aspx?direct=true&db=aph&AN=25907089&site=ehost-live (accessed 7 September 2011).
Westerman, W. (1998) 'Central American Refugee Testimonies and Performed Life Histories in the Sanctuary Movement', in R. Perks and A. Thomson (eds) *The Oral History Reader*, New York: Routledge.

Chapter 7

'I didn't know if this was sanctuary'
Strategic adaptation in the US New Sanctuary Movement

Grace Yukich

Religious activists from around the country gather in a small Los Angeles church for the 2007 'National Convening' of the New Sanctuary Movement (NSM). In the 1980s, the church provided refuge to undocumented immigrants from Central America as part of the US Sanctuary Movement. Today, more than 20 years later, over 60 activists sit in metal folding chairs arranged in a semi-circle around a poster at the front of a gymnasium. The poster reads: 'Sanctuary is not a building. It is rooted in faith and nurtured by prayer and conscience.' A small, white woman in her fifties stands and speaks, her words jointly translated into Spanish – one of many signs reminding activists of why they are here.

She points to the poster and ties it to the 1980s Sanctuary Movement, asking everyone to think about how the NSM builds on sanctuary's legacy. She calls out, 'How many people here participated in the first movement?' and around ten people raise their hands. But when the group begins to sing 'De Colores' – a Spanish-language song popular in the 1980s – I feel like the only person in the room who does not already know it by heart. People sing and sway happily, lost in the music and the feelings its meaning evokes in them.

After the song, the leader exclaims, 'I can almost smell the '80s again!' and asks participants in the 1980s movement to share their experiences. A Latino man jokes about continuing the struggle 'but with whiter hair now', though he is quick to add that he is happy to see young faces in the room. A Jewish activist from New York says, 'The first movement was the most profoundly transformative experience of my life, personally and politically. My hope is that the NSM will build on the original and will create community like the first one.' The spell of nostalgia and collective effervescence is broken, though, when a hand goes up in the air, followed by an activist asking difficult questions. 'But how is the New Sanctuary Movement going to right the mistakes of the first Sanctuary Movement?' she asks. 'Is sanctuary even the right approach for what we're facing?'

The practice of sanctuary has a long history, making it a powerful religio-political symbol. It was the central strategy and primary tactic of the 1980s Sanctuary Movement, a US movement of churches, synagogues, and other groups giving safe haven to refugees fleeing civil wars in Central America (cf. Coutin 1993; Cunningham 1995; Smith 1996). In the early twenty-first century, the NSM aims to breathe new life into sanctuary's tradition of mobilizing the power of religious authority to challenge the moral and legal authority of the state (Cunningham 1995).

The NSM emerged in May 2007 as a reaction to growing conflict around immigration in the US.[1] It is an interfaith network of faith communities with approximately 30 local coalitions nationwide seeking to liberalize immigration policy and transform native-born religious communities. In the NSM, religious activists 'give sanctuary' to carefully selected mixed-status immigrant families, in which at least one person is undergoing deportation proceedings and the others are citizens or legal residents of the US.

In the 1980s Sanctuary Movement, most sanctuary recipients were recent arrivals who needed transportation, housing, resettlement assistance, food and clothing – in fleeing violence, they entered the US seeking immediate humanitarian aid more than residency or citizenship (see Perla and Bibler Coutin, Chapter 5 in this volume). Churches and synagogues temporarily housed immigrants in their buildings, protecting them against authorities until they could be moved to a safer place. In contrast, the NSM highlights the struggles of immigrants who are long-term US residents with local family and community ties, careers, and homes (see Caminero-Santangelo, Chapter 6 in this volume). They do not need humanitarian aid or a place to hide *en route* to a safer location; instead, they seek legalization and naturalization that will allow them to continue living and working in the US locales they consider home. The traditional sanctuary offer of aid, shelter, and protection in the form of temporarily living in a church is therefore less appealing and less useful for today's undocumented population, as I discuss below. As a result, the NSM has struggled to re-imagine sanctuary to meet the demands of a new political environment.

Social movement scholars agree that the adoption of new strategies and tactics in response to a shifting environment is possible but difficult (Minkoff 1999; McCammon 2003; McCammon *et al.* 2008). However, strategic adaptation is typically discussed as though it is a *decision* that movements make rather than a *process* of *attempted* adaptation that may have varying levels of success, depending on factors both internal and external to the movement. Additionally, few scholars have examined the consequences associated with new movements seeking to adapt old, well-known strategies and tactics to new political contexts when those same strategies are central to the movement's identity. Given the apparent inability of sanctuary to meet the needs of many of today's undocumented immigrants, why did activists choose sanctuary? How does it operate today on matters of identity, strategy, and tactic compared to past incarnations? How has the NSM tried to adapt sanctuary to the current context, with what degree of success, and with what consequences for the movement?

To answer these questions, I conducted ethnographic research with the NSM, primarily with the New York City and Los Angeles coalitions, from August 2007 to January 2009. I participated in movement meetings, vigils, protests, immigration check-ins, fundraisers, and informational town hall sessions in faith communities. I also interviewed 48 movement participants in NYC and LA and 22 potential participants who were recruited by the movement but chose not to join.

My research reveals that the NSM seeks to capitalize on sanctuary's power as a religious symbol, but that activists also recognize the necessity of finding 'the right approach for what we're facing', forcing them to struggle to adapt sanctuary to a political context that differs from the immigration environment of the 1980s. Their efforts demonstrate that a movement's reading of the political context and related decision to adapt is only the first step in a *process*, one that involves struggle and that may fail.

Like an older movement whose adaptation efforts are restricted by its widespread identification with certain symbols, strategies, and tactics, sanctuary's powerful history is an obstacle to strategic adaptation, since religious activists already have assumptions about what sanctuary means. And as a nascent social movement organization, the NSM lacks the resources and networks to successfully disseminate a new understanding of sanctuary among potential recruits. Uncertainty and confusion have resulted from the movement's choice to adopt and adapt sanctuary as its core identity and strategy, impairing the NSM's ability to recruit new members, to build commitment among existing members, and to construct and sustain a unified group identity. My findings highlight both the power of sanctuary as a historic symbol and practice and the difficulties involved in significantly altering the shape of its practice on a large scale.

Choosing and changing movement strategy

Social movement scholars disagree about how best to define strategies and tactics. Some use the concepts virtually interchangeably; others bristle at this practice, arguing for the need to clearly distinguish them (cf. Minkoff 1999; Ganz 2000; McCammon 2003; King and Cornwall 2005). Most commonly, tactics are conceptualized as concrete movement practices such as sit-ins, marches, or letter-writing. Definitions of strategies are more diverse. Some define strategy as simply the sum of a movement's tactics (King and Cornwall 2005), while others conceive of strategy as a general approach to activism, such as protest, advocacy, or service provision (Minkoff 1999). While such distinctions are important for theorizing movement activities and outcomes, they can obscure the possibility that a single symbol might organize a movement as identity, strategy, and tactic at once. This is precisely the role that sanctuary plays for the NSM.

Today, sanctuary has become the core identity and moniker of the NSM. However, sanctuary as it has often been historically practised both in the US and elsewhere is not the movement's primary tactic.[2] Instead, the word 'sanctuary' refers to a general strategy entailing both legal, non-confrontational tactics and more marginally legal, disruptive ones, including housing and hiding immigrants in churches, synagogues, and mosques. Reflecting its various concrete shapes, in my analysis, the word 'sanctuary' denotes identity, strategy, or tactic, depending on how it functions for activists in the setting described.

In choosing concrete practices and general approaches to activism, social movement organizations make selections for reasons beyond political goals (see Polletta 2008). For instance, Nepstad's (2004) study of the Plowshares Movement shows how the religious beliefs of movement members influence their tactical choices, suggesting that religious activists might be expected to choose strategies and tactics with religious resonance, even if they are not politically efficacious.

Once movements initially commit to particular strategies and tactics, there are both positive and negative consequences for altering approaches. Scholars of organizational change have long emphasized structural inertia, stressing the obstacles organizations face in making any far-reaching changes (Hannan and Freeman 1984). Nonetheless, social movement research suggests some movements are able to adapt strategies and tactics to better fit a political environment, and those who engage in strategic adaptation and tactical innovation are more likely to achieve their goals rapidly (McAdam 1983; McCammon 2003; McCammon et al. 2008). But accounts stressing the adaptation of strategies and tactics to a political context at times depict this as a *decision* that movements make based on knowing the environment (McAdam 1983; McCammon et al. 2008) rather than as a *process* that may be difficult to implement and unsuccessful.

Research suggests that social movement organizations (SMOs) are not equally equipped to enact changes, and different types of alterations have different implications. Building on organizational theory, Morris argues that 'the extent and distribution of internal social organization will determine the extent to which innovations in collective strategy and tactics are adapted, spread, and sustained' (1981: 746). Studies emphasizing the 'liability of newness' suggest that older, more formalized organizations are better able to enact changes because their resources and networks can diffuse innovations (cf. Freeman et al. 1983; Minkoff 1999; Morris 1981). At the same time, these organizations are inhibited by their age, formalization, and recognized identity, which make it harder to change their practices – a characteristic Ganz (2000) calls the 'liability of senescence'. When it comes to flexibility, newer organizations have the benefit of less routinization and a less recognized relationship between the organization and its main strategies and tactics (ibid.). However, they also lack the resources to disseminate information about changes to the movement's identity, structure, and activities, making creative change, no matter how brilliant, difficult to implement.

Taken together, this research indicates that major changes in the meaning and shapes of certain strategies and tactics could enhance a movement's success and survival if these adaptations help it fit the changing political context, though some studies depict adaptation as a decision rather than a process with varying levels of success. Existing scholarship also suggests that organizational age and formalization may influence the ability of SMOs to successfully adapt their strategies, even when they recognize the importance of doing so and are committed to adaptation. But research is divided as to whether newness or age is the greater liability in attempts to adapt strategy. Missing from these debates is discussion of how the age and public resonance of symbols, strategies, and tactics might interact with organizational characteristics in shaping the capacity to respond to the current political context.

Deciding on sanctuary

Discussions about forming a new religious movement for immigrant rights began in early 2006 after passage of The Border Protection, Anti-Terrorism, and Illegal Immigration Control Act (HR 4437) in the US House of Representatives. Popularly known as the Sensenbrenner Bill, the legislation would have made it illegal to aid undocumented immigrants. Fearing that the bill might also pass the Senate, making it law, religious supporters of undocumented immigrants became increasingly concerned about what the legislation would mean not only for immigrant communities but also for religious values and practices. Clergy and Laity United for Economic Justice (CLUE), a faith-based workers' rights organization in Los Angeles, helped facilitate initial discussions about how to respond to the Sensenbrenner Bill and what they saw as the anti-immigrant culture that gave rise to its passage. Rev. Alexia Salvatierra, CLUE's Executive Director and one of the first national organizers of the NSM, explained:

> CLUE's stock and trade – the way that we respond to any social crisis – is always by asking what the particular contribution of the faith community is. So we don't want to do what other people are doing, we want to do what we can uniquely contribute. So we began to ask ourselves what that was.

The people in LA responsible for initial organization of what became the NSM were committed to finding a way to 'uniquely contribute' to the political and cultural debates surrounding the Sensenbrenner Bill's passage as people of faith.[3] The identities and commitments among early activists to a religious identity and moral vision made them more likely to choose core movement identities, strategies, and tactics that would allow them to achieve both their goal of liberalizing immigration policy and the more implicit religious goal of transforming religious communities.

The practice of offering refuge in sacred places, like houses of worship or designated cities, to people pursued by the state or other authorities stretches back through the Middle Ages (see Shoemaker, Chapter 1 in this volume) to ancient times (see Cunningham 1995). In modern times, US authorities are not legally bound to respect sanctuary. Rather, they have a legal right to enter religious buildings to apprehend people fleeing state authorities. Still, its practice has emerged at several key points in US history, since authorities have typically hesitated to enter churches to pursue fugitives because of religion's special public and moral status. Prior to the 1980s, when sanctuary took the shape of temporarily housing Central American refugees in religious properties to protect them from deportation, churches gave refuge to fugitive slaves during the Civil War as part of the Underground Railroad and protected draft resisters and AWOL soldiers during the Vietnam War (Cunningham 1995). In 2006, when religious immigrant rights activists sought a core identity, strategy, and tactic around which to organize, this was the image of sanctuary in the American public consciousness.

Because of its public visibility and relatively recent history, the 1980s Sanctuary Movement is particularly well known among progressive religious activists. Sanctuary was part of the religious repertoires of early NSM activists, so they already understood how to use it – an important part of their eventual decision to choose it as identity, strategy, and tactic (McAdam *et al.* 2001). Despite the symbol of sanctuary being religiously resonant, some activists were initially wary because they believed it had become less effective in the post-9/11 political context. An LA organizer related:

> At that point [an activist priest] was pretty much a steady drum beat in L.A. about 'we have to go back to the Sanctuary Movement.' But that had been the historic sanctuary congregation which had been known for having all kinds of people sleeping there, you know, thousands of undocumented members, and we think that it probably made sense for his church to do some form of sanctuary. But I think I had the image of, you know, opening the doors and thousands of people coming into each congregation and not being able to do anything for them ... You know, so it was like I thought we were gonna have lots of people come into our congregations and then ICE [Immigration and Customs Enforcement] is gonna come in and pick them all up. And what good will that do? So, no, I really didn't see it as something that was going to work.

Activists perceived at least two important differences between the 1980s and the 2000s: first, the needs of immigrants differed; second, immigration enforcement had become more stringent.

During the 1980s, sanctuary activists focused on undocumented immigrants from Central America seeking asylum in the US (Coutin 1993; Cunningham 1995; Smith 1996). As recent arrivals in the US, their resources for avoiding deportation and obtaining legalization were limited – indeed, some had no possessions, creating a need not only for legal status but also for basic necessities like food, shelter, and clothing (Smith 1996). Aside from whether taking sanctuary in a church furthered their ultimate goal of legalization through asylum, temporarily staying in a church helped meet their more immediate needs for temporary housing and nourishment. As such, whatever the pros and cons of sanctuary as a tactic for legalization, it benefitted immigrants seeking humanitarian aid.

In the 2000s, the US still attracts asylum-seekers in need of basic economic aid in addition to legalization, but by 2006 the number of people seeking asylum in the US had decreased compared to the 1980s (UNHCR 2001, 2011). In contrast, the number of undocumented immigrants entering the US had increased by 75 percent from the 1980s to the early 2000s (Passel and Suro 2005; Passel and Cohn 2010).[4] In 2009, over half of these undocumented immigrants had been living in the US for ten years or longer, and 85 percent had been in the country for at least five years (Passel and Cohn 2010). Thus, in the 2000s, a larger proportion of people seeking legalization, whether asylum-seekers or unauthorized migrants, do not need shelter or humanitarian aid, only 'papers'. Most of today's undocumented immigrants have lived in the US for years and already have homes, families, and jobs. Moving into a church, synagogue, or mosque would not satisfy their needs, which are less varied than those of the Central American immigrants seeking asylum during the 1980s. In fact, it might unnecessarily complicate their lives by forcing them to leave their homes, jobs, and families to engage in a practice that may or may not lead to legalization.

The US government's approach to immigration in the 2000s has also changed significantly compared to the 1980s (Brotherton and Kretsedemas 2008). The Department of Homeland Security, created by the Bush administration following 9/11, became the new home for immigration regulation. Unlike the Immigration and Naturalization Service (INS), the immigration regulation agency during the 1980s, the newly formed ICE is housed in a department whose *raison d'être* is to protect the nation's security. Immigrants are legally constructed as more than outsiders: they are potentially dangerous criminals or terrorists threatening the US. At the same time, since the 1980s the number of undocumented immigrants in the US has risen dramatically (Passel and Suro 2005; Passel and Cohn 2010). In response, the US government vastly increased spending on enforcement and began stepping up efforts to detain and deport undocumented immigrants (Brotherton and Kretsedemas 2008). For instance, between 2001 and 2007, deportations from the US increased by 69 percent (US DHS 2009). Combined with the possibility of the Sensenbrenner Bill's passage, which would increase penalties for aiding undocumented immigrants, the 2000s context was riskier both for undocumented immigrants and those assisting them.

As a result, despite experience with, and knowledge of, sanctuary as a strategy, early activists initially decided it was not a good fit for the situation they were facing. They flirted with a handful of other strategies and tactics, such as educating congregations or lobbying, but found these activities lacked the religious resonance they needed for recruiting religious people and reaching the movement's religious and political goals. Thus, an absence of other effective options made early activists rethink using sanctuary. They began considering using the religious symbolism of sanctuary and strategically adapting its meaning to better fit the current environment.

Redesigning sanctuary for a new context

In 2006, an undocumented immigrant named Elvira Arellano entered public sanctuary in a church in Chicago (see Caminero-Santangelo, Chapter 6 in this volume). While Arellano's case was traditional in some ways – she had moved into a church building – it also brought attention to current problems facing undocumented immigrants. Rather than staying in the church alone, she was living there with her US citizen son, a situation highlighting the growing number of mixed-status families threatened with separation by US deportation practices (Passel and Cohn 2009).

Because of Arellano's example, early NSM activists' ideas about sanctuary began to shift. For instance, rather than seeing it solely as temporarily sheltering people in religious buildings, what NSM activists call 'physical sanctuary' (see also Rehaag 2009), they began conceiving of it as a broader, more abstract idea of sacrificial, potentially risky immigrant–congregation partnerships focusing on mixed-status families, calling it 'radical accompaniment'. Stepping outside of the historic meaning of sanctuary this way enabled early activists to embrace sanctuary as identity and strategy.

Once it decided on sanctuary in late 2006, the developing coalition of Los Angeles activists still had to determine how to fit this vision of sanctuary to undocumented immigration today. Based partially on the sanctuary model used by Arellano, they decided New Sanctuary would not be open to all undocumented immigrants, only those whose cases might strike ordinary citizens as unfair due to their otherwise exemplary records. Recipients would be carefully selected mixed-status families, in which at least one member was undocumented and undergoing deportation proceedings and the others are US citizens, so that if the law were enforced, the family would be split up.[5] Selected families would 'go public' to draw attention to the injustices of immigration policy. In return, the NSM would offer legal, spiritual, and financial support or other forms of radical accompaniment. Only in the direst circumstances would immigrants move into religious properties. Activists hoped this new strategy would avoid the difficulties of immigrants moving into religious buildings, while using the symbolic power of sanctuary to capture media attention and religious support. Thus, the new version of sanctuary is a collection of tactics, only one of which is the traditional practice of sanctuary. While some of its tactics are legal and non-confrontational, such as offering immigrants spiritual support and legal representation, others are more marginally legal and disruptive, such as 'physical sanctuary'.

The Center for Human Rights and Constitutional Law has provided the NSM with legal justification for the tactic of sanctuary, arguing that it should be legal in today's context as long as congregations do not attempt to conceal undocumented immigrants taking sanctuary.[6] Still, many NSM activists do not fully trust this opinion since it has not been tested in the courts, advising members to treat physical sanctuary as an act of civil disobedience.[7] Potential recruits, who are mostly ignorant of the legal opinion, typically assume that physical sanctuary is illegal because some 1980s Sanctuary Movement activists received criminal convictions for their activities. In the eyes of current and potential activists, the legality of church-based sanctuary is uncertain, leading to perceptions of physical sanctuary as a practice with probable legal repercussions. As a result, New Sanctuary activists work hard to publicly emphasize sanctuary as radical accompaniment taking many forms, including 'physical sanctuary'.

In contrast, during the 1980s Sanctuary Movement, 'physical sanctuary' was the primary tactic for the movement. Rather than sanctuary representing a general approach to movement strategy, its embodiment in the 1980s was more disruptive and its overall legality more questionable, as demonstrated by the trials and convictions of several sanctuary providers during the 1980s (Cunningham 1995). As such, the new conception of sanctuary represents a significant alteration in the meaning of a well-known symbol, an attempt to adapt it from a tactic with a specific shape and practice to a strategy that includes many tactics.

Because of sanctuary's long and well-known history as a risky tactic involving housing people in religious buildings, this process of re-imagining sanctuary has been difficult. The NSM shares characteristics with younger movements in that it launched only in 2007, is relatively informal, and has few resources and networks that can disseminate this new understanding. At the same time, by adopting a sanctuary identity, the NSM explicitly connects itself to past sanctuary movements. As the next section demonstrates, this association creates a constraining effect similar to those faced by older movements: the public has particular ideas about a 'sanctuary movement', making it hard to change those meanings in a wide-reaching, persuasive way.

The consequences of strategic adaptation

Immediately after the nostalgic gathering of the 2007 national NSM at the beginning of this chapter, another session is taking place that involves local coalitions reporting to everyone on their current activities. An African American woman in her forties and an Asian woman in her late teens stand together at the front of the room. They have travelled from North Carolina to learn more about what NSM involvement will mean. They describe their coalition's relationship with an undocumented family from Liberia. They are in touch with the family on a regular basis and are trying to find ways to help them. Still, one of the women explains with uncertainty, 'I didn't know if this was *sanctuary*. I see myself as part of that family, offering support they need.'

A white pastor in his fifties, a participant in the 1980s Sanctuary Movement and an NSM leader, pipes up: 'Sanctuary is not one thing. It's a multi-dimensional response by communities of faith to hurting people.' Another person agrees, assuring the woman that there is 'no typical sanctuary family because there is no typical immigrant family', and that there will not be a single appropriate response, a single legal answer for everyone. Others add that sometimes there is no legal solution for undocumented families, and the response of religious communities must be to simply stand with them. The North Carolina women slowly nod, though they both squint as though unconvinced by their responses. After the gathering, while they continued working with immigrants, they did not become more deeply involved in the NSM.

Discussions of what sanctuary means today, and leaders' assertions that sanctuary now means something different compared to the 1980s, are common in the NSM, especially when newcomers are present. As a young, relatively unorganized activist network, NSM leaders have insufficient resources to adapt people's understandings of sanctuary on a wide scale. Instead, many potential recruits assume sanctuary will take its 1980s shape, making them hesitant to get involved. The biggest concern among the people I interviewed who did not join the NSM was that they might be pressured to give immigrants shelter in religious buildings and might therefore be participating in something illegal. While the strategy of 'new sanctuary' includes more than traditional or 'physical' sanctuary, when the NSM has been unable to get this understanding across to potential participants, it has often failed to obtain their support.

Thus, many potential activists are either confused about what counts as sanctuary or they assume it is 'old sanctuary' and seek to avoid the risks involved. Further, some think NSM leaders are being disingenuous about sanctuary's flexibility, believing the new model is designed with the ultimate goal of a congregation housing a family on their property. A woman whose congregation got involved but personally chose not to join explains her decision:

> I was expecting ... a conversation and not recruitment. I feel that we were recruited and not invited into the process, invited into conversation, or asked, 'What's your congregation like? How can we get them involved in the New Sanctuary Movement in a way that feels relevant and comfortable to them?' I mean not comfortable as in easy, but as in ... a circle into a square hole ... it's forcing on us a way of doing this other thing that I don't think necessarily fits.

In her eyes, the model for sanctuary is already set and it is supposed to look the way it looked in the 1980s. She is unconvinced that NSM organizers value a variety of sanctuary forms – even after multiple 'education sessions' about their work.

The new version of sanctuary as radical accompaniment has not caught on in many quarters. As the North Carolina newcomer's statement 'I didn't know if this was sanctuary' suggests, many potential participants are confused about whether their partnerships with immigrant families count as 'sanctuary' if they are not housing those families in their churches, synagogues, or mosques. Others express doubts about whether the NSM is genuinely interested in various forms of sanctuary, since they perceive its structure as geared toward supporting immigrants moving into religious properties. As this evidence indicates, choosing a symbol with such a long, powerful legacy has led to tensions that have constrained movement growth.

Conclusion

The NSM is not merely a revival of the 1980s Sanctuary Movement – rather, its activists are struggling to adapt sanctuary as an identity, strategy, and tactic for the current political context. Even though early activists knew it did not fit today's environment, they used sanctuary because they were committed to forming an explicitly religious movement and sanctuary was the most prominent option in their religious repertoires. However, to fit the political context, they had to design a new type of sanctuary that would better address existing immigration issues. Thus, activists were aware of the need to adapt and made the decision to do so: but the decision alone was not enough to ensure successful adaptation, so a process of struggling to adapt ensued.

Despite leaders' attempts to redesign sanctuary in a clear and unified way, a good deal of confusion remains among NSM activists, potential recruits, and the general public regarding what constitutes sanctuary in the NSM. While lack of growth can partly be attributed to the hostile political climate, the NSM's inability to fully diffuse new understandings of sanctuary is also creating problems with recruiting new activists and with cultivating commitment among those who join.

The case of the NSM affirms earlier research stressing the role of religion in choosing strategies and tactics. But it also provides a new way of thinking about the relationship between movement characteristics, strategic adaptation, and outcomes. As an organizationally young movement, the NSM has struggled to adapt sanctuary because of its lack of resources and networks, affirming research on the liability of newness. Yet, ironically, its choice of an older, well-known strategy interacts with its organizational newness to create a liability of senescence as well. The NSM's choice of the symbol of sanctuary clearly connects it to past movements, constraining its ability to redefine itself for a new context. This suggests that it is not only the age of an SMO that matters for its flexibility: the age and renown of a movement's organizing symbol influence these factors as well, interacting with organizational age and formalization in shaping the process of strategic adaptation.

Though a symbol's strong legacy can make activists more likely to choose it, that same legacy may make it as difficult to adapt to a changing context as the age and formalization of the organization itself. While sanctuary's historic legacy, symbolic power, and resonance can help recruit religious activists and shape public conversations, this chapter suggests that adaptations of sanctuary may work best in older, more formalized SMOs with the resources and networks to diffuse atypical incarnations of sanctuary.

Notes

1 See www.newsanctuarymovement.org.
2 While sanctuary has taken a variety of shapes throughout history, including the 1980s Sanctuary Movement, it is typically understood as the provision of refuge in sacred

buildings (Lippert and Rehaag 2009). Even multifaceted movements like the 1980s Sanctuary Movement are best known for this aspect of sanctuary, even if this legacy is a simplified version of a more complex reality. For instance, Perla and Coutin's (2009) re-examination of the legacies and origins of the 1980s Sanctuary Movement, which they call the US-Central American Sanctuary Movement in order to highlight its transnational nature, was necessary because the movement's US-based church sanctuary practices are better known in public and scholarly circles than its Central American-based practices.

3 During 2006, the Senate version of the Sensenbrenner Bill (S. 2611) failed to pass, so that neither became law.
4 From 1980 to 1989, an average of 57,389 people per year applied for asylum in the US (see United Nations High Commissioner for Refugees 2001: 1 and 25, for data on number of cases). These numbers must be multiplied by 1.45 to calculate the number of individual applicants, since there are an average of 1.45 persons per case, as discussed in ibid.: vi). In 2006, 51,880 people applied for asylum in the US, a 9.5 percent decrease since the 1980s (United Nations High Commissioner for Refugees 2011: 15). In comparison, from 1981 to 1990, an average of 400,000 people per year migrated to the US without authorization (Passel and Suro 2005: 54). But by the period leading up to the Sensenbrenner Bill's passage, 2000–2004, that number had risen to an average of 700,000 people per year, a 75 percent increase (Passel and Cohn 2010: 5).
5 Merit-based approaches have also recently been adopted in Canadian sanctuary practices, though these changes have been parallel developments rather than coordinated efforts (Lippert 2009; Rehaag 2009).
6 See www.newsanctuarymovement.org/legal.
7 See page 3 of UUA Issue Brief on the NSM at www.uua.org/documents/washingtonoffice/sanctuary_issuebrief.pdf.

References

Brotherton, D.C. and Kretsedemas, P. (eds) (2008) *Keeping Out the Other: A Critical Introduction to Immigration Enforcement Today*, New York: Columbia University Press.

Coutin, S. (1993) *The Culture of Protest: Religious Activism and the U.S. Sanctuary Movement*, Boulder, CO: Westview Press.

Cunningham, H. (1995) *God and Caesar at the Rio Grande: Sanctuary and the Politics of Religion*, Minneapolis: University of Minnesota Press.

Freeman, J., Carroll, G.R. and Hannan, M.T. (1983) 'The Liability of Newness: Age Dependence in Organizational Death Rates', *American Sociological Review*, 48: 692–710.

Ganz, M. (2000) 'Resources and Resourcefulness: Strategic Capacity in the Unionization of California Agriculture, 1959–66', *American Journal of Sociology*, 105: 1003–62.

Hannan, M.T. and Freeman, J. (1984) 'Structural Inertia and Organizational Change', *American Sociological Review*, 49: 149–64.

King, B.G. and Cornwall, M. (2005) 'Specialists and Generalists: Learning Strategies in the Woman Suffrage Movement, 1866–1918', *Research in Social Movements, Conflicts and Change*, 26: 3–34.

Lippert, R. (2009) 'Whither Sanctuary?', *Refuge*, 26: 57–67.

Lippert, R. and Rehaag, S. (2009) 'Introduction: Sanctuary in Context', *Refuge*, 26: 3–6.

McAdam, D. (1983) 'Tactical Innovation and the Pace of Insurgency', *American Sociological Review*, 48: 735–54.

McAdam, D., Tarrow, S. and Tilly, C. (2001) *Dynamics of Contention*, Cambridge: Cambridge University Press.

McCammon, H.J. (2003) '"Out of the Parlors and Into The Streets": The Changing Tactical Repertoire of the U.S. Women's Suffrage Movements', *Social Forces*, 81: 787–818.

McCammon, H.J., Chaudhuri, S., Hewitt, L., Muse, C.S., Newman, H.D., Smith, C.L., and Terrell, T.M. (2008) 'Becoming Full Citizens: The U.S. Women's Jury Rights Campaigns, the Pace of Reform, and Strategic Adaptation', *American Journal of Sociology*, 113: 1104–47.

Minkoff, D. (1999) 'Bending with the Wind: Strategic Change and Adaptation by Women's and Racial Minority Organizations', *American Journal of Sociology*, 104: 1666–703.

Morris, A. (1981) 'Southern Student Sit-in Movement: An Analysis of Internal Organization', *American Sociological Review*, 46: 744–67.

Nepstad, S.E. (2004) 'Disciples and Dissenters: Tactical Choice and Consequences in the Plowshares Movement', *Research in Social Movements, Conflict, and Change*, 25: 139–59.

Passel, J. and Cohn, D. (2009) *A Portrait of Unauthorized Immigrants in the United States*, Washington, DC: Pew Hispanic Center.

——(2010) *U.S. Unauthorized Immigration Flows Are Down Sharply Since Mid-Decade*, Washington, DC: Pew Hispanic Center.

Passel, J. and Suro, R. (2005) *Rise, Peak, and Decline: Trends in U.S. Immigration, 1992–2004*, Washington, DC: Pew Hispanic Center.

Perla, H. and Coutin, S.B. (2009) 'Legacies and Origins of the 1980s US-Central American Sanctuary Movement', *Refuge*, 26: 7–19.

Polletta, F. (2008) 'Culture and Movements', *Annals of the American Academy of Political and Social Science*, 619: 78–96.

Rehaag, S. (2009) 'Bordering on Legality: Canadian Church Sanctuary and the Rule of Law', *Refuge*, 26: 43–56.

Smith, C. (1996) *Resisting Reagan: The U.S. Central America Peace Movement*, Chicago: University of Chicago Press.

United Nations High Commissioner for Refugees (2001) *Asylum Applications in Industrialized Countries: 1980–1999*, Geneva: UNHCR.

——(2011) *Asylum Levels and Trends in Industrialized Countries, 2010*, Geneva: UNHCR.

U.S. Department of Homeland Security (2009) *2008 Yearbook of Immigration Statistics*, Washington, DC: US Government Printing Office.

Part III

Sanctuary movements and practices in Europe and Canada

International comparative and case studies

Chapter 8

Holy territories and hospitality
Nordic exceptionality and national differences of sanctuary incidents

Jill Loga, Miikka Pyykkönen and Hanne Stenvaag

The history of Nordic sanctuary practices

Church sanctuaries have reappeared in Nordic countries during the past 30 years. These sanctuary incidents relate to the second and third waves of post-Second World War immigration.[1] Almost all church or parish sanctuaries in the Nordic countries during this period were provided to rejected asylum-seekers.

Today, there is no *formal* legal ground for church asylum in the Nordic countries; the practice is founded on old customs and norms. However, these norms have a long legal history both in the profane legal system and religious understanding.

The oldest traces of asylum rights in Scandinavian countries can be found in the Act of Eric (1189/90). This includes descriptions of punishment for people who attack a church refuge. In the first Norwegian legislative assembly, the formal Gulating Laws[2] and the second Borgarting Laws,[3] church asylum is described as honouring Jesus Christ and the requirement not to offend the church, and the churchyard. In these ancient laws the priest's duty to help fugitives and outlaws was also expressed. These two normative grounds were institutionalised in church laws as *reventia loci* (meaning the inviolability of holy territory or 'asylon') and *intercession* (meaning the priest's duty to help people in distress and to show hospitality or 'asylos') (Loga 1998).

Church sanctuary[4] existed as a formal legal institution in Scandinavia until 1537. During the Lutheran Reformation, both legality and legitimacy of this institution disappeared as the religion was institutionalised as part of the state.

Even though the formal foundation of church sanctuary, both as a holy ex-territorial area and a humanitarian duty by a servant, disappeared from state law after the Reformation in Scandinavia, these norms have remained in Protestantism. Most central to the ethics of Luther is the altruistic principle of 'loving your neighbour', and from this, follow hospitality and charity. While the number of church sanctuary incidents decreased after the Reformation, drawing on these Lutheran principles sanctuary incidents nonetheless occasionally occurred, mostly during wars and revolts.

The ties between state and the Church have been close in the Nordic countries, and the modern practices must still be seen in this light. Most of the sanctuary incidents in Scandinavia have taken place within the Lutheran majority churches, still closely tied to the state, and thus producing exceptional dilemmas.[5]

In this chapter we observe modern sanctuary practices related to refugees in four Nordic countries: Denmark, Finland, Norway and Sweden. The chapter is mainly based on former research performed by the authors in Finland and Norway. The data used varies from personal interviews with asylum-seekers and sanctuary providers, to survey data, Church documents and media accounts. First, we briefly describe the different actors in sanctuary politics, and then proceed with country-specific case observations. We focus on the characteristics of sanctuary incidents and the public debates concerning them, their legitimacy and institutionalisation. In the conclusion, we identify the differences and similarities between countries.

Parties involved in Nordic sanctuary politics

Today sanctuary practices in Nordic countries usually involve rejected asylum-seekers. The rejected asylum-seekers' 'opponent' in sanctuary incidents is the state with its migration laws, administrative practices and bodies, and authorities. The civic and church-related actors involved form a loose collective of actors and ideas, which was called a 'sanctuary movement' in previous sanctuary studies (e.g. Wiltfang and McAdam 1991; Cunningham 1995).

Sanctuary providers are normally Lutheran congregations and their employees or volunteers, but the national leaders of Churches have played a central role in the public discussions on sanctuary incidents and practices. Other sanctuary actors are refugee support groups, women's associations, human rights, multicultural and social service organisations, and political activists.

The media is also significant in Nordic sanctuary incidents. Media attention arises when sanctuary providers and supporters attempt to publicise specific cases. Most Nordic sanctuary incidents today are 'sanctuaries as exposure' (Weller 1989) since the representatives of the congregations and civic organisations publicise cases through media appeals. In Finland and Norway, for instance, the media has supported congregations, civic organisations and asylum-seekers and opposed the immigration authorities and the police, especially when women and children are involved. This has not, however, meant that the tone in public debate has been only favourable to sanctuary practices. Right-wing parties have argued that churches should stay out of public politics. Moreover, during the heated debates in Norway during the 1990s, this argument was also made by government officials, and left-wing parties and church representatives.

Sanctuary incidents in Nordic countries

Denmark

The first modern sanctuary incident in Denmark happened in 1987. Eighty asylum-seekers from Lebanon established a sanctuary and started a hunger strike in Maria Church in Copenhagen. This sanctuary lasted only four days, as the refugees were promised that their safety would be secured before any deportation, and that their asylum applications would be reopened. To prevent police from entering the church, the congregation declared an 'ongoing service of prayer', thus defining the sanctuary provision as an act of solidarity (see also Millner, Chapter 4 in this volume), more than defining it as a holy territory or a sacred space (Bollmann 1992).

From 1991 to 1992, around seventy stateless Palestinians stayed for half a year in Copenhagen's Blågårds and Enghave Churches. Many priests and pastors from different denominations, including some bishops in the Danish Church, appealed to the authorities to let the group stay for humanitarian reasons. The active supporters of this sanctuary consisted of different groups, from grass-root anarchists, active church members, trade unionists, civic organisations, to neighbours. This time, the situation was solved politically by granting the refugees permission to stay in Denmark (Christensen 1992).

It took 17 years for the next sanctuary incident to appear, in 2009 in Brorson church in Copenhagen (Kirkeasyl 2011). The sanctuary was instituted after an agreement was signed, which allowed forced returns from Denmark to Iraq. This agreement included a group of approximately 270 Iraqi refugees who had been living in Denmark for up to 10 years, as they had not returned to Iraq despite negative decisions on their asylum applications. Sixty of them formed this sanctuary group which stayed three months in the protection of the church. Their supporters established an organisation, *Kirkeasyl*. Media discussions revealed that the local congregation and pastor were eager to 'de-politicise' their role, stating that they were only following the Christian tradition of helping people in need, and therefore had responded positively to the request for sanctuary from the refugees. The appeal for permission to stay in Denmark for humanitarian reasons for the whole group of Iraqis was supported by numerous organisations such as Amnesty International and Save the Children, the major newspaper *Politiken*, more than 100 pastors, and the organisation 'Grandparents for Asylum'.

The Brorson sanctuary incident ended dramatically when the police entered and shut down the sanctuary on the night of August 13, 2009. The police action towards the Brorson sanctuary was followed by large demonstrations, and different initiatives to find other ways of helping the refugees, for example, helping them to find work permits in Denmark. All this actualised a debate about how to understand church sanctuary. There were two factions in the Church. The majority faction argued that the Church was offended by the authorities, and that the church as a place for service and prayer should be respected. The other faction, called 'Church, know your place!', drew on Luther to argue that the Church should respect state authorities (Lodberg 2010). The police act of entering the church split the Danish Social Democrats, with its leader Thorning Schmidt in support of the action, while the former prime minister Nyrup Rasmussen condemned the action, stating 'the border for normal humanity and decency was broken'.[6]

The debate on the Brorson sanctuary, on the one hand, was characterised by the harsh tone in the Danish debate about refugees and integration. One example of this is the Danish church and integration minister Rønn Hornbech, who stated: 'I don't understand, why they don't seek refuge in the mosque ... For me, it is completely baroque, that Muslims that belong to a people, who persecute Christians, seek refuge in a Christian church.'[7] On the other hand, the debate was also characterised by a traditional understanding of the Lutheran doctrine of separation between Church and state, requiring the Church to refrain from involvement in political questions.

As we will see, the sanctuary incidents in Denmark differ from those in Finland and Norway. There have been only a few sanctuary incidents in Denmark, and these incidents appear to involve less institutionalisation. The sanctuaries have all consisted of large homogenous groups of refugees, have received much media interest, and have been of short duration.

Finland

Modern sanctuary practice was non-existent in Finland from the civil war to the 1970s. Most incidents before the 1990s did not end up in institutional reports, history books or other media. They were occasionally organised by parishes or churches, but more often by priests and other church workers or active citizens. The space of sanctuary was usually the homes of these people or other concealed spaces organised by them.

The most well-known case during the 1990s involved a priest offering shelter to rejected Bangladeshi asylum-seekers in the Cathedral of Helsinki and organising a hunger strike for them in 1996. The protest ended without confrontation or the need to enter sanctuary, though despite the wide and favourable publicity, the asylum applications were eventually rejected and the asylum-seekers were deported.

According to an immigration worker of the Lutheran Church and a women's organisation worker, altogether approximately sixty people have received sanctuary since the beginning of the 1970s in Finland. The Evangelical-Lutheran Church and its congregations select suitable asylum-seekers from the applicants. Congregations and church employees choose to help those whose background stories seem believable (Pyykkönen 2009). However, the selection is also based on publicity criteria, especially recently, when the Finnish 'sanctuary as exposure' (Weller 1989) policy was adopted. Almost all those selected have been women, as their mistreatment by immigration authorities is seen as the most damaging. The backgrounds of the sanctuary subjects and applicants have varied from Russians and former Yugoslavians to Africans and people from the Middle East. Most often they are from countries with high rates of refugee emigration.

The Finnish Ecumenical Council (FEC) published its guidance instructions called *Church as Sanctuary* in 2007. According to these instructions, the ethical hospitality principle (the 'asylos') is primary in Finnish sanctuary practice, but the holiness (the 'asylon') of the church space is also recognised as part of the process. In the instructions, the FEC (2007: 10–11) takes a stand for sanctuary as exposure by claiming open sanctuaries – meaning information sharing to both media and public authorities – guarantee more efficient treatment of the asylum-seekers' cases.

After these instructions, which attracted media attention as a new kind of challenge to the state's sovereignty to control its borders, sanctuary applications increased. Many incidents gained wide media attention and an increasing number of cases ended with positive results. However, thus far only one-third of the cases have resulted in deportation withdrawals. Although the FEC, which consists of representatives of all Christian Churches, published the sanctuary instructions, the Lutheran Church and its congregations are the main religious party to be officially involved in sanctuary politics in recent years, while Orthodox congregations have been involved in only a few sanctuary incidents.

The two best-known sanctuary incidents in Finland are Naze Aghai's case (2007–8, right after the publication of the FEC's instructions) and the so-called 'grandma cases' (2009–10). In the first incident, Iranian Kurd and political activist Naze Aghai ended up securing a temporary residence permit after two years of bouncing between a reception centre and a congregation's sanctuary in Turku, rounds of administrative and court appeals, and church and civic struggle attracting influential media attention. The residence permit came after the administrative court of Helsinki overturned the Finnish Immigration Directorate's deportation decision in May 2008. The grandma cases ended differently: in June 2010, a few days before the Finnish Immigration Service gave their final decision on Irina Antonova's visa renewal, her relatives took her to an elderly care facility in Russia, where she later died in August 2011. The 'Egyptian grandma', Eveline Fadayel, died just two months after the Directorate of Immigration issued her one-year residence permission. Both incidents involved up to two years of struggle: Antonova spent a couple of months publicly in 'symbolic sanctuary'[8] in Munkkivuori congregation, while Fadayel spent three months underground in Lintula Orthodox Convent. Relatives, supporters and congregation activists organised several court appeals for both grandmas and even the European Court of Human Rights (ECHR) gave a favourable decision on Fadayel's case.

Both central church sanctuary elements – the holy territory and the duty to help fugitives – were used by congregation activists in the above cases, in addition to humanitarian reasons. The duty to help 'neighbours' was the main argument when the congregation's opposition to Finnish laws and administrative decisions was justified. This argument was also used by the congregation activists and church representatives when the decisions on taking people into sanctuary were considered. The church as holy territory was also used when the decision was made in congregations, but as a public matter this argument became especially important when police and other authorities left the congregation territories in peace. Both church and civic sanctuary activists cited humanitarian reasons, stating that deportation would mean death, illness and, in Naze's case, torture of the persons in sanctuary. Both cases generated significant publicity. Family members, human rights lawyers and supporters appealed to the ECHR for the grandmas and started media campaigns to influence Finnish Immigration Service decisions. The church and its representatives, human rights activists, many civic organisations, and politicians, including the Finnish President Tarja Halonen, and Finnish and Russian media criticised migration officials and courts over their decisions. On May 31 2010, two thousand people demonstrated in Helsinki to protest at the deportation decisions.

Since Naze's case, immigration authorities and police have cooperated with church workers (Pyykkönen 2009: 25). The authorities ask congregation workers to monitor the health of individual asylum-seekers. Several times the Evangelical-Lutheran Church has been asked to evaluate the possible destinies of asylum-seekers in their countries of origin if they were deported, to clarify asylum-seekers' backgrounds in ambiguous situations, and to report on the conditions in the countries of origin, before a deportation decision is made.[9] After Naze's case, the Advisory Board of the Finnish Immigration Service, with external members from the Ecumenical Council, the Lutheran Church and several civic organisations, was created. Thus, church actors have an institutionalised position in Finnish asylum-seeker politics, though the sanctuary practice is still not officially recognised by the authorities.

Norway

Contemporary sanctuary practices in Norway began in earnest in February 1993 in the city of Tromsø, when two families and five young men fleeing military service from Kosovo received protection in the Lutheran congregation of Elverhøy (Vetvik and Omland 1997; Loga 1998). What may have prompted this sanctuary incident was a decision by the Norwegian Government that all Albanian asylum-seekers from Kosovo would have their applications turned down. This decision was criticised by the general public and within the Church. Soon after the establishment of a few sanctuaries, the Department of Justice stated the police as a basic principle would not remove refugees from the churches. Shortly after this statement, several congregations followed the example of Elverhøy, and by November 1993 as many as 140 congregations in Norway were housing approximately 650 Albanian asylum-seekers from Kosovo.

These actions were followed by a heated debate in Norway, consisting of both criticism by church officials of the government's immigration policy and also public criticism of the state church as an exceptional institution in a modern democracy. Within a state church, sanctuary practices appeared to be a medieval custom made legal by priests and other official employees. The parallel actions in 140 congregations all over the country made the phenomenon appear to be a political movement and a collective act of civil disobedience. In the beginning of the debate, the church described sanctuary provision as a matter of saving lives: returning Albanian asylum-seekers to Kosovo at this time would have put their lives at risk (Bue 1993a, 1993b; Loga 1998). Leaders of the Church and priests in congregations argued that the irresponsibility of the government called for humanitarian and Christian ethical action by the Church. Referring to information from their own sources, the congregations and collaborating humanitarian civic organisation claimed the situation for the Albanians in Kosovo was critical.

The sanctuary incidents in 1993 were local initiatives but they triggered a grass-roots movement that spread rapidly. During this period, the majority of sanctuary incidents occurred in congregations of the Church of Norway, a state church, but sanctuary provision has taken place in other denominations of churches as well.

How was it possible for the Church to so openly resist state sovereignty in the early days of contemporary sanctuary practice? When the situation had almost reached its peak, the Bishops Conference wrote a letter to the congregations, arguing the Church's role as a 'holy territory' was the basic idea underlying sanctuary practice, thus moderating the ethical arguments of helping people in distress. One main reason for emphasising the argument of the Church as a holy territory could have been to de-politicise church actions (Johansen 2004). Later the congregations emphasised the ethical arguments in sanctuary provision (Vetvik and Omland 1997; Johansen 2004).

Negotiations between the government and the decision-making bodies of the Church leadership ended in a compromise with the creation of a joint statement, 'Felleserklæringen', in November 1993. As a result of this joint statement, 670 people left the churches, and during the same year the Bishops Council signed a statement to stop sanctuary practices (Vetvik and Omland 1997; Loga 1998; Mellomkirkelig råd 1998). The outcome was that 2500 asylum-seekers from Kosovo had their applications reconsidered, and of these, approximately 2000 received a residence permit.

However, the promise and compromise between the Church and the government did not last very long. Already in February 1994, the number of sanctuary incidents began to rise again, and by March the number of refugees in churches had risen to more than 200. In the following two years no new resolutions were proposed and the debates returned more frequently and gradually became more heated with a new peak in 1996. Some priests continued to highlight humanitarian duties, while others who had carried on this practice in their congregation for some years started to question its function. The decision-making bodies of the Norwegian state Church, which had entered a compromise with its head and financier, the government, were not perceived as having a legitimate role to play in this issue by the local levels of the organisation. Therefore, the different local congregations were more or less left to their own devices, while the public debates gradually shifted to the legitimacy of this old institution, the state Church.[10] At this time the public was not entirely supportive of church sanctuary and the acts of the Church more generally. There were also voices arguing the Church had abandoned the compromise with the Ministry of Justice.

In October 1996, a new government was established and the Ministry of Justice was led by a former critic of the strict refugee policy, a former policewoman, Anne Holt. While the new Prime Minister Torbjørn Jagland proclaimed that sanctuaries are 'a medieval practice which allows a few people to sneak into Norway through the door of the Church',[11] the new Minister of Justice, Anne Holt, was faced by great expectations by the different actors of the 'church asylum movement'. New perspectives and critical voices brought the debate to a head, and the Minister of Justice was pushed to intervene. The solution was presented on December 9, 1996. Minister Anne Holt invited all the families with children to exit the churches and she promised that those who immediately contacted the nearest police station would have their asylum applications reconsidered. And with this amnesty, she echoed her predecessor: 'This will happen only once.'[12] This amnesty was a unilateral political decision by the government, and not a compromise between two factions. This ended the period of 'the church asylum movement' or a broad and collective sanctuary practice in Norway. And it reduced the temperature of ongoing debates and the difficult situation for both the Church and government subsided. Still, sanctuary practices did not cease in Norway.

In 1998, the Church of Norway published a report on the sanctuary experiences, including guidelines for future sanctuary provision (Mellomkirkelig råd 1998). The report focused on the problematic aspects of sanctuaries, and the refugees are described as 'guests who refuse to leave'. The focus was still on the church as a 'holy territory' or a 'sacred space', and it reported that a congregation has an obligation to enter dialogue with persons seeking refuge. But the congregation's role is also understood as passive, the refugees are understood to be imposing their problem on the church, and the solution is to strongly emphasise that sanctuary is meant to be temporary. During this period, congregations had different attitudes and experiences. Some congregations decided to close their doors to asylum-seekers, and some perceived the refugees in their church almost to be squatters. In 1999, the Ministry of Justice changed their guidelines, providing a measure for the police to remove refugees from a church if requested to do so by the congregation.

Interviews with persons engaged in sanctuary work, from both 1993–96 and 2000–2001, show their main motivation for carrying out this work was assisting refugees in difficult situations (Loga 1998; Johansen 2004). Most of the persons involved belonged to the actual congregation, and they linked their engagement with their Christian faith. Their main focus was ethical reasons. Most informants were involved in refugee politics for the first time during their engagement in organised religious activities.

After the amnesty in 1996, the number of refugees in sanctuaries remained between approximately 30–80 persons until 2004. In 2004, the political debate on children as asylum-seekers was raised again, and the result was an agreement, where families with children who had been in Norway for more than three years would have their cases reopened. This included refugees in sanctuaries, and some families were allowed to stay in Norway after years of living in a church. In December 2004, there were only two refugees in sanctuary in churches in Norway. After 2004, the number of refugees in sanctuaries has been fewer than 10 most of the time, with a small increase to around 20 in 2009 and 2010. Characteristic of this whole period is that refugees in the sanctuaries were a heterogeneous group from different countries and with very different backgrounds. Thus, the focus on the individual stories has become vital. In addition, sanctuary incidents have tended to be of long duration. The longest one involved Shalah Valadi, from Iran, who lived for seven years in the Pentecostal church in Mysen, until she received permission to stay in 2007.

Torjussen (2008) identifies the changing attitudes of the Church as the most likely reason for the decline in sanctuary incidents in Norway after the 1990s. There has also been a shift from the majority of sanctuary incidents involving the Church of Norway in the early period, to the majority involving Free Churches later on. Even if the numbers of sanctuary incidents in Norway have constantly decreased, the idea of sanctuary is established in public debate and it remains a possibility for refugees in need. As the group of unreturnable refugees in Norway has risen over recent years, churches have again become places for public appeals for these groups, through hunger strikes, tents camped as protest at the walls of central churches, and asylum marches following old pilgrimage paths.

Sweden

In the most recent guide for congregations working with questions of refugees and immigration, the Church of Sweden does not write much about church sanctuary. What they write mainly refers to the question of hiding refugees, pointing out that it is not illegal to help hidden refugees, as long as it is not for economic reasons (Svenska kyrkan 2008: 32). However, in Sweden, we find the apparently most stable sanctuary in all the Nordic countries.

Alsike monastery, a small Lutheran monastery with three nuns, located in the countryside near Uppsala, has been a refuge for rejected asylum-seekers since 1978. At the entrance, there is a sign announcing that the Alsike monastery is a 'sanctuary for refugees in danger', referring to Genesis 4:15 and Matthew 25:35.[13] On two occasions since the founding of the church, in 1981 and 1993, refugees have been arrested in the monastery. Of the 36 refugees arrested in Alsike in 1993, 13 were returned to their home countries, while the rest of the group were allowed to return to the monastery, and were later granted residence permission in Sweden. This incident was heavily discussed in the media, both because it involved children, but also because it raised the question of whether it is acceptable to establish this kind of refuge, and whether it is acceptable for the police to raid a monastery or a church. The prime minister warned that the police should be careful, because of the special role the Church plays (Wicklin 2005). Officially, the conclusion was that the authorities and the police were authorised to act as they did. On the other hand, there has not been any similar incident since 1993, even if the Alsike monastery has continued its publicly well-known sanctuary activity.

As well as the continuous sanctuary in Alsike, there have been at least seven examples of sanctuary incidents in Swedish churches, stretching from a group of more than 100 Turkish and Bulgarians staying in different churches in Helsingborg for a number of months in 1990, to the most recent case in 2011, where a group of Ethiopian refugees refused by Norway, lived for two months in Adolf Fredriks Church in Stockholm, before being returned to Norway. In 1995, there was an incident similtar to the Danish sanctuaries, where 50 Bosnian-Croatian refugees stayed in a church in Karlskrona for six weeks, before the Swedish government decided to return this group of refugees, at the time consisting of about 5000 asylum-seekers, to Croatia. Due to an escalation in the conflict in Former Yugoslavia, the return deportations were stopped.

The sanctuary with the longest duration in Sweden was in Åsele, a small community in Northern Sweden, where two Kurdish families from Turkey lived in the church for 16 months in 1993. After this period in the church, they moved to a house in the village of Åsele, and during this period, they were arrested by the police. Most of the family members had to return to their home country,[14] but still there was contact and solidarity work in the community, and some of the children were later allowed to finish their studies in Sweden.

One special incident was the Ucklum case from 1999, where ten children from a Kurdish family were in sanctuary, while their parents lived underground (Nordblom and Demir 2001). The church was kept under surveillance from the police, and deportation of the children was announced. In the end, the children received permission to stay for humanitarian and medical reasons.

The concept of 'refugee-hider' arose in Sweden during the early 1990s, when groups and networks organised themselves around sanctuary activities (Wicklin 2005). According to Hebert and Jacobsson (1999), the refugee-hiding movement is heterogeneous and less political than other groups practising what can be interpreted as civil disobedience. The means and reasons for becoming a refugee-hider depend on the context, and are often a spontaneous reaction to a specific situation. The arguments and reasoning of the refugee-hiders are not uncommon among activists and congregations involved in Norwegian sanctuary incidents. The Swedish Church as an organisation has not been hiding refugees, but the role of individuals attached to the Church is often mentioned, and many refugees in difficult situations do contact the Church. To count the numbers of hidden refugees and refugee-hiders is of course a difficult task. Judging from the visibility of refugee-hiding in the public debate, and the existence of refugee-hiding networks in Sweden, it seems to have been more frequent than in Norway. On the other hand, 'exposure sanctuaries' have been much more common in Norway than in Sweden.

The Easter declaration in 2005 is noteworthy. At this time the debate was in full swing surrounding the phenomenon of refugee children reacting to their situation with an extreme state of apathy. A reform of the Swedish juridical processes for asylum-seekers was also on its way. The Swedish Ecumenical Council engaged in these debates was critical of the present system, especially in respect to children, and asked for an amnesty, a new chance, for all the hidden refugees. The response was overwhelming, around 160,000 signatures were collected, and the issue was debated publicly. Even if it did not result in a general amnesty, a temporary law made it possible for 30,000 hidden refugees to apply for a reopening of their cases, receiving more generous treatment.

Conclusion

The first actual sanctuary after the Second World War in a Nordic country was in the Swedish Alsike monastery in 1978. In Norway, the first incident took place in a Protestant Church, Lambertseter in Oslo, in 1987. Denmark was the first Nordic country with a public sanctuary practice, in Blågård Church during 1991–92. The Danish case was a model for the 'sanctuary wave' in Norway during 1993–94. In Finland, public sanctuary provision started in 1996, but the actual 'sanctuary movement' (Cunningham 1995) did not emerge until the 2000s. The sanctuary seekers in Nordic incidents have not been centred in any specific countries or regions, but have, with few exceptions, been from those countries from where the majority of the European refugee migration come.

The number of asylum-seekers in sanctuaries has been highest in Norway, especially during the 1990s. Finland is the country with the lowest rate of sanctuary incidents, which corresponds to a lower population of asylum-seekers. However, during the past five years the number of cases has been similar in Norway and Finland: 10–20 per year. In Denmark, the group aspect has been dominant. This is also true of Norway in the early days of the movement, but this later changed to an individual focus. In Finland, the individual focus has been dominant from the beginning. In Sweden, the types of incidents have been more varied. Certain sanctuary practices in Denmark, Norway and Sweden have been triggered by changed policies regarding the return of groups of asylum-seekers, and have thus been linked to demands for policy reforms or amnesty for an entire group.

There are two central ways of legitimising churches' sanctuary practices in Nordic countries: the ex-territorial argument and ethical humanitarianism. Both arguments have normative grounds in old customs. In Norway, the ex-territorial arguments have been explicit, especially in official church documents. On this understanding, congregations are obliged to respond to fugitives. However, there is no formal obligation to help, which has left the congregations and asylum-seekers in the situation that some describe as 'a guest who refuses to leave'. This means that the 'asylos', the servants of the holy territories, are left to themselves to make a personal judgement on humanitarian grounds, or a judgement on behalf of the congregation, to help or not.

In all Nordic countries, the Church acts as a political critic of the state's immigration policies through the holy territory argument, even if they have a more or less formalised or institutionalised agreement with the governments. The holy territory argument can be understood as a political critique of the state's immigration policies, even if the political critique is more obvious when the ethical argument is dominant. The Church uses a public building to undermine state sovereignty over border control and the action of police. The ex-territorial argument has been powerful in Finland as well, but there, the ethical argument has been dominant. This is mirrored in the two key features of Finnish sanctuary incidents: first, that congregations make decisions on specific cases and there is no general 'welcome fugitives principle'. Second, Finnish sanctuary practices have only rarely occurred in church buildings, but instead in apartments organised by the sanctuary activists, which often are owned by congregations.

The state and the police have been reluctant to actively intervene in Nordic sanctuary incidents, even if there have been examples of this in Sweden and Denmark. A probable explanation for this is the position of the Church in Nordic countries as an integral part of the state where the holy territory (the 'asylon') is government property and the humanitarian servants (the 'asylos'), who are protecting refugees, are official employees. Thus, the legitimacy and the political handling of sanctuary practices are different from practices in other countries where the religion is organised more autonomously in civil society. In Norway, the government has stated most clearly that refugees will generally not be arrested by the police in churches. Exceptions can be made if the church asks the police to remove the refugees from the church, but this has only occurred in a few incidents, and has not led to a public debate. In Finland, there is no such clear statement by the state authorities, but no police interventions in sanctuaries have taken place. Several asylum-seekers have, however, been caught by the police when they temporarily left sanctuaries to run errands, such as medical appointments. In Denmark and Sweden, it is clearly more risky to take sanctuary, and sanctuaries are more often 'concealment-like' (Weller 1989) hiding places than in Norway or Finland.

The internal debates within churches have also changed over time. In Norway, at the beginning of the sanctuary movement, the local and the central level of the Church shared the same perspective. Later, there was a split between the top and local levels in the Church organisation, stemming from the agreement the Church leadership had made with the government. From this point on, sanctuary provision occurred non-systematically and did not have the character of a movement. The congregations were left to their own devices with their practices without the broad support of the Lutheran Church. In Denmark, Finland, and Sweden internal debates have taken place about how to understand the role of the Church in refugee-related questions, but without a clear division of perceptions between top and grass-roots level.

There have been public debates in all Nordic countries regarding whether the churches should oppose state policies or not. Churches have been cautious about making statements indicating that church sanctuary is an official part of their repertoire. On the one hand, many political parties and the related civic organisations are in favour of an active and critical role for the churches and congregations with regard to strict state policies due to humanitarian reasons. Loud and growing anti-immigration parties have, on the other hand, argued that churches should not oppose state laws and practices. Our sense, in recent years, is that the attitudes among the larger public and the media have become more critical of church sanctuary practices. However, the practice is now established as an informal, partly legitimate possibility for refugees in Nordic countries. In this sense, sanctuary practices also reflect local grass-roots-related activism and critical opposition to national immigration policies.

Notes

1 See Geddes (2003: 17–19) for details.
2 Gulatingsloven, ca. AD 900.
3 Borgartingsloven, tenth century AD.
4 In Scandinavia, the concept 'church asylum' is more commonly used.
5 Norway and Finland have Lutheran state churches. Denmark and Sweden have so-called national churches. The Church of Norway formally changed from a state church into a national church on 21 May 2012.
6 *Politiken*, 17 August 2009.
7 According to *Kristeligt Dagblad*, 16 June 2009.
8 The congregation was prepared to provide shelter, in the event that deportation appeared likely.
9 Notes from the 'Church as Sanctuary Practice in Congregations' network meeting of 23 February 2009.
10 From the Reformation in 1536–37.
11 Prime Minister Jagland, cited in *Aftenposten*, 10 November 1996.
12 Minister of Justice, Anne Holt, cited in *Aftenposten*, 9 December 1996.
13 Genesis 4:15 refers to the story of Cain, who is deemed to be a restless wanderer, but still is marked by God, so that no one would kill him. Matthew 25:35 refers to the judgment, where Jesus says: 'I was a stranger, but you invited me in.'
14 Three of the family members were not at home, and stayed underground in Sweden.

References

Bollmann, K. (1992) 'Asyltanken – et historisk rids', *Kritisk Forum for Praktisk Teologi*, 49: 11–20.
Bue, B. (1993a) 'Kyrkjeasyl', *Kritisk Jus*, 4(93): 153–4.

——(1993b) 'Kyrjeasylet er avvikla', *Kritisk Jus*, 4(93): 219–21.
Christensen, E. (1992) 'Efter 154 døgns kirkeasyl', *Kritisk Forum for Praktisk Teologi*, 49: 105–12.
Cunningham, F. (1995) *God and Caesar at the Rio Grande: Sanctuary and the Politics of Religion*, Minneapolis: University of Minnesota Press.
Finnish Ecumenical Council (2007) *Kirkko turvapaikkana* [Church as Sanctuary], Helsinki: Suomen ekumeeninen neuvosto.
Geddes, A. (2003) *The Politics of Migration and Immigration in Europe*, London: Sage.
Hebert, N. and Jacobsson, K. (1999) 'Olydiga medborgare? Om flyktinggömmare och djurrättsaktivister', *SOU 1999*: 101.
Johansen, H. (2004) 'Kirkeasylets teologi: et grasrotsperstekti', unpublished master's thesis, University of Tromsø.
Kirkeasyl (2011) *Kirkeasyl: en kamp for ophold*, Frederiksberg: Bogforlaget Frydenlund.
Lodberg, P. (2010) 'Palæstinensere og irakere i kirken – kirkeasyl på dagsordenen', *Kritisk Forum for Praktisk Teologi*, 122: 7–21.
Loga, J. (1998) *Mellom erfaring og kategori: en studie av kirkeasylets aktualisering i Norge*, Report No. 67/99, Bergen: Institutt for Administrasjon og Organisasjonsvitenskap.
Mellomkirkelig råd (1998) *Kirkeasyl: erfaringer, dilemmaer og veien videre: Rapport fra et utvalg nedsatt av mellomkirkelig råd for den norske kirke*, Oslo: Den Norske Kirke.
Nordblom, T. and Demir, E. (2001) *Andrum i Ucklum*, Göteborg: Församlingsförlaget.
Pyykkönen, M. (2009) 'Deportation vs. Sanctuary: The Rationalities, Technologies, and Subjects of Finnish Sanctuary Practices', *Refuge*, 26(1): 20–32.
Svenska kyrkan (2008) *Vägledning för dig som arbetar med flykting-och invandringsfrågor i en församling i Svenska kyrkan*. Available at: http://www.svenskakyrkan.se/default.aspx?id=552755 (accessed 18 November 2011).
Torjussen, E. (2008) 'A Historical Perspective on Church Asylum', unpublished Master's thesis, University of Oslo.
Vetvik, E and Omland, T. (1997) *Kirkeerfaring med kirkeasyl*, KIFO-rapport Nr. 4/94, Trondheim: Tapir Forlag.
Weller, P. (1989) 'Sanctuary as Concealment and Exposure: The Practices of Sanctuary in Britain as Part of the Struggle for Refugee Rights', paper presented at The Refugee Crisis conference, Oxford, January.
Wicklin, M. (2005) 'Flyktinggömmarna', in D. Qviström (ed.) *Välgrundad fruktan*, Örebro: Bokförlaget Cordia AB.
Wiltfang, G.L. and McAdam, D. (1991) 'The Costs and Risks of Social Activism: A Study of Sanctuary Movement Activism', *Social Forces* 69(4): 987–1010.

Chapter 9

The rise and features of church asylum in Germany

'I will take refuge in the shadow of thy wings until the storms are past'[1]

Wolf-Dieter Just

Introduction: German asylum policies

'Persons persecuted on political grounds shall have the right of asylum.' This was the wording of the old Article 16 of the German Basic Law from 1949,[2] a generous unconditional rule. The constitutionally guaranteed right to asylum in Germany was the result of the painful experiences of the history of political persecution during the time of National Socialism. At that time some of the authors of the Basic Law had been refugees themselves and knew what it meant to be a refugee. Article 16 granted individuals the absolute entitlement to protection and thus the fundamental right to asylum. Therefore, the asylum legislation of the Federal Republic of Germany was one of the most extensive in Europe. Until the last third of the 1970s, this generous right was undisputed. However, the number of refugees coming to Germany was comparatively small then, according to the BAMF (Bundesamt für Migration und Flüchtlinge) (BAMF 2011: 11). Most came from East European countries. During the Cold War, they were seen as a living proof of the superiority of the Western liberal democratic system over the state socialism of the Eastern bloc (ibid.: 11).

This attitude changed, however, when in the late 1970s the number of applications for asylum increased and more and more refugees began arriving from Turkey and 'Third World' countries (e.g. Sri Lanka, Eritrea, Afghanistan) (Church Office of the Evangelical Church in Germany and the Secretariat of the German Bishop's Conference in co-operation with the Council of Christian Churches in Germany 1997: 18f). In 1980, for the first time, more than 100,000 refugees applied for asylum in Germany (BAMF 2011: 11). The German government reacted with several restrictions: visa obligations for most countries of origin, banning asylum-seekers from gaining employment, and lowering their living conditions (Kopp 2002: 27f). For a while, this had the desired effect: the conditions for asylum-seekers in Germany were 'sufficiently' deterrent, their numbers decreased (BAMF 2011: 11). A few years later, however, the numbers increased again (ibid.: 11) evoking a fierce discussion on Article 16 of German Basic Law. On the one hand, Christian Democrats wanted to delete the article from the Constitution, arguing it was too liberal and made it impossible to restrict the influx of asylum-seekers. Social Democrats and the Green Party, on the other hand, defended the article on humanitarian grounds, reminding the public of the obligations from German history (Herbert 2001: 298ff). This discussion escalated when, after the reunification of Germany and the collapse of the Eastern bloc, Germany received an unprecedented number of asylum applications: 256,000 in 1991 and then 438,000 in 1992 (BAMF 2011: 11). Most of the asylum applicants arrived from the former Soviet Union, East European countries and the Former Yugoslavia (Church Office of the Evangelical Church in Germany and the Secretariat of the German Bishop's Conference in co-operation with the Council of Christian Churches in Germany 1997: 19). There was a growing hostility toward foreigners, particularly asylum-seekers, among the German population that culminated in violence in certain places: night-time arson attacks on housing facilities of asylum-seekers and foreigners harrassed on the streets (ibid.: 10).

The German government responded with massive restrictions on the asylum law and an amendment of the Constitution. This reform of 1993 is popularly known as the 'asylum compromise'.[3] Article 16 was replaced by Article 16a. The new article formally upholds the right of asylum, but circumscribes it, however, significantly by safe-third-country and safe-country-of-origin regulations. The safe-third-country policy requires that an asylum-seeker passing through a 'safe third country' before arriving in Germany should be denied asylum and sent back to the first safe country. Safe third countries include all EU Member States, Norway, and Switzerland. As Germany is surrounded by states deemed 'safe', in theory, no person entering Germany by land has the right to asylum (Kopp 2002: 35). The safe-country-of-origin policy instructs German authorities to reject any application from an asylum-seeker from a country listed as 'safe', or where the German government does not find a risk of persecution (ibid.: 35).

Due to this amendment, the constitutional entitlement to asylum has become almost meaningless.[4] Consequently, after 1993, the number of asylum applications began to decline rapidly. In 1994, the number of applications dropped to less than 130,000; in 2000 to 77,000; in 2007 to 19,000. In recent years numbers have increased but only slightly (BAMF 2011: 11).

In the past two decades asylum policies have become more and more Europeanized. The need to 'harmonize' national asylum policies in the EU arose due to the lifting of internal border controls between most EU Member States through the Schengen Free Travel Accord (1985) (Kopp 2002: 51f; see also Walters 2002). So far, this harmonization has involved a number of legal instruments covering issues such as which Member State is responsible for hearing an asylum claim (according to the 'one state only principle'), the procedures to be used in reviewing the asylum claim, and the living conditions of asylum-seekers pending a decision (Kopp 2002: 51ff).

The Common European Asylum System (European Commission Home Affairs 2011) has not eliminated differences in the way Member States treat asylum-seekers and refugees. Member States are united, however, in their determination to defend the EU against unwanted immigrants and refugees. The continent has been turned into a 'fortress'. In 2004, a European Union agency for external border security was founded: Frontex,[5] equipped with about 113 vessels, 26 helicopters, 22 fixed-wing aircrafts and modern surveillance and detection technologies to combat 'illegal' immigration (Leonard 2011: 16). It is responsible for coordinating the activities of the national border guards to ensure the security of the EU's borders with non-Member States. It has been widely criticized by NGOs and the European Church Asylum Movement since its operations block asylum-seekers from claiming protection under the 1951 Refugee Convention:

> The militarizing of Europe's outer borders, the practically unfulfillable [sic] conditions for legal entry and repulsive living conditions for immigrants continue to be a system abhorrent toward refugees. The attempt to find protection in our countries has cost the lives of thousands. In our society, however, reports on refugees drowning in the Mediterranean, suffocating in containers, or taking their own lives in deportation centers are met by what Hanna Arendt called 'the curse of indifference'.
>
> (GECCA 2010b)

How did the German church asylum movement come about? A brief history[6]

It is against this background that the German church asylum movement came into being. It began in November 1983. The Protestant parish of Heiligkreuz (Holy Cross) in Berlin took in three Palestinian families facing deportation to Lebanon, which was experiencing a civil war. This was the first church asylum incident to occur in Germany. The action was successful – at the end the families were permitted to stay in Germany (Just 1993: 111).

Parishes in other parts of Germany followed this example. One spectacular case occurred in a church in Hamburg in 1984. The parish was trying to protect Susan Alviola, the wife of a Philippine sailor, and her two children from deportation – without success. The woman was violently arrested and removed from the church by sixty policemen (Ginsbttrg 1984). That same evening the family was deported to Manila. This action of the police and the local government outraged the public and became known throughout the country (ibid.). Due to numerous protests, some by prominent figures, violent breaking of a church asylum became a rare exception. This type of state reaction is still widely seen as 'disproportionate' (GECCA 2007).

Since the end of the 1980s, the number of church asylum cases has increased in Germany, due to growing numbers of refugees and the restrictions on the basic right of asylum. The first church asylum networks were built at local and regional levels. In February 1994, the 150 participants of a nation-wide church asylum conference in the Evangelische Akademie Mülheim an der Ruhr decided to found the 'German Ecumenical Committee on Church Asylum' (GECCA). The participants came from all regions of Germany, from Protestant and Catholic congregations, free churches and monasteries. They met under a verse from Psalm 57: 'In the shadow of thy wings I will take refuge'.

The German Ecumenical Committee on Church Asylum (GECCA)

The initiative came at the right time for asylum-seekers. As mentioned above, the right to asylum had been drastically reduced in 1993. NGOs involved in lobbying for refugees had experienced their strongest setback and were demoralized. In this situation the church asylum movement created new hope and energy, showing that refugee support groups were not powerless.

The new organization was intended as a network of committed individuals and parishes ready to provide church asylum. Its goal was to provide a platform for a continuous flow of information within the network and sharing of experiences; documentation of church asylum cases; legal and practical advice and mutual support; theological reflection; lobbying for support in churches and congregations; organization of seminars and training courses about church asylum; public relations and political protest against the restrictive German asylum policies. (Just and Sträter 2003: 146);

According to GECCA, church asylum is understood:

> as a form of temporary protection for refugees without legal residence status who would face unacceptable social hardship, torture or even death if forced to return to their country of origin. During church asylum, all relevant legal, social and humanitairian aspects are examined. In many cases it turns out that the authorities' decisions need to be revised, thus giving a new asylum procedure a chance of success.
>
> (GECCA 2007: 2)

Through GECCA's activities, sanctuary became a well-known faith-based form of action protecting refugees from deportation. Information was widely spread through a number of conferences, training courses and publications. One flyer gives answers to basic questions like: What is church asylum? Is church asylum likely to be successful? How long does church asylum take? What is expected from parishes? Does a parish need to do it all on its own? How is church asylum financed? Are there legal consequences for the parishes? Is church asylum made public? At the end some basic principles of church asylum were formulated, on which GECCA members agreed:

Basic principles of church asylum

- Parishes offering church asylum are committed to serving people who face danger of physical harm or to their freedom in case of a deportation or

for whom a deportation would entail unacceptable and inhuman social hardship.
- These parishes also fight for the right to human dignity, freedom and protection from physical harm laid down in the German Constitution.
- Parishes offering church asylum place themselves between refugees and the public authorities which have to carry out the deportation in order to gain time for further negotiations, for recourse to legal remedies, for a careful examination of the need for protection and for a fair asylum procedure. Parishes offering church asylum make their work public in most cases and never use violence. They do not claim exemption from German jurisdiction and the state can exercise its access right at any time in order to carry out the deportation. The parishes use publicity, mainly via the media, in order to protect refugees and to make their course of action transparent, explaining their goals and taking their fair share of responsibility.
- By making their work public, parishes offering church asylum show that their action in individual cases is also aimed at fairer asylum policies in general.
- 'Church asylum' is the last legitimate resort … for a parish in order to protect refugees for a limited time and to bring about a timely re-examination of their protection status as guaranteed by the state.

(GECCA 2007)

Due to GECCA's activities, sanctuary has since been reflected upon in many church groups and congregations. More and more parishes have granted sanctuary to refugees if there was reasonable doubt concerning their safe return. As a result of the courage of parishes providing asylum, thousands of refugees have already escaped deportation, possibly even torture or death (Just and Sträter 2003: 141ff; 164ff; GECCA 2008).

GECCA has a board and a steering committee with members from all regions of Germany, Protestant, Catholic, and free churches. It has Berlin offices with an executive secretary. Most work, however, is done by volunteers. The Committee is financed through fees paid by its members, donations and subsidies from Protestant and Catholic churches.

GECCA has regular contacts and exchanges with sanctuary movements and groups in Europe,[7] the USA and Canada. In 2008, a delegation from GECCA visited sanctuary groups in Arizona and North Mexico, to study their support work for migrants in the Sonora desert on the US–Mexican border. In 2009, a group from Tucson, Arizona, came for a return visit to Germany to study church asylum work in Germany. After this the US delegation continued to Malta and learned about the situation of refugees barred from entry at the external borders of the EU. In 2010, GECCA organized an international conference in Berlin called 'New Sanctuary Movement in Europe' (GECCA 2010a). The conference attracted participants from various European countries, the USA and Canada. At the end of the conference the *Charta of the New Sanctuary Movement in Europe* was adopted, with a number of pledges to help refugees in need (GECCA 2010b).

Creating an organizational structure for the German sanctuary movement has proved to be advantageous in many respects. Congregations considering granting sanctuary for refugees can access a network and an office for legal, theological and practical advice. They can also learn through this network and office about other congregations with similar sanctuary cases and draw on their experience. Moreover churches and congregations in Germany are challenged to define their position on current asylum policies and their social and ethical responsibility. It is for these reasons that church asylum cases are more common in Germany than in countries without a permanent organizational structure for sanctuary. Since the foundation of the nation-wide sanctuary network, there have been about sixty church asylum cases per year during the 1990s, and there are currently about thirty ongoing. About 75 per cent of all sanctuary cases result in preventing the deportation of the refugees concerned (Just and Sträter 2003: 141ff; 164ff; GECCA 2008).

The position of churches in Germany

The practice of asylum within the church was, and continues to be, controversial. As a result, sanctuary often leads to conflicts not only with public authorities, but also within churches. The sanctuary movement, however, has succeeded in convincing church officials of the ethical legitimacy and necessity of sanctuary. In their *Joint Statement Regarding the Challenges of Migration and Displacement*, Churches in Germany take a common stand on church asylum. They consider it legitimate in specific, single cases. Sanctuary has to be 'ultima ratio' – after the use of all legal means to prevent the violation of human rights and the threat to life in the country of return have failed:

> But with this the Churches neither claim an area for themselves outside the law nor do they deny the State the right to enforce its decisions, including within church buildings. According to their own understanding, it is the task of the Church to get involved in advocacy where rights of persons are violated and where there is a duty to stand besides persons under pressure. The practice of so-called 'Kirchenasyl' (sanctuary) is among other things a question to politics as to whether the laws concerning foreigners and asylum seekers protect people who have come to us individually, and preserve them from persecution, torture and even death. Congregations which take a stand for the realisation of these human and basic rights therefore do not question the State under the rule of law but make a contribution to the preservation of legal peace and the basic values of our society. For their stand for ethical principles which belong to the foundations of our faith, generally they deserve support and recognition.
> (Church Office of the Evangelical Church in Germany and the Secretariat of the German Bishop's Conference in co-operation with the Council of Christian Churches in Germany 1997: 75)

Conflicts with state authorities and how sanctuary practices are legitimized

Nevertheless sanctuary is a breach of law in the eyes of its opponents. In a number of cases, the clergy and members of church boards responsible for providing church asylum had been charged with 'supporting illegal stay of foreigners' (Morgenstern 2003: 189). In most cases they have been formally acquitted of such charges, but some have faced fines. In one particular case, a priest was harshly fined 4000 German Marks (ibid.: 189). Whether granting of church asylum is a punishable act under Section 96 of the Residence Act[8] is still disputed among politicians and jurists (Müller 1999: 191ff). Perhaps at some point the German Federal High Court will clarify this issue. For the time being, however, the GECCA has tried to avoid litigating this issue, due to worries that a negative ruling would be detrimental to its work.

The debate over whether sanctuary is a breach of the law, is best understood less as a legal matter and more as a political question. The sanctuary movement argues that it is not aiming to question the rule of law but rather to defend it. They see themselves as legitimized not merely by reference to Christian ethics, because they recognize that such arguments do not suffice in political discussions, debates within the wider society, and conversations with government departments and judicial courts. They see their practices as legitimized by the highest norm of the German Constitution: the respect for human dignity as a duty of all governmental authorities.[9] Moreover, they note that the Constitution commits the German people to human rights that 'shall bind the legislature, the executive, and the judiciary as directly applicable law' (Article 1.3).

In the case of deportation where people's dignity and human rights are at risk and their person, life, freedom and security are threatened, it is the churches' position that such people are constitutionally entitled to protection. If the state fails to offer such protection, others must step into help. As the former Protestant Bishop of Berlin, Wolfgang Huber, explained, sanctuary is 'subsidiärer Menschenrechtsschutz' (a human rights protection subsidiary) that comes into play when the state does not fulfil its duties (Huber 2003). In addition to Article 1 of the German Basic Law, the church asylum movement can also call upon Article 4: the freedom of conscience and freedom of religion. There is a Christian obligation to lend assistance to people in need, which is one of the driving forces behind church asylum. No legal rule can undo the fact that a Christian conscience is bound so strongly by the Word of God that it may come into conflict with the actions of the state. The right to freedom of conscience and religion requires the state to refrain, wherever possible, from limiting such conscience-based actions.

Opponents of sanctuary counter this argument by explaining that deportation of people who could be in danger of bodily harm, loss of life and freedom, torture, inhumane or degrading treatment or punishment is forbidden by the UN

Convention Relating to the Status of Refugees (Geneva Convention) and to the European Convention of Human Rights. As a result, these opponents contend that church groups are wrong to say that sanctuary is needed to provide a human rights protection subsidiary.

If it was the case that deportation practices always followed this international law, then perhaps sanctuary would not be needed. But the reality is very different. Sanctuary remains necessary for the following reasons.

First, the latest 2010 Amnesty International Report included stories of deportations from Germany into detention and torture, e.g. in Syria (Amnesty International 2010: 142). Two Eritrean deserters suffered harrowing conditions when they were deported from Germany in September 2010. Moreover the Romani, who are currently deported in large numbers from France and Germany to Kosovo and Romania, await massive discrimination in the job and housing markets, in the educational system and in health care (Knaus 2011). These examples show how church asylum remains necessary. Second, no government agency and no court is immune from fatal mistakes or overstepping boundaries where their power is applied. In our context, these mistakes mean, for example, that grave errors of judgment by institutions can happen even in well-designed asylum processes. Sanctuary movement communities are, as a rule, better informed about the dangers posed by potential deportation, because these communities take much more time to speak with the person concerned, build trust and learn why they fled. As a matter of fact, quite often hearings of the federal office are of a miserable quality. GECCA studies examining sanctuary success and failure demonstrate how problematic the procedure for granting the right of asylum often is. The re-examination of individual cases showed how refugees' reasons for seeking asylum or the potential persecution resulting from deportation do exist, which were initially overlooked in the governmental procedure for granting the right of asylum (Just and Sträter 2003: 164ff; GECCA 2008).

Sanctuary is also necessary due to the Dublin II Regulations of the EU. About a third of all asylum-seekers in Germany are subject to this regulation, which determines the EU Member State responsible to examine an application for asylum lodged in one of the member states by a third country national. The goal is to avoid so-called 'asylum shopping' – a term coined by the Federal Office for Migration and Refugees.[10] Only one EU Member State is responsible for the asylum procedure. As a rule, it is the EU Member State that allowed the entry, or specifically, did not *prevent* entry of the asylum-seeker in question. The regulation largely affects the states with EU external borders – particularly those to the south and the east. Asylum-seekers who flee to another EU country can be transferred back to the country of the original point of entry. This has two precarious consequences: each EU state seeks to rid itself of as many refugees as possible to other Member States. The majority of refugees arrive in states on the south and east borders of the EU. These states are overwhelmed by refugee applications. Furthermore, according to the Dublin II Regulation, the majority of refugees from EU states are transferred back to those countries. The majority of Dublin II refugees in Germany, for example, are transferred back to Poland and Italy (BAMF 2011: 43). States at the external borders try to prevent the entry of refugees into the EU through particularly harsh tactics. At least 17,738 people have died since 1988 along the European borders, according to Fortress Europe (Fortress Europe 2011). Working with the EU border security, Frontex, states fend off refugees by preventing the initiation of the asylum and by ensuring their living conditions are poor. Refugees in Greece and Italy, for example, do not receive a procedure for granting the right to asylum even close to European standards. The European Court on Human Rights has found this with respect to Greece. According to the Court, the detention conditions and living conditions for asylum-seekers transferred under the Dublin II system are 'inhuman and degrading' – violating Articles 3 and 13 of the European Convention on Human Rights.[11]

Recently transfers normally ruled under the Dublin II Regulation have been prevented through sanctuary. This is made easier by the fact that according to the regulation, these transfers must occur within a six-month period. Afterwards the reponsibility of the procedure for granting the right to asylum is given to the state in which the refugee currently is residing. With the help of sanctuary, it has been repeatedly successful to bridge this six-month period and to prevent a transfer.

What impact does church asylum have on congregations?

The experiences of congregations granting church asylum are various. In some cases controversies and conflicts arose within the congregation – especially when the decision to grant sanctuary was not unanimous. In other cases there have been violent attacks on church buildings by right-wing extremists.

In most cases, however, the experience is positive. Members of congregations typically join together in common action, which strengthens their cohesion. Their Christian faith is given a practical expression, the life in the congregation is activated and there are some important learning processes that occur.

First of all, congregations learn from direct encounters with refugees. They get to know them not as anonymous 'floods' or asylum swindlers threatening German society, but as human beings with an individual face. Members of the parish listen to their stories, learn about the cruel fate in their home countries, the dramatic experiences during the flight, the restrictive life conditions in Germany, their fears of being deported back. This human encounter provokes feelings of profound compassion and the desire to help.

Congregations learn about the reasons for flight, and the political situation in countries of origin. They start to gain as much information as possible about the respective country of origin in order to explain and justify *vis-à-vis* the public and the authorities, why they grant sanctuary and why these refugees need protection. In some cases members of sanctuary congregations have even travelled to the respective country in order to gain first-hand information about the dangers refugees are facing in case of deportation.

Congregations also learn about the German and European asylum laws and policies. They learn how narrowly 'political persecution' is defined by state officials, how restrictive the criteria for recognition are, how humiliating the living conditions for refugees in Germany are – bad accommodation, restrictions on movements, welfare not in cash but in kind[12] transfers. Through these experiences many members of the congregations become critical of German asylum policies and laws and some get politically involved.

Members of the congregation discover in a new way the relevance of their Christian faith for daily life in the society. Reading the Bible they discover that it is full of stories about migrants and refugees.[13] In the large Codes of Law of the Hebrew Bible the protection of the 'stranger' is granted an essential spot: 'You shall not wrong an alien, or be hard upon him; you were yourselves aliens in Egypt' (Exodus 22, 21). 'When an alien settles with you in your land, you shall not oppress him. He shall be treated as a native born among you, and you shall love him as a man like yourself, because you were aliens in Egypt' (Leviticus 19:33–4).

Congregations may also learn how challenging the commandment to love your neighbour may become. They understand what it means, that God became man, identifying himself with those who are hungry, thirsty, strangers, naked, sick and in prison. 'I tell you this: anything you did for one of my brothers here, however humble, you did it for me' (Matthew 25:40). Thus, in times of sanctuary, the spiritual life of the congregation gains a new quality. Worship services get new meaning and relevance due to Bible readings, the stories of the refugees, the prayers for them and the appeals for help. The close link between faith and action becomes clear and challenging.

Conclusion

In quantitative terms, sanctuary in Germany is insignificant. Between 2001 and 2007, for example, 299 cases of church asylum were documented (GECCA 2008: 8) – although hugely significant for the refugees concerned, this is just a drop in the ocean compared with the number of those deported from Germany,[14] or even the many thousands who have died at the external borders of Europe. Yet the symbolic value of church asylum is high. Most cases of sanctuary draw a lot of public attention and stimulate many discussions and controversies about asylum policies and the conflict between the legality and legitimacy of sanctuary practices. In many cases both the media and the public have reacted with understanding and respect[15] – probably one reason for the high rates of success (Just and Sträter 2003: 148ff; GECCA 2008).

As long as German and European asylum policies continue to be insufficient to protect asylum-seekers from unacceptable social hardship, torture or even death, there will be congregations in Germany that grant sanctuary. They feel obliged by their Christian conscience and see sanctuary as the last chance to resist injustice. They are encouraged by the fact that in most cases church asylum is successful and the authorities' decision needs to be revised. They are not aiming to question the rule of law but rather to defend it – referring to the inviolable character of human dignity and human rights. In doing so, they bear concrete witness to the Christian commitment to people in distress and contribute to the preservation of legal peace and the basic values of German society.

Notes

1 Psalm 57:1.
2 The Basic Law is the Constitution of the Federal Republic of Germany.
3 It is called a 'compromise' because support from the opposition in parliament was needed for the amendment of the Constitution (a two-thirds majority is required). After difficult negotiations, a compromise with the Social Democrats was achieved.
4 Now the Geneva Refugee Convention, to which all EU countries have subscribed, has more relevance for refugee protection.
5 Frontex means the 'European Agency for the Management of Operational Cooperation at the External Borders of the Member States of the European Union'.
6 Cf. Just and Sträter (2003: 141–63) and Mittermaier (2009).
7 Contact and exchange occur especially with groups and movements in Scandinavian countries, the Netherlands, Belgium, France, Switzerland and Austria.
8 According to Section 96 of the German Residence Act, it is punishable with a prison sentence up to 5 years, if a person assists a foreigner in entering German territory illegally or supports their illegal stay. In practice, this pertains foremost to smuggling foreigners into German territory. A new administrative rule exempts those who provide social assistance or medical aid to undocumented migrants (Allgemeine Verwaltungsvorschrift zum Aufenthaltsgesetz vom 18 September 2009). But what about people involved in church asylum? This is unclear. Most judges, however, have refrained from punishing church asylum providers, because according to Article 4,1 of the German Basic Law, the 'Freedom of faith and of conscience … shall be inviolable' (Müller 1999: 202).
9 Article 1 of the German Basic Law:

> (1) Human dignity shall be inviolable. To respect and protect it shall be the duty of all state authority. (2) The German people therefore acknowledge inviolable and inalienable human rights as the basis of every community, of peace and of justice in the world. (3) The following basic rights shall bind the legislature, the executive, and the judiciary as directly applicable law.

10 The term shows the disrespect and belittlement of the experience of those who often have fled brutal violence and anguish.
11 The case concerned the expulsion of an asylum-seeker to Greece by the Belgian authorities in application of the Dublin II Regulation (European Court on Human Rights 2011).
12 According to Section 3 of the Asylbewerberleistungsgesetz (law governing Benefits of Asylum-Seekers), benefits should usually be granted in kind.
13 Almost all important figures in the Bible have at some times been migrants or refugees: Abraham, Jacob, Joseph and his brothers, Moses, Ruth, King David, Elijah, Jeremiah, Jesus, and Paul.

14 In 1994, sixty refugees were protected through sanctuary in Germany, while 35,000 were deported! (Just and Sträter 2003: 150).
15 Cf. Morgenstern's evaluation of opinion polls on sanctuary (Morgenstern 2003: 242f).

References

Amnesty International (2010) *Amnesty International Report 2010: Zur weltweiten Lage der Menschenrechte*, Frankfurt: Fischer Verlag.
BAMF (2011) *Das Bundesamt in Zahlen*, Nürnberg: author.
Church Office of the Evangelical Church in Germany and the Secretariat of the German Bishop's Conference in Co-operation with the Council of Christian Churches in Germany (eds) (1997) '… *And the Stranger, Who Is at Your Door*', Bonn: author.
European Commission Home Affairs (2011) *Asylum: Building a Common Area of Protection and Solidarity*. Available at: http://ec.europa.eu/home-affairs/policies/asylum/asylum_intro_en.htm (accessed 22 October 2011).
European Court on Human Rights (2011) *Factsheet 'Dublin Cases'*. Available at: http://www.echr.coe.int/NR/rdonlyres/26C5B519-9186-47C1-AB9B-F16299924AE4/0/FICHES_Affaires_Dublin_EN.pdf (accessed 27 December 2011).
Fortress Europe (2011) *Fortress Europe*. Available at: http://fortresseurope.blogspot.com/2006/02/immigrants-dead-at-frontiers-of-europe_16.html (accessed 7 September 2011).
GECCA (2007) *Basic Information on Church Asylum*, Berlin: GECCA. Available at: http://www.kirchenasyl.de/6_publikation/6-1_unsere/download/kurzinfo_englisch.pdf (accessed 29 August 2011).
——(2008) *'Sonst wär ich nicht mehr hier!' Eine empirische Untersuchung über Kirchenasyl und Gästewohnungen*, Berlin: GECCA.
——(ed.) (2010a) 'Documentation of the Conference: New Sanctuary Movement in Europe, 7–10 October, Berlin'. Available at: http://www.kirchenasyl.de/1_start/English/documentation-annual%20meeting2010.pdf (accessed 29 August 2011).
——(2010b) *Charta of the New Sanctuary Movement in Europe*, Berlin. Available at: http://www.kirchenasyl.de/1_start/Kasten%20Aktuelles/Charta-english.pdf (accessed 29 August 2011).
Ginsbttrg, H.J. (1984) 'Behörde ohne Gnade', *Die Zeit*, 30 November. Available at: http://www.zeit.de/1984/49/behoerde-ohne-gnade (accessed 30 December 2011).
Herbert, U. (2001) *Geschichte der Ausländerpolitik in Deutschland*, München: Beck.
Huber, W. (2003) 'Vorwort', in W.D. Just and B. Sträter (eds) *Kirchenasyl: Ein Handbuch*, Karlsruhe: von Loeper, pp. 7–13.
Just, W.D. (ed.) (1993) *Asyl von Unten. Kirchenasyl und ziviler Ungehorsamkeit: ein Ratgeber*, Reinbek: Rowohlt.
Just, W.D. and Sträter, B. (eds) (2003) *Kirchenasyl: Ein Handbuch*, Karlsruhe: von Loeper.
Knaus, V. (2011) *No Place to Call Home: Repatriation from Germany to Kosovo as Seen and Experienced by Roma, Ashkali and Egyptian Children*, UNICEF Kosovo, Pristina. Available at: http://www.unicef.de/fileadmin/content_media/presse/110826-roma-studie/Roma-Studie-Englisch-2011.pdf (accessed 22 October 2011).
Kopp, K. (2002) *Asyl*, Hamburg: Europäische Verlagsanstalt.
Leonard, S. (2011) 'Frontex and the Securitization of Migrants through Practices', in Migration Working Group Seminar, European University Institute, Florence, 9 February. Available at: http://www.eui.eu/Documents/RSCAS/Research/MWG/201011/SLeonardspaper.pdf (accessed 22 October 2011).

Mittermaier, V. (2009) 'Refuge in Europe? Church Asylum as Human Rights Work in Fortress Europe', *Refuge*, 26(1): 68–70.
Morgenstern, M. (2003) *Kirchenasyl in der Bundesrepublik Deutschland*, Wiesbaden: VS-Verlag.
Müller, M.H. (1999) *Rechtsprobleme beim 'Kirchenasyl'*, Baden-Baden: Nomos.
Walters, W. (2002) 'Mapping Schengenland: Denaturalizing the Border', *Environment and Planning D: Society and Space*, 20(5): 561–80.

Chapter 10

Ethnography of relationships among church sanctuary actors in Germany

Hiroshi Oda

Introduction

> The hearing of the first eligibility officer was tough. He tried to find mistakes or faults in my wording. In another hearing by the second officer the interview was conducted in a relaxed atmosphere. He listened to me. He knew my pain.

I would like to begin this chapter with an account of the story of a refugee, Ahmed (a pseudonym), which was told to me during an interview we had together in 2003. I met him at his apartment. He was about 30 years old and gave the impression he was a bit of an introvert. His room was quite bare except for a few pieces of furniture. This was because he had just been granted asylum by the state and was liberated from church sanctuary which had lasted almost four years. In the quotation above, Ahmed compared the two eligibility officers who heard him: the first rejected him and the second recognized his application. What was the reason the first decision was overturned?

Listening to the stories of refugees plays an important part in asylum – whether it is state asylum or grass-roots sanctuary. Rolf Heinrich, a pastor who has been engaged in the church sanctuary or *Kirchenasyl*[1] movement in Germany, wrote that refugees are people with a unique story and unchangeable dignity; they are not 'cases'. Dealing with cases during an examination procedure does not recognize the person's individuality, their biography and dignity. Because true encounters are necessary for this recognition (Heinrich 1998: 31), he suggested that modalities of relationship with refugees in church sanctuary and bureaucratic asylum procedures differ from one another.

The aim of this chapter is to investigate what kind of relationship exists between church sanctuary's various actors. The methodology for this investigation is to introduce a unique story of a refugee and then gradually combine contextualization and theoretical considerations with it. At the expense of generalization, we can gain a heuristic perspective and an attitude to concretely understand the refugee's voice. This is an 'ethnography of the particular' (Abu-Lughod 1991) with a special emphasis on the narrative mode of presentation.

After a story of a Kurdish refugee is recounted, several theoretical themes are discussed: credibility, compassion, sovereignty and hospitality. First, I consider how credibility is differently constructed in various contexts of the state asylum procedures as well as grass-roots church sanctuary. Compassion for refugees is obvious among church sanctuary supporters. Several German supporters insisted they found elements of the refugee in themselves and therefore the relationship between them and refugees was fluid. This type of relationship between self and other was remarkable in my field research and strongly distinguished it from the interaction of immigration control and asylum procedures. Although compassion is ingrained in Article 16 of the German Basic Law, the rights of foreigners have been restricted by state sovereignty. As a result, a confrontation has emerged that has made grass-roots sanctuary for refugees necessary. In the final section of this chapter, I argue that church sanctuary is a manifestation of local communities' potential for hospitality.

The story of a refugee

I conducted my field research on the subject of church sanctuary in Germany mainly from 2002 to 2003. In March 2003, I visited the Federal Office for Recognition of Foreign Refugees (now the Federal Office for Migration and Refugees) in Nuremberg which has jurisdiction over asylum procedures in Germany. There were a few staff workers I met there who spoke quite negatively about church sanctuary, with comments like, 'I have never observed a successful case of church asylum [sanctuary] at all.' They indicated the reason for this sentiment was that 'only the Federal Office has information which is necessary to form an appropriate judgment on an application of asylum'. I felt a bit discouraged after hearing these negative comments, and thought my study might be meaningless.

About two weeks later, I visited an officer at a municipal immigration authority in the Ruhr district in North Rhine-Westphalia. He said, to my surprise, that church sanctuary 'is meaningful and that if new evidence of a persecution is to be found, it would give grounds to open-up a re-examination into problematic cases at the Federal Office'. He went on to mention a particular case in which an asylum application had once been denied and a deportation order was issued. While the refugee was protected in a church sanctuary, his follow-up application was eventually accepted. The refugee finally received a reversed judgment and became a 'person entitled to asylum' from the Federal Office.

I would like to reconstruct this drama on the basis of materials given by a non-governmental organization (NGO) supporting refugees with the refugee's permission.

This refugee, Ahmed, was born in a town in eastern Turkey. Under the influence of his brother he became a sympathizer of a Kurdish political party in the 1980s. He ran a grocery store and distributed political leaflets to party members. In the early 1990s he took part in a strike to protest at the killing of intellectuals and dissidents in Kurdistan. He was soon arrested and held in a police station. Over a two-month period he was detained and tortured. After his release he continued his political activities. During his short absence the police raided his grocery store. It was at this point, he decided to escape from the town to Istanbul. From there he reached Germany by land.

His application for asylum was filed immediately after he entered Germany. His first hearing at the Federal Office was conducted about one and a half years later. His application was denied and he was told to leave Germany voluntarily within one month or otherwise risk deportation to Turkey. He then filed an action in the administrative court. It took three and a half years for a verdict rejecting his action. He then felt he had no choice but to go underground.

Later he was arrested in Germany and sent to a detention centre to begin his deportation process. By this time, it was almost a full seven years since he had entered Germany. On the day he was about to be deported by air to Turkey, he managed to escape through a deportation bus window and he then fled into a church community and found shelter at a rotating church sanctuary.

Rotating church sanctuary (or *Wanderkirchenasyl*) is a special form of church sanctuary especially in the North Rhine-Westphalia area in which a group of Kurdish refugees move from church to church every several weeks (Ökumenische Bundesarbeitsgemeinschaft Asyl in der Kirche 2004). From January 1998 to 1999, 493 Kurdish asylum-seekers supported by the campaign 'No human being is illegal' (*Kein Mensch ist illegal*) travelled from one local church community to another protesting their demands to stop the deportation of Kurds to Turkey. This demand, however, was refused by local politicians in January 1999, which led to the failure of a group solution and the end of this special organized movement.

Soon after, single cases had to be laboriously re-examined again. Near the end of February 2004, 397 people received a stable residence status recognition. 39 people among them were entitled to full asylum based on Article 16a of the Basic Law. Ahmed was one of them. Ahmed moved between two church communities in a German city with other Kurdish refugees, finally settling in one community. In the beginning he was unable to leave the parish hall for fear of being arrested. To his good fortune, a pastor and some supporters negotiated with the municipal authority and the local police office, and soon he was allowed to move inside the administrative area in this German city.

During his time in church sanctuary, a social worker and Ahmed scrutinized his documents. They found that two digits of the date on his escape from his hometown to Istanbul had been transposed in the first hearing transcript. Hypothetically speaking, he left his hometown on 12/09 (September 12th), but in the transcript, the two digits, '2' and '9' had been transposed in an error (thus, 19/02=February 19th). This error suggested his escape from his hometown was earlier than the date of the police raid on his grocery store that had been the reason for his escape.

This small but tragic error had grave consequences for Ahmed. Because of it, the first eligibility officer ruled that the 'credibility of the entire statements of the applicant failed'. His supporters pleaded and asked the Federal Office to start a new asylum procedure for Ahmed. The second hearing was conducted eight years later. This second officer did not interrogate or question Ahmed about the exact dates, but simply added them as background information to his account on his political activities and torture.

What was different from the first hearing to the second is that the narrative on Ahmed's experience in prison, including torture, became very long and detailed. While in the first transcript there are only three lines, in the second, there are 73. The second officer asked Ahmed about these differences:

OFFICER: Why didn't you tell these experiences in prison during the first asylum procedure?
AHMED: At that time I was in a confused mental state. I am an introverted person. If I talked about this time in prison, I would be emotionally hurt. During the first procedure I couldn't come out of my shell.

His answer above suggests that the timing of a hearing and the psychological state of the applicant can influence a hearing (see also Cameron 2010). At the end of the second hearing, which was 155 minutes (the first hearing was only 75 minutes), Ahmed confesses his anguish and feelings. It is evident that his authentic voice heard here under excruciating circumstances points to a critical annotation of the German asylum system:

> I have a lot of thoughts within me. But it's not possible for me to express all these thoughts. What happened in Turkey and the life in illegality in Germany distressed me. I can say that I feel as if I have become a criminal. I cannot lead a normal life. I thought about taking my own life, and I made an attempt at suicide. I have no right to live in Turkey or in Germany. If I had no fear for my life in Turkey, I wouldn't have had to live illegally in Germany for three years. I had no economic problems in Turkey.

Two modes of credibility

Social construction of credibility

Ahmed's application was refused by the first officer for the reason that his statement was 'not credible'. The officer documented his decision: 'The applicant didn't make it credible to have been exposed to political persecution in Turkey and to fear the future on his return there.' But nine and a half years later, the second officer from the same governmental institution filed the opposite decision: 'The applicant made it quite credible that he had been exposed to a politically motivated persecution in Turkey.'

In the context of the German asylum procedure, an applicant is required to make a statement. It must be coherent and credible (*schlüssig und glaubhaft*). The verdict of 'credibility' is so crucial that the entire asylum procedure is decided upon it.

What was the difference between the two decisions concerning 'credibility'? No new evidence about persecution was submitted for the second application, other than the discovery of the transposed dates on his transcript, which made the second hearing possible.

The reason for the first officer's refusal was the temporal inconsistency in Ahmed's statement. Here chronological accuracy is the decisive criterion of credibility. On the one hand, according to Schmidt and Arslan (2002), the understanding of time is repeatedly referred to in assessing credibility in the German asylum procedure. Assigning such importance to time is deeply rooted in German culture:

> In Germany – perhaps more than in any other country – people structure their days, weeks, years, and indeed much of their whole life through the moments and units of time. Chronological reliability is seen as an essential factor for the shaping of trust and an extremely important factor for positive images, reliability, interest and credibility.
>
> (ibid.: 7)

On the other hand, 'the exact and coherent account of concrete moments ... in the chronological reconstruction of events is necessary when compiling a credibility verdict. However, for many refugees, it is impossible even from a cultural perspective' (ibid.: 8). This is due to a nonlinear concept of time predominant in the regions from where refugees flee (ibid.: 8). Nevertheless:

> in the German asylum procedure, judges and eligibility officers often demand an exact account of the chronological events and dates and then go on to draw their conclusion on the inaccuracy and inconsistency from statements made by the refugees. In most cases, conclusions drawn were deemed incredible.
>
> (ibid.: 8)

Schmidt and Arslan see 'culture' from an essentialist point of view. In fact, a chronological accuracy was overemphasized by the first officer as a criterion for the judgment of credibility.

Schmidt and Arslans' observations are valid for a formal context like the asylum procedures. There are, however, other aspects of temporality in the everyday German context, for example; circulating time (Christmas and birthdays are very important) and approximate time (a train could be often delayed). Also, eligibility officers are not necessarily 'programmed' with the linear and exact time concept. Such normative cultural elements could be absent in particular situations. The second officer had shown his agency and did not overemphasize the criterion of chronological accuracy.

The hearing of an asylum procedure is a complex interaction, where many factors are at work, including the applicant's psychological state, the competence of an interpreter, the attitude of an eligibility officer, the timing of the hearing, the domestic political–economic situation, and the diplomatic relationship between the country of origin and the country in which the applicant seeks asylum (see also Rehaag 2008).

The decision of credibility by the officer is influenced by these psycho-sociopolitical factors. Nevertheless, the hearing abides by the bureaucratic principles of accuracy and impersonal relations. Applicants are considered suspect and any errors or mistakes are counted against them. Such credibility assessments are inhuman and narrow-minded. Is there an alternative means of determining the credibility of asylum applicants?

Credibility in an intimate sphere

One pastor who protected Ahmed in sanctuary said:

> Kurdish refugees stayed for six weeks in our community. They came out of their anonymity and gave their names, showed their faces and shared their personal life stories with us. They knew that people would sympathize with them for what they had been through … The atmosphere made … it … possible for refugees to tell their stories. For example, a Kurdish woman shared her personal tragedy of being raped in Turkey with a German female supporter. Until then, she had kept it secret from her husband and other refugees and even from the German officers who had interviewed her.

With respect to 'credibility', this pastor commented:

> If we know a refugee who wants to be protected in our community and is anxious about being deported to his/her home country, it is a good enough reason to follow up on a church sanctuary for a refugee. To begin with, we believe and trust a refugee's story at the risk of possibly being deceived later. It is not necessary for us to examine the credibility of a refugee's story. We only look into a refugee's story in detail and carefully check whether all legal procedures had been completed.

Another pastor from another region took a different stance on 'credibility'. His church community does not offer church sanctuary until they are convinced of credibility. In this community, church sanctuary for a Tamil family from Sri Lanka was examined. At first, they conducted a 'cross-fire interrogation'. Some contradictions were found, but the pastor and other church representatives were convinced that, overall, this refugee family's story was credible.

As part of the church sanctuary process in Germany, a supporter group is organized. Supporters would come forward, mainly from the specific church community concerned and work voluntarily. For rotating church sanctuary (*Wanderkirchenasyl*) in which the refugee Ahmed was protected, about 25 people belonged to such a group. They cared for the refugees' needs; they gave food and mattresses, collected donations, found lawyers as well as physicians who treated refugees at no cost. They took turns watching out for police officers, and simply communicated and listened to the refugees. Personal encounter and contact with the refugees provided supporters with a profound and concrete understanding of the refugees' suffering. They came to know refugees as real people with real human names and faces (these caring practices in Germany are remarkably similar to those documented in Canada by Lippert (2006), who characterizes them as 'pastoral').

Such relationships are termed the 'intimate sphere', which refers to a continual relationship mediated by the attention on the concrete other (Saito 2003: vi). Through the personal encounters and contacts in this sphere, the supporters and refugees formed credibility assessments different from the bureaucratic approach. They developed face-to-face relationships and listened attentively to each other. The interactive process allowed for deeper and often more accurate understandings of credibility.

Compassion and church sanctuary

Compassion: sensing the pain of others

Ahmed reported that the second eligibility officer sympathized with 'his pain'. Sensing pain, suffering and fear can be reduced to the simple word: 'compassion'. The compassion of church community members worked as a driving force behind church sanctuary practices. One supporter mentioned his family history and wartime experience as a reason for his engagement in church sanctuary; his father had come from Poland to the Ruhr district as a migrant and during the Second World War this supporter escaped air-raids with his mother. This memory provided him with incentives to participate in church sanctuary. Other elderly people in the same church community related their own experiences of fleeing, expulsion and difficulty in settling in the Ruhr district, when they discussed whether it was right to shelter refugees. In these cases, personal memories of suffering were recalled in encounters with refugees, and these memories strengthened their compassion for the refugees. There were other supporters who did not connect their actions with personal suffering, but instead with the Christian sense of obligation to help people in need.[2] Compassion could be assigned to a stable personal character ('she is a compassionate person'), but it can also refer to a dynamic phenomenon, especially if it depends on the image of others to whom a compassionate feeling is directed.

In the case of church sanctuary in this community, a direct encounter with refugees reduced negative stereotypes about 'illegal economic refugees' among community members, and provided them with a concrete understanding of the painful predicament of these refugees (see also Lippert (2006) on the Canadian context).

The concept of compassion has attracted attention in the field of peace education (Forges 1997); it begs the question: how can one understand or imagine the pain of victims of historical violence like the Holocaust or sex slavery during the Second World War? This question is connected to the theoretical problem of self–other relationships.

Fluid relationships among church sanctuary actors

During my study of church sanctuary in Germany, one of the most interesting theoretical discoveries is in a statement by supporters indicating that they were able to find elements of the refugee or the stranger in themselves.

To an outsider, two kinds of church sanctuary actors are clearly distinguished: namely German supporters and foreign refugees. However, from an internal point of view, the relationships between self and other are more fluid. Here are their statements:

> Through my experiences in church sanctuary, what I personally think very important is the discovery of a stranger in myself. I conduct church sanctuary not from the so-called 'neighbourly love', but from such recognition, as it is said in the Old Testament, 'Because you were strangers ... '.

These are the words of a pastor engaged in the rotating church sanctuary through which Ahmed had been once sheltered. He did not mention his personal experience during an interview with me, but emphasized that some supporters from his church community remembered their own experiences of flight and suffering through encounters with other foreign refugees and these memories motivated them to help refugees.

Another pastor from a different city who sheltered a Pakistani refugee family told me:

> The Bible is full of stories of refugees. A more important point is: We ourselves are a community of refugees. The origin of this community was religious refugees who fled here from the Rhineland, Holland, Switzerland and France in the seventeenth and eighteenth centuries because of their Protestant Reformed denomination, and economic refugees who came from Pfalz in the middle of the eighteenth century. From this history of our community, we have an obligation to help refugees. It is not trifling that we are just a community of refugees. The passage from Exodus in the Old Testament was transposed to our community—'because you were strangers in the land of Egypt'.

Along with the Judaeo-Christian tradition of being a refugee, she added to the character of her parish as a community of refugees and connected this to their involvement in church sanctuary.

In these narratives, the relationships between supporters and refugees are not asymmetrical, such as the strong shows the weak mercy (see also Millner, Chapter 4, and Darling and Squire, Chapter 13 in this volume). Rather, the supporters and refugees share their pain with each other. The German supporters feel the pain of foreign refugees as their own pain. In other words, the supporters participate and suffer with the refugees. The distinction between them is neither clear nor dichotomous, but is fluid and replaceable. This type of compassionate relationship between self and other is remarkable in German church sanctuary and strongly distinguished from the interaction of immigration control and asylum procedures. I next re-examine the genesis and peculiarity of state sovereignty from the window of church sanctuary.

Questioning sovereignty

Compassion in the German Basic Law

Sensitivity to others' pain is not merely an individual trait of an eligibility officer, nor only the attitude of church sanctuary supporters. Article 16 of the German Basic Law itself, on which the German asylum procedures are based, had been conceived to ensure compassionate sensitivity in cases. In this aspect, asylum as a legal institution and a grass-roots sanctuary movement are not opposed to each other, but instead have similar traits: 'Persons persecuted on political grounds shall have the right of asylum.' This provision was written in the second paragraph of Article 16 of the Basic Law of the Federal Republic of Germany, enacted in 1949.

The right of asylum in the constitutions of countries like France has been within the jurisdiction of state sovereignty. But in the German Basic Law, it is stipulated as a right of a foreign individual and the state has an obligation to grant asylum to them. In this respect, Article 16 is ground-breaking (Honma 1985: 18). Concerning individual asylum rights, a Copernican change from the right of the state to the right of an individual was accomplished in the German Basic Law. Behind this intrinsic change, there were many personal experiences of German politicians and jurists who designed and finally implemented the German Basic Law.

This was obviously evident in the history of the origins of the Basic Law for the Federal Republic of Germany. Friedrich Wilhelm Wagner (1894–1971), a member of the Parliamentary Council, sought asylum in France and in the US during the Nazi period. He recalled his and his colleagues' exile experiences during the Council in 1948: 'We were very lucky that we found accommodation abroad, and that thereby we escaped from Hitler and his henchmen' (Kreuzberg and Wahrendorf 1992: 52). From these experiences as refugees, he wanted to introduce the article on the right of asylum into the Basic Law of the new Germany. He defined this right as 'a right which is granted to a foreigner who cannot live any more in his own country' (ibid.: 50).

Another member of the Parliamentary Council, Carlo Schmid (1896–1979), argued that the practice of asylum should be essentially different from immigration control:

> To grant asylum is always a question of generosity. If one wants to be generous, one has to risk being mistaken about one person. This is another side of asylum and probably in this side there is also dignity of such an action.
>
> (ibid.: 44)

Several authors of the German Basic Law personally knew pain, misery and suffering as foreign refugees. A pioneering feature of Article 16 lies in this compassion for others and the willingness to restrict state sovereignty for the protection of refugees.

National order of things

Asylum comes from the ancient Greek word *asylos*, which means 'inviolable'. The Roman Empire permitted the right of asylum or sanctuary to the Christian Church by the emperor's edict in AD 399 (on the later medieval period, see Shoemaker, Chapter 1 in this volume). After the birth of the sovereign state in the seventeenth century and the development of nation-states, sanctuary granted by the Christian Church was restricted and abolished (Abe 1986: 320–1).

The sovereign nation-states then appropriated sanctuary or asylum as a political protection of a foreign refugee on the basis of the inviolability of their territory. As a result of the division of the land and the monopolization of political power in each territory by the sovereign states, a 'national order of things' has emerged (Malkki 1995). Classification through the national attributes is now influential and familiar in the modern world. People who deviate from this order of sovereign states, such as a displaced and stateless person, are seen as anomalies and placed in a state without human rights (Agamben 1998; see also Czajka, Chapter 3 in this volume).

In this historical context, the uniqueness of the asylum right in the German Basic Law becomes obvious. It was a challenge to restrict a state sovereignty in favour of the right of a foreign individual. In reality, this ideal has been restricted as immigration control has been enhanced. In 1983, the first church sanctuary in Germany was conducted (see Just, Chapter 9 in this volume) and this German version of the sanctuary movement spread not only nationwide but also into neighbouring countries. After this, two sorts of asylum (state asylum and church asylum, namely sanctuary) co-existed in Germany. The major dilemma of state asylum is that it had to operate on conflicts between the protection of human rights and immigration control, as well as between state sovereignty and the right of the individual. These two asylums are a manifestation of the conflict between the state sovereignty and human rights. But if we return to the origin of the Article 16 of the German Basic Law, these two asylums share the same feeling of compassion for foreign refugees and there is no fundamental difference between them.

From this real conflict, however, 'refugees threatened with deportation' or 'refugees not recognized as refugees' can appear. They are liminal entities, as Turner described, that: 'are neither here nor there; they are betwixt and between the positions assigned and arrayed by law' (Turner, 1969: 95). In this phase, a church sanctuary seeks to bring such liminal entities back to a position assigned by law, namely legal resident status. Church sanctuary itself is a liminal space that local actors open amid the national order of things by exercising their agency (de Certeau 2002).

From church sanctuary to hospitality

Hospitality in human history

In this final section, I would like to briefly consider what implications can be drawn from my field research. Church sanctuary or the sanctuary movement is a relatively marginal phenomenon in the contemporary world. Sanctuary is a special form of hospitality. Several scholars have pointed out the close relations between hospitality and sanctuary (Henssler 1954; see also Darling and Squire, Chapter 13 in this volume). A peculiarity of contemporary sanctuary is related to the characteristics of a guest; a fugitive is received.

Entertaining and protecting strangers, namely hospitality, have been universal customs in human history. In his pioneering work, Morgan (1881) reported on the law of hospitality and its general practice among Native Americans. Quoting a Moravian missionary, Heckwelder, Morgan described the cosmological background of hospitality practised by them:

> [The Great Spirit] made the earth and all that it contains for the common good of mankind ... Everything was given in common to the sons of men ... Everyone is entitled to his share. From this principle, hospitality flows as from its source ... They give and are hospitable to all, without exception, and will always share with each other and often with the stranger, even to their last morsel.
>
> (Heckwelder, cited in Morgan 1881: 49)

In this spiritual world-view, everything is originally given by the Deity, and does not belong to a particular person. Hospitality is the act of sharing these things with strangers.

In Western Kenya in Africa, there was a unique system of hospitality '*abamenya*' (Wagner 1970; Matsuda 1999). This Maragoli word refers to a vagabond or a stranger. Communities in this region used to accept *abamenya* as a village member. Community members could leave their village and be easily accepted in another one. Such open human mobility was a normal state in this area. There was no solid distinction among 'ethnic groups' or 'tribes'.

Abamenya had served as a local peace resource. Anthropologist Matsuda evaluates its relevance as follows: 'This is a wisdom of African society made to avoid a total ethnic conflict' (Matsuda 1999: 100). In fluid relationships, people were not fixed to any monolithic identity. Therefore conflict between them did not develop into a total war, like the First and Second World Wars. In other words, *abamenya* can be regarded as a local deterrent against war. The British colonial government prohibited this local custom of *abamenya* and introduced a resident registration system for gathering taxes and labour forces as well as indirect rule. As a result, a fixed unit of people, or so-called 'tribe', was politically invented.

From an anthropological perspective on hospitality, how contemporary sanctuary is marginalized and how people have been deprived of the right to hospitality by a sovereign state or colonial government become visible. There is a parallel relationship between the prohibition of the non-state sanctuary in modern Europe by the sovereign state and the prohibition of the local customs of hospitality in African society by the European colonial governments. Through these restrictions of human mobility, a national and colonial order of things has emerged. In this historical context, the contemporary sanctuary is seen as a movement to call state sovereignty over human mobility into question and to restore a certain level of the right of hospitality to the local community.

The potential of the local community

We shall return to the story of church sanctuary for Ahmed. Local community members found an error in his hearing transcript and made the re-examination of his case possible. They supported Ahmed and other refugees over a long period in face-to-face relationships (see also Lippert 2006: 96–8). Official asylum procedures can never provide such intimate and personal protection because of impersonal relations associated with the bureaucracy.

Church sanctuary asks the question, what kind of protection should be offered to refugees? Like the discussion about credibility, two types of protection emerge: institutional protection based on the legal system and personal protection that goes on in human relationships. We anthropologists know how important it is to have face-to-face relationships with local people, which are often developed through personal introductions. This is, of course, not only practical for successful field research but also for one's personal security. Such relational protection cannot be replaced by official permission.

Foreign refugees live in a local community in a host country. The local people can become acquainted with refugees and from these relationships can offer substantial human protection to refugees. Church sanctuary is a salient example of this. Compassionate hospitality (Oda 2006) by the local community does not always conflict with the state system. Rather, it can help actualize the ideal of the German Basic Law or the Universal Declaration of Human Rights.

Conclusion

Starting from the story of a refugee, we have reflected on what played the decisive role in his entitlement to asylum. Compassion from the face-to-face encounter and fluid relationships in church sanctuary is important. In the course of our consideration, we called the state sovereignty over human mobility in question and recognized the universality of hospitality in human history.

Jacques Derrida (1997) criticized the tendency to punish people who help foreign refugees for 'the guilt of hospitality'. Immigration control by the state authority is absolute. A private person and a local community possess no right of hospitality for a 'foreigner' against the decision of the state. But is no *abamenya* system possible in our contemporary world?

The story of Ahmed showed the limitations of state asylum procedures and the capabilities of the local communities to accept and protect foreign refugees. Without the engagement by these community members, many refugees have been deported and exposed to risk. Church sanctuary by the local actors cannot be replaced by state asylum. There are unique features in church sanctuary, like credibility construction in the intimate sphere, compassion and fluid relationships between self and others. These features are rooted in the old and universal culture of hospitality. For this reason, church sanctuary and the sanctuary movement provide us with valuable clues to reconsider the relationships between the local and the national and to envision a future global human society beyond the conventional national order of things.

Acknowledgements

I am extremely grateful to all those who cooperated in my field research in Germany. This research was supported by the Grant-in-Aid for Scientific Research of the Ministry of Education, Culture, Sports, Science and Technology, Japan, in 2002 and 2003 (Encouragement of Young Scientists (B)). I am indebted to Mr Geoffrey Thompson in Sapporo for editing the English draft. Responsibility for the text rests entirely with me.

Notes

1 *Kirchenasyl* is the German version of church sanctuary. In contemporary Germany, it means temporary protection of a foreign refugee from physical danger resulting from deportation by a church community.
2 However, I also met some community members who were against church sanctuary because they believed in the German legal system's infallibility.

References

Abe, K. (1986) 'Asyl no Shiso' [On the Thought of Asylum], in *Chusei no Hoshi no Shitade [Under the Stars of the Middle Ages]*, Tokyo: Chikuma-Shobo, pp. 315–22.

Abu-Lughod, L. (1991) 'Writing against Culture', in R.G. Fox (ed.) *Recapturing Anthropology: Working in the Present*, Santa Fe, NM: School of American Research Press, pp. 137–62.

Agamben, G. (1998) *Homo Sacer: Sovereign Power and Bare Life*, Palo Alto, CA: Stanford University Press.

Cameron, H.E. (2010) 'Refugee Status Determinations and the Limits of Memory', *International Journal of Refugee Law*, 22(4): 469–511.

De Certeau, M. (2002) *The Practice of Everyday Life*, Berkeley, CA: University of California Press.

Derrida, J. (1997) *Cosmopolites de tous les pays, encore un effort!* Paris: Editions Galilée.

Forges, J. (1997) *Éduquer contre Auschwitz: Histoire et mémoire*, Paris: Editions Sociales Françaises.

Heinrich, R. (1998) 'Kirchenasyl als politische Aktion? Sozialethische Reflexionen und Schlussfolgerungen', in *Wanderkirchenasyl für ein Bleiberecht kurdischer Flüchtlinge aus der Türkei*, Köln: Ökumenisches Netzwerk Asyl in der Kirche in NRW e.V., pp. 25–34.

Henssler, O. (1954) *Formen des Asylrechts und ihre Verbreitung bei den Germanen*, Frankfurt am Main: Vittorio Klostermann.

Honma, H. (1985) *Kojin no Kihonken toshiteno Higoken [Right of Asylum as a Basic Right of an Individual]*, Tokyo: Keiso-Shobo.

Kreuzberg, H. and Wahrendorf, V. (1992) *Grundrecht auf Asyl: Materialien zur Entstehungsgeschichte*, 2nd rev. edn, Hamburg: Heymann.

Lippert, R.K. (2006) *Sanctuary, Sovereignty, Sacrifice: Canadian Sanctuary Incidents, Power and Law*, Vancouver: UBC Press.

Malkki, L.H. (1995) 'Refugees and Exile: From "Refugee Studies" to the National Order of Things', *Annual Review of Anthropology*, 24: 495–523.

Matsuda, M. (1999) *Teikou Suru Toshi [Anthropology of Resistance]*, Tokyo: Iwanami-Shoten.

Morgan, L.H. (1881) *Houses and House-Life of the American Aborigines*, Washington, DC: Government Printing Office.

Oda, H. (2006) '"Because We Are a Community of Refugees": An Ethnographic Study on Church Asylum in Germany', *Journal of Graduate School of Letters* (Hokkaido University) 1: 17–29. Available at: http://eprints.lib.hokudai.ac.jp/dspace/bitstream/2115/5760/1/1–2_ODA.pdf (accessed 21 December 2011).

Ökumenische Bundesarbeitsgemeinschaft Asyl in der Kirche (ed.) (2004) *Asyl in der Kirche: Eine Dokumentation*, Karlsruhe: Von Loeper Literaturverlag.

Rehaag, S. (2008) 'Troubling Patterns in Canadian Refugee Adjudication', *Ottawa Law Review*, 39: 335–65.

Saito, J. (ed.) (2003) *Shinmitsuken no Politics [Politics of the Intimate Sphere]*, Kyoto: Nakanishiya-Shuppan.

Schmidt, M. and Arslan, E. (2002) 'Glaubwürdigkeit in der interkulturellen Kommunikationssituation des Asylverfahrens', *ASYLMAGAZIN*, October: 5–9. Available at: http://www.asyl.net/fileadmin/user_upload/beitraege_asylmagazin/AM2002-10-05-Schmidt-Arslan.pdf (accessed 21 December 2011).

Turner, V. (1969) *The Ritual Process: Structure and Anti-Structure*, Chicago: Aldine.

Wagner, G. (1970) *The Bantu of Western Kenya*, Oxford: Oxford University Press.

Chapter 11

The emergence of the Ontario Sanctuary Coalition

From humanitarian and compassionate review to civil initiative

Hilary Cunningham

Between 1990 and 1997, I conducted intensive research as an anthropologist with the Sanctuary Movement based in Tucson, Arizona. A good deal of my time was spent focusing on the activities of the refugee-transporting wing of the movement – otherwise known as the sanctuary 'underground railroad'. This had been established in the early 1980s to assist fugitives fleeing violent civil wars in Central America and to provide them with 'safe houses' in the United States or safe passage to Canada. The research was not without its challenging and in some cases hair-raising moments – the railroad had to constantly evade the attention of US Border Patrol officers as well as their Mexican counterparts, and as my research progressed, the border itself became increasingly militarized and violent. This research resulted in an ethnography exploring the U.S. Sanctuary Movement (Cunningham 1995) and shortly after its publication, the activities of the Tucson underground began to significantly wane.

Following my work in the United States, I received a research grant to explore sanctuary activities in Canada. In 1997 I moved with my family to Toronto, Ontario, and several weeks later, I once again found myself in a church basement – this time attending the weekly meetings of the Ontario Sanctuary Coalition. I was there at the invitation of Romero House – a registered charity and community of four homes in Toronto, founded in 1992 by Sister Mary Jo Leddy, which provided housing as well as legal and social services to refugee claimants in Canada.

Romero House was named after Archbishop Oscar Romero – a prelate and an outspoken critic of political violence and oppression in El Salvador who was assassinated by the members of the ruling military junta in 1980. As it turned out, Romero was a figure I was well acquainted with – the first church to declare Sanctuary for Central Americans in the United States (the very church where I conducted my original research on the underground railroad) declared itself a sanctuary on the anniversary of Romero's murder, March 25.

Romero House received government funding to provide housing and other services to those seeking refugee protection in Canada and awaiting their hearings. The organization was staffed largely by volunteers and was deliberately built on the model of a 'community'. Each of the four Romero homes housed approximately 10–15 refugee claimants, and volunteers lived in the houses (i.e., 'in community') along with the families. Through this arrangement, Romero House underscored the importance of an intimate and daily exchange of experiences among refugees and volunteers, exemplifying Romero House's desire for Canada to put a 'face' on refugee issues.

My fieldnotes from this period indicate that the main item on the agenda at my first meeting with the Ontario Sanctuary Coalition was the case of a Kurdish refugee claimant – Sami Durgun. Sami had arrived in Canada as a visitor in 1988 and in the following year made a refugee claim. In 1991, the Immigration and Refugee Board (IRB) turned down his refugee claim and in 1993 he was also refused a minister's permit – a discretionary procedure allowing immigration officials to waive regular immigration requirements on humanitarian and compassionate grounds. According to Romero House records, the IRB insisted that as Sami had 12 siblings still residing in Turkey, he could obviously return there and live safely. The IRB also suggested that he could 'pretend' not to be a Kurd and hence secure his safety. Sami, who attributed the non-existent 12 siblings to a translation error,[1] had participated in two public hunger strikes in support of the Kurdish cause and in 1991 had been filmed by TV Ontario during a demonstration in front of the Kurdish Embassy. Such activities had made him a well-known Kurdish activist in Canada.

After a long and complicated fight, Sami was finally granted refugee protection and landed immigrant status late in 1993. By March 1998, however, Sami – then 35 years of age – had still not received his landed documents and was awaiting the outcome of a further security check by the Canadian Security Intelligence Services (CSIS). With no immediate action on the horizon, Sami was desperate – in particular, his diploma from a completed business course had been held up because of his immigration status and he had been forced to turn down several jobs. Lamenting that he was in an 'immigration limbo' and that his life was fast becoming intolerable, Sami declared that he was ready 'to take a stand'. With the encouragement of several Romero House volunteers at the meeting, Sami agreed to hold an around-the-clock vigil in front of federal immigration offices in downtown Toronto.

I recall that the corner of University Avenue and Dundas Street, where Sami initially held his vigil, was extremely cold that March – unfortunately it was also a natural wind tunnel. Both my husband and I spent several nights with Sami – ducking in and out of 24-hour coffee shops, stamping our feet and clapping our hands to stay warm, and then helping Sami fold up his cot at 6:30 a.m. to make way for employees entering the building. As the days went by and as immigration officials stubbornly refused to budge, we listened with some misgivings as Sami told a news reporter: 'I'm going to stay here until I get landed status. I have nothing else to do. I don't like to do this kind of action, but there's only one hope. This is the only option open' (Black 1998: B3).

I well remember my son – who was 4 years old at the time – listening wide-eyed to some of our conversations about Sami and his strategy to force the

Canadian government to recognize his existence. As the freezing weather persisted, we grew discouraged and then eventually alarmed. I particularly recall him asking me one night as I tucked him into bed what 'hy-po-ther-mia' meant – his child's voice extremely careful to repeat each of the syllables distinctly.

Sami Durgun's stand in the bitter and biting cold outside of Immigration Canada offices was an extraordinary eye-opener for me – anthropological and otherwise. It turned out to be a quick and effective initiation into what sanctuary was and had become in Canada over the 1990s.

Immigration and refugee reforms

I had already come into contact with several Canadian sanctuary workers during my fieldwork with the Arizona and Texas-based wings of the US Sanctuary Movement – but through them I had acquired a somewhat different conception of what sanctuary in Canada entailed. Among US-based participants, Canada was largely regarded as the 'overground' terminus of the US underground railroad – a place where refugees were not only likely to be well received and subject to fair adjudication, but also much more likely to have their cases accepted. Indeed, many refugees and their families who came through the US-based sanctuary network were clandestinely directed along 'the line' to church communities and social service organizations in Canada which then 'hosted' refugee claimants awaiting refugee status in Canada. Among US sanctuary workers, Canada was often spoken of in glowing terms and as a destination of hope and liberation for many of the refugees traveling the underground railroad.

Despite this strong regard for – and some might argue romanticization of – Canada's refugee system and policies (see also Young, Chapter 16 in this volume), however, I soon learned that Canada was fast losing its reputation as a safe haven. In many respects, Sami Durgun's case typifies changes that were taking place, and his importance for sanctuary efforts in southern Ontario is directly linked to the new developments within Canada's refugee determination process during the late 1980s and early 1990s.

Closing the refugee door

On April 7, 1993, Sami Durgan received the following letter from a supervisor at Employment and Immigration Canada:

> Dear Client,
>
> This is in reference to your request, pursuant to subsection 114(2) of the Immigration Act, for an exemption from the Governor-In-Council of subsection 9(1) of the Immigration Act on humanitarian and compassionate grounds.

Following a thorough and sympathetic review of all the circumstances of your case, it had been determined that there are insufficient humanitarian, compassionate and other grounds to warrant requesting such an exemption. Consequently, it will be necessary for you to submit an application for permanent residence at a Canadian post abroad, as required by the Immigration Act. Until such an application has been filed, no further consideration can be given to your case.

As your status will expired [sic] on 11 February, 1991, you are required to leave Canada. Failing that, normal enforcement procedures will be initiated.

(Letter from K. Kemp, A/Supervisor, Toronto Central CIC, to Sami Durgan. April 07, 1993, Employment and Immigration Canada)

Sami was one among a group of 24 Toronto-based refugee claimants who received similar letters from the Government of Canada requesting that they leave the country. Devastated by the letter, Sami Durgan had, in many respects, found himself in a Canada that was significantly reorganizing and reorienting its immigration practices.

Over the late 1980s and early 1990s, new legislative and administrative measures profoundly recast Canadian refugee policy. The emphasis on overseas determination, for example, as well as stricter criteria for case reviews, gave refugee determination a much more restrictive character. Reflecting broader shifts in public discourse, the bureaucratic culture also went through several significant changes as the system itself became re-oriented toward identifying fraud and abuse – in other words, identifying those who were 'working the system' and taking advantage of Canada's 'generosity'. These developments also reflected concerns that refugee claims had become a method for avoiding immigration screening and that Canada had lost control over its immigrant selection process (see Pratt and Valverde 2002).

While the reasons for these shifts are complex and multi-faceted, *controlling* the refugee process was part and parcel of a broader effort to *control* the Canada–US border (see Pratt 2005). Such developments in Canada echoed the spirit of border enforcement occurring along the US–Mexico border. Throughout the 1990s, US officials exerted pressure on the Canadian government to do 'something' about its 'lax' borders. As a result, many of the new refugee determination procedures that were adopted by the Conservative-led government during this period resonated with 'border control' concerns – namely by recasting refugees as 'security risks'.

Legislation such as Bills C-55, C-84 and C-86, for example, significantly altered the ways in which refugee adjudication worked, and among the most controversial of the new regulations were new screening mechanisms that gave frontline immigration officials greater powers to limit full access to the refugee determination system. The new laws also gave the Minister of Employment and

Immigration the power to interdict and ultimately turn away vessels suspected of transporting refugee claimants – a new ministerial power that in part reflected Canada's sovereignty anxieties after two ships carrying Tamil and Sikh refugees were abandoned on its east coast in the late 1980s.

Many critics of these new measures saw Canada's refugee policy becoming nativist, alarmist and restrictive, taking a radical turn from the more liberal-democratic tradition of 'universal access' to the refugee determination process. For those active in refugee resettlement, such as the volunteers and staff at Romero House, these legislative and cultural changes significantly altered their roles in refugee matters, particularly as their energies were re-directed toward interfacing with the intricacies of the new adjudication process itself.

Offering sanctuary

Romero House documents from September 1992 to March 1996 are illustrative of the striking changes that occurred in Canadian refugee policy over this period.[2] Some of the most vocal critics of the new refugee determination procedures were congregations and church-based social justice organizations (often called 'coalitions'), many of which had previous and long-standing involvement with refugee issues (for an overview and descriptions of these coalitions, see Lind and Mihevc 1994). As refugee protection was increasingly denied and deportation notices multiplied, some turned their attention to the US Sanctuary Movement as well as a growing European Sanctuary Movement. By the Spring of 1993, 'sanctuary' was clearly in the air in Ontario and other parts of Canada (see Matas 1988; Stastny and Tyrnauer 1993). Between 1990 and 1991, for example, two congregations within the United Church of Canada offered sanctuary to refugee claimants (both of whom had received deportation orders), and in 1992, the 34th General Council of the United Church of Canada (acting on a petition from one of its congregations) affirmed 'the moral right and responsibility of ... congregations to provide sanctuary to legitimate refugee claimants who have been denied refugee status'. In the following year, the Social Affairs Commission of the Ontario Conference of Catholic Bishops declared: 'The decision in conscience to offer sanctuary, which is a decision of the last resort, is part of every major faith tradition.'

The Romero House group likewise started to explore sanctuary for some of its refugee families under immediate threat of deportation. In the Summer of 1992, it arranged for 'protective asylum' for two families:

> [These families] were 'hidden' by religious communities and ecumenical groups throughout Ontario. This meant that their room and board and living expenses were provided by church groups throughout the province. The Canadian Auto Workers provided money for their living expenses.

Doctors and hospitals volunteered their medical services. These refugees were in safe keeping because of the decency of so many people.

('Public Inquiry into Immigration Canada is in the National Interest.' Memo to the Canadian Council on Refugees from the Ontario Sanctuary Coalition, November 13, 1993)

In the Spring of 1993, as Sami Durgan and others like him received removal notices, several churches and coalitions in southern Ontario decided to meet to *explicitly* discuss sanctuary. The meeting confirmed that church and advocacy groups were experiencing similar problems: legitimate refugee claimants were being put under notice of removal and church members in particular felt that it was unethical to allow the deportation of people at real risk of imprisonment, torture and quite possibly death if they returned to their countries of origin. (On some of the issues involved in church-based determinations of refugees, see Rehaag 2006.)

At the meeting, participants from Romero House reported that many of their refugee cases had become difficult and frustrating – of central concern was the dramatic shift in Canada's Humanitarian and Compassionate Review (HCR) proceeding, a legal mechanism that allowed the Minster of Immigration to intervene. Although used sparingly, a Minister's HCR for deportation reprieve was an intervention refugee advocacy groups often relied upon in their most extreme cases.

Although only a relatively small number of their cases had undergone HCR, Romero House stated that it had enjoyed reasonable success with this mechanism, but that it had recently discovered (under the Conservative-led government of Brian Mulroney) that even this option was being quickly curtailed:

> It is difficult to discern the reasons for the sea change from this generally respectful relationship which guaranteed at least for the most desperate a measure of 'natural justice' ... In any case, there was a virtual shutdown on humanitarian and compassionate requests ... Refugee advocates found that if they made an H and C request to the Minister's Office they were told that such decisions had been delegated to local immigration officers at 'hearings and appeals', i.e. enforcement. When refugee advocates contacted these local immigration officers, they were told that no decision could be made without a permit from the Minister.
>
> (Ontario Sanctuary Coalition, Chronology: Efforts to Protect Refugees, May 1992–93. No year of publication specified on original document.)

While reviewing a series of documents – letters, faxes, briefs – produced by the Ontario Sanctuary Coalition between 1992 and 1996, I noted that one principal frustration of church groups was not only a sense of being excluded from the refugee determination procedure at all stages, but also treated with what they often perceived as absolute disdain by government officials. As sanctuary advocates became increasingly knowledgeable of and involved in the bureaucratic workings of the refugee determination process, they also began to document the negligence of some lawyers as well as instances of bias among the IRB members. In one case, a claimant's lawyer fell into a sound sleep during her hearing. In several others, the background information on a claimant's country of origin was woefully outdated or simply unavailable. This state of affairs led many refugee advocates to the conclusion that Canada's refugee determination system was suffering from both carelessness of counsel and the capricious bias of some IRB members:

> [T]he only positive decision I saw was in a case that I thought was very problematic. The case involved a Nigerian man who had been out of his country for 15 years and who had married a Polish woman. They lived there for 10 years and had two children who were Polish citizens. The man claimed that he had been discriminated against in Poland. The IRB felt that this did not amount [to] persecution. However, he was accepted under the PDRCC review [a post review] with no mention of these particulars – only a collection of articles about recent developments in Nigeria. I asked the lawyer involved why she thought this case was accepted. Her reply was, 'What can I say? It was the week after the murder of Ken Saro-Wiwa. There was sympathy for Nigerians.'
> (Memo sent to Susan Davis and Michael Malloy from the Ontario Sanctuary Coalition (Mary Jo Leddy and Michael Creal), March 26, 1996)

As HCR requests, in particular, were ignored or left languishing, church groups began to experience both an ethical and procedural estrangement from the Canadian refugee determination process. Several refugee advocates began to identify what they felt was the 'first indication that civil servants were somewhat contemptuous of the political authority/public interest in these [refugee] matters'.[3] As discussions continued among refugee advocacy groups in southern Ontario, the Toronto-based Romero House decided to formalize its identity by joining with several other groups – naming themselves the Ontario Sanctuary Coalition (see also Lippert 2006: 25–6, 70–1). They also began to hold weekly meetings at the Church of the Holy Trinity adjacent to a major shopping complex, the Eaton Centre, in downtown Toronto.

Declaring sanctuary

The decision to formalize sanctuary as a strategy to protect refugees had its providence in a series of important events occurring between June 1992 and May 1993. In June of 1992, as deportation orders proliferated, refugee claimants from around the city of Toronto literally began showing up on Romero House doorsteps – 'at all hours' as one document reports.[4] Acting as an impromptu Refugee Board,[5] volunteers and social workers quickly conducted interviews with the refugees and assessed the information they provided:

> Refugees began showing up in the early morning and late evenings of the offices and homes of various advocacy groups. The claims of these refugees had been refused by the immigration and refugee board and their appeals to the federal court had been rejected. They had received deportation orders. These refugees came to Amnesty International, Vigil and Romero House. In at least 90–95% of the cases that we received, we concluded that the refugees were not at risk and that we would try to help them in every humanitarian way short of making a special claim to the Minister of Immigration. Of the refugees we remained concerned about, we knew that some of them had had their legitimate claims refused because of negligent lawyers, incompetent [sic] translators or clearly biased board members.
> ('Public Inquiry into Immigration Canada is in the National Interest': memo to the Canadian Council on Refugees from the Ontario Sanctuary Coalition, November 13, 1993)

In cases felt to involve a clear risk, Romero House staff made last-minute appeals to local immigration officials and to the Minister of Employment and Immigration. Yet, as their efforts continued to fail, refugee advocates began to make quiet offers to find refugees places to live in the US – places where they felt refugees might have a better chance of blending into an underground economy. While this was a rather extraordinary reversal of affairs – especially given that Canada had, until this point, been seen as the sanctuary terminus – many refugee families were reluctant to explore this option. After much discussion – and as mentioned earlier – the sanctuary coalition decided to 'hide' two families, one in a house provided by a religious community and the other in an apartment provided by an ecumenical group. As these and other refugee families went into hiding, the congregation of Holy Trinity started to raise money through private donations and an extensive sanctuary support network was established.

Moving toward public sanctuary

The immediate build-up to the public declaration of sanctuary in Ontario took place between November 1992 and May 1993. Five months after the two families went into hiding, their refugee claims remained outstanding. Supporters began to wonder anxiously how long the situation would go on. An appeal was made through June Callwood, a distinguished Canadian journalist, directly to the Prime Minister's office, and documents supporting the asylum claims for 23 files were personally delivered to an executive assistant on November 27, 1992. In February 1993, Romero House received a letter from the then 'new' Minister of Employment and Immigration, Pauline Browse, stating that two refugees had been given Minister's permits, but also that 13 of the cases had been rejected.

As a result, several meetings were arranged between Sanctuary Coalition members and Immigration and Refugee officials – the former demanding an explanation for the refusals. The Sanctuary Coalition account of this period suggests these meetings were often far from fruitful:

> It was clear to us that Minister Browse had not read the files and was unaware of some issues. At one point she asked us, 'What happens to the refugees that are deported to Buffalo?' She seemed surprised to learn that families were being separated.
> (Ontario Sanctuary Coalition, 'Additions to Chronology: Efforts to Protect Refugees, May 1992–93')

In April 1993, three of the Romero-sponsored refugees who had been promised a ministerial review received deportation orders. Urgent appeals were made to the Minister's office, but the deportations went ahead and two families were sent to Buffalo. Romero House volunteers and staff accompanied the families:

> On May 6/93 we informed Minister Browse that the immigration officials had deported two families and had separated another family in spite of serious documentation about their safety. It was a time of deep shame for us as Canadians. We knew we would never, could never, do it again. We wanted all the bureaucrats who had dealt with these human beings as pieces of paper, who had never to face them, to be present at the moment when these decent human beings were carted off in a security van.
> ('Public Inquiry into Immigration Canada is in the National Interest': memo to the Canadian Council on Refugees from the Ontario Sanctuary Coalition, November 13, 1993)

Symbolic sanctuary

> We are here today to say that extraordinary measures must now be taken to protect the lives of genuine refugees. These people must rely on the decency of Prime Minister Mulroney and his willingness to intervene personally on their behalf. They may have to rely on our willingness to declare sanctuary – a place of protection for refugees.
> Today we make a promise to these refugees: WE WILL NOT ABANDON YOU.
> (Press release: 'A Promise of Civil Initiative to Protect Refugees', Ontario Sanctuary Coalition, Monday, May 31, 1993)

As the removals and deportations continued, and as relations between refugee advocates and government representatives remained strained, the Ontario

Sanctuary Coalition decided to publicly declare sanctuary. Mary Jo Leddy, then a Catholic Sister of Zion, announced that unless the government acted on the review of the outstanding 23 cases, churches across Ontario were prepared to offer refugees sanctuary – but it was a kind of sanctuary that differed significantly from the practices of the US Sanctuary Movement (see Cunningham 1995; Perla and Coutin, Chapter 5 in this volume). As a result, refugee advocates began to explore and explicitly discuss different models of sanctuary, including that of church-based sanctuary offered by the Tucson group with whom I had worked. Some models, however, were rejected:

> We decided that the American model was not appropriate in this context, i.e., placing refugees publicly within a church building. We felt that it was not appropriate because churches were always trying to move the refugees up to Canada. We opted more for the World War II model in which Christians hid those refugees whose lives were in danger. We began to offer Sanctuary without announcing what we were doing.
> (Ontario Sanctuary Coalition, 'Additions to Chronology: Efforts to Protect Refugees, May 1992–93')

Ontario Sanctuary Coalition members had in fact contacted members of the Tucson-based Sanctuary Movement in order to explore sanctuary options. Some Ontario delegates acknowledged that many US sanctuary groups had successfully provided sanctuary in church buildings – thereby challenging states to violate not only sacred spaces, but also First Amendment rights to freedom of religious expression. Many of them, however, felt this tactic would be unlikely to work in Canada owing to its different religious culture and lack of formal church–state separation protocols. Without the same history of heightened church–state tensions, coalition members argued, Canadian government officials were much more likely to simply walk into churches to find refugee claimants. As a result, the Ontario Sanctuary Coalition decided to adopt 'symbolic' sanctuary – or what others called 'phantom' sanctuary.

Consequently, during the May 1993 press conference, pictures of the refugees in hiding were hung inside the Church of the Holy Trinity, but the exact location of where the refugee families were staying was not disclosed.

Civil initiative

The principle of sanctuary that the Ontario Sanctuary Coalition invoked – that of *civil initiative* rather than *civil disobedience* – was a direct result of their contact with the Tucson-based wing of the US Sanctuary Movement and, in particular, the writings of sanctuary-founder and Quaker, Jim Corbett.

The concept itself had a rather tumultuous history in the US Sanctuary Movement as it lay at the core of a key difference between the two main factions of the movement. At first, US church groups had envisioned sanctuary more in terms of the civil disobedience tradition of Henry David Thoreau and Martin Luther King, Jr., i.e., one broke the law as a matter of conscience and in so doing, brought about change in bad or immoral laws. After consulting with secular legal groups (particularly the American Civil Liberties Union), however, members of Tucson's Sanctuary network began to explore the concept of civil initiative – a tradition rooted in the Nuremberg Trials in which citizens were encouraged to disobey inhumane governments.

Using the principles of this second tradition, Tucson Sanctuary groups began to argue that the US government was in violation of its own domestic as well as international laws regarding the treatment of refugees. In such circumstances, US citizens were morally and legally obligated – i.e., they had to take the civil *initiative* – to uphold those laws even if their governments did not. As a result, Tucson Sanctuary workers developed a key legal argument: offering sanctuary was not breaking the law, but rather upholding existing laws regarding asylum.[6]

Although many Ontario Sanctuary Coalition members had long-standing connections to non-violent direct-action traditions of civil disobedience among the peace and justice networks of the 1980s, civil initiative seemed more in tune with the kinds of advocacy in which they were engaged. Drawn deeply into the bureaucratic cultures, politics and practices of refugee governance and determination, the Ontario Sanctuary Coalition built an argument that would allow it to function, in some respects, like a 'state within a state' – but a state that adhered to Canada's commitments to international refugee protocols. At the same time, the Ontario Sanctuary Coalition maintained its identity as an advocate for reform – in subsequent years mounting a demand for public inquiry into refugee adjudication, the implementation of a merit-based review for refugee claims, as well as a Supreme Court challenge regarding Charter Rights.

Conclusion: sanctuary as a 'state within a state'

The notion of sanctuary as a kind of state-within-a state is an intriguing one – and something that has been developed as a distinctive feature of the Ontario Sanctuary Coalition. Although Ontario-based notions of sanctuary draw upon the standard fare of sanctuary – i.e., a political and cultural separation of church–state, the human right to freely express one's religious beliefs, the sanctity of sacred space and humanitarian asylum – in some respects, it also relocates the essence of state sovereignty by taking it out of the hands of a government-sanctioned official and moving it into moral space of the 'ordinary' citizen.

Yet the religious nature of sanctuary has meant that church and state are often to be found in close quarters. Such entanglements are embedded in the 1993 press release that the Ontario Sanctuary Coalition released as it declared 'symbolic' sanctuary:

In the past year, we have seen some genuine refugees deported, sent on the long journey back to the arbitrary detention, torture and death they tried to escape. These people are not just 'cases' to us. They are human beings with names and faces. Their tears are like yours and ours. We have gone with the refugees to the 'removals' units. Husbands and wives have been separated. We have seen fathers shackled in front of their children, children put in 'detention'.

In the name of God, in the name of Canada, this must stop. We have been, we are, more decent than this.

The state within the state, then, can also be seen a condition of compassion and deep moral commitment to those who are rendered invisible within massive structures of governance – structures too often fraught with bureaucratic indifference and incompetence.

The concept of civil initiative remains at the core of current Ontario Sanctuary coalition activities – most of which have remained focused on assisting refugees as they move through Canada's refugee circuit as well as legal reform of refugee determination in Canada. Although sanctuary has taken many different forms and valences in Canada (see Lippert, 2006, 2009), historically the Ontario Sanctuary Coalition is among the first Canadian network to form a 'sanctuary social movement'. Drawing on the experiences of sanctuary practices in the American south-west, yet responding to a significant remolding of asylum practices in their own backyard, so to speak, the Ontario Sanctuary Coalition carved out a distinctive set of religio-political practices suited to their own circumstances (see also Yukich on the NSM, Chapter 7 in this volume).

The significance of what they aspired to be – and continue to strive toward – came home to me with the celebration of Sami's *finally* victorious citizenship bid. It had been a long, long road for him, and for those who had accompanied him. But his smile after his success – a smile that continually faltered between joy and anguish and one whose ambiguity could only be captured in tears – was an expression of just such a unique entanglement between 'God' and 'Nation'. Sami had experienced the space of secular sanctuary as place of deserved 'refuge and protection' – but with a more spiritual understanding of sanctuary as a space of compassion, witness and ultimately friendship.

Notes

1 Sami's asylum hearings, in fact, had been cancelled four times owing to problems with translators.
2 These documents were kindly given to me by Mary Jo Leddy, founder of Romero House, refugee advocate and author of several books detailing the plight of Canadian refugees and the Ontario Sanctuary Coalition (see Leddy 1997, 2010).
3 Interestingly, this disenchantment with bureaucracy has some strong parallels to experiences of US-based sanctuary activists who also began to think about sanctuary as a political response to what they regarded as a flawed and increasingly restrictive refugee determination process.

4 Of particular concern were Eritrean refugees from opposition parties whose cases were being rejected on the grounds of insufficient evidence. Refugee advocates put together information establishing grounds for a reopening of the cases but were informed in a letter from the Immigration and Refugee Board that new or previously unavailable information did not constitute grounds for reopening a hearing.
5 In this respect, refugee advocates were adopting the role of state-actors to fulfill Canada's legislative responsibilities. This was to become central to their legal argument for sanctuary—that of civil initiative. See also Lippert (2006) on this issue and his discussion of sanctuary as a sovereign para-state.
6 Critics of civil initiative claimed that it undercut the compelling political statement that only civil disobedience could make. See *Basta!* Editor's Note, January 1985, p. 1.

References

Black, D. (1998) 'Refugee Staging Chilly Protests', *The Toronto Star*, 16 March, p. B3.

Cunningham, H. (1995) *God and Caesar at the Rio Grande: Sanctuary and the Politics of Religion*, Minnesota: University of Minnesota Press.

Leddy, M.J. (1997) *At the Border Called Hope: Where Refugees Are Neighbours*, Toronto: HarperCollins.

——(2010) *Our Friendly Local Terrorist*, Toronto: Between the Lines.

Lind, C. and Mihevc, J. (1994) *Coalitions for Justice: The Story of Canada's Interchurch Coalitions*, Ottawa: Novalis.

Lippert, R. (2006) *Sanctuary, Sovereignty, Sacrifice: Canadian Sanctuary Incidents, Power and Law*, Vancouver: University of British Columbia Press.

——(2009) 'Whither Sanctuary?', *Refuge*, 26(1): 57–67.

Matas, D. (1988) 'Canadian Sanctuary', *Refuge*, 18(1): 14–17.

Pratt, A. (2005) *Securing Borders: Detention and Deportation in Canada*, Vancouver: University of British Columbia Press.

Pratt, A. and Valverde, M. (2002) 'From Deserving Victims to "Masters of Confusion": Redefining Refugees in the 1990s', *The Canadian Journal of Sociology/Cahiers canadiens de sociologie*, 27(2): 135–61.

Rehaag, S. (2006) 'Bordering on Legality: Canadian Church Sanctuary and the Rule of Law', *Refuge*, 26(2): 43–56.

Stastny, C. and Tyrnauer, G. (1993) 'Sanctuary in Canada', in V. Robinson (ed.) *The International Refugee Crisis: British and Canadian Responses*, London: Macmillan.

Chapter 12

Religious sanctuary in France and Canada

Caroline Patsias and Nastassia Williams

Introduction

In this chapter, we compare two instances of religious sanctuary provided by Catholic parishes in Canada and France: the Église Saint-Jean de la Croix in Montreal and the Église Saint-Bernard in Paris. We explore which of two conceptions of political obligation, liberal or republican, is adopted by the principal actors: political authorities, representatives of the Catholic hierarchy, church members and citizens. Religious sanctuary reveals tensions in the right to asylum, involving respect for human rights, popular expressions of increasing anxiety about security, activist social movement support for the demands of asylum-seekers, and the logic of the state. The analysis of religious sanctuary provides an opportunity for a broader examination of political obligation and its limitations in contemporary society.

Religious sanctuary refers to protection offered by churches to a person under threat. Sanctuary grows out of the sacred mandate of religious institutions. Many have proposed that sanctuary existed in ancient Greece (Lippert 2005), and it was only towards the seventeenth century, with the rise of secularism and the progressive conquest by the state of the monopoly on political authority, that the recognition of religious sanctuary began to be challenged. The phenomenon nevertheless persisted, and it has recently resurfaced with the sanctuary movement of the 1980s in the United States (see Perla and Bibler Coutin, Chapter 5 in this volume). While the US example is the most well known, sanctuary practices have occurred elsewhere, including in Europe, Canada and Australia (Tazreiter 2004; Lippert and Rehaag 2009).

In contemporary society, sanctuary practices typically involve persons whose applications for immigration or refugee status have been rejected and for whom the church is the last recourse prior to deportation. Aside from delaying deportation, these asylum-seekers hope to compel the authorities to review their cases by drawing media attention to their cause and, in turn, gaining public support. Sanctuary practices have antagonized some state officials, who see them as challenging state power. For example, in 2004, the former Canadian minister for citizenship and immigration Judy Sgro (Bronskill 2004) stated, '[F]rankly if we start using the churches as a back door to enter Canada, we're going to have huge problems' (Wilson 2004). The minister emphasized dangers posed by sanctuary practices to immigration policy: in her view, sanctuary challenged the sovereignty and universality of the law (ibid.). Consistent with this position, police forced entry into a Protestant church (the Église Unie Saint-Pierre) in Quebec City that same year to arrest Algerian asylum-seeker Mohamed Cherfi following the rejection of his appeal for refugee status (Wilson 2004; Wyatt 2004).

Such state reactions are reminders that religious sanctuary raises the question of obedience versus resistance to the authorities. The choice of these terms is not arbitrary: questioning civil obedience implicitly refers to the issue of civil disobedience. Thoreau ([1849] 1948) was famously charged with 'civil disobedience' when he refused to pay his taxes to protest US slavery laws and the US war against Mexico. The term remains associated with the emblematic figure of Mahatma Gandhi and the non-violent struggle for independence in India, as well as the US civil rights movement. Civil disobedience is a conscious and intentional infraction of the law in the name of principles that transcend the law (Bedau 1961). Yet, as Rehaag (2009) and others have pointed out, for ecclesiastical actors, granting sanctuary is not necessarily an act of civil disobedience. Rather, it may reflect the need to review the rejected claimant's case in order to avoid deportation that would contravene various norms, including, for example, international refugee law or natural law. This is why we prefer, in the context of religious sanctuary, the terms 'resistance to authority' and 'political obligation' over 'civil disobedience'.

Religious sanctuary also needs to be understood within a wider debate on immigration. In the face of potential new waves of refugees and in an age marked by economic and financial crises, nations have adopted restrictive policies variably modulated according to the asylum-seeker's country of origin (Wihtol de Wenden 1994). Governments fear that the status of political refugee will be perverted to the benefit of economic migrants from poor countries.

There are two major currents of conceptualization of political obligation: liberal and republican-participatory. These divergent visions have influenced the positions taken by various actors on religious sanctuary. How do the new problematics of immigration in modern democracies affect these visions and conceptions of religious sanctuary? In other words, what are the visions being asserted in a world where containing the flow of immigration is a state priority?

Our aim here is to assess how the different visions of political obligation overlap and how these visions shed light on the practices of, and the discourse about, religious sanctuary. We will explore this duality by comparing two incidents of religious sanctuary: in the Église Saint-Bernard in Paris and the Église Saint-Jean de la Croix in Montreal. France and Canada are two countries with very different political heritages: Canada is marked by a liberal tradition, whereas France boasts republican roots. Are their respective positions on religious sanctuary converging despite the traditions specific to each country? Which factors account for the similarities or differences – is it the category of the actors in question or their nationality? Finally, how have citizens actively involved in religious sanctuary redefined political obligation, and how have they legitimized their actions?

Perspective

Religious sanctuary studies have typically been approached from a social movement perspective and interpreted as a new variant of church–state conflict (Wiltfang and McAdam 1991). This emphasis on the religious dimension of sanctuary has encouraged the neglect of other aspects, such as the meaning of religious sanctuary in terms of governance and political obligation (Lippert and Rehaag 2009).

In this regard, we would like to analyze the overlap of ideological matrices between different actors and the levels at which they act, within a political system characterized by economic liberalism and restricted mobility rights among populations. Our research casts new light on how the 'fringes' contribute to redefine the limits of political obligation. Ultimately, this analysis represents an initial exploration of the convergences and divergences between sanctuary practices in two countries. It will serve to determine how much, if at all, national heritage comes to bear on the matter or whether Canada and France have adapted in similar ways to the international context.

Research strategy and methodology

Our comprehensive, comparative approach reflects our intent to clarify the meanings different actors attribute to religious sanctuary and the underlying conceptions of democracy. As our two cases illustrate, we approach the provision of religious sanctuary as an 'incident' during which asylum-seekers physically occupy ecclesiastic establishments and remain there to avoid deportation (Lippert 2005). Our intention is to bring to the fore the reactions of the actors involved in these sanctuary crises – namely, the political authorities, the churches and their members, and some citizens.

We have selected two examples that fulfil our study's objectives. First, both involve irregular immigrants who faced deportation either because legal changes affected their status or because their application was rejected. They attempted to avoid deportation by seeking refuge in a church. Second, France and Canada are two countries with divergent political traditions – republican and liberal, respectively – whose immigration policies and associated rights to asylum have both recently taken a more restrictive turn. To grasp the viewpoints of the actors involved, we consulted the websites of the relevant organizations (the Catholic Church, migrant and rights advocacy groups, etc.) and reviewed the press coverage surrounding the cases. Secondary sources were particularly helpful in understanding the Église Saint-Bernard occupation in Paris: Blin (2005, 2010) not only related the facts but also studied various actors involved. We also interviewed the director of the Office for Social Justice of the Archdiocese of Montreal, who had negotiated on behalf of the Church in the case of the refugee claimants at the Église Saint-Jean de la Croix.

Reflecting this methodology, the remainder of the chapter is divided into three sections: the first presents the liberal and republican perspectives on political obligation; in the second, we focus on the two sanctuary experiences in Montreal and Paris within the framework of the liberal and republican traditions; finally, we conclude with a discussion of the tensions these episodes bring to light regarding evolving democratic processes, the relationship to authority and national sovereignty.

Political obligation: liberal and republican

Liberal democracy and political obligation

For liberals, sovereignty is dissociated from the law. Law must be based on what is just and not, first and foremost, on the expression of the popular will. Sovereignty is not embodied in the capacity to stipulate the law. It is much more important for the law to remain the expression of reason and liberty than that of the popular will – a will that has the potential of becoming tyrannical. This conception accounts for the rejection of sovereignty as a hegemonic principle. In the liberal vision, power in all its all forms must be subject to constraints, regardless of its origin, popular or otherwise. Political liberty is seen as a means to protect individual liberties. It is therefore understandable that liberalism has traditionally been associated with negative freedom (i.e., the maximum freedom that individuals can have by virtue of the law) and the protection of private life from government intrusion (Berlin 1969; Lacroix 2003). This desire to preserve individual freedom justifies the importance attributed to the defence of individual rights. The consequences of this defence are twofold: on the one hand, the liberal vision focuses on the procedural dimensions of democracy to the detriment of substance (Sartori 1973; Manin 2002); on the other hand, respect for rights can leave room for disobedience of the law and recourse to illegal or violent actions, despite the traditional opposition of liberals to more direct forms of popular participation.

Since any consensus of what constitutes the Good is impossible – or at least very hard to attain in modern societies, characterized as they are by a pantheon of values – for liberals, only respect for democratic procedures guarantees respect for individual rights and civic co-existence. According to the liberal point of view, collective choice is not subject to any vision of the Good or to any other substantial criterion (Jones 1983).

Because liberalism imposes limitations on authority, even that of democratically elected governments, political disobedience is a legitimate tool against democratic legislation that fails to respect the fundamental rights of individuals.

Inversely, any act of disobedience, be it active or passive, becomes nearly indefensible if fundamental rights are not at issue (Dworkin, 1985). Liberals, however, impose constraints on disobedience as well, first and foremost being the stringent condition that no rights should be infringed in pursuing such action. Moreover, aside from their traditional aversion to collective protest, liberals must come to terms with another major dilemma. Though disobedience can be a means to draw attention to issues of fundamental rights (in the broadest sense possible), it clashes with liberal respect for procedures. This is why liberal thinkers remain cautious about the leeway granted for disobedience, imposing a second criterion of acceptability – namely, that the rights violations in question be sufficiently grievous (Rawls 1971; Dworkin 1985; Habermas 1990). Much of the difficulty with respect to identifying occasions when civil disobedience is permissible according to liberal understandings involves the concrete assessment of the gravity of the rights violations at issue. However, a more basic question can also be posed: is disobedience only acceptable when enacted in defence of rights? Advocates of the republican vision of democracy would answer no.

Republican democracy and political obligation

For participatory republicans, democracy cannot be reduced to a set of procedures. Of course, they acknowledge that respect for rights and procedures is a fundamental aspect of democracy. However, they also believe a 'strong democracy' (Barber 1984) requires effective citizen participation in the nation's decision-making and governance – participation that cannot be reduced to the electoral process and the establishment of preferences (Mouffe 2000). Popular sovereignty, then, is not expressed solely by default, which is to say by deciding who gets to govern come election time (Bohman and Rehg 1997), but also positively through involvement in decision- and policy-making procedures. Republican thinkers view the tie between the state and democracy through the notion of popular sovereignty, which is what guarantees the expression of the people's will and the democratic nature of the state. The freedom that citizens possess resides, then, in their capacity to participate in elaborating laws and not merely in the possibility of escaping from the control of the state (Arendt 1994).

This vision of democracy explains how republican thinkers understand civil disobedience. Such disobedience no longer serves the sole objective of contesting rights violations; it must also compensate for democratic deficits or a loss of sovereignty (Markovits 2005). These terms designate situations where popular sovereignty either was not engaged or needs to be engaged anew. Examples include when public policy has not been approved by the citizenry, when changes to an initial project have not been open to popular consultation or, similarly, when the situation at the origin of policy discussions has changed. The participatory-republican vision of democracy, whereby the legitimacy of the democratic regime depends on the full exercise of popular sovereignty, therefore requires that the popular voice expresses itself once again. This view opens a door for civil disobedience (Singer 1973; Markovits 2005). As it is directly associated with the exercise of sovereignty, civil disobedience in this conception is not perceived as a means of last resort. However, by the same token, civil disobedience emerges as intrinsically limited. Its principal objective is to fill a democratic deficit, not to react to the results of a policy itself. Moreover, while disobedience contributes to expand democracy by allowing sovereignty to be extended, it also poses its own threat to sovereignty.

By challenging the laws of the people, does disobedience not weaken the popular sovereignty that motivated it in the first place? Excessive resistance to authority could, by colonizing the entire sphere of political activity, supplant all other legal forms of political action and thus undermine the consolidation of democracy that civil disobedience is meant to foster. Paradoxically, republicans find themselves in a dilemma similar to that of liberals: What measure of democratic deficit justifies recourse to disobedience?

These theoretical understandings of civil disobedience are part of the ideological background when instances of civil disobedience – and debates over civil disobedience – occur in modern democracies. As a result, they can clarify some issues raised by religious sanctuary in modern democracies. We will now examine two instances of sanctuary, in Paris and in Montreal, respectively, to illustrate these issues and how the positions of the actors in question drew on both the liberal and the participatory-republican perspectives.

Comparing two sanctuary experiences

The Église Saint-Bernard experience (Paris)

By the end of the 1990s, France was embroiled in a heated debate over immigration policy and national security. The right-wing government of the time was calling for a hardening of the existing Pasqua and Méhaignerie immigration laws (named after successive interior ministers, Charles Pasqua and Pierre Méhaignerie). Although proposed legislation ultimately came to naught, it encountered only light opposition besides that of the French Catholic and Protestant Churches, which had both campaigned since 1992 for greater openness towards immigrants (Blin 2010).

In this context, in June 1996, 312 refugee claimants – mostly Malians and Senegalese – took asylum in the Église Saint-Bernard. They were supported not only by associations (e.g., advocacy groups, community groups and NGOs) and church representatives, but also by high-profile public figures (politicians, philosophers, actors) who participated in negotiations with the government. Ten undocumented immigrants began a hunger strike to put pressure on the government and civil society (Bantman 1996; Simonnot 1996). The movement gained momentum and received substantial media coverage following the hunger-strikers' forced evacuation to hospital.

On 23 August 1996, the government decided to adopt a hard-line approach: the police forcibly entered the sanctuary, and 210 occupants were arrested. In all, 109 undocumented immigrants received visas to stay in France, among them eight single adults who had been denied political asylum and 101 parents of children born in France and entitled to French nationality by virtue of the *droit du sol*. Altogether 35 per cent received legal resident status in France (Blin 2010: 110).

The Église Saint-Bernard sanctuary incident engendered two contradictory discourses that did not merely grow out of the opposition between the government and advocacy groups. The latter, in fact, were themselves divided on a number of issues. One major disagreement concerned the regularization of the undocumented immigrants. Part of the movement, supported by the mediation committee, wanted to apply the criteria established by the government in judging beforehand whether cases were valid. This would have given applicants with children or a spouse already possessing French nationality an advantage over single candidates who had been denied the right of asylum (Bernard and Herzberg 1996). Others in the movement, however, felt that this strategy was tantamount to accepting the policies of the government instead of contesting their legitimacy. For this more radical segment of the movement, the undocumented immigrants were engaged in a political battle that went beyond the mere fact of asking to be regularized; their action also constituted a challenge against existing North–South relations and the immigration policies that resulted from the North–South power imbalance.

The aim, then, was not just to regularize the Saint-Bernard asylum-seekers but to go further by calling on all undocumented immigrants to unite and mobilize a broader base of support for the cause (Bernard 1996). This division was also the consequence of the profile and values of the groups concerned. *SOS-racisme*, an anti-racist organization founded in 1984 with close links to the Socialist Party, preferred a reformist approach, while the groups *Droits devant* (Rights First), the *Comité des Sans Logis* (Committee of the Homeless) and the *Ligue des droits de l'Homme* (Human Rights League) demanded more radical political changes. These tensions and the diversity in the adopted positions also reflected the different degree of institutionalization of the groups and the competition to represent the cause of refugees to the government (Blin 2005).

The political class was divided as well. In May 1993, in reaction to the general resistance of the Catholic Church towards the laws bearing his name, Interior Minister Charles Pasqua made the following statement: 'We are not in Saudi Arabia! This means that the government will not allow clerics to dictate the law in a nation that is a secular republic, not a den of ayatollahs' (Blin 2010: 70; our translation). The right-wing governing party kept to its initial hard line. At the same time, there was division on the left of the political spectrum as well. Within the Socialist Party, a consensus was slow to emerge, and then-party leader Lionel Jospin declined to participate in demonstrations of support for the undocumented immigrants (Perrignon 1996). Yet the movement garnered popular support, with polls showing 46 per cent of the French population in favour and 36 per cent against. Paradoxically, 68 per cent of the same population rejected the idea of relaxing the Pasqua laws (Blin 2010: 100). In other words, though French civil society was sensitive to a specific situation, as a general matter, it continued to support hard-line immigration policies.

The Église Saint-Jean de la Croix incident (Montreal)

In 1998, following a church service, 17 Chileans decided to occupy the Église Saint-Jean de la Croix in central Montreal (in a neighbourhood known as Petite-Patrie) and begin a hunger strike to obtain asylum in Canada (Dumas 1998). The parish council, with the support of the archbishop of Montreal, refused to ask the authorities to evict them. The Saint-Jean de la Croix sanctuary incident needs to be examined against a political backdrop characterized by both a tightening of Canadian refugee admission criteria and a shift in the political profile of asylum-seekers, as illustrated by the case of these Chileans who had fled not from a communist regime but from a democratic republic – albeit one where the practice of torture was well documented (Montpetit 1998).[1]

Lawyers and advocacy groups defending Chilean immigrants' interests condemned the Immigration and Refugee Board (IRB) for failing to sufficiently consider the merits of each claim separately. To their eyes, IRB members applied the same approach in all cases and invariably reached the same conclusion (Patsias, interview with Brian McDonough, directeur de l'Office de la pastorale sociale, à l'Archevêché de Montréal, Montreal, 14 July 2011). Another point was that the IRB judgements ignored the complexity of the political situation in Chile and the real abuses that threatened the rights of asylum-seekers in their own country. The objective of the hunger strike by the Chileans in the Montreal sanctuary was to protest against the iniquity of their treatment by the administrative authorities. At the same time, a committee including representatives of the Catholic archdiocese of Montreal and well respected members of civil society approached federal and provincial immigration departments, condemning the manner in which the refugees' claims had been processed (Dumas 1998). Complicating matters further was the political environment: a sovereignist party was in power at the provincial level, meaning that relations with its federal counterpart were problematic. In the end, the solution agreed upon was that Ottawa would examine the files of refugees who qualified for a Quebec selection certificate (*Certificat de sélection du Québec*: CSQ). André Boisclair, at the time Quebec's Minister of Relations with Citizens and of Immigration said:

> This process [the examination of the hunger strikers' CSQ applications] has nothing to do with the legitimacy of their demands for refugee status, which fall under federal jurisdiction. Its aim rather is to identify the candidates who meet the Quebec selection criteria in the 'skilled worker' category.
>
> (Montpetit 1998; our translation)

Of the 80 Chileans who filed applications under this process, 23 obtained a CSQ, but not all of them then went on to submit their forms to the federal authorities. This raised doubts, including among the refugee claimants' advocates, about the veracity of some of the refugees' situations that had been described in the direst of terms.

The Chilean refugee claimants received the support of the church's parishioners, but, as in France, this support was not unequivocal. Some on the parish council remained hostile to the immigrants; they were fearful of adopting a position that, by contesting the rules, could threaten the system as a whole. Special treatment for the Chileans of the Saint-Jean de la Croix parish might cause prejudice to genuine refugees who followed the rules. Others questioned the veracity of the stories recounted by the asylum-seekers. Finally, traces of racism and anti-communism were discernible (Patsias interview with Brian Donough). These attitudes reflected those of the general population and part of the political class. While the federal minister of immigration worried that the situation could set a bad precedent, opposition among elected members of the provincial legislature was just as firm, particularly from Minister Boisclair, who held the seat in the church's riding. Beyond the federal argument, Boisclair did not accept the action taken by the Catholic Church, which, to his eyes, defied the sovereignty of the state and undermined order in the community (ibid.).

Comparing the French and Canadian cases

The discourse of the groups supporting the undocumented immigrants at the Église Saint-Bernard reflected both the liberal vision of rights advocacy and a challenge to the authority of the state. While delivered on behalf of the defence of rights, the discourse also included an explicit vision of the Good in connection with the notion of domination and with a condemnation of the relationship of subordination between the countries of the developed North and those of the low-income South. Moreover, rifts among the advocacy groups and among the asylum claimants themselves showed that the division between liberal and republican discourses was not reflected cleanly in the division between the state and civil society. Those who defended selecting the asylum-seekers who should be granted sanctuary at times implicitly echoed the positions of the political actors, condemning the radical positions and militancy of the extreme leftist groups (Blin 2010: 81). This discourse was reminiscent of the prudence liberals typically harbour towards obeying the law and of their distrust of collective struggle, with its potential for social disorder. The Catholic Church, too, was divided on the issue. While the episcopate had earlier called for the expulsion of the asylum-seekers from the Église Saint-Ambroise (Prieur 1996; Blin 2010), the Saint-Bernard parish priest, with the backing of the church hierarchy, decided to support the cause of the asylum-seekers.

The Canadian case, too, ran up against the challenge of determining whether the refugee claimants should be entitled to asylum. In France, negotiations with the government were principally conducted by ideologically engaged advocacy groups with a professional approach to such causes. In Canada, they were led by the Church.[2] According to the various churches, certain factors justified granting asylum. Above all, the absence of an appeal in the refugee determination process ran counter to the liberal principle of rights. As well, the very heavy burden of proof fell entirely on the claimant, who was often in a precarious situation to begin with. In this regard, church representatives pointed out a lack of sensitivity in the application of the law. In other words, the intent was not to challenge the legitimacy of the law, but rather to contest a fastidious application of the law oblivious to the situation of *these* refugees. This desire to avoid conflict, which reaffirmed the primacy of the law, was emblematic of a liberal vision and arguably amounted to sanctioning the government's general immigration policies – if not the specific application of those policies in particular cases (Rehaag 2009).

The difference between the communities harbouring the refugees influenced the discourse and roles of the actors. In France, the church provided a place of refuge but had little or no say in the demands made and in the negotiations with the government. Media attention was focused on the committee of public figures and especially the leaders of the advocacy groups and those of the asylum-seekers themselves. The civil society groups that mobilized in support of the refugee claimants consisted largely of these professionalized groups, with the citizen in the street remaining essentially outside of the debate. Bearing witness to a more republican perspective, some aspects of the discourse that revealed a specific notion of the Good and of social relations owed much to the presence of these politically engaged groups, some of which were labelled as being on the far left of the political spectrum.

In Canada, however, it was the Church and its secular representatives who were most involved in negotiations with the authorities. Moreover, while the community supporting the refugees certainly included advocacy groups, it was made up above all of individual citizens. For example, the priest had to present his case to his parish council, which consisted of laypersons living in the neighbourhood. The sociological and ideological profile of these laypersons differed from that of members of the French groups in the Église Saint-Bernard episode. In Canada, support was motivated by moral values, an attachment to the Catholic tradition of helping the needy, the notion of a superior law and perceived injustice. Yet the parish council remained, like the neighbourhood residents themselves, committed to the idea of respect for legality. Unlike the French groups, they were not made up of activists defending immigrants' rights or fighting for greater social justice. In such a context, determining whether the stories recounted by the asylum-seekers were in fact true became crucial to obtaining the support of the community.

Finally, in both cases, the reaction of the authorities and their discourse was the same: the law had to be respected, as did territorial borders. A vision of immigration emerged in France and Canada that sprang from the necessity of controlling South–North migration. This was true even in Canada, traditionally a country of immigration. Furthermore, in Canada, as in France, the ambivalent attitudes within the general population demonstrate the impact of a discourse that, beginning in the 1980s, depicted political refugees as fraudulent immigrants and an unnecessary burden on taxpayers (Blin 2010). In France, this economic argument was compounded by a more cultural one related to the universal nature of the Republic and its distrust of pluralistic identities. Lastly, in both cases, the state was reluctant to make any exceptions to its immigration policies, which reflected the ambivalence observed in the general population.

Conclusion

Comparing these two sanctuary incidents from the liberal and republican perspectives allows us to gain a better grasp of the nature of sanctuary in modern societies from three different angles: (1) church–state relations; (2) the citizen's relationship to authority; and (3) the shifting relationship between rights and sovereignty under the influence of immigration issues. We sought first to interpret the two cases in light of the classic opposition between church and state. In both examples, this opposition had to be qualified, much as Lippert (2005) argued before us. Indeed, on closer inspection, the attitude of the churches and of the others actors involved was far from a challenge to state sovereignty. Though these actors might have affirmed they were acting in the name of a higher law, divine law was never invoked; at most, these parties made reference to natural rights. The discourse of the French groups supporting the refugee claimants was unmistakably secular – the higher principle invoked being that of human rights. From this view, the liberal discourse clearly came to the fore, the corollary of an era in which human rights arguments became pre-eminent (Taylor 1989). However, the separation of powers and respect for republican sovereignty were acknowledged implicitly. While authority was challenged, the confrontation was only on account of the authority's limitations, that is, its inability to accommodate exceptions within a general rule. Put differently, sanctuary challenged the law's application, not its underlying principles. In the Canadian example, the Church pleaded for a more humane assessment of the cases that would allow greater consideration of the particular situation of the asylum-seekers in question. In other words, what it questioned was the 'violence of abstraction' (Terestchenko 1992). Recognizing that authority was challenged only insofar as the demands made were for an exception to the rule must not, however, lead us to underestimate how the practice of sanctuary can carry the seeds of resistance to power. After all, exceptions to a rule can lead to the rule being changed or circumscribed. In France, though the human rights discourse and the idea of moral regulation were indeed both present, they were accompanied by an idea of the Good. This explained the more political and ideological dimension of the arguments put forth – namely, the North's subordination of the South and the supremacy of popular sovereignty and freedom over national sovereignty. One can see a similar phenomenon at work in the

1980s US-Central American Sanctuary Movement, where injustice towards particular asylum-seekers was read against a broader context, including relations of subordination between the global North and South (Perla and Bibler Coutin, Chapter 5 in this volume).

This nuance in the discourses was reflective not so much of fundamental differences in the political cultures of the two countries as of the particularities of the communities in Montreal and Paris that supported the asylum-seekers. In Montreal, the community was composed of local citizens residing in the neighbourhood who sat on the Saint-Jean de la Croix parish council or otherwise belonged to the church. In France, the protests were led by well honed advocacy groups specializing in advocating around such causes and pushing a much broader agenda. Moreover, our analysis underscored the hybrid nature of the discourses and the overlap between liberal and republican perspectives. The way in which immigration issues have changed has unquestionably reinforced the vision of the sovereign state as guarantor of the security of national borders and monopolistic holder of the right to bestow citizenship. At the same time, however, state sovereignty is being eroded to the benefit of 'pockets' of sovereignty where citizens assert their vision of justice and contest the state when it drifts too far from social realities. This erosion of the state is reflected in religious sanctuary, which is an expression of resistance to authority. We need to reconsider referring to the sanctuary movement as civil disobedience, regardless of what the actors themselves think. The sanctuary movement represents a form of resistance to authority and the claim for a sphere of autonomous action independent of institutionalized power structures, a circumscribed re-assessment of governance and its excesses. Thus, contemporary religious sanctuary also teaches us something about more general changes that have swept through political life in recent times and the spheres in which individual citizens have a say in what is just (Rosanvallon 2008).

Notes

1 Following a visit to Chile, Canadian Prime Minister Jean Chrétien indicated that Canada would lift visa requirements for Chileans travelling to Canada. This led to a substantial number of Chileans applying for asylum in Canada. However, of the 2629 refugee status applications filed in Montreal, only 50 were accepted (Berger 1997).
2 The Church's involvement in such cases dates back to the Vietnamese boat people who entered Canada in the 1970s (see Lippert 1998). The government of the day had called upon ecclesiastical institutions to help accommodate these refugees.

References

Arendt, H. (1994) 'La désobéissance civile', in H. Arendt, *Du mensonge à la violence*, Paris: Pocket.
Bantman, B. (1996) 'Les dix continuent la grève de la faim', *Libération*, 24 August, p. 6.
Barber, B. (1984) *Strong Democracy: Participatory Politics for a New Age*, Berkeley, CA: University of California Press.

Bedau, H.A. (1961) 'On Civil Disobedience', *Journal of Philosophy*, 58: 653–61.
Berger, F. (1997) 'Des vols spéciaux pour les Chiliens refusés', *La Presse*, 7 June, p. A1.
Berlin, I. (1969) *Four Essays on Liberty*, Oxford: Oxford University Press.
Bernard, P. (1996) 'Les associations accueillent avec réserve le projet gouvernemental sur l'immigration', *Le Monde*, 11 October, p. 10.
Bernard, P. and Herzberg, N. (1996) 'Aucun barbelé, aucune loi n'arrête les courants d'air!', *Le Monde*, 19 November, p. 12.
Blin, T. (2005) 'Les sans-papiers de Saint-Bernard', *Mouvement social et action organisée*, Paris: L'Harmattan.
——(2010) *L'invention des sans-papiers*, Paris: PUF.
Bohman, J. and Rehg, W. (1997) *Deliberative Democracy: Essays on Reason and Politics*, Cambridge, MA: MIT Press.
Bronskill, J. (2004) 'Ottawa veut cesser l'asile dans les églises', *Le Soleil*, 26 July, p. A10.
Dumas, H. (1998) 'Chiliens réfugiés dans une église', *La Presse*, 18 September, p. A7.
Dworkin, R. (1985) *A Matter of Principles*, Cambridge, MA: Harvard University Press.
Habermas, J. (1990) 'Le droit et la force', in J. Habermas, *Écrits politiques*, Paris: Cerf.
Jones, P. (1983) 'Political Equality and Majority Rule', in P. Jones, *The Nature of Political Theory*, Oxford: Clarendon Press.
Lacroix, J. (2003) *Communautarisme versus libéralisme: quel modèle d'intégration politique?* Brussels: Éditions de l'Université libre de Bruxelles.
Lippert, R.K. (1998) 'Rationalities and Refugee Resettlement', *Economy and Society*, 27(4): 380–406.
——(2005) *Sanctuary, Sovereignty, Sacrifice: Canadian Sanctuary Incidents*, Vancouver: University of British Columbia Press
Lippert, R.K. and Rehaag, S. (2009) 'Sanctuary in Context', *Refuge: Canada's Periodical on Refugees*, 26: 3–6.
Manin, B. (2002) 'L'idée de démocratie délibérative dans la science politique contemporaine. Introduction, généalogie et éléments critiques', *Politix*, 15: 57–37.
Markovits, D. (2005) 'Democratic Disobedience', *The Yale Law Journal*, 114: 1897–1952.
Montpetit, C. (1998) 'Réfugiés Chiliens', *Le Devoir*, 11 September, p. A4.
Mouffe, C. (2000) *The Democratic Paradox*, New York: Verso.
Perrignon, Judith (1996) 'L'immigration, sujet glissant pour le PS', *Libération*, 24 December, p. 12.
Prieur, C. (1996) 'De Saint-Ambroise à Saint-Bernard, cinq mois de négociations avortées', *Le Monde*, 22 August, p. 5.
Rawls, J. (1971) *A Theory of Justice*, Cambridge, MA: Harvard University Press.
Rehaag, S. (2009) 'Bordering on Legality: Canadian Church Sanctuary and the Rule of Law', *Refuge: Canada's Periodical on Refugees*, 26: 43–56.
Rosanvallon, P. (2008) *La Légitimité démocratique. Impartialité, réflexivité, proximité*, Paris: Le Seuil.
Sartori, G. (1973) *Théorie de la démocratie*, Paris: Armand Colin.
Simonnot, D. (1996) 'Le Noël au Soleil des sans-papiers. Ceux de Saint-Bernard se sont retrouvés à la Cartoucherie', *Libération*, 26 December, p.10.
Singer, P. (1973) *Democracy and Disobedience*, Oxford: Clarendon Press.
Taylor, C. (1989) *Sources of the Self*, Cambridge: Cambridge University Press.
Tazreiter, C. (2004) *Asylum Seekers and the State: The Politics of Protection in a Security-Conscious World*, Aldershot: Ashgate.
Terestchenko, M. (1992) *Les Violences de l'abstraction*, Paris: PUF.

Thoreau, H. D. ([1849] 1948) *On the Duty of Civil Disobedience*, New York: Holt, Rinehart and Winston. (Originally published in 1849 as *Resistance to Civil Government*). Available at: http://publicliterature.org/books/civil_disobedience/1.

Wihtol de Wenden, C. (1994) 'The French Response to the Asylum Seeker Influx, 1980–93', *Annals of the American Academy of Political and Social Science*, 534: 81–90.

Wilson, D. (2004) *Sanctuary in the Spotlight*. Available at: http://www.ucobserver.org/justice/2004/09/sanctuary_in_the_spotlight/.

Wiltfang, G and McAdam, D. (1991) 'The Costs and Risks of Social Activism: A Study of Sanctuary Movement Activism', *Social Forces*, 69: 987–1010.

Wyatt, N. (2004) 'Deported Algerian Arrested in Québec Church Must Return: Coalition', *Canadian Press*, 9 March.

Part IV

Emergent realms
Cities of Sanctuary and military sanctuaries

Chapter 13

Everyday enactments of sanctuary
The UK *City of Sanctuary* movement

Jonathan Darling and Vicki Squire

Introduction

Sanctuary cities have been the focus of considerable attention in the US and Canadian contexts. Both countries have long-standing traditions of sanctuary movements as well as a plethora of localised urban collectives that assert rights to sanctuary within the city (see, for example, Cunningham, Chapter 11, Mancina, Chapter 14, Ridgley, Chapter 15, and Young, Chapter 16 in this volume). Notwithstanding occasional episodes of church-centred sanctuary (see Cohen 2003), the UK has seen much less interest in the development of sanctuary cities. Indeed, it is only in recent years that a coordinated movement, *City of Sanctuary*, has emerged across the UK to define a range of urban environments as key sites for the practice of sanctuary. This chapter provides an overview of *City of Sanctuary*, setting out the broad aims of the movement as well as drawing on our research into the movement's activities in the city of Sheffield.[1] In focusing on the Sheffield case, the chapter explores how key activities, such as the facilitation of voluntary opportunities, can be understood both as reflecting and as creating possibilities for disruptive acts of sanctuary. These disruptive acts are explored through an emphasis on *everyday enactments* of sanctuary as forming relations which are not always-already imbued with traces of domination but are continuously open to challenge. Our interest is in the ways that these everyday enactments are detached from, and thus potentially disrupt, the relations of privilege that are embedded in the formal articulation of the movement as promoting a cultural shift towards valuing 'hospitality'. Specifically, we draw out the tensions between everyday enactments of sanctuary and formal practices of hospitality in *City of Sanctuary*, as a means to both forefront and challenge the uneven relations that constitute the UK sanctuary movement.

The chapter proceeds in four parts. First, we examine the activities of *City of Sanctuary* by providing an overview of its organisation, ideals and practices. In so doing, we draw distinctions between the formal articulation of sanctuary found in this movement, and the broader 'patchwork' of everyday enactments of sanctuary manifest across Sheffield and beyond. The limitations of this formal approach form the focus of the second part of the chapter. The third part sets out how *City of Sanctuary* activities might be understood as creating opportunities for everyday enactments of sanctuary that disrupt the assignment of positions associated with relations of hospitality. Here we explore the temporality of sanctuary through considering the regulatory potentials of 'waiting' as an imposed practice which conditions the lives of those seeking asylum (see Conlon 2011; Schuster 2011). We then consider how volunteering potential questions such as governmental temporalities of waiting. Drawing attention to the significance of tensions within *City of Sanctuary* activities, we then turn to the work of Henri Lefebvre (1996) on the 'right to the city'. We argue that Lefebvre helps to highlight how routines of work, travel and occupation can be of particular significance for challenging uneven relations embedded in sanctuary practices. Specifically, we consider Lefebvre's work as a frame for understanding how everyday enactments of sanctuary might be tied to a notion of inhabiting the city. We suggest that this facilitates an appreciation of how everyday enactments of sanctuary can cut across the positions and assumptions of hospitality. Let us begin, however, by introducing *City of Sanctuary*.

City of Sanctuary: movement or patchwork?

In 2007, Sheffield became a *City of Sanctuary* with the support of the City Council and over 100 local organisations. While Sheffield was the first city in the UK to achieve official status as a *City of Sanctuary*, it is by no means the only place in the UK where sanctuary has been enacted. The creation of a place as a *City of Sanctuary* is based on the commitment of member organisations and groups, as well as on support from local politicians and the active participation of asylum-seekers, refugees and refugee groups. As such, localised groups across a variety of cities and towns have been formed under the name of *City of Sanctuary* in recent years. The movement is a means by which actions that intervene in the field of asylum politics are facilitated, consolidated and unified. Indeed, in October 2011, a national network of local groups in 17 towns and cities formed part of this 'movement to build a culture of hospitality for people seeking sanctuary in the UK' (*City of Sanctuary* 2011). At the time of writing, Bristol, Sheffield and Swansea were the only cities with official status as a *City of Sanctuary* (ibid.). Nevertheless, the movement is clearly more far-reaching than this 'official' articulation would imply.

So what precisely constitutes a place as a *City of Sanctuary*? There is both a more formal and a more *informal* answer to this question. Formally, the primary aim of the movement is to 'influence policy-makers and public attitudes throughout the country' (ibid.), yet to achieve this, *City of Sanctuary* favours processes of cultural change over political lobbying or campaigning (Barnett and Bhogal 2009: 83; see also Squire 2009a, 2011; Darling 2010). To qualify 'officially' as a *City of Sanctuary*, a place has to: gain resolutions of support from local groups and organisations; involve local refugee communities in the movement; achieve the support of the City Council and produce a strategy for greater inclusion of refugees and people seeking sanctuary in the city (Barnett and Bhogal 2009: 79). Much work goes into creating a place of sanctuary before official status is gained. For this reason an understanding of the less formal dimensions of *City of Sanctuary* is central in understanding how a place is constituted as such.

At a less formal level, the constitution of a city or town as a *City of Sanctuary* takes a variety of forms depending on the specific location of groups involved. One of the key impulses driving the movement is the encouragement of a localised approach, through which the movement's activities are embedded in the specificities of the urban context (see Darling 2010; Squire and Darling forthcoming). Despite these local specificities, however, there are similarities in the activities of *City of Sanctuary* across the UK, such as in the organisation of cultural events like community gardening or social evenings. These are designed to foster relationships between those taking sanctuary and other people who are present in the city. In addition to such activities, there is a strong emphasis on the creation of volunteering opportunities for those who are denied the right to work or who face barriers to entering the job market. Educating local residents about the challenges facing those taking sanctuary is also frequently emphasized.

One aspect common to each activity is that they create opportunities for everyday encounters between individuals and groups present within the city. However, though significant, the role of *City of Sanctuary* itself should not be overstated. One could perhaps say that *City of Sanctuary* is also a product of everyday encounters: it reflects and further develops the possibilities for such encounters rather than simply providing opportunities for them. Indeed, one could say it is a product both of those encounters that emerge from political and social activities by existing groups (such as the Northern Refugee Centre in the Sheffield case), as well as of those that emerge out of social and personal connections formed within a city of dispersal[2] and resettlement (including those associated with religious groups or congregations of various denominations). To develop an understanding of the significance of *City of Sanctuary* in these terms is not simply to understand it as a movement with official qualification standards and formal aims and objectives. It is to understand *City of Sanctuary* as a patchwork formation that emerges from, and feeds into, less formal everyday encounters. This prompts us to consider the political significance of such encounters and the possibilities they provide in challenging the uneven relations embedded in sanctuary practices. It is to the limits of the movement's formal emphasis on a 'culture of hospitality', however, that we turn to next.

The limits of a 'culture of hospitality'

Everyday enactments are of particular interest as a site through which to explore *City of Sanctuary*. These enactments provide a means to consider acts of sanctuary that diverge from the formal representation of the movement as fostering a 'culture of hospitality'. The latter, we suggest, is a politically limiting approach that is bound to rationalities of power that produce uneven relations between guest and host (Squire 2011; Squire and Bagelman 2012; Squire and Darling forthcoming). Indeed, it is in the formal articulation of the movement as centred on intercultural events and the promotion of a 'culture of hospitality' that the uneven relations embedded in sanctuary practices are evident. In part, this is because practices of hospitality do little to redress or contest the distinctions of position, status and privilege which inform the exclusionary politics of asylum evident in states such as the UK (see Squire 2009b). Rather, what comes to surface through valorising welcome is not only the privilege some have in welcoming others, but also the assumed indebtedness of those 'guests' who are 'welcomed' or hosted (see Chan 2005; Darling 2009, 2011a). Practices of sanctuary that remain wedded to notions of gratitude or indebtedness are problematic precisely because they maintain subordinate positions for those being 'offered' sanctuary.

A culture of hospitality is particularly problematic where it is bound to the valorisation of individual contribution, since this can carry over embedded privileges into governmental practice by limiting the scope of welcome to those deemed morally or socially 'worthy'. A celebration of the potential or actual contributions made by asylum-seekers and refugees is central to some of *City of Sanctuary*'s campaign materials (see Darling 2010). This serves as a means to present those seeking sanctuary as 'good' and 'worthy' citizens, as figures 'deserving' of sanctuary (see also Sales 2002). Yet valorising the contributions of those seeking asylum or taking refuge in the city once again risks positioning asylum-seekers and refugees as dutifully repaying a debt imbued through the 'offer' of sanctuary, as well as subordinated in his or her need for this 'offer' of sanctuary in the first place. The formal language and practice of *City of Sanctuary* therefore extend a pastoral logic (see Lippert 1998, 2005a: 89–140), and can be understood as being mobilised in terms that both depoliticise and regulate the presence of asylum-seekers and refugees (see Squire and Bagelman 2012).

While the formal message of this form of sanctuary politics is potentially limiting, it is notable that within Sheffield such a message was also questioned. For example, in interviews during the movement's initial work, city councillors David and Julie expressed concern at the approach of *City of Sanctuary*;

> I just have this fear that they're [*City of Sanctuary*] talking to the converted ... and they haven't broadened their horizons. Because, I genuinely don't believe that in general terms they talk to Joe Public in the street, they're the people they should be talking to ... they're talking to a quite closed audience and they're not going to be challenged as much there.
>
> (David, interview, 2007)

David's concern that the methods of *City of Sanctuary* are too often focused upon garnering support among groups and individuals who would be expected to support values of sanctuary and hospitality are furthered by Julie, who states:

I think they'll have to step up a gear, as they won't really grab that many people's attention just working in that locale, but of course it's not so challenging here, there is no backlash.

(Julie, interview, 2006)

The difficultly highlighted here for *City of Sanctuary* is that in speaking only to those who may already support their aims implies there is a lack of dialogue, debate and criticism. Indeed, a number of politicians in the city expressed concern about how the movement would extend their message to more diverse groups.

If, as David suggests, the majority of individuals and groups reached by *City of Sanctuary* are expected to be supporters of such an initiative, such as refugee organisations, universities and local churches, then the argument regarding cultural change is weakened. Moreover, the way the movement is formally articulated fits dominant agendas, not only in terms of the articulation of *City of Sanctuary* as a movement for hospitality but also in its articulation as a 'mainstream' movement. *City of Sanctuary* seeks to promote opportunities for interaction between those seeking sanctuary and other Sheffield residents. It aims in particular to celebrate the contributions of refugees to the city, and to allow those seeking sanctuary to be supported as far as possible within the constraints of the UK's dispersal policies. As such, the kinds of cultural activities promoted fit well with Sheffield's image as a cosmopolitan and inclusive city. This image is promoted through The Sheffield City Strategy 2010–20 (Sheffield First Partnership 2011), which highlights an 'inclusive' and 'vibrant' city in which 'people feel welcomed, valued and can fully participate'. The lack of negative response that Julie notes might thus be read as a consequence of the relatively conservative nature of *City of Sanctuary*, also reflected in the explicit refusal to engage in more traditional 'political' activities such as lobbying and protest.[3]

In its emphasis on fostering a culture of hospitality and practices of welcome, the *City of Sanctuary* movement is thus relatively easily subsumed under a dominant discourse of the 'tolerant' nation. This not only offers an explanation for the lack of backlash noted in Sheffield, but also highlights the limits of *City of Sanctuary* as a movement. In its formal articulation, the movement would seem to do little to effectively challenge or resist the exclusionary nature of asylum discourse and practice in the UK (Squire 2009b). Indeed, in uncritically maintaining the position of the city as a site of dispersal politics (see Darling 2011b), *City of Sanctuary* might be understood as actively propagating such exclusions by allowing supporting organisations, practices and councillors to be part of a 'sanctuary city' without politicising its status. Yet even accepting these limitations, we perceive tensions in the way sanctuary is enacted that warrant further attention. Our primary interest is not in assessing the *City of Sanctuary* movement, but in exploring how tensions in its 'patchwork' formation are indicative of the disruptive potential of everyday enactments of sanctuary. In the next section we discuss these everyday enactments of sanctuary.

Everyday enactments of sanctuary

As we have noted, in contrast to sanctuary incidents such as those examined by Randy Lippert (2005a, 2005b) in the Canadian context, *City of Sanctuary* Sheffield does not actively engage in the material or physical provision of accommodation or protection (see also Yukich on the US New Sanctuary Movement, Chapter 7 in this volume). Rather, such work is undertaken by a range of other local organisations. It might thus be tempting to suggest that *City of Sanctuary* represents little more than a collective of organisations and individuals who promote values of hospitality but who do not effectively practise sanctuary. However, this overlooks how the activities of *City of Sanctuary* both emerge from, and create possibilities for, everyday enactments of sanctuary in a more diffuse sense. There are three points that we want to summarise here as a means to set out our understanding of *City of Sanctuary* as a patchwork of everyday enactments that potentially invoke more disruptive acts of sanctuary. We do not focus on the specificity of these disruptive acts here, since they are detailed elsewhere (Squire 2011; Squire and Bagelman 2012; Squire and Darling forthcoming), but rather we draw out some points of significance in highlighting everyday enactments of sanctuary.

Rightful presence

The first point relates to how everyday enactments of sanctuary entail disruptive claims to justice or presence. That is, they involve enactments of 'rightful presence', whereby those taking sanctuary assume or enact claims that disrupt the uneven relations between guest and host (Squire and Darling forthcoming). We suggest that this occurs through a 'making present' of interconnected histories and geographies, thus invoking a form of relational justice (see Dikeç 2001). The activities of *City of Sanctuary* are not primarily significant for the development of a movement promoting rightful presence or for the emergence of a campaign for justice on behalf of those seeking refuge. Rather, these activities are significant for the disruptive 'acts' through which those taking sanctuary make claims to a 'right to have rights' (see Isin 2008). Thus, activities such as museum exhibitions, blogging workshops and speakers' events are important in so far as they emerge from, and provide conditions for, enactments of sanctuary that challenge or trouble uneven relations of guest and host. In other words, we want to highlight the ways that claiming or assuming presence as rightful disrupts broader historical and geographical patterns of privilege. This might be understood as an informal dimension of *City of Sanctuary* that exceeds its official remit. As such, it disrupts the formal articulation of sanctuary as a form of hospitable engagement and shows the political potential of everyday activities of *City of Sanctuary*.

Networks and encounters

The second point we want to highlight relates to the significance of the network-building dimension of the movement, which is important to the engagements that *City of Sanctuary* fosters among organisations, individuals and community groups. While this form of network-building is limited in its reach, it nonetheless provides for encounters between those taking sanctuary and other groups that may be more 'established' within the city. We are not suggesting here that such encounters are necessarily 'positive' (see Closs Stephens and Squire 2012), although in this case they are of significance since they potentially challenge processes of isolation associated with dispersal (Squire 2009b). Indeed, for some, such encounters are seen as a distinctly positive dimension of *City of Sanctuary*, as Ilya, an asylum-seeker, describes:

> It's brilliant work, it's, like, to bring together locals and foreigners and to say, look, we're human beings and we can live together without offending each other and we have a lot to share and we can work together ... [the council's decision to join] is a recognition of the fact that these people are a part of Sheffield.
>
> (Ilya, interview, 2007)

Ilya's positive account of the work of *City of Sanctuary* in Sheffield contrasts with that of David and Julie in that the movement's very existence is articulated as providing a sense of hope through the discursive articulation of practices of solidarity which involve a shared investment in the city. While we make no normative claims about the nature of the relations fostered through the network-building dimension of the movement, we do want to suggest the encounters that emerge through such connections may create opportunities for relations that disrupt the privileges associated with hospitable sanctuary practices.

Taking, not waiting to receive, sanctuary

The final point here relates to the significance of *City of Sanctuary* activities as a means by which sanctuary can be creatively enacted or 'taken', rather than merely passively received (see Squire and Bagelman 2012). This requires a little more discussion than the previous points, since temporality is a relatively neglected dimension in the analysis of sanctuary (but see Bagelman 2012; Lippert 2005a: 143–5, 154, 171). In analysing the 'time politics' of asylum in the UK, Saulo Cwerner (2004: 73) argues that the 'diverse temporalities' of everyday life are subsumed within a focus on the speed of the asylum process, such that the 'temporal complexity' of asylum as a process is overridden by a desire for asylum adjudication processes to work 'faster'. Here different rhythms of movement, mobility, recuperation and counselling fade from importance in the light of a dominant framing of speed as the key tempo of asylum processing. However, while a dominant rhythm of asylum is this process of speeding up, this is in part matched by a very different temporality for those awaiting decisions. For those seeking sanctuary, the 'speeding up' of asylum is interwoven with the apparent 'slowing down' of daily life (Cwerner 2004).

The everyday temporal rhythms of the asylum process are summarised by Andrew who, reflecting on his experiences of the asylum system, stated:

> In the beginning, it was really depressing, I can't really go anywhere … you're just sitting there in a house waiting for the Home Office decision which you didn't know when, who and when they're gonna write. I mean, every time I was receiving any sort of papers, official papers, they were all of [a] negative kind … you just get refusals all the time … they're just getting rid of the case, but … it's actually your life at stake when you read those papers … So after waiting for a couple of years, it became really hard to understand … it's a constant uncertainty, every single day you don't know what's gonna happen.
> (Andrew, interview, 2010)

In the UK, restrictions applied to the lives of those seeking asylum are often manifest in terms that prevent participation in certain forms of urban life. Asylum-seekers often have little or no means to travel, for example, and the denial of a right to work means this central routine of everyday life is denied in favour of a largely undifferentiated temporality of waiting. Waiting, as articulated by Andrew, presents an uncertain and isolating experience that can feed into processes whereby asylum-seekers are related to as passive recipients of hospitality, rather than as political agents in their own right. Such imposed passivity also suggests a process of supplication (see Bagelman 2011), through which the uncertainty of waiting is attached to a performed position of earnestly 'seeking' or 'requesting' sanctuary. The imposition of waiting upon those seeking sanctuary, and the management of their everyday lives through restrictions on work and travel are indicative of how the regulation of temporality can become a means of state control (see Shapiro 2000). Indeed, Deidre Conlon (2011) has suggested that the temporal dimensions of authority imposed through awaiting asylum decisions constitute a means of regulating the politics of (im)mobility, with the logic of waiting having become one of the 'weapons in the battle to deter' those seeking asylum (Schuster 2011: 411).

So, to what extent might the very logic and practice of enforced waiting provide opportunities for more disruptive enactments of sanctuary? Alison Mountz (2011) suggests that within the processes of temporal containment or marginalisation associated with waiting there exist opportunities for resistance. In particular, she argues that waiting may invite activism and produce spaces of political possibility through which the contradictions in, and failures of, struggles to govern (im)mobility are brought to wider attention. How far do the activities of *City of Sanctuary* disrupt practices of state deterrence? It does not appear to us as though there are sustained or collectively organised tactics of resistance at play in the formal practices of *City of Sanctuary*, which may have serious implications for the movement's wider political effects. However, a consideration of how *City of Sanctuary* activities involve disruptive 'takings' of sanctuary through everyday enactments may nevertheless be fruitful. Specifically these activities develop insights into the possibilities for more sustained collective struggles around processes of temporal management along with the uneven relations that these both reflect and reproduce. We suggest therefore that a consideration of the tensions between the formal articulation of sanctuary and informal everyday enactments of sanctuary is critical in understanding the potential and limitations of the sanctuary 'patchwork' of which *City of Sanctuary* activities form a part.

The role that volunteering plays in this process is particularly telling, because it allows us to draw attention to the potentialities of everyday enactments of 'taking' sanctuary, as well as the limitations of such enactments where they are not consolidated through more sustained collectively organised forms of resistance. *City of Sanctuary* has established links with local businesses, charities and community groups in order to coordinate and facilitate volunteering among asylum-seekers. For example, opportunities were created in a community gardening organisation, in a central Sheffield café and with a local refugee NGO for individuals to spend time working alongside other Sheffield residents. In reflecting on such opportunities, Catherine suggests that:

> [T]he process was a very long one because it was a long waiting period. For me, it was five years of waiting with no answer, with nothing to rely on … it was a bit difficult and a bit shocking. But during that time I just did volunteering work and that kept me going and it made me forget about the waiting time.
>
> (Catherine, interview, 2010)

Here, Catherine's volunteer work allowed her to 'forget' the process of waiting rather than entirely escape it. Similarly, Rodrigo highlights how the connections made through volunteering were crucial in dealing with the frustrations of the asylum system. When asked about what frustrations he had encountered, he noted:

> I've been here for the last one year and among others was the waiting period, seems to be quite long and quite stressful, and you find yourself living in the … uncertainty. You do not know the outcome of the decisions, so it's quite stressful. But on the other hand, I felt I should keep busy by getting engaged and doing volunteering with various organisation[s], and by so doing, I find it's lovely meeting new friends, different cultures, ways of coping up, you know, that is how I thought things should be, and that's how I kept myself busy.
>
> (Rodrigo, interview, 2010)

For Rodrigo, as well as for Catherine, volunteering offers a means of coping with the logic of waiting built into the asylum system, rather than an escape or a more sustained challenge to the uneven relations that constitute sanctuary as such.

Nevertheless, volunteering also appears to feature in more disruptive terms, as a means not only to meet other people and share concerns and knowledge, but also to tap into a different rhythm of city life. Sanctuary, in this regard, might be understood as being taken in ways that potentially subvert the relations of privilege associated with the logic of waiting and state deterrence. Here the slowed down rhythm of life associated with the isolating effect of dispersal was brought into contact with many rhythms that mark everyday life for Sheffield's inhabitants – those of a regular commute to work, the contours of a working day, and the encounters offered through volunteering. It is in this sense that volunteering might be understood as a significant dimension of the 'minor' politics that are embedded in everyday enactments of sanctuary (see Squire 2011). We do not mean to suggest here that such enactments feature as a radical overturn either of the logic of waiting embedded in the asylum system or of the uneven relations of guest and host that ultimately render some as volunteers and others as paid workers. However, we do suggest that there remain disruptive dimensions to these enactments of sanctuary in the form of processes of taking a position within the city, which effectively challenge the uneven relations embedded in the formal articulation of *City of Sanctuary* as a movement of hospitality. To explore such possibilities, we turn to literature on the 'right to the city' (Lefebvre 1996).

The right to the city

Lefebvre's (1996) notion of the 'right to the city' might provide one way to explore the potential of everyday enactments of sanctuary in relation to the activity of volunteering, introduced above. The notion of a right to the city implies 'the participation of the urban citizen in the political life, management, and administration of the city' (Dikeç 2001: 1790). As such, it suggests a conception of citizenship not based upon civic duty or belonging, but which is open to all and is claimed through the act of participation itself (Lefebvre 1996; Purcell 2006). Lefebvre's 'right to the city' thus names a renewed focus on the production, appropriation and use of urban space by those who inhabit it, which is 'earned by living out the routines of everyday life in the space of the city' (Purcell 2002: 102). For Lefebvre (1996), the city is a compositional arrangement of varied rhythms, temporalities, routines and relations, which form both the space of the city and the everyday texture of urban existence. It is to this compositional imaginary of urban space that a right to the city is orientated as a means to valorise participation within the city as it is constantly reproduced in daily life.

Returning to the example of volunteering discussed by Catherine and Rodrigo, we can see some resonances with this idea. In engaging with the city through participating in the routines of everyday life, those taking sanctuary become part of the compositional enactment of urban life – a compositional enactment that entails multiple routines, rhythms and forms of occupation. For Catherine and Rodrigo, the 'keeping busy' of volunteering is in the first instance an embodiment of routine and repetition through which some frustrations and closures of imposed waiting are addressed on a daily basis. Yet, it is not simply routines, but also the breaking of routines, that is important. The 'time politics' of asylum and its routines of waiting (Cwerner 2004) are here challenged through the enactment of a right to be part of the city via an engagement with its routines. Everyday enactments such as these bear an account of the urban inhabitant which is not reliant upon distinctions of status or belonging, and thus potentially disrupts the categories of host and guest. The inhabitant is one who takes part in the everyday enactment of the city through its routines, practices and rhythms and at the same time is constituted politically, in part, through such an engagement with the city. Indeed, as Purcell (2002: 102, original emphasis) argues 'the right to the city empowers urban *inhabitants*' and is 'defined by everyday experience in lived space' (ibid.: 106).

To address those taking sanctuary as urban inhabitants potentially facilitates an understanding of everyday enactments of sanctuary in terms that reject embedded assumptions about the indebted guest. Rather than guests or celebrated conditional presences, Catherine and Rodrigo might be understood as inhabitants whose daily routines are integral to the texture of urban life in Sheffield. Their involvement in volunteering in this regard disrupts the temporal logic of waiting, which disqualifies asylum-seekers and refugees from enacting urban inhabitancy. As such, an alternative reading of voluntary work might be developed here that challenges the idea that it is an activity that reinforces embedded privileges. Lefebvre's (1996) focus upon the political and productive salience of urban inhabitancy is helpful here because it potentially fosters an appreciation of the shifting and dynamic nature of everyday enactments of sanctuary, in terms that favour neither mobility nor settlement as norms or ideals. Thus, it neither discriminates against those who inhabit the city for fleeting periods, nor fixes routines in ways that overlook either the dynamic nature of urban life or the relations of sanctuary examined here. Nevertheless, the voluntary nature of the work placements organised by *City of Sanctuary* remains problematic in so far as it remains bound to uneven relations and articulated as part of a contributory process. Hence patterns of privilege are less overturned here as they are challenged in partial and ambiguous terms. Our conclusion is by no means final in this regard, since we detect both possibilities and limitations in the everyday enactments that make up the informal patchwork of sanctuary within which *City of Sanctuary* is bound.

Conclusion

In this engagement with *City of Sanctuary*, we have not offered an appraisal of the movement's practices or of its re-conceptualisation of sanctuary within the city. Rather, we have considered the 'patchwork' of which *City of Sanctuary* is a part, specifically as a means to think about the limits and opportunities of everyday enactments of sanctuary in Sheffield in challenging established 'host–guest' relations. The sanctuary practices we have examined in many respects draw upon and further entrench established relations of privilege, along with the uneven relations implied by the formal articulation of *City of Sanctuary* as a 'hospitable' movement. Yet such relations can also be partially challenged or resisted in everyday enactments of sanctuary, such as in the voluntary work of Catherine and Rodrigo discussed here. We have suggested that to understand those taking sanctuary as 'urban inhabitants' is one way of exploring activities such as volunteering as more disruptive enactments of sanctuary. Though ambiguous and often temporary, highlighting everyday enactments implies that sanctuary relations are not necessarily always-already imbued with traces of privilege or domination, but are rather continuously open to challenge. To expose these 'breaks' or openings is both to challenge the articulation of *City of Sanctuary* as 'apolitical' and to highlight the importance of critically confronting the rationalities of power within which those enacting sanctuary are caught. The activities of *City of Sanctuary* can be understood as offering opportunities for, as well as limiting, the enactment of sanctuary in terms that offer a more sustained challenge to uneven relations within which the 'time politics' of asylum are embedded. While the resistances and challenges we have pointed to here are limited and partial, they nonetheless remain disruptive. As such, they pose ways of thinking about how the uneven relations embedded within contemporary practices of sanctuary might undergo a more sustained challenge (see also Czajka, Chapter 3 in this volume). On our reading, it is the informal dimensions of *City of Sanctuary* that are of most interest, since they do not necessarily comply with the formal articulation of hospitality. Rather, in the informal activities and everyday enactments of *City of Sanctuary*, we see the possibilities of alternative perspectives on sanctuary that reject the assumptions and exclusions implied within a framework of hospitality. It is from these informal, momentary and often prosaic enactments of sanctuary that a politics of sanctuary that challenges the presumptions and privileges of the 'hospitable host' might be envisaged.

Acknowledgements

Many thanks to all those members of *City of Sanctuary* who contributed to this research. Thanks also to Louise Richards and Ruth Healey whose support in carrying out the interviews was invaluable, and to Gabi Kent of Angel Eye Media. Thanks to Randy Lippert and Sean Rehaag whose engaging and constructive comments have helped to refine our argument in this chapter.

Notes

1 The chapter is based upon research undertaken by both authors on the Sheffield *City of Sanctuary* movement. Darling's research took place between October 2006 and August 2007 and involved interviews with asylum-seekers and refugees in Sheffield,

together with local councillors, politicians and *City of Sanctuary* members (see Darling 2010). Squire's research formed part of the *Mobile Solidarities* study (see Squire 2011), which involved interviews with ten *City of Sanctuary* organisers and participants in the Spring and Summer of 2009 and 2010, together with documentary analysis of *City of Sanctuary* material (see Squire 2009a).

2 Dispersal here refers to the practice of relocating asylum-seekers around an 'asylum estate' of accommodation throughout the UK so as to avoid an 'over-burdening' of provision on the South-East of England. This practice, in place since 1999, has been argued to have destabilising effects on those seeking asylum via enforced mobility and insecurity, it is also argued to act as a means of regulatory deterrence as accommodation is offered with no choice over the location provided (see Gill 2009; Squire 2009b; Darling 2011b).

3 In this respect, *City of Sanctuary* might be viewed as more conservative than some sanctuary movements in the US and Canada. Here sanctuary incidents have been coupled with public protests, anti-deportation actions and wider modes of disruptive campaigning which, formally at least, fall outside the remit of *City of Sanctuary* (see Coutin 1993; Lippert 2005b).

References

Bagelman, J. (2011) 'The Point of Sanctuary? Cutting Across a Statist Ontology', paper presented at The International Studies Association Annual Convention, Montreal.

——(2012) Cities of Sanctuary: A State of Deferral, Unpublished PhD thesis, The Open University, UK.

Barnett, C. and Bhogal, I. (2009) *Becoming a City of Sanctuary: A Practical Handbook with Inspiring Examples*, Sheffield: Plug and Tap.

Chan, W.F. (2005) 'A Gift of a Pagoda, the Presence of a Prominent Citizen, and the Possibilities of Hospitality', *Environment and Planning D: Society and Space*, 23: 11–28.

City of Sanctuary (2011) *About City of Sanctuary*. Available at: http://www.cityofsanctuary.org/about (accessed 21 October 2011).

Closs Stephens, A. and Squire, V. (2012) 'Politics through a Web: Citizenship and Community Unbound', *Environment and Planning D: Society and Space*, 30.

Cohen, S. (2003) *No One Is Illegal: Asylum and Immigration Control, Past and Present*, Stoke on Trent: Trentham Books.

Conlon, D. (2011) 'Waiting: Feminist Perspectives on the Spacings/Timings of Migrant (Im)Mobility', *Gender, Place and Culture*, 18: 353–60.

Coutin, S.B. (1993) *The Culture of Protest: Religious Activism and the U.S. Sanctuary Movement*, Boulder, CO: Westview Press.

Cwerner, S.B. (2004) 'Faster, Faster and Faster: The Time Politics of Asylum in the UK', *Time & Society*, 13: 71–88.

Darling, J. (2009) 'Becoming Bare Life: Asylum, Hospitality and the Politics of Encampment', *Environment and Planning D: Society and Space*, 27: 649–65.

——(2010) 'A City of Sanctuary: The Relational Re-Imagining of Sheffield's Asylum Politics', *Transactions of the Institute of British Geographers*, 35: 125–40.

——(2011a) 'Giving Space: Care, Generosity and Belonging in a UK Asylum Drop-In Centre', *Geoforum*, 42: 408–17.

——(2011b) 'Domopolitics, Governmentality and the Regulation of Asylum Accommodation', *Political Geography*, 30: 263–71.

Dikeç, M. (2001) 'Justice and the Spatial Imaginary', *Environment and Planning A*, 33: 1785–1805.

Gill, N. (2009) 'Governmental Mobility: The Power Effects of the Movement of Detained Asylum Seekers around Britain's Detention Estate', *Political Geography*, 28: 186–96.

Isin, E.F. (2008) 'Theorizing Acts of Citizenship', in E.F. Isin and G.M. Nielsen (eds) *Acts of Citizenship*, London: Zed Books.

Lefebvre, H. (1996) *Writing on Cities*, trans. and ed. by E. Kofman and E. Lebas, Oxford: Blackwell.

Lippert, R. (1998) 'Rationalities and Refugee Resettlement', *Economy and Society*, 27: 380–406.

——(2005a) *Sanctuary, Sovereignty and Sacrifice: Canadian Sanctuary Incidents, Power and Law*, Vancouver: University of British Columbia Press.

——(2005b) 'Rethinking Sanctuary: The Canadian Context, 1983–2003', *International Migration Review*, 39: 381–406.

Mountz, A. (2011) 'Where Asylum-Seekers Wait: Feminist Counter-Topographies of Sites Between States', *Gender, Place and Culture*, 18: 381–99.

Purcell, M. (2002) 'Excavating Lefebvre: The Right to the City and Its Urban Politics of the Inhabitant', *Geojournal*, 58: 99–108.

——(2006) 'Urban Democracy and the Local Trap', *Urban Studies*, 43: 1921–41.

Sales, R. (2002) 'The Deserving and the Undeserving? Refugees, Asylum Seekers and Welfare in Britain', *Critical Social Policy*, 22: 456–78.

Schuster, L. (2011) 'Dublin II and Eurodac: Examining the (Un)Intended(?) Consequences', *Gender, Place and Culture*, 18: 401–16.

Shapiro, M. (2000) 'National Times and Other Times: Re-Thinking Citizenship', *Cultural Studies*, 14: 79–98.

Sheffield First Partnership (2011) *The Sheffield City Strategy 2010–20*. Available at: http://www.sheffieldfirst.org.uk/city-strategy (accessed 21 October 2011).

Squire, V. (2009a) 'Mobile Solidarities: The *City of Sanctuary* Movement and the Strangers into Citizens Campaign'. Available at: http://www.open.ac.uk/ccig/news/mobile-solidarities-the-city-of-sanctuary-movement-and-the-strangers-into-citizens-campaign (accessed 20 October 2011).

——(2009b) *The Exclusionary Politics of Asylum*, Basingstoke: Palgrave Macmillan.

——(2011) 'From Community Cohesion to Mobile Solidarities: The *City of Sanctuary* Network and the Strangers into Citizens Campaign', *Political Studies*, 59: 290–307.

Squire, V. and Bagelman, J. (2012) 'Taking not Waiting: Space, Temporality and Politics in the *City of Sanctuary* Movement', in P. Nyers and K. Rygiel (eds) *Citizenship: Migrant Activism and the Politics of Movement*, London: Routledge.

Squire, V. and Darling, J. (forthcoming) 'The "Minor" Politics of Rightful Presence: Justice and Relationality in *City of Sanctuary*', *International Political Sociology*, 7: 2013.

Chapter 14

The birth of a *sanctuary-city*
A history of governmental sanctuary in San Francisco

Peter Mancina

Across the United States in the early 1980s through the mid-1990s, religious congregants and order members of a variety of faiths decided to take firm action to help Salvadoran and Guatemalan refugees enter the US and resettle their families in 'public sanctuaries' (Coutin 1993; Cunningham 1995, 1998). The congregants did this in defiance of US immigration authorities that had denied over 90 per cent of the asylum requests from Guatemalans and Salvadorans fleeing the violence of US-supported anti-communist military regimes (Bau 1985; Coutin 1993; Crittenden 1988). Sanctuary activists throughout the country claimed that the US federal government, by denying these claims for political reasons, was breaking international and domestic refugee law. As a result, some sanctuary activists stepped in to unofficially restore legal order by stationing volunteers in Mexican border towns as informal immigration agents to interview refugees and choose those whom they would help cross the border. Others throughout the country set up safe houses and publicised refugee testimonies to a national audience. The sanctuary movement's hope was to pressure the US Department of State to end its active involvement in the Central American civil wars and also to pressure the Immigration and Naturalization Service (INS) to stop deporting Central American refugees fleeing the violence.

In San Francisco, California, a city farther from the border, the sanctuary movement was less focused on helping refugees cross into the US and more focused on easing refugee transition to American life and organising local citizens to oppose US foreign and immigration policy (Perla and Bibler Coutin, Chapter 5 in this volume). San Francisco's sanctuary movement also cultivated alliances with key officials in the municipal government, effectively incorporating them into the movement as sanctuary activists. The city government became a key ally of the movement, providing venues from which the movement could amplify the voices of refugees and counter the discourse and policing practices of the INS. Through the work of city officials and grassroots sanctuary leaders, the sanctuary movement infused the municipal government's culture of tolerance towards immigrants with the sanctuary movement ethics of providing 'support, protection, and advocacy' (Catholic Social Services 1982: 6) for undocumented refugees. Informed by this ethical framework, the municipal government then assembled a regulatory apparatus, a *sanctuary-city*, to manage and improve the precarious situation of undocumented Central American refugees. This effectively institutionalised sanctuary as a governmental strategy, an 'art of government' (Foucault 1991), for governing a mixed-status city population.[1]

This apparatus was set in motion through the passage of two pieces of *sanctuary-city* legislation, the 'City of Refuge' resolution (1985) and the 'City of Refuge' ordinance (1989). This legislation required municipal employees to cease all participation in immigration policing and provide city services to all city residents including undocumented refugees in an 'immigration status-blind' manner. These prohibitions and the provision of normal city services as *sanctuary-city services* linked municipal departments, agencies, and commissions with sanctuary movement organisations. Leaders of these sanctuary organisations provided technical assistance to city agencies and also served on the commissions that monitored *sanctuary-city* compliance. In this manner, governmental sanctuary in San Francisco remained legal, routine, institutional, and sustained rather than *exceptional* (Lippert 2005; Ridgley 2011). This chapter will trace the history of how these activists brought about these developments in their local government, resulting in legally significant changes that affected the lives of countless thousands of undocumented refugees and immigrants in the decades that followed.

Research for this chapter included the consultation of ten archival collections of the personal and organisational papers of Bay Area sanctuary congregations, Archdiocesan organisations, and church officials working on sanctuary; three personal collections of San Francisco sanctuary organisers; archival collections of the newspaper *El Tecolote* and the San Francisco Catholic Archdiocese's newspaper *The Monitor*; and the meeting minutes of the San Francisco Board of Supervisors and the Human Rights Commission. I also conducted 15 interviews with sanctuary movement organisers, parishioners, and governmental officials involved in municipal sanctuary work during the 1980s and 1990s.

The San Francisco sanctuary movement and the cultivation of governmental sanctuary

In the early 1980s, the San Francisco Bay Area became one of the emerging centres of the US sanctuary movement. Responding to the needs of an estimated 60,000–100,000 Central American refugees in the Bay Area, community organisers employed by the San Francisco Catholic Archdiocese's Catholic Social Service (CSS-SF) and the Commission on Social Justice's Latin American Task Force (LATF) worked with religious leaders in over 65 churches, synagogues, and religious orders to educate them on the wars in Central America, the plight of refugees, and possible forms of communal action (including public sanctuary) to improve the situation. With the support of the San Francisco Archbishop John Quinn, the organisational space and resources of the Archdiocese were made available to sanctuary organisers to build an urgent action network of social workers, lawyers, health services providers, employers, and private family 'sponsors' that addressed the life-sustaining needs of refugees. They also organised a political network of labour unions, institutional church officials, and local government officials to publicly 'protect, defend, and advocate' for the rights of undocumented refugees. Following valued guidance from refugee and immigrant rights organisations such as the Central American Refugee Committee (CRECE) (Perla and Bibler Coutin, Chapter 5 in this volume) and most importantly, from community partners in Central America, sanctuary workers mixed legal advocacy and community education with efforts toward policy changes granting political asylum and voluntary departure status to refugees.

From 1980 to 1982, CSS-SF, LATF, and the Ad Hoc Committee to Stop the Deportations (AHCSD), an organisation that allowed CSS-SF and LATF to join forces with a variety of community groups, organised public demonstrations, speaking events and public discussions, delegations to speak with local immigration officials, labour strikes, informational mailings, Congressional letter writing, vigils and media work, and assistance to refugees both in San Francisco and Central America. They also began outreach to the San Francisco municipal government to educate certain officials in powerful positions about the Central American wars; repression of Central American religious leaders, peasants, and dissidents; and the systematic deportation of legitimate, but legally unrecognised political refugees.

In particular, movement leaders targeted progressive members of the San Francisco Board of Supervisors, the city's legislative body made up of leaders who from 1978–80 were voted into their positions by the district populations they represented, and from 1981–2000 were elected through city-wide voting. In addition to determining the city budget and passing the city's laws, this body had the power to pass resolutions that served as statements of political opinion, moral orientation, and legal directives for practical government business. The Board's meetings, which were open to the public, served as a venue where sanctuary movement leaders and undocumented refugees provided testimony on the wars in Central America, INS deportation policies, and the experience of refugees in the city. This testimony was addressed directly to the city's lawmakers, influencing them in their decisions to cooperate with or oppose state and federal policy, including immigration policy and foreign policy.

Community groups that wished to pass particular legislation or to influence the allocation of city funds worked directly with Supervisors and with leading legislative aides in their offices. From the beginnings of 1980, CSS-SF, LATF, and AHCSD worked to develop relationships with two newly elected progressive Supervisors: Nancy Walker, who represented District Nine, including the predominantly Latino Mission District, and Harry Britt, who represented District Five, including Dolores Heights and the Castro. Over the next decade, these two Board members went on to present 33 of the city's 50 resolutions and ordinances that supported sanctuary movement efforts, instituted sanctuary practices in daily department procedures, and formally honoured sanctuary movement leaders. Among these pieces of legislation were calls for an end to US aid for the Salvadoran military junta; the withdrawal of US military personnel from Central America; support of self-determination and human rights for the citizens of El Salvador; and federal recognition of refugees from El Salvador and Guatemala as 'political' refugees, the provision of asylum or extended voluntary departure status to them, and a halt to their deportations. In preparation for presenting this legislation to the Board, Supervisors Walker and Britt periodically requested background information from CSS-SF on refugees from El Salvador, invited CSS-SF organisers and refugee leaders to speak at public hearings, and worked with the organisers on campaign strategies to gather support for sanctuary policy initiatives.

In 1982, after two years of successful organising with these municipal officials and following the declarations of public sanctuary at five congregations in the nearby East Bay in March, CSS-SF, LATF, and AHCSD leaders began to reach out to congregations and religious orders in San Francisco to discuss the possibility of declaring public sanctuary. From 1982–84, an extensive 'house meeting' campaign was conducted wherein CSS-SF organisers, accompanied by CRECE leaders, met with members of parishes and religious orders in their private homes to educate them about the wars in Central America, the plight of refugees, and about the practicalities of managing a public sanctuary. Sanctuary services and activities that congregants were invited to participate in included providing refugees with food, shelter, medical and psychological care, education and tutoring, and employment; helping refugees to process political asylum applications; raising funds for bail bonds for detained refugees; educating the parish and city community on Central America and refugee needs; supporting appropriate legislative reform; maintaining contacts with other sanctuary communities; praying for specific needs of the refugees and for the success of sanctuary work; creating liturgies to sustain and inspire their own efforts; lobbying in Washington; traveling to Central America and reporting to US audiences; and aiding the resettlement of displaced people in El Salvador. Congregants were also invited to ask questions, raise concerns, provide congregation-specific action plans, and most importantly to reflect on what it means to be a Christian, Jew, Buddhist, Unitarian, or Quaker in the context of oppression. Sanctuary organisers and congregants referred to this process of intense moral reflection as a 'discernment process', a religious process of identifying a decision that must be taken on a spiritual issue so as to resolve that issue. Sanctuary discernment processes lasted for six months to one year, after which CSS-SF and CRECE stepped back, leaving individual congregations to organise a communal vote to decide whether or not to become a public sanctuary.

By 1984, seven San Francisco congregations and religious orders had declared public sanctuary[2] and joined together to form the San Francisco Sanctuary Covenant (SFSC). SFSC was one of the Bay Area's seven 'Sanctuary Covenant Communities'[3] – coordinating councils that planned events and campaigns among sanctuary congregations in individual cities or groups of adjacent cities. SFSC coordinated activities and strategising among sanctuary congregations of a variety of faiths located in the San Francisco Archdiocese's area of oversight, which included congregations in San Francisco, San Rafael, and Burlingame. Drawing on the organisational structure already established by the East Bay Sanctuary Covenant (EBSC), SFSC consisted of a steering committee on which two representatives from each sanctuary congregation and two representatives from CRECE and CSS-SF participated. Like each of the other Bay Area Covenant Communities, SFSC sent delegates to the meetings of the Northern California Sanctuary Churches (NCSC), an informal regional communications council through which Bay Area sanctuary congregations stayed connected to each other and to developments in the national movement.

As new congregations carried out their discernment processes and voted in favour of declaring public sanctuary, membership in SFSC increased from seven members in 1984 to 11 members by 1985,[4] 14 members by 1986,[5] and 19 members by 1989.[6] Both SFSC and NCSC facilitated the decentralisation of power in the movement by investing communal resources and information in the base membership of sanctuary congregations.

SFSC members shared experiences, analysis, and reflection on their sanctuary work, and developed strategies for media work, legislative and political action, service programmes, and education and outreach to other local congregations. SFSC served as a mechanism with which members could build congregational strength, autonomy, and the ability to act in a complementary and communal manner rather than serving as a bureaucratic top-down, decision-making body. The immediate goals of SFSC were to respond to emergencies in Central America through letter writing and telegram campaigns; to offer 'support, protection and advocacy' on behalf of the refugees in San Francisco; to produce a monthly newsletter to inform sanctuary congregants and supporters about current events in Central America, refugees in the US, and the status of sanctuary work; and to pass legislation that would end all US aid supporting the war in El Salvador and end the deportations of Salvadoran refugees.

Instituting governmental sanctuary

In November of 1985, SFSC began to work with Supervisor Walker to launch a grassroots campaign persuading the Board of Supervisors to pass a resolution declaring San Francisco a 'City of Refuge' for Salvadoran and Guatemalan refugees. This became the city's first step towards instituting the sanctuary movement practices of publicly providing undocumented refugees life-sustaining services and space to build their lives anew in San Francisco. Following sanctuary resolutions that had already been passed by city councils in Berkeley, Los Angeles, West Hollywood, Seattle, Olympia, Chicago, St. Paul, Madison, Burlington, Cambridge, Ithaca, and New York City, SFSC proposed that the San Francisco resolution mandate city employees to refrain from cooperation with the INS in immigration policing through gathering and distributing immigration status information. This would effectively encourage refugees to use the city's emergency police, fire, and health services, as well as social services and public schools with less fear of being turned in to the INS.

In the wake of the indictments of 16 sanctuary workers in Texas and Arizona in January 1985 (Cunningham 1995), the City of Refuge campaign served to unite the San Francisco sanctuary movement's base members at the then-11 sanctuary congregations, reinvigorate them in a time of legal uncertainty, and show the country that the movement in the Bay Area was unwavering in its commitment to 'protect, defend, and advocate' for the rights of undocumented refugees. It also gave them the opportunity to educate other District Supervisors and then-Mayor Dianne Feinstein about the plight of Central American refugees, the sanctuary movement, and the national sanctuary cities campaign.

This education would be multi-faceted. At the grassroots level, CSS-SF sanctuary organisers who also worked as staff for SFSC began to work with parish sanctuary committees to educate parishioners on the proposed City of Refuge resolution. Educating this base occurred through house meetings similar to those that CSS-SF organised for sanctuary congregations in their discernment processes in the early to mid-1980s. These organisers asked parishioners to in turn educate the undecided Supervisors and Mayor by sending in postcards and making direct phone calls in favour of the resolution. Organisers also educated and collected signatures of nearly 50,000 San Francisco residents so that if the Board and the Mayor rejected the resolution, SFSC would have enough citizen support to put the resolution on the general elections ballot in November 1986.

At the governmental level, in consultation with Supervisors Walker and Britt, SFSC sent small delegations to meet with each Supervisor, the Mayor, and the Chief Officers of city departments that worked directly with the public such as the Police, Sheriff, Public Health, and Education departments. The delegations included four sanctuary organisers: Father Peter Sammon and Sister Kathleen Healy of St. Teresa's Catholic Church; Eileen Purcell, lead sanctuary organiser of CSS-SF's Central American Refugee Organising Project (CAROP); and Lana Dalberg, staff person hired by SFSC specifically for the City of Refuge campaign. The delegations also included a Salvadoran refugee from CRECE who had provided first-hand war testimony to congregants in the initial 1982 house-meeting efforts, and Marc Van Der Hout, the movement's most prominent lawyer and co-founder of the pro-sanctuary legal organisation, the Father Moriarty Central American Refugee Project.

In the meetings, these delegates introduced the Central American refugee issue, the sanctuary movement, and the City of Refuge campaign; and solicited the support of the politician or department head. SFSC maintained relationships with ally Supervisors through weekly written, telephone, and personal visits, and provided them with a steady stream of updated info on the campaign and the sanctuary movement. Additionally, SFSC leaders worked closely with Supervisors on the Board's Human Services Committee to review other cities' sanctuary city resolutions and to draft recommendations for San Francisco's resolution and potential methods of monitoring its enforcement.

In evaluating the influence of this outreach on city officials, SFSC wanted to make a lasting and personal impression with regard to the refugee issue and the need for governmental sanctuary. As a result, they organised delegation trips to Central America where city officials could personally witness the effects of war and the causes of Salvadoran exile. Sending delegations to Central America had long been a powerful method for 'converting' potential sanctuary workers to a life of deep conviction for supporting the anti-deportation cause and helping refugees (Coutin 1993). In February 1984, the already-sympathetic Supervisor Walker had joined CSS-SF organisers on such a delegation for 10 days in Nicaragua, El Salvador, and Honduras. In late November 1985, SFSC and CSS-SF invited officials previously unaffiliated with the movement, Assemblyman (and later San Francisco Mayor) Art Agnos and Supervisor Doris Ward, on a trip to El Salvador with Father Sammon. They visited refugee camps and church organisations that were helping refugees, areas of the countryside where bombing was occurring up to four times per week, and prisons where political prisoners were being tortured (Sammon and Purcell 1998). The impact of these experiences motivated these officials to provide powerfully authoritative testimonies on the plight of refugees and the need for sanctuary-city policy at special Board hearings leading up to the Board's vote. This experiential conversion of governmental officials into dedicated sanctuary politicians allowed the movement to further infuse sanctuary ethics in governmental discourse, to promote governmental projects in support of refugees, and to defend sanctuary from legal attacks that came from within City Hall.

On 9 December, Supervisor Walker presented the City of Refuge resolution to the Board and two weeks later on 23 December it passed by an 8–3 vote. Most notably, the resolution stated that:

> the City and County of San Francisco finds that immigration and refugee policy is a matter of Federal jurisdiction; that federal employees, not City employees, should be considered responsible for implementation of immigration and refugee policy.
>
> ... the City and County of San Francisco urges the Mayor, and the Chief Administrative Officer, to advise the commissions and departments under their respective jurisdiction of this fact of law; and that the Mayor is urged to affirm that City Departments shall not discriminate against Salvadoran and Guatemalan refugees because of immigration status, and shall not jeopardise the safety and welfare of law-abiding refugees by acting in a way that may cause their deportation ...
>
> ... the implementation of the provisions of this resolution by employees and agencies of the City and County of San Francisco remain consistent with federal statute, ordinance, regulation or court decision and, provided further, the City and County of San Francisco is not, in adopting this

resolution, encouraging its employees and citizens to violate any local, state, or federal laws'

(San Francisco Board of Supervisors 1985: 1–4)

Though it did not explicitly redefine city department procedures, the resolution transformed the normal, institutional day-to-day services that these departments provided San Francisco residents into governmental *sanctuary services* that could be extended to undocumented Salvadoran and Guatemalan refugees. The resolution also served as a reference point for governmental legislators considering future legislation, manners of engaging the local immigrant population, and assessing the effects of federal initiatives to incorporate city employees in federal–municipal joint projects. However, it was largely moral and symbolic in its purpose, rather than legally binding. It created no institutional oversight body, no chain of command, no procedures for serving refugees, and no guidelines for when or how disciplinary action should be administered to non-compliant city employees.

Over the next three years, San Francisco's sanctuary-city status provided government officials a moral standard that governmental action should measure up to with regard to the rights of undocumented residents. Moving beyond the struggle for immigrant and refugee rights, the 'sanctuary-city' became defendable itself. It provided activists and politicians a point of focus for political work, encouraging them to continue to elaborate ways of making San Francisco a place where all residents, including the undocumented, could thrive free from discriminatory treatment and fear. The sanctuary-city concept was extended and reapplied by the municipal government to support, protect, and advocate for other sectors of society such as South African and Namibian refugees fleeing apartheid, sexual minorities, and conscientious objectors to war.

Enforcing governmental sanctuary

By late 1988, the City of Refuge resolution had still not been fully translated into explicit departmental policy changes appropriate to serving refugees, or disciplinary procedures that could ensure city employee compliance. Despite San Francisco Sheriff Michael Hennessey's progressive stance in support of the 1985 resolution, Sheriff's Department officers in San Francisco jails maintained the practice of providing the names of all Latino inmates to the INS so that they could interview them. Police officers also on occasion accompanied INS agents on raids in the Latino immigrant community.

In this context, the newly elected Mayor Art Agnos looked to the long-time community advocate, SFSC Chair, and guide of Agnos' El Salvador delegation trip in 1985, Fr. Peter Sammon, to help him bring changes to the city government's treatment of its diverse residents. In November 1988, Mayor Agnos personally appointed Father Sammon to be a Commissioner on the San Francisco Human Rights Commission (HRC). This government body was first created in the mid-1960s to give effect to the rights of every inhabitant of the city and county to equal economic, political and educational opportunity, to equal accommodations in all business establishments, and to equal service and protection by public agencies.

The HRC was charged with providing reputable, expert advice and assistance to the City and County, in particular, the Mayor and the Board of Supervisors. The commission's responsibilities included research into emerging social issues affecting minorities in the city, advocacy for human rights issues, and investigation and mediation of complaints of governmental discrimination and non-compliance with minority-related ordinances. The HRC was also responsible for providing outreach, technical assistance, referrals, expert advice, and training to city officers, departments, and community organisations to implement ordinances governing the provision of city services to minorities.

Within the city governmental structure, HRC resolutions carried 'clout' on city and national issues due to the fact that its 11 Mayoral-appointed Commissioners were recognised in the city as politically powerful and charismatic community advocates. While they might not have had full legal authority as Commissioners to demand that departmental action be taken, their moral authority gave them the power to speak frankly with city officials and persuade them to make changes. Serving four-year terms, each Commissioner provided leadership for, and set policy by means of, participation on one of the HRC's five issue-oriented Standing Committees. These committees provided for the in-depth study and exploration of issues, and invited community involvement in the discussion on how these issues should be dealt with by the municipal government. Committees invited expert community speakers to present opposing points of view whenever discussing an issue before the commission, and recommended that the HRC take positions on specific pieces of city, state, and federal legislation.

When Fr. Sammon was appointed Commissioner, he was assigned the position of Chair of the 'Social Issues/Police Liaison Committee' (SI/PLC), which worked with the Police Commission to oversee police conduct in issues of discrimination. Under the direction of Commissioner Sammon, SI/PLC focused on issues related to immigration and undocumented residents, law enforcement and public safety, housing, prejudice-based violence, and unemployment. Sammon kept a vigilant eye on police violations of the City of Refuge resolution, and invited sanctuary movement organisers and lawyers to testify in favour of HRC resolutions supporting sanctuary initiatives.

In the summer of 1989, two incidents called into question the efficacy of the city's sanctuary resolution: in June, San Francisco police officers photographed CRECE leaders during a protest and gave the pictures to the Salvadoran Consulate, and in July, San Francisco police officers and Alcohol Beverage Control officers worked directly with the INS to raid a local salsa club, *Club Elegante* (Ridgley 2008). These two actions threatened the atmosphere of trust that the sanctuary resolution was intended to create between the community and the

SFPD, and among other things had the potential to silence undocumented witnesses of crimes from talking or interacting with police and other city authorities. In response, Commissioner Sammon brought these issues to the HRC and began to lead a governmental effort to legally enforce institutionalised sanctuary in city departments that worked directly with immigrants. The purpose of this was to make sure that departments working directly with immigrants could no longer disregard the City of Refuge resolution, and as a result, to re-establish undocumented residents' trust in the municipal government. This trust would allow undocumented people to feel safer to call the police, an ambulance, or a fire truck, and therefore reduce the threat of crime, health hazards, and fires, ensuring public order and promoting the general welfare of all San Francisco residents.

Working with Jim Gonzalez, the city's first Guatemalan-American District Supervisor and a former Catholic seminarian, sanctuary movement lawyer Ignatius Bau, CRECE refugee leader Carolina Castaneda, Sister Kathleen Healy, Commissioner Sammon, and his HRC staff aide Don Hesse began to revise the City of Refuge resolution. In order to strengthen the mechanisms for its enforcement, this team, with the advice of the City Attorney, opted to turn it into an ordinance of the city's Administrative Code. This drafting was first done as an HRC SI/PLC project that the HRC would vote on and then refer to the Board of Supervisors to pass into law. Before it was voted on, Commissioner Sammon invited Bau, Healy, and Casteneda to present the ordinance to the HRC. The ordinance commended public church sanctuaries for their work with refugees, and mandated that no department, agency, commission or employee of the City and County of San Francisco shall use city resources to:

1. assist or cooperate in their official capacity with any INS investigation, detention, or arrest procedures, public or clandestine, relating to alleged violations of the civil provisions of the federal immigration law;
2. assist or cooperate in their official capacity with any investigation, surveillance or gathering of information conducted by foreign governments;
3. request information about or disseminate information regarding the immigration status of any individual;
4. condition the provision of services or benefits by the City and County of San Francisco upon immigration status except as required by federal or state statue, regulation or court decision.
(San Francisco Human Rights Commission 1989)

After HRC approval in September of 1989, the ordinance was reviewed by the Board's Human Services Committee, and in October it was presented to the full Board by Supervisors Gonzalez, Walker, Alioto, and Britt. The Board voted unanimously to approve it, and Mayor Agnos signed it into law. At the time, the main presenter of the ordinance, Supervisor Gonzalez, was Chair of the Board's Finance Committee, and therefore, would personally review and authorise city department budgets, taking into account complaints regarding non-compliance with the sanctuary ordinance. This sent a powerful message to departments and agencies that breaking this city law might result in budget cuts and as a result, departments, including the police, were cooperative.

Within two months, all government applications, questionnaires and interview forms used in relation to benefits, services or opportunities had been reviewed and all questions regarding immigration status other than those required by federal or state statute, regulation or court decision, were deleted. Mayor Agnos sent each appointing officer of the City and County of San Francisco a memo requiring him or her to inform all employees under her or his jurisdiction of the prohibitions in the sanctuary ordinance, the duty of all of her or his employees to comply with its prohibitions, and the disciplinary action that would be administered to employees who failed to comply with the ordinance. However, the form disciplinary action would take was left in the hands of department heads. Each city and county employee was then sent a written directive from the City Attorney Louise Renne informing them of the city's sanctuary prohibitions and advising them to contact the City Attorney for any technical guidance they might need on implementing sanctuary.

While the original 1985 City of Refuge resolution had not established an enforcement or monitoring body, the 1989 ordinance designated the HRC's SI/PLC, then headed by Commissioner Sammon, as the main governmental body in charge of reviewing compliance with the mandates of the ordinance. In particular, the SI/PLC, with the support of the Mayor, conducted investigations of instances of noncompliance or when a complaint alleging noncompliance had been lodged. They could then mediate conversations between the parties involved to assess whether there was a violation. If they determined that a violation had occurred, they could work directly with the departments to make the necessary procedural changes to bring the department into compliance. However, the SI/PLC was not given the power to impose specific sanctions for violators.

In the year following the passage of the sanctuary ordinance, Commissioner Sammon and Don Hesse worked with department heads to develop specific changes to policy and procedure manuals for city employees who worked directly with undocumented immigrants and refugees. Sammon and Hesse also participated in educating and training city employees on these department-specific procedural changes related to the sanctuary ordinance as well as on issues facing the undocumented. Departments most involved in the workings of the sanctuary-city apparatus were the Police, Public Health, Fire, Social Services, Education, and the District Attorney's Office. However, governmental sanctuary enforcement efforts most urgently focused on modifying the work of the Police.

SFPD officers were forbidden from stopping, questioning, or detaining any individual solely because of the individual's national origin, foreign appearance, inability to speak English, or immigration status. In the course of traffic enforcement, investigations, and taking reports, officers could not ask for immigration status documents, nor could they assist the INS in the enforcement of immigration laws unless there was a significant danger of personal injury to INS agents or threat of serious property damage during an INS raid. Nor could officers assist the INS in transporting people suspected solely of violating federal immigration laws. They could not cooperate with foreign governments in any investigation, surveillance, or information-gathering project unless it was related to an investigation into a violation of city, county, state, or federal criminal laws.

Over time, city employees who previously had thought it their duty as citizens to report undocumented immigrants to the INS began to treat immigration status as 'irrelevant' to providing their department's services. Others had already viewed it irrelevant before the sanctuary-city was created. As a result, some were reluctant to participate in writing explicit sanctuary policies or attend SI/PLC trainings that they found to be a waste of time. Nonetheless, these departments accepted the responsibility of serving *all* San Francisco residents, including the undocumented.

Conclusion

In San Francisco during the 1980s, sanctuary movement leaders helped assemble and coordinate a network of sanctuary congregations and sympathetic politicians to 'support, protect, and advocate for' unauthorised Central American refugees. Due to the success and public recognition of this work, these leaders were called upon by the municipal government to help assemble and coordinate a *sanctuary-city* apparatus, a network of governmental departments, agencies, officials, and front-line employees to manage the precarious situation of undocumented refugees in the city. This linked the ethics, knowledge, discourse, practices, and social networks of the grassroots sanctuary movement with those of the municipal government. Governmental sanctuary required city employees to refrain from acting outside of municipal jurisdiction and from acting outside of the law when serving undocumented residents. By forbidding city employees from engaging in intrusive surveillance, information gathering, and distributing of the details of refugee legal status, the municipal government was able to provide life-sustaining municipal services to undocumented refugees and to advocate on their behalf in public arenas. Such sanctuary practices encouraged undocumented residents to remain healthy, trusting, law-abiding, and cooperative with municipal agents, and therefore, these practices were used as morally imbued techniques for city management, maintenance of public order, and promotion of the general welfare.

Acknowledgements

This work is funded by The National Science Foundation and The Wenner-Gren Foundation. Many thanks are due to The Graduate Theological Union

Archives, the Dominican Sisters of San Rafael, the Presentation Sisters of San Francisco, the San Francisco Archdiocese Archives, *El Tecolote*, and the San Francisco Human Rights Commission for allowing me to consult their archival collections. Thank you to Eileen Purcell for sharing her personal documents and to Zina von Bozzay, Eileen Purcell, Lana Dalberg, and the editors of this volume for reading previous drafts of this chapter.

Notes

1. For further discussion of immigration governance 'apparatuses', see Mancina (2011) and Feldman (2011).
2. These were the Sisters of the Presentation, St. Teresa's Catholic Parish, the Dominican Sisters of San Rafael, First Unitarian Church, the American Friends Meeting of San Francisco, and Noe Valley Ministry.
3. In Northern California, the other Covenant Communities were organised in the 'East Bay' (coordinating Oakland, Berkeley, Albany, Hayward, and San Leandro); in Marin County (coordinating Marin City, Mill Valley, and Novato); in the 'South Bay' (coordinating Palo Alto and Los Altos); in Sonoma (coordinating Petaluma and Santa Rosa); in the San Joaquin Valley (coordinating Fresno and Visalia); and lastly, a Covenant to coordinate Sacramento and Davis.
4. New members by 1985 were the 7th Avenue Presbyterian Church and the Franciscan Brothers and Fathers in San Francisco, Sisters of Mercy in Burlingame, and the Sisters of Notre Dame in Belmont.
5. New members by 1986 were St. John of God Catholic Church, St. Francis Lutheran, and the Redemptorist Fathers.
6. New members by 1989 were St. Boniface Catholic Church, Sisters of the Holy Name, and the Jewish Congregations Ahavat Shalom and Sha'ar Zahav. Additionally, the San Francisco Jewish Sanctuary Coalition joined as an affiliate organisation.

References

Bau, I. (1985) *This Ground Is Holy: Church Sanctuary and Central American Refugees*, New York: Paulist Press.

Catholic Social Services (1982) 'Central American Refugees: A Grant Proposal' [Grant Proposal], October 1982, personal collection of Eileen Purcell, San Francisco, California.

Coutin, S.B. (1993) *The Culture of Protest: Religious Activism and the U.S. Sanctuary Movement*, Boulder, CO: Westview Press.

Crittenden, A. (1988) *Sanctuary: A Story of American Conscience and the Law in Collision*, New York: Weidenfeld and Nicolson.

Cunningham, H. (1995) *God and Caesar at the Rio Grande: Sanctuary and the Politics of Religion*, Minneapolis: University of Minnesota Press.

——(1998) 'Sanctuary and Sovereignty: Church and State along the U.S.-Mexico Border', *Journal of Church and State*, 40(2): 371–86.

Feldman, G. (2011) *The Migration Apparatus: Security, Labor, and Policymaking in the European Union*, Stanford, CA: Stanford University Press.

Foucault, M. (1991) 'Governmentality', in C. Gordon and P. Miller (eds) *The Foucault Effect: Studies in Governmentality*, Chicago: University of Chicago Press.

Lippert, R. (2005) *Sanctuary, Sovereignty, Sacrifice: Canadian Sanctuary Incidents, Power, and Law*, Vancouver: University of British Columbia Press.

Mancina, P. (2011) 'Crisis-Management: Tzeltal-Maya Migration and the Foucauldian Apparatus', *Dialectical Anthropology*, 35(2): 205–25.

Ridgley, J. (2008) 'Cities of Refuge: Immigration Enforcement, Police, and the Insurgent Genealogies of Citizenship in U.S. Sanctuary Cities', *Urban Geography*, 29(1): 53–77.

—— (2011) 'Refuge, Refusal, and Acts of Holy Contagion: The City as a Sanctuary for Soldiers Resisting the Vietnam War', *ACME: An International E-Journal for Critical Geographies*, 10(2): 189–214.

Sammon, P. and Purcell, E. (1998) '"Peter Sammon," interview by Eileen M. Purcell', February 13, 1998, transcript, *Sanctuary Oral History Project*, Graduate Theological Union, Berkeley, CA.

San Francisco Board of Supervisors (1985) 'Resolution 1087-85 (Cal-1985)'. Available from The Graduate Theological Union Archives, Gustav Schultz Sanctuary Collection, Box 1, Folder 44.

San Francisco Human Rights Commission (1989) 'Meeting Minutes'. Available from San Francisco Human Rights Commission Archive, Box 95-04-19-04, Folder '7/13/89 HRC Minutes Materials'.

Chapter 15

The city as a sanctuary in the United States

Jennifer Ridgley

Introduction

This chapter provides an introduction to the history and politics of city sanctuary in the US. It traces the changing substance and meaning of sanctuary as it has been incorporated into the legal and institutional spaces of local governments. City sanctuary was first invoked in the US in the 1970s, when the City of Berkeley, California, declared itself a sanctuary for navy soldiers resisting the war in Vietnam. Since that time, local governments have drawn on biblical and faith-based ideas of sanctuary to support a variety of groups, including military personnel, refugees, and non-citizens. While cities have mobilized sanctuary in different ways depending on local contexts and political organizing, sanctuary policies also share common logics and histories. Attempts to transform cities into spaces of sanctuary can thus be seen as an ongoing and persistent political strategy in the US.

Much of this strategy has centred on the passage and maintenance of sanctuary policies. These policies include symbolic declarations of city space as sanctuary, restrictions on the use of local resources for enforcing federal law, and policies to ensure all city residents have equal access to rights and entitlements. During the 1970s and 1980s, city sanctuary policies also included expressions of support for the faith-based movements which were providing sanctuary to war resisters and Central American refugees.

The history of city sanctuary is thus not entirely separate from faith-based sanctuary movements. Local policy-makers have drawn legitimacy from the same biblical and religious traditions that have inspired church sanctuary, and religious organizations across the country have played an important role in early campaigns for sanctuary policies. The idea of the city as a space of refuge was thus very much a product of faith-based organizing. But city sanctuary also has been shaped by legal, political, and institutional contexts somewhat unique to the city. Throughout the 1980s and 1990s, cities had to negotiate the complicated political and legal terrain that characterized their relationship to federal immigration law and their role as service providers. As I will discuss, city sanctuary was gradually transformed, becoming less connected to faith-based ideas of refuge and asylum. Local campaigns supportive of war resisters, immigrants, racialized groups, and human rights also have been important to the history of city sanctuary.

The purpose of this chapter, then, is to highlight some diverse movements and political logics that have come together to produce city sanctuary in the US, and how sanctuary has changed over time. It provides background on the history of sanctuary policies during the 1970s and 1980s, and describes how city sanctuary has shifted from its original religious origins to become more associated with policies limiting local involvement in the enforcement of federal immigration law. As I will discuss, this shift has occurred as local governments have responded to the legal and institutional norms of city governance and their relationship to federal law. But city sanctuary also has been redefined by the immigration authorities, federal policy-makers, and anti-immigration politics. These transformations raise important questions for how we understand the city as a sanctuary in the US.

City sanctuary in the US has received significantly less scholarly attention compared to church sanctuary; there is a lot to learn about how sanctuary has been mobilized in specific places and times (see also Darling and Squire, Chapter 13, and Yukich, Chapter 7, in this volume). A comprehensive account of city sanctuary in the US is not possible here. Instead, I focus on several key moments of political struggle. These examples were chosen because they illustrate the diverse ways sanctuary has been invoked by cities, but also because they highlight the different political logics that have constituted city sanctuary in the US over time.

This chapter begins with the events that led to Berkeley's 1971 sanctuary policy in support of soldiers who were refusing to fight in the Vietnam War. It examines how city sanctuary was constituted at the intersection of church-based sanctuary and antiwar organizing within the navy, and how it was later reshaped to support the Central American Sanctuary Movement. I then focus on the struggles over sanctuary in San Francisco (see also Mancina Chapter 14 in this volume) and New York City during the major immigration reforms of the 1980s and 1990s, and how city sanctuary re-emerged in the context of post-9/11 security initiatives.

Cities of refuge

According to biblical traditions, six ancient Cities of Refuge were set aside for people who sought protection from punishment if they accidentally killed someone:

> Then ye shall appoint you cities to be cities of refuge for you; that the slayer may flee thither, which killeth any person at unawares.
>
> And they shall be unto you cities for refuge from the avenger; that the manslayer die not, until he stand before the congregation in judgment.

> ... These six cities shall be a refuge, both for the children of Israel, and for the stranger, and for the sojourner among them: that every one that killeth any person unawares may flee thither.
>
> (Numbers 35: 10–14)

Religious scholars have described Cities of Refuge as places where the exceptional circumstances surrounding the killing could be carefully considered, and the pace of justice slowed down to ensure a just trial. Sanctuary movements in the US have drawn on this tradition, understanding Cities of Refuge as places where people could flee until the demands of justice could be met (Bau 1985; MacEóin 1985).

While contemporary supporters of city sanctuary have only rarely suggested these ancient traditions held legal bearing on their actions, biblical passages and religious histories of sanctuary and refuge have served as a reference point and source of legitimacy for cities interested in protecting the rights of people who have a complicated, and problematic, relationship to federal law. Soldiers facing charges under the Uniform Code of Military Justice for objecting to the war, refugees threatened with deportation by the Immigration and Naturalization Service (INS), and non-citizens who have been long-term residents in the US have all been subjects of city sanctuary policies. References to and discussion of religious tradition and biblical passages in these cases can be understood as a way of thinking through and interpreting sanctuary in relation to contemporary contexts, however, rather than adherence to strict doctrine. Biblical and religious traditions have provided some inspiration for local governments that have declared themselves Cities of Refuge, but so too have other political and legal trajectories. Indeed, as sanctuary has been brought into the legal and institutional spaces of local government, its moral and religious histories have been progressively de-emphasized.

The city as a sanctuary for antiwar soldiers

In 1971, the City of Berkeley, California, declared itself a sanctuary for soldiers on the aircraft carrier *USS Coral Sea* who were resisting the Vietnam War. In the Fall of 1971, the *Coral Sea* arrived at the naval air station at Alameda in preparation for deployment to Vietnam. Resistance against the war among navy personnel had been growing as the navy's fleet of aircraft carriers was called upon to play a more significant role in the bombing (Cortright 2005). Antiwar organizing on the *Coral Sea* had come together around Stop Our Ship (SOS), a group of soldiers trying to prevent their aircraft carrier from participating in the war.

While the *USS Coral Sea* engaged in sea trials and prepared for its departure to Vietnam, the SOS movement circulated petitions, published an underground newspaper, outreached to other navy ships, and eventually organized rallies and protest actions at NAS Alameda in partnership with the civilian antiwar movement (Anon 1971a; Anon 1971b; SOS 1971; Stop that Ship 1971). However, opportunities for protest actions and political expression were severely curtailed for navy personnel. On board the aircraft carrier, the ship's Executive Officer confiscated SOS petitions, and regulations were introduced prohibiting the distribution of literature not first censored by the Captain, a move that many saw as a violation of their Constitutional right to free speech (Crewmembers of the *USS Coral Sea* 1971a; Anon 1971c; SOS Petition 1971). Soldiers who transgressed the norms of military discipline to circulate SOS materials or express opposition to the war were disciplined, beaten, transferred, or incarcerated (Crewmembers of the *USS Coral Sea* 1971a, 1971b; Anon 1971d; *Coral Sea* Officers 1971; SOS Petition 1971).

Crew members of the *USS Coral Sea* who did not believe they should be forced to participate in the war were thus in a difficult position. They asserted a moral obligation to voice their opinions about the war and that their freedom of speech was protected by the US Constitution (SOS Petition 1971). The military authorities believed that soldiers were obligated to fight unless they went through the process of gaining formal Conscientious Objector (CO) status. Approval for CO status was notoriously difficult to obtain and because the legal definition of CO was so limited, soldiers knew there was a good chance their applications would be refused. Rev. Gus Shultz, pastor of the University Lutheran Chapel in Berkeley, described the limited choices available to the crew of the *Coral Sea* and suggested a sanctuary alternative:

> One issue important in this case is that young men who have entered the military and encountered unexpected circumstances have changed their views concerning war. Now they face almost impossible alternatives: continue to participate in killing, start the long and uncertain process for obtaining CO status, while processing CO continue to participate in killing, or become a federal criminal by taking unauthorized absence or going AWOL ... Killing or crime; that is the choice they are given. Traditional civil and religious sanctuaries are the place for arbitrating and exposing such injustice.
>
> (University Lutheran Chapel n.d.)

Since the late 1960s, a number of church congregations in the US had been offering sanctuary to draft resisters and soldiers refusing to serve in Vietnam (Foley 2006). Some congregations reasoned that the authorities would be less willing to enter religious spaces to make arrests. Others hoped that any arrests made in sacred spaces would 'dramatize the religious and moral basis of opposition to the war' (Fiske 1968: E5). In October 1971, the University Lutheran Chapel in Berkeley joined 17 congregations in California and announced they would provide sanctuary to soldiers refusing to fight 'to fulfill our religious heritage and facilitate the liberties guaranteed by the First Amendment of the Constitution of the US, and to provide one alternative for military personnel who wish to act on their beliefs' (Berkeley Church Offers Sanctuary to Military Dissenters n.d.). Church sanctuary in California expanded at this time as the SOS movement requested more sanctuaries be established for navy personnel stationed at the various air bases along the coast.

On November 8, 1971, just before the ship was scheduled to leave the Bay Area, the City of Berkeley passed a resolution offering sanctuary to *Coral Sea* soldiers. The resolution declared the city's support for those refusing to serve and for the churches providing sanctuary, and stated that the City would provide its own facility for sanctuary in cooperation with the University Lutheran Chapel and its supporting congregations (City of Berkeley 1971). Although none of the crew publicly took Berkeley up on its offer, the resolution represented a reworking of sanctuary in the secular spaces of the city. Most important for the legacy of city sanctuary in the US was the fifth point of Berkeley's resolution:

> That no Berkeley City Employee will violate the established sanctuaries by assisting in investigation, public or clandestine, of, or engaging in or assisting arrests for violation of federal laws relating to military service on the premises offering sanctuary, or by refusing established public services.
>
> (City of Berkeley 1971)

Berkeley's policy went on to become a model for city sanctuary policies in support of Central American refugees during the 1980s, which restricted cooperation with the INS.

The City of Berkeley was well known for its left politics, and its declaration of sanctuary was a popular initiative. US Attorney James Browning threatened to prosecute members of the Berkeley City Council for encouraging desertion (Moore 1971), but religious leaders in the Bay Area responded to these criticisms by suggesting the city was exerting its moral authority and responsibility where traditional procedures of the federal state had failed (Jennings 1971). The city responded to Browning's threat somewhat differently. The City held up sanctuary as a response to its moral responsibilities to act in the face of what many perceived to be an illegal and unjust war, but also 'to indicate the belief of the Berkeley City Council that the continuation of the war adversely affects the city's ability to deal with important urban problems' (City Council Supports *USS Coral Sea* Resistors n.d.). Here, then, we begin to see hints of sanctuary being portrayed as a response to the tensions between federal policy and municipal governance, a theme I will return to shortly.

The city as a sanctuary for Central American refugees

During the 1980s, religious sanctuary was invoked by faith communities again, this time to support people who were fleeing violence and persecution in Central America and to challenge the US government's refusal to grant asylum (see Perla and Bibler Coutin, Chapter 5 in this volume). Faith communities provided housing, legal assistance, transportation and other forms of support to Central Americans who were trying to avoid arrest and deportation. While conservative politicians and federal immigration authorities cast those without status as illegal or criminal, the Sanctuary Movement held that the US government was transgressing the law by detaining and deporting people who had a 'reasonable fear of persecution', in violation of US and international refuge law (Altemus 1987–88).

Sanctuary among church congregations and synagogues in the US in the early 1980s evoked minimal reaction from the federal authorities, but this changed as the movement expanded, developed a more trenchant critique of US foreign policy in Central America, and was sympathetically covered by national media (Cunningham 1995). In January 1985, tensions between the federal government and the Sanctuary Movement reached a new intensity when a group of participants were indicted on felony charges of conspiracy and alien smuggling. Eleven people involved with the Sanctuary Movement, including many nuns and priests, were eventually tried in a high profile case that received a great deal of media attention across the country. During the trial, it became clear the arrests were the result of an extensive joint undercover operation between the FBI and the INS that involved infiltration of church gatherings and organizing meetings (Coutin 1995).

National media coverage of the surveillance, arrests, and trial brought a lot of attention to the Sanctuary Movement and to US involvement in the violence in Central America (Coutin 1995). This, in turn, opened up space for the further expansion of sanctuary into the institutional and political spaces of local government. Advocates and supportive officials pushed back against the criminalization of sanctuary work and adopted resolutions that expressed official support for Central American refugees and the local congregations in their communities that had become involved in the movement.[1] From 1985 to 1987, more than 20 cities and two states (New York and New Mexico) declared themselves sanctuaries for Central Americans, and expressed support for the faith-based Sanctuary Movement.[2] Many modelled their policies on Berkeley's 1971 declaration of sanctuary, and placed limits on local involvement in the investigation of alleged violations of immigration law by Salvadoran and Guatemalan refugees. Contrary to the initial goals of the FBI and the INS, then, the criminalization of the Sanctuary Movement helped revive sanctuary, fuelling its expansion into US cities.

San Francisco as a sanctuary

The first city sanctuary policies in the 1980s were largely symbolic statements of support for the Sanctuary Movement and Central American refugees. At the time, the federal government rarely called upon local police or resources to enforce immigration law, and INS activities in most cities went unnoticed by most residents. In the years that followed, however, growing preoccupation with illegal immigration in the US and the 1986 passage of the Immigration Reform and Control Act (IRCA) began to influence the way immigration enforcement was carried out in the US interior. The IRCA contained provisions for a large-scale legalization programme and represented an intensified focus on enforcement, dramatically increasing resources for the INS. Indeed, the budget and staff of the INS doubled between 1986 and 1990 during a time when many other government agencies experienced significant cuts to funding (Wells 2004). Waves of immigration raids occurred in many cities, often targeting Latino communities. This led to changes in the substance and meaning of city sanctuary.

San Francisco, for example, had declared itself a City of Refuge for Central American refugees in 1985, but there were several high profile incidents since that made it obvious local authorities were still providing assistance to the INS (Bau 1994; Wells 2004). From 1986 to 1989, federal immigration raids in the city increased, and there were growing complaints about civil rights violations by INS personnel. Of particular concern for many residents was the alleged targeting of Latino residents, and the possibility that city officials were being implicated in racial profiling (Miyasato 1989). By September 1989, advocates in San Francisco were suggesting that the Latino community was under a 'state of siege', and urged the city to distance itself from the INS (Romero 1989).

In response to these concerns, the San Francisco Board of Supervisors strengthened their City of Refuge policy, entrenching it into the city's Administrative Code. Local police, and city and county staff were prohibited from inquiring or disseminating information about a person's immigration status unless it was affirmatively required by federal or state statute, regulation, or court decision. City officials were also required to review and revise all applications, questionnaires, and forms used by the city, removing questions about immigration status wherever possible (City and County of San Francisco 1989). Sanctuary in the city thus began to take on a more concrete, if more bureaucratic form, as local officials discussed the everyday practices needed to change to comply with the new ordinance.

In the hearings and press coverage surrounding the revised ordinance, sanctuary discourse also shifted away from a focus on Central American refugees. Advocates asserted the new City of Refuge ordinance was a civil rights policy, reflecting the principle 'that all persons residing within the city and county have fundamental human, civil and constitutional rights which must be respected' (Romero 1989: 5). The Board of Supervisors suggested the policy was important because immigrants and refugees who viewed city officials as agents of the INS would be afraid to report crimes or illnesses which, in turn, would jeopardize the health and safety of all residents (San Francisco Board of Supervisors 1989: 3). Sanctuary had a new role in the city, connected less to the specific struggles of Central American refugees, and more to local government operations, reflecting broader concerns about racial profiling, civil rights, health, and security.

San Francisco's 1989 Ordinance is still a part of the city's Administrative Code, although it has been revised several times. During the early 1990s, reflecting a growing convergence between anti-crime and anti-immigrant discourses, sanctuary policies across the country were publicly attacked by opponents who accused local governments of protecting criminals and attracting illegal immigrants who drain public resources. Federal policy-makers, local police, and immigration officials who were critical of city sanctuary policies began to play a more significant role in defining the substance and meaning of sanctuary in public discourse as they honed in on the aspects of sanctuary policies that limited cooperation with the INS, or restricted information sharing with the federal government. Officials at the INS, for example, began to argue that sanctuary policies were impeding public safety by limiting the flow of information about 'aliens' who had been convicted of crimes, and Congress debated several crime bills which had been amended to outlaw city sanctuary policies. In San Francisco, sanctuary was blamed for overcrowded jails and the California Office of Criminal Justice Planning threatened to withhold up to $4 million in funding if the city's sanctuary policy was not repealed. As a result, the ordinance was revised to remove some prohibitions on police identifying or reporting people suspected of violating the civil provisions of immigration law if they were in custody after being booked for the alleged commission of a felony (see Bau 1994, for a detailed account of events surrounding these changes).

In 1996, conflicts over city sanctuary came to a head when federal immigration reforms – including The Illegal Immigration Reform and Immigrant Responsibility Act and the Welfare Reform Act – directly attacked city sanctuary policies, purporting to void local laws that prohibited state and local agencies from sharing information with the INS. These 'anti-sanctuary' provisions led to conflict with the City of New York, in particular, which unsuccessfully challenged the new provisions in court.

New York City as a sanctuary

New York City's first attempt to define the role that municipal staff, police and service providers should play in immigration law enforcement was in 1985, when Mayor Koch issued a memorandum to all city departments declaring that city employees should not report their contact with someone who is undocumented to the INS unless the person 'appears to be engaged in some kind of criminal behavior' (Merina 1985: 1). Koch's directive laid the groundwork for New York City's policies on sharing information with the INS for years to come. It was later formalized into several different Executive Orders and reissued by Mayor Dinkins and Giuliani. At the time, the Mayor's spokespeople denied the memo had anything to do with sanctuary, but other city officials told the press it was, in part, a response to public hearings that involved discussions about the situation of Central American refugees and the movement that had emerged to support them (Lindsey 1985; Merina 1985; Schmalz 1985).

Regardless of any immediate connections Koch's directive might have had to sanctuary during the 1980s, by the time Congressional representatives were discussing the 1996 immigration reforms, New York City was coming up in policy debates as an example of a sanctuary city that should be targeted for sanctions. In federal policy circles, city sanctuary had become virtually synonymous with local policies that limited cooperation and information sharing with the INS, regardless of whether cities themselves had invoked sanctuary.

Then New York City Mayor Rudolph Giuliani was a vocal, if perhaps unlikely, critic of the 1996 immigration reforms, and he accused the federal government of directly targeting New York City with its anti-sanctuary provisions (*Filipino Reporter* 1996). In the press, Giuliani emphasized how restrictions on cooperation and information sharing benefited the public health and safety of the entire city, arguing that it was only after the passage of the order that the city was able to convince undocumented migrants to report crimes and seek medical help (Mullins 1996). No mention was made of the historical roots of city sanctuary, or its connections to faith-based organizing across the country. In its legal challenge, the city focused on questions of municipal governance, unsuccessfully arguing that federal anti-sanctuary provisions were undemocratic and unconstitutional, insofar as they represented a lack of respect for local political processes (*City of New York v. US* 179 F.3d 29 [2nd Cir. 1999]). The City of New York lost its case against the federal government, appealed the judges' decision, and finally lost its appeal in 1999.[3]

The city as a sanctuary after 9/11

The next time tensions over city sanctuary came to a head was after 2001. National security concerns converged with a resurgence of anti-immigration politics in the US, and federal efforts to involve local police in the enforcement of immigration law were renewed. High profile media personalities like Lou Dobbs and Bill O'Reilly attacked sanctuary cities, accusing them of harbouring criminals and terrorists. These attacks resonated with the rhetoric of harbouring and safe haven that surrounded the War on Terror, and sanctuary began to take on a more sinister meaning in public discourse.

Despite protestations from city officials that they had never had a sanctuary policy, New York City became a target of anti-sanctuary organizing after a Congressional Research Service report listed it as a sanctuary city (Seghetti *et al.* 2004). In December 2002, a woman was abducted and assaulted in Queens, New York. It was later made public that a number of the assailants were not only undocumented, but had criminal histories and had been in the custody of the NYPD on several different occasions. The anti-immigration lobby seized on the event and blamed sanctuary for the violence (Subcommittee on Immigration, Border Security, and Claims 2003).

However, other ideas of city sanctuary have resurged since 9/11. In November of 2001, local police across the country were asked to help the FBI question 5000 Middle Eastern men, most of whom were in the US on temporary visas. The men were not suspected of any crime, but were selected because they fit 'criteria of persons who might have knowledge of foreign-based terrorists', based on factors such as gender, age and national origin (Office of the Attorney General 2001: 1). Interviewees were asked about their political beliefs, and police were asked to call the INS if they suspected the men were violating any immigration-related regulations.

The plans for mass questioning sparked protest from civil liberties and immigrants' rights groups who were concerned about racial profiling and mass detentions (Richissin 2001). While most local police forces agreed to participate, a handful refused. Sanctuary policies from the 1980s that prevented local police from collecting information about a person's immigration status if they have not been charged with any crime were reinvigorated as a form of resistance to the mass questioning.[4] Indeed, many cities across the country have reaffirmed their sanctuary policies since 2001 as a response to perceived attacks on civil liberties (National Immigratoin Law Center 2004), and sanctuary policies became an axis of organizing during the large-scale demonstrations for immigrants' rights that occurred across the country in 2006 and 2007.

Conclusion

The idea of the city as a space of sanctuary has been mobilized by local governments during several major waves of political organizing in the US. Berkeley during the Vietnam War era, and cities declaring sanctuary for Central American refugees in the mid-1980s explicitly linked their sanctuary policies to faith-based movements. Biblical ideas of the ancient Cities of Refuge to which accused people could flee resonated with those seeking justice for groups existing in a problematic or complicated relationship to federal law. While antiwar soldiers and refugees were the original subjects of city sanctuary in the US, it was later extended to non-citizens more broadly and racialized groups who have been targeted by immigration law enforcement.

As city sanctuary became more explicitly connected to debates about information sharing and cooperation between various institutions of government, cities defended their policies through appeals to the necessities of municipal governance, and the health and safety of residents. In the process, city sanctuary has been transformed away from its religious roots and into a more institutionalized mechanism of local government. This transformation has also been shaped by critics of sanctuary, who have fuelled a political discourse linking sanctuary to the harbouring of criminals, local government failure to enforce the law, and threats to national security. In addition to faith-based traditions, then, city sanctuary also has been constituted by more secular movements and political trajectories. For example, antiwar resistance within the US Navy and movements for immigrants' rights were important to the history of city sanctuary in the Bay Area. Cities have invoked sanctuary as a civil rights strategy, and a form of resistance to the post-9/11 security agenda. In order to understand the city as a space of sanctuary in the US, then, more research is necessary to unpack how sanctuary has been shaped by different social movements and political struggles in particular historical moments and places, and how this, in turn, has transformed the substance and meaning of sanctuary more broadly.

Notes

1 For example City of Berkeley, Resolution No 52, 596-N.S Declaring Berkeley a City of Refuge (1985), City of Los Angeles, Sanctuary Resolution, November 27, 1985 (original resolution), Oakland Resolution No 63950 C.M.S. (July 8, 1986), and City of Madison, Wisconsin, Resolution reaffirming support for efforts to refugees fleeing El Salvador and Guatemala (1985). Olympia, WA, Ithaca, NY, and Burlington, VT, also passed policies commending sanctuary workers.
2 These cities included Berkeley, Los Angeles, Oakland, San Diego, San Francisco, and West Hollywood, California; Burlington, Vermont; Cambridge, Massachusetts; Chicago, Illinois; Ithaca and Rochester, New York; Madison, Wisconsin; Olympia, Washington; Duluth and St. Paul, Minnesota; and Takoma Park, Maryland.
3 The city claimed that new federal prohibitions violated the Tenth Amendment and the Guarantee Clause of the US Constitution because, among other things: they usurped states' and local governments' administration of the core functions of government; interfered with the ability of local government entities to regulate their own workforces; and compelled them to enact and enforce a federal regulatory program.
4 This occurred in, among other cities, Portland and Corvallis, Oregon; San Francisco and San Jose, California; and Seattle, Washington.

References

Altemus, M. (1987–8) 'The Sanctuary Movement', *Whittier Law Review*, 9: 684–721.
Anon (1971a) 'Alameda at 5am. Military Personnel 1971–72, 1988, 1990', Box 1, Folder 2, Gustav Shultz Sanctuary Collection, 1971–72, 1981–90, Graduate Theological Union, University of California, Berkeley.
——(1971b) 'SOS Rally Promotes Slowdown at Alameda Naval Station', *The Daily Californian*, 10 November, p. 12.
——(1971c) '*USS Coral Sea* Sets Sail Amid Protests', *American Report*, November 26. Container 8, Folder 23, Pacific Counseling Service and Military Law Office, 1969–77. Bancroft Library, University of California, Berkeley.
——(1971d) 'From the Belly of the Beast', *A Warship Can Be Stopped* (Newspaper): 2 (original on file with author).
Bau, I. (1985) *This Ground is Holy: Church Sanctuary and Central American Refugees*, New York: Paulist Press.
——(1994) 'Cities of Refuge: No Federal Preemption of Ordinances Restricting Local Government Cooperation with the INS', *La Raza Law Journal*, 7: 50–71.
Berkeley Church Offers Sanctuary to Military Dissenters (n.d.) 'Press Release. Military Personnel 1971–72, 1988, 1990', Box 1, Folder 5, Gustav Shultz Sanctuary Collection, 1971–72, 1981–90, Graduate Theological Union, University of California, Berkeley.
City and County of San Francisco (1989) 'Ordinance 375–89 Amending the Administrative Code by Adding Chapter 12H Thereto, Affirming San Francisco's Status as a City and County of Refuge, and Prohibiting the Use of City and Country Resources to Assist in Enforcement of Federal Immigration Laws. September 28, Legislative File 97–89–42', Clerk of the Board, City and County of San Francisco, CA.

City Council Supports *USS Coral Sea* Resistors (n.d.) 'Military Personnel 1971–72, 1988, 1990', Box 1, Folder 3, Gustav Shultz Sanctuary Collection, 1971–72, 1981–90, Graduate Theological Union, University of California, Berkeley.

City of Berkeley (1971) *Resolution No. 44.784-N.S. November 9, 1971. Further Statement of Policy of Berkeley City Council with Respect to Sanctuary for Men of the USS Coral Sea*. City of Berkeley, CA.

Coral Sea Officers (1971) 'Press Release November 9', Container 8, Folder 23, Pacific Counseling Service and Military Law Office, 1969–77, Bancroft Library, University of California, Berkeley.

Cortright, D. (2005) *Soldiers in Revolt: GI Resistance During the Vietnam War*, Chicago: Haymarket Books.

Coutin, S.B. (1995) 'Smugglers or Samaritans in Tucson, Arizona: Producing and Contesting Legal Truth', *American Ethnologist*, 22(3): 549–71.

Crewmembers of the *USS Coral Sea* (1971a) 'A Statement to the Press by Crewmembers of the *USS Coral Sea*, October 11', Container 8, Folder 21, Pacific Counseling Service and Military Law Office, 1969–77, Bancroft Library, University of California, Berkeley, CA.

—— (1971b) 'A Statement to the Press by Crewmembers of the *USS Coral* Sea, December 9', Container 8, Folder 23, Pacific Counseling Service and Military Law Office, 1969–77, Bancroft Library, University of California, Berkeley.

Cunningham, H. (1995) *God and Caesar at the Rio Grande: Sanctuary and the Politics of Religion*, Minneapolis: University of Minnesota Press.

Filipinio Reporter (1996) 'Giuliani Vows Fight Vs. Illegal Alien Law', 19 September, p. 6.

Fiske, E.B. (1968) 'Church, Sanctuary and War Resisters', *New York Times*, p. E5.

Foley, M.S. (2006) 'Sanctuary! A Bridge between GI and Civilian Protest against the Vietnam War', in M.B. Young and R. Buzzanco (eds) *A Companion to the Vietnam War*, Malden, MA: Blackwell Publishing, pp. 416–33.

Jennings, R.P. (1971) 'A Pastoral: Re Sanctuary Offered to Sailors of the *USS Coral Sea*. November 13, 1971', Military Personnel 1971–72, 1988, 1990. Box 1, Folder 2, Gustav Shultz Sanctuary Collection, 1971–72, 1981–90, Graduate Theological Union, University of California, Berkeley.

Lindsey, R. (1985) 'Aid to Aliens Said to Spur Illegal Immigration', *New York Times*, 23 December, p. A1.

MacEóin, G. (1985) 'A Brief History Of The Sanctuary Movement', in *Sanctuary: A Resource Guide for Understanding and Participating in the Central American Refugees' Struggle*, San Francisco: Harper and Row, pp. 14–32.

Merina, V. (1985) 'Cities vs. the INS Sanctuary: Reviving an Old Concept', *Los Angeles Times*, 17 November, p. 1.

Miyasato, M. (1989) 'S.F. Hispanics Protest INS Raid of Nightclub', *The San Francisco Chronicle*, 26 January, p. A5.

Moore, W. (1971) 'No "Sanctuary" for Berkeley Council', *San Francisco Chronicle*, 12 November, p. 11.

Mullins, E. (1996) 'US Is Discriminating Against Immigrants', *Irish Voice*, 29 October, p. 8.

National Immigration Law Center (2004) 'Introduction and Background: Sample Language for Policies Limiting the Enforcement of Immigration Law by Local Authorities'. Available at: http://www.nilc.org/immlawpolicy/Local-Law/sample%20policy_intro%20brief_nov%202004.pdf (accessed 1 February 2008).

Office of the Attorney General (2001) 'Memorandum: Interviews Regarding International Terrorism', unpublished memorandum, 9 November.

Richissin, T. (2001) 'Critics Seek Limit to Terror Inquiries', *The Sun*, 22 December.

Romero, M. A. (1989) 'Testimony on Behalf of the Mexican American Legal Defense and Education Fund Before the Human Services Committee, Board of Supervisors, City and County of San Francisco. September 28, Legislative File 97-89-42', Clerk of the Board, City and County of San Francisco, CA.

San Francisco Board of Supervisors (1989) 'Press Release: Board of Supervisors Hearing on San Francisco City and County of Refuge Ordinance', unpublished Legislative File 97-89-42, Clerk of the Board, City and County of San Francisco, CA.

Schmalz, J. (1985) 'Koch Faults U.S. Policy on Illegal Immigration', *The New York Times*, 19 October, p. A31.

Seghetti, L.M., Viña, S.R. and Ester, K. (2004) *Enforcing Immigration Law: The Role of State and Local Law Enforcement*, Washington, DC: Congressional Research Service.

SOS (1971) *Good Times*, IV.30, 15 October. Available at:http://shapingsf.ctyme.com (accessed 15 May 2008).

SOS Petition (1971) 'Container 8, Folder 21, Pacific Counseling Service and Military Law Office, 1969–77', Bancroft Library, University of California, Berkeley.

Stop That Ship (1971) *Good Times*, IV.32, 12 November. Available at: http://shapingsf.ctyme.com (accessed 15 May 2008).

Subcommittee on Immigration, Border Security, and Claims (2003) *Hearing on New York City's 'Sanctuary' Policy and the Effect of Such Policies on Public Safety, Law Enforcement, and Immigration*. Hearing, February 27, Washington, DC: GPO.

University Lutheran Chapel (n.d.) 'One Man Accepts Sanctuary (Press Release)', Military Personnel 1971–72, 1988, 1990. Box 1, Folder 2, Gustav Shultz Sanctuary Collection, 1971–72, 1981–90, Graduate Theological Union, University of California, Berkeley.

Wells, M.J. (2004) 'The Grassroots Reconfiguration of U.S. Immigration Policy', *International Migration Review*, 38: 1308–47.

Chapter 16

Seeking sanctuary in a border city
Sanctuary movement(s) across the Canada–US border

Julie E.E. Young

The Detroit/Windsor Refugee Coalition (DWRC), now known as Freedom House, sits at the base of the Ambassador Bridge that connects Detroit, Michigan, to Windsor, Ontario. Located in downtown Detroit, the building is visible across the river in Windsor. This contemporary shelter for people seeking asylum in the United States is the institutionalization of local sanctuary efforts that took place in the late 1980s. Connected to the wider, US-based sanctuary movement, the DWRC began as a loose network of advocates who contested US policy in Central America and assisted people to cross the border into Canada by making a claim for refugee status. Members of this coalition strategically used Canadian and US legal frameworks and re-conceptualized the international boundary line that both divides and joins this border city.

The emergence of the DWRC in the 1980s and its ongoing, material presence in the contemporary border city help us to think about how solidarity is worked out across international boundary lines: the relationships that are possible, the spaces that are produced, and the implications of such collaboration. This chapter focuses on refugee advocacy across the Detroit (US)–Windsor (Canadian) border in the late 1980s. I examine the possibilities for refuge in a border city, where the international boundary line weighs heavily on the landscape, with a presumption that this spatial relationship matters for how refuge is conceived and worked out.

Border-city sanctuary

The geographic location of a border city underscores the spatial negotiations involved in practices of sanctuary. Seeking refuge literally requires that an individual cross an international boundary line and make a claim on another state for protection. However, the practice of refuge entails more than this literal act of border crossing, and it is more than a status that is sought and granted. Refuge is a process, and the specifics of its geography matter. The Detroit–Windsor border city was drawn into negotiations of refuge due to its location on the Canada–US border and because of connections to the wider US-based sanctuary movement.

Jacques Derrida (2001) urges us to look to the city in navigating the relationship between state sovereignty and individual claims for refuge, arguing the city should serve as a refuge in ways the nation-state cannot. Rather than considering refuge only as dependent on a hospitable state, it is important to understand refuge as negotiated and contested by a range of actors at various scales and in relation to different places and moments. Derrida suggests that 'cities of refuge' are already in existence through the ways in which residents of the city are reshaping membership. Here, 'the city' refers not to a distinct level of state governance, but rather to a political space through which it is possible to reframe ideas and practices of belonging and solidarity (Isin 2007; Young 2011).

Interesting examples of how refuge has been negotiated can be found in various practices of 'sanctuary'. Several researchers have focused on negotiations of sanctuary and precarious legal status within state space; for example, the US-based sanctuary movement (Coutin 1993; Cunningham 1995), 'cities of sanctuary' initiatives (Ridgley 2008; Darling 2010; Squire 2011), and taking sanctuary in a religious institution (Lippert 2005; Rehaag 2009). My research is located in a different space of negotiations: I focus on the Canadian 'end' of the US-based sanctuary movement and efforts to help people access Canadian territory to make a refugee claim during the mid- to late-1980s. Refuge by official definition requires the crossing of a boundary from one state to another; however, the individuals seeking refuge in this case had already left their 'countries of origin' and sought safety in another country (the US). Yet, this place was not safe because they were unable to secure formal recognition of their right to remain and risked detention and deportation as they lived in legal and social limbo.

Sanctuary work begins with the recognition that a given place cannot provide safety for some people and the consideration of different options – taking sanctuary in churches or other institutions, sanctuary-city declarations and practices, and moving to another state's territory. The first two options are more obvious contestations of the state's policies and practices. The third option reads like a capitulation: rather than contesting policies and practices where one is, the aim is to find refuge across the border in another state's territory. Unlike taking sanctuary in a church or benefiting from a sanctuary-city declaration, both of which contest the current system by claiming the right to presence in that place, moving to another state's territory entails entering another system and working within its terms.

Nonetheless, the migration of refugees may change those terms. Catherine Nolin (2006: 106) describes how Central American refugees arriving in the late 1980s transformed the geography of refuge in Canada. She argues these refugees redefined the spaces of refuge 'from "asylum control" in the Canadian embassies and consulates ... to "asylum demand" at the country's border' (ibid.: 107). New social and political spaces were created through the actions of people seeking refuge at the international boundary line. The location of these individuals at the boundary line and the visibility of their claims are significant.

This 'asylum-demand'-at-the-border option becomes available because of the geography of the place. What is different about the sanctuary-related efforts I examine is that the territory encompassed by this refugee advocacy is a border city. Windsor and Detroit sit on either side of an international boundary line between two different states; yet, it is possible to consider Detroit–Windsor as one place that is simultaneously separated and joined by the border. Indeed, this is part of what is noteworthy about the Detroit–Windsor refugee advocacy work in the 1980s: individuals on both sides of the border worked together despite the international boundary line, taking part in a joint project to assist refugees from Central America as they sought safety in the area. Their efforts underscore the utility of working as though these two cities were one place, and I argue that seeing this place as one border city reclaims the border for refugees as it contests state practices.

Part of the argument for situating this research in this border city has to do with the significance of (in)visibility to the negotiation of refuge and border control more broadly. The state makes its border control practices increasingly difficult to locate: the border moves out as a way for states to prevent people from arriving and making claims for refugee status, but the border also simultaneously moves in as states try to track down people who have circumvented pre-emptive interdiction measures (Walters 2006; Isin and Rygiel 2007; Hyndman and Mountz 2008; Mountz 2010). These spatial strategies include the imposition of visas on particular countries, the designation of 'safe third countries', and the involvement of local police in enforcing immigration laws.

The border, moreover, is enforced in mundane ways that do not often draw attention; this is not incidental, but strategic. Joseph Carens (1997: 33) argues that the invisibility of state interdiction practices operating in routine, bureaucratic ways helps to avoid discussion of the contradiction between principle and practice in asylum law: 'Unlike open interdiction, the force that lies behind a refusal to grant someone a document or to permit someone to board an airplane is so much a part of everyday life that it is largely invisible and difficult to communicate effectively.' Routine practices of border control remove people – and the reality of their exclusion – from sight (Macklin 2005; Watt 2006).

In this context of mobile borders, the international boundary line becomes a strategic site at which to challenge state border control policies and practices. It is strategic precisely because of its visibility. This would seem obvious: the boundary line is the most visible manifestation of both the concept and the practice of state borders. And yet, it is precisely at these physical lines demarcating the edges of territories where 'the border' is often taken for granted. In a confrontation between state sovereignty and individual mobility, the former wins out (Hyndman 2004; Dauvergne 2008), and discussion of alternative visions is often foreclosed.

The sanctuary movement in Canada

US intervention in El Salvador and Guatemala in the 1980s meant that the US government was hesitant to accept refugees fleeing regimes it was supporting. Responding to the US role in the conflicts in Central America, a network of advocates and religious organizations established the 'sanctuary movement' to assist these individuals to enter, remain in, and/or leave US territory. By 1987, more than 440 sites throughout the US had been declared 'sanctuaries' (Cunningham 1995). Most people engaged in the sanctuary movement considered their work to be acts of 'civil initiative', in that they were upholding a law the government refused to uphold (i.e., the 1980 US *Refugee Act*) rather than breaking the law through acts of civil disobedience.

While much has been written about the US-based sanctuary movement (see in particular: Coutin 1993; Cunningham 1995; see also Perla and Bibler Coutin, Chapter 5, Caminero-Santangelo, Chapter 6, and Yukich, Chapter 7 in this volume), very little was recorded about Canadian involvement in this network beyond brief but intriguing references. For example, Hilary Cunningham (1995: 216, n. 26) reveals, in a footnote, that refugees who were considered 'high-risk' because they had been arrested in the US for immigration violations were 'bonded mainly out of south Texas and became wards of Quaker groups working with the Canadian government'. Many of these accounts also mention a 'clandestine Underground Railroad' and a more 'officially recognized route [known] as the Overground Railroad' that assisted Guatemalans and Salvadorans in reaching the Canadian border (Elbow 1992; Coutin 1993; Cunningham 1995; Nolin 2006: 106). Sanctuary workers regularly evoked the legacy of the Underground Railroad that helped fugitive slaves escape the US in the nineteenth century to lend legitimacy to their actions (Cunningham 1995). These limited details position Canada in a particularly benign light. Indeed, Randy Lippert (2005: 22) argues the success of the US-based sanctuary movement 'presupposed more liberal Canadian refugee policies that provided Central American refugees with a greater likelihood of legal acceptance as refugees'.

The distinction between Canadian and US legal treatment of refugees from El Salvador and Guatemala is evident in much higher acceptance rates for refugee claims in Canada at the time. In 1985, for example, the US government was 'granting asylum to 3 per cent of Salvadoran applicants and fewer than 1 per cent of Guatemalan applicants' (Cunningham 1995: 205), while the Canadian rates were 60 per cent and 70 per cent respectively (García 2006). Canada's acceptance rates demonstrate a different interpretation of the Refugee Convention and of the political situations in these two countries. Between 1983 and 1985, more than five thousand Salvadorans and one thousand Guatemalans were recognized as refugees in Canada (Lemco 1991). In relation to these different stances in Canada and the US, some people were guided to the northern border of the US through the 'Overground Railroad'.

There are limited recorded details about this network and this allows a particular view of Canada to emerge. It sustains what I term the 'Canadian humanitarian imaginary' – the powerful narrative that Canada has a generous and welcoming policy towards refugees, and no further examination is required. It is true that through sanctuary work, as well as on their own, many Central Americans found refuge in Canada when they could not find it in the US; it is also true that these negotiations were taking place in a period where Canadian policy was shifting. In 1987, the Canadian government introduced changes to refugee policy that dramatically affected individuals seeking refuge at the border, including the introduction of the *Refugee Deterrents and Detention Bill* (C-84) (see Lippert 2005: 51–4; Pratt 2005: 98–102). Officials removed El Salvador and Guatemala from the moratorium on deportations list, implemented a visa requirement for these countries, and instituted direct-backs to the US, meaning that people would have to wait there until their hearing date, often several weeks away. Many people who had previously been able to enter Canada and make a refugee claim were dissuaded from doing so, and individuals returned to the US could be subject to detention and deportation while they awaited their hearing in Canada (Lemco 1991; Pratt 2005).

As both the US and Canadian governments were making it more difficult for refugees to cross their shared border, advocates in several cities on or near the Canada–US border responded (Lippert 2005: 23). I focus on the informal network that assisted refugees in the Detroit–Windsor area. The border city became an active and important site in this work because of its strategic location.

Local advocacy responses in Detroit–Windsor

In the context of sanctuary work in the late 1980s and in contrast to the US side of the border, the Canadian side of the border was produced as a space of refuge because the Canadian legal framework offered a dependable pathway to secure status for people who had escaped wars in Central America and were living precariously in the US. While the suite of administrative changes enacted by the Canadian government in early 1987 made it more difficult to access the refugee determination system (see Lippert 2005: 53–4; Pratt 2005), the door was not completely shut and many people were able to successfully achieve refugee status in Canada after making a claim at the Canada–US border. Related to this geographical positioning was a concern with the optics of border crossings that were facilitated by local advocates, influenced by the logic of the wider sanctuary movement. Advocates focused on 'overground' routes and methods, strategically mobilizing Canada's refugee policies to enable people to leave the US and gain secure legal status across the border. In addition, local sanctuary efforts created a space of refuge that spanned the international boundary line, relying on cooperation between organizations and individuals on both sides of the Detroit River.

The work of Detroit–Windsor-based organizations and individuals focused on three main areas: lobbying, solidarity and public education, and sanctuary-related initiatives. Advocates affiliated with this network focused on contesting US and Canadian foreign and refugee policies. They lobbied the municipal councils in both cities to respond to government policies. They carried out teach-ins and demonstrations, organized conferences and forums, and turned to theatre productions to raise awareness about the implications of US and Canadian policies for Central America. They also engaged in a range of activities related to the wider sanctuary movement, from participation in caravans, speaking tours, and organizing efforts, to convincing Detroit City Council to declare a City of Sanctuary in 1987. Finally, local advocates assisted Central Americans to cross the border into Canada by making a refugee claim.

Local organizations involved in this work included the Windsor Central American Refugee Sponsorship Network (WCARSN) that emerged around 1981, and the Detroit/Windsor Refugee Coalition (DWRC) that came together around 1983. Separately and, starting in 1983, together, these groups arranged for private sponsorship of Central Americans seeking entry to Canada from the US via the Windsor–Detroit border crossings. This collaborative effort emerged in 1983 when two lawyers, one in Windsor and one in Detroit, 'learned Salvadorans seeking refugee status were being sent back to the US by Canadian immigration authorities in Windsor' (Powless 1984). After these lawyers had successfully assisted two refugees to cross into Windsor, the WCARSN joined forces with the DWRC. From that time, the group comprised of 'church members, lawyers, social workers, and interested residents established "safe houses" to hide Salvadorans. They gathered donations to develop a revolving bail fund and posted notices in Spanish American communities informing "illegals" of their rights' (ibid.). The WCARSN was dissolved in 1985 but the DWRC continued the work, with the support of churches, community groups, and individuals in both cities.

The Detroit Sanctuary Coalition (DSC) and the Third World Resource Centre (TWRC) in Windsor were also active at the time. The DSC organized in Detroit in connection to the national sanctuary movement towards the goals of offering sanctuary to refugees from conflicts in Central America, educating the US public about the effects of its government's policies in the region, and changing these policies. The TWRC's focus was on public education about the situations in Central America, including US and Canadian policies in the region. Both groups organized community education workshops and events, which included opportunities for refugees to give testimonials. Beginning in 1981, the TWRC helped to organize an annual event to commemorate the death of Archbishop Oscar Romero of San Salvador (Anon 1987; Reaume, personal communication, June 2010). In December 1983, St. Rita's Catholic Church in Detroit was declared a sanctuary and hosted a family from El Salvador for several years (Reuther archives, Box 3, Folder 37: MICAH; reports, correspondence, 1980–86). In 1987, a member of the TWRC wrote a play entitled, 'Scream Out, Screen Out', which dramatized a refugee determination hearing. Both a play and a teach-in, it was performed during the University of Windsor

Law School moot court in October 1987 (Reaume, pers. comm., June 2010). The play was also performed in February 1988 at a youth event at the Faculty of Education, University of Windsor. Three hundred students from twenty local schools attended the forum on the topic of 'The World's Refugee Problem'. The play was performed by a local grade 12 drama class (TWRC archives, Box 2, Folder 4: Third World Resource Centre Newsletter, No. 36, Mar.–Apr. 1988).

Members of solidarity and advocacy groups from both sides of the border took advice from one another and participated in demonstrations, teach-ins, and other public events together. For example, in 1982, organizers from the Detroit-based Michigan Interfaith Committee on Human Rights spoke at the high school human rights forum on refugees in Windsor. Members of Windsor's TWRC demonstrated against US foreign policy outside Cobo Hall in downtown Detroit where US Secretary of State George Shultz was speaking. In August 1987, in response to Canadian refugee policy changes, an event was held at a church in nearby Hamtramck, Michigan, on how to organize in response to US and Canadian policies *vis-à-vis* Central America; it was attended by both Windsor- and Detroit-based advocates (Reaume, pers. comm., June 2010).

As the US and Canadian governments were tightening their borders, the DWRC focused on assisting individuals to make a refugee claim at the border. The coalition found places for people to live in Detroit while awaiting their refugee hearings in Canada, and offered assistance, such as legal support at refugee hearings and in interactions with government departments, once they were in Canada awaiting the final outcome of their claim (Gutschi 1986). The DSC outreached to make people aware of the DWRC's 'sanctuary' work (Reuther archive, Box 6, Folder 6: Detroit Sanctuary Coalition Project, 1988). Organizers in Detroit also had great success with their local lobbying, culminating in the 30 September 1987 proclamation of Detroit as a City of Sanctuary (Walter Reuther Library, Archives of Labor and Urban Affairs, Organization in Solidarity with Central America Collection, Box 3, Folder 5: Detroit Sanctuary Coalition, 1986–87).

From this brief overview, we see that local advocates engaged in a variety of initiatives and used a range of approaches in their advocacy and solidarity work. The optics of legality underlying their efforts and the border-spanning character of their advocacy work are two key aspects of the sanctuary-related organizing occurring in Detroit–Windsor in the late 1980s. Optics of legality refers to the sense that the legitimacy of people's presence in this border city could be restored by accessing the Canadian refugee system, despite having little chance of being accepted through the US system. Border-spanning refers to the geography of their work and its implications: the international boundary line emerged as a strategic site for contestation of the refugee and foreign policies of both countries.

From demonstrations and teach-ins to sanctuary declarations and human rights forums, a main goal of the local network was to bring public awareness to the dire situations in Central America and related issues faced by those forced to seek safety in the US. This concern with visibility is evident in the archival records, where documentation of refugee testimonials, teach-ins, and public events figure prominently. At a different scale, the collaborative work of Detroit–Windsor-based advocates brought visibility to the precarious situations of Central Americans in the US.

Individuals involved in the Canadian end of the sanctuary movement were careful to situate their work as facilitating the 'legal' movement of people across the border from the US into Canada. Advocates focused on so-called 'overground' routes and methods to enable people to leave the US and gain secure legal status across the border. This included such actions as encouraging people the US government considered 'illegal aliens' to make claims for asylum in the US or apply for a 30-day temporary visa to remain in the US while awaiting their refugee hearings in Canada. For those who had deportation orders outstanding against them in the US, advocates suggested that individuals advise the Immigration and Naturalization Service of their voluntary departure as they crossed the border to attend their refugee hearings in Canada.

Detroit–Windsor-based advocates drew from the strategy employed by the wider, US-based sanctuary movement. Until the sanctuary movement brought public attention to their presence within the US, people who had left the conflicts in El Salvador and Guatemala and were living in the US had been detained and deported with impunity. Public declarations of sanctuary at churches and synagogues in the US began in 1982. The arrest and prosecution of eleven sanctuary workers in 1985–86, in what became known as 'the Sanctuary Trial', increased media coverage and public awareness of the US government's involvement in conflicts in both countries and treatment of asylum-seekers within its borders. Sanctuary members hoped that drawing attention to their work would 'force the government to address their concerns' (Cunningham 1995: 31). The sanctuary movement contested the US administration's approach to these refugees by characterizing their own work as legal and responding to the US government's failure to uphold its legal obligations.

The sanctuary movement and its local incarnation in Windsor–Detroit brought attention to these refugees who were being disappeared by the US government – either actively (through detention and deportation) or indirectly (through the dissuasive effect of low acceptance rates for asylum claims and heightened immigration enforcement that encouraged people to remain undocumented). Assistance provided to Central American refugees meant these particular individuals were not disappeared in the border control machinery. Rather, they were brought within the legal framework in order to cross the border and hopefully achieve status in Canada. This was possible because of distinct interpretations of refugee policy for Central Americans in the US and Canada. Canada was a place where their legal status, as undocumented immigrants in the US, could be made more secure by entering the Canadian refugee determination system.

This emphasis on legality was a crucial element of the work of the DWRC. Their efforts were characterized by a concern with the optics of border crossings: entry to Canada was to be achieved via officially sanctioned means. On one hand, this focus on assisting people to enter the refugee determination system in Canada perpetuates the link between legality and perceptions of legitimacy, in the sense that authorized entry confirms that the need for refuge is genuine. To a certain extent, use of the immigration systems in both countries leaves their rules unquestioned. Early discussions from the 'El Salvador Study Group' of the First Presbyterian Church in Ann Arbor, Michigan, provide insight into this concern over the perceived legality of particular kinds of sanctuary work:

> The idea of our church openly defying the government by offering illegal sanctuary, as a few churches around the country were doing, was emphatically rejected by our conservatives. But even they seemed ready [to] consider actions within the law, such as sending money to the border in Arizona for legal aid for refugees. We agreed to invite speakers and to continue reading books and articles in the effort to reach consensus.
> (Bentley Historical Library, Mary Hathaway papers; Box 3, Folder 11: Deliverance)

On the other hand, this understanding of the optics of legality is noteworthy. Similar to the framing of sanctuary work in the US, local advocates recognized that working within the legal framework helped to legitimate their efforts, in the sense that it was more difficult to dismiss their work as 'unlawful'. That is not to say that use of 'underground' methods would have been less legitimate. In terms of its role in broadening the base of people who were sympathetic to their advocacy and interested in effecting change, this decision to work through 'legal' means could be described as strategic. Advocates wanted to draw attention to the situation so that their government's actions could not be ignored by highlighting that, for many undocumented persons living in the US, the route to safety involved crossing the border into Canada.

Related to this strategic mobilization of the legal framework is another key implication of Detroit–Windsor-based advocacy from this period: the emergence of a border-spanning space of refugee advocacy points to the international boundary line as a strategic site for making the state's exclusions visible. Advocates sought to shift the debate around asylum and to secure the safety of refugees. That they had to do so by helping refugees leave the US is crucial. The majority of persons assisted by local advocates travelled the 'overground' route to Canada; only two families entered church sanctuaries in Detroit in this period.

Rather than deep collaboration among organizations assisting refugees in the Detroit–Windsor area in the 1980s, there were loose connections and regular exchanges of information between advocates on both sides of the border (Logan, personal communicatiom, September 2009; Reaume, pers. comm., June 2010).

There was, however, recognition that refugees had better chances of securing permanent status and would be safer in Canada. Local advocates established cross-border relationships to carry out this goal. The name of one actor in particular – the Detroit/Windsor Refugee Coalition – signals the significance of the border-city relationship to its work: although paid staff and most volunteers were Detroit- or Michigan-based, the coalition worked by establishing contacts in Windsor to assist refugees at the border and as they settled into the city. Churches and community members in both cities participated in this work. In a *Windsor Star* article from 23 February 1987, three days after some of the Canadian policy changes came into effect, two Windsor-based volunteers indicated they would work with 'Detroit churches and refugee organizations to arrange accommodations [in Detroit] for the would-be refugees' who had been directed back to the US by Canadian officials (Priest 1987). This collaboration, although relatively informal, ad hoc, and personal, evolved into an enduring organization. Rather than disappearing when the focus of displacement shifted to other contexts in the 1990s, the DWRC remained active and – as outlined earlier – found a permanent home in a former convent at the base of the Ambassador Bridge.

This materialization of the sanctuary work and border-spanning relationships of refugee advocacy signals a key innovation of local efforts in the late 1980s. It was not only that, by entering the Canadian refugee system, the city of Windsor became a sanctuary; although Windsor was certainly positioned as a place of refuge through the coalition's involvement in helping people across the border into more secure legal positions. It was also the involvement of people on both sides of the river that was significant: border-spanning relationships helped to make this work happen. Moreover, it was not just that they had to collaborate in order to help individual refugees get safely to Canada; it was that they worked together across the boundary line. Local advocates created an alternative vision of the spaces for refuge that are possible around an international boundary line. A key piece of the work was that it conceived of the two cities within the same framework of getting particular people to safety. Their work re-conceptualizes the border. Rather than treating it only as an obstacle to be crossed, the border-spanning work of Detroit-Windsor-based advocates reframed the boundary line as a point of connection in addition to one of separation. In a tentative way, DWRC members offered a glimpse of a potential 'border city of refuge' where two cities on either side of a boundary line were envisioned as one place.

Reframing 'safety' in North American space

This Detroit–Windsor-based advocacy is instructive in two key respects. First, the conceptualization of its work as linked across the Canada–US border opened alternative spaces of sanctuary and had (potentially) lasting impacts on how people in both cities worked with refugees and immigrants, although ever-tightening border controls have made collaborative work across the border more difficult in the past decade. Second, its understanding of the optics of working within the legal framework legitimated the DWRC's work and the wider sanctuary movement, making it harder to dismiss advocates and refugee claimants as law breakers. At the same time, this approach reinforced the notion that legitimate border crossings were 'legal' ones. Taken together, these elements highlight the contradictions of sanctuary and border control. On one side, even people working to overcome the state's exclusions help to perpetuate the system of categorization that legitimizes particular movements over others. On the other, their work takes place in the same place (a border city) and different places (a city cut through by a boundary line). Advocates seemed to view their border-city connections as a drawing together, not only as a separation, pointing to the possibility of a different kind of space of refuge. Their involvement in assisting refugees did not stop at their side of the international boundary line.

These political and geographical negotiations matter because of the particular context of visibility and proximity offered by a border city. This movement (the DWRC and other local advocates contesting US and Canadian policies) finds this geography (the border city) because it needs it – the proximity, the distinct policy frameworks, and the centrality of two urban centres. In a sense, it is an accident of geography that allows this movement to emerge and create a space of refuge here. The international boundary line running through this border city fuels the practices of local advocates. The border is an obstacle that separates places but it is also a point of connection. This contradictory character of a border city emphasizes the fragility of relationships that span boundary lines and points to the difficulties of sustaining such linkages.

Since this period, there have been substantial changes to border control policy that have further restricted access to Canadian territory for refugees. A key change is that in the interim, Canada has declared the US a 'safe' country for refugees under the 2004 Canada-US *Safe Third Country Agreement (STCA)*.[1] While the *STCA* essentially treats the US and Canada as one space for the purposes of asylum, the boundary line is further entrenched for people seeking to cross the border under its terms. The Agreement forecloses legal options for individuals seeking refuge across this boundary line.[2] By closing a legal route of entry to Canada to many refugees, it is likely that it has caused some to turn to 'underground' modes of entry as they seek safety (Pratt 2005; Mountz 2010). While there is no doubt that a policy like the *STCA* complicates collaboration on refugee advocacy, it could provide the rationale for precisely that kind of integration of efforts across the boundary line. These further restrictions of access to Canadian space could also inspire stronger relationships for advocacy and contestation, particularly in a pair of cities that has to a certain extent functioned as one place. The legacy of the DWRC and other local organizing in the late 1980s is the glimpse of a border city of refuge, in which the border is reclaimed for refugees.

Acknowledgements

This chapter is based on research done for my dissertation, entitled 'Border city of refuge: Refugee advocacy and the reframing of the Windsor–Detroit border' (Department of Geography, York University). The research received funding support from the Social Science and Humanities Research Council and the Ontario Graduate Scholarship.

Notes

1 In fact, Canada proposed safe third country provisions in one of the bills put forward in 1987 (Bill C-55, the *Refugee Reform Bill*), but they were not implemented likely due to the controversial question of whether or not Canadian officials could list the US as a 'safe' country (Dirks 1995).
2 The *STCA* contains several exceptions that allow individuals to make claims at the border in particular circumstances.

Archives consulted

Bentley Historical Library, University of Michigan, Ana Arbor, Michigan, Mary Hathaway papers.
City of Windsor Municipal Archives.
Third World Resource Centre archives, Global Resource Centre/Ten Thousand Villages, Windsor, Ontario.
Walter Reuther Library, Wayne State University, Detroit, Michigan, Archives of Labor and Urban Affairs, Organization in Solidarity with Central America Collection.

References

Anon (1987) 'Ex-Refugees Mark Death of Archbishop', *Windsor Star*, March 23, p. A5.
Carens, J.H. (1997) 'The Philosopher and the Policymaker: Two Perspectives on the Ethics of Immigration with Special Attention to the Problem of Restricting Asylum', in K. Hailbronner, D.A. Martian, and H. Motomura (eds.), *Immigration Admissions: The Search for Workable Policies in Germany and the United States* (pp. 3–50), New York: Berghahn Books.
Coutin, S.B. (1993) *The Culture of Protest: Religious Activism and the US Sanctuary Movement*, Boulder CO: Westview Press.
Cunningham, H. (1995) *God and Caesar at the Rio Grande: Sanctuary and the Politics of Religion*, Minneapolis, MN: University of Minnesota Press.
Darling, J. (2010) 'A City of Sanctuary: The Relational Re-Imagining of Sheffield's Asylum Politics', *Transactions of the Institute of British Geographers*, 35(1): 125–40.
Dauvergne, C. (2008) *Making People Illegal: What Globalization Means for Migration and Law*, Cambridge: Cambridge University Press.
Derrida, J. (2001) 'On Cosmopolitanism', in J. Derrida, *On Cosmopolitanism and Forgiveness*, London: Routledge.
Dirks, G.E. (1995) *Controversy and Complexity: Canadian Immigration Policy during the 1980s*, Montreal: McGill-Queen's University Press.

Elbow, G.S. (1992) 'The Overground Railroad: Central American Refugee Flows to Canada', in D.G. Janelle (ed.) *Geographical Snapshots of North America*, New York: The Guilford Press.

García, M.C. (2006) *Canada: A Northern Refuge for Central Americans*, Migration Information Source. Available at: http://www.migrationinformation.org/Feature/display.cfm?id=390 (accessed April 28, 2012).

Gutschi, M. (1986) 'Offering a Warm Welcome to Refugees', *Windsor Star*, October 7, p. C6.

Hyndman, J. (2004) 'The (Geo)Politics of Gendered Mobility', in L.A. Staeheli, E. Kofman and L. Peake (eds) *Mapping Women, Making Politics: Feminist Perspectives on Political Geography*, New York: Routledge.

Hyndman, J. and Mountz, A. (2008) 'Another Brick In The Wall? Neo-*Refoulement* and the Externalization of Asylum by Australia and Europe', *Government and Opposition*, 43(2): 249–69.

Isin, E.F. (2007) 'City.State: Critique of Scalar Thought', *Citizenship Studies*, 11(2): 211–28.

Isin, E.F. and Rygiel, K. (2007) 'Abject Spaces: Frontiers, Zones, Camps', in E. Dauphinée and C. Masters (eds) *Logics of Biopower and the War on Terror: Living, Dying, Surviving*, (pp. 181–203) Basingstoke: Palgrave.

Lemco, J. (1991) *Canada and the Crisis in Central America*, New York: Praeger.

Lippert, R.K. (2005) *Sanctuary, Sovereignty, Sacrifice: Canadian Sanctuary Incidents, Power, and Law*, Vancouver: University of British Columbia Press.

Macklin, A. (2005) 'Disappearing Refugees: Reflections on the Canada-US Safe Third Country Agreement', *Columbia Human Rights Law Review*, 36: 365–426.

Mountz, A. (2010) *Seeking Asylum: Human Smuggling and Bureaucracy at the Border*, Minneapolis: University of Minnesota Press.

Nolin, C. (2006) *Transnational Ruptures: Gender and Forced Migration*, Burlington, VT: Ashgate.

Powless, L. (1984) 'A Long Road to Freedom', *Windsor Star*, July 28, p. D1.

Pratt, A. (2005) *Securing Borders: Detention and Deportation in Canada*, Vancouver BC: UBC Press.

Priest, L. (1987) 'Border Closed to 22 Refugees', *Windsor Star*, February 23, pp. A1, A4.

Rehaag, S. (2009) 'Bordering on Legality: Canadian Church Sanctuary and the Rule of Law', *Refuge*, 26(1): 43–56.

Ridgley, J. (2008) 'Cities of Refuge: Immigration Enforcement, Police, and the Insurgent Genealogies of Citizenship In US Sanctuary Cities', *Urban Geography*, 29(1): 53–77.

Squire, V. (2011) 'From Community Cohesion to Mobile Solidarities: The *City of Sanctuary* Network and the *Strangers Into Citizens* Campaign', *Political Studies*, 59(2): 290–307.

Walters, W. (2006) 'Border/Control', *European Journal of Social Theory*, 9(2): 187–204.

Watt, S. (2006) 'Formal and Practiced Citizenships: "Non Status" Algerians and Montreal, Canada', unpublished thesis, York University, Canada.

Young, J.E.E. (2011) '"A New Politics of the City": Locating the Limits of Hospitality and Practicing the City-As-Refuge', *ACME: An International E-Journal for Critical Geographies*, 10(3): 534–563.

Chapter 17

Framing militant sanctuary practices in Afghanistan and Iraq, 2001–11

Michael A. Innes

Introduction

At a speech at the International Institute of Strategic Studies (IISS) on 2 October 2009, General Stanley McChrystal, then Commander of US and NATO forces in Afghanistan, encouraged an audience of listeners to question 'generally accepted, bumper sticker truths' about the country and the war being fought there (McChrystal 2009). McChrystal's comments came a week after journalist David Martin profiled him on the US weekly news show *60 Minutes*, and several weeks into a vigorous public campaign by McChrystal to drum up support for a resource-intensive counterinsurgency plan then still awaiting White House approval. He was cashiered the following summer (Cooper and Sanger 2010).

McChrystal's blunt speech at the IISS is illustrative. In his introductory remarks, he offered barbed criticism of a proposal to abandon Afghanistan – 'Chaos-istan' – that would let it degenerate into a 'Somalia-style haven of chaos' to be contained but not occupied. The remark was a curious one. For eight years prior, Afghanistan had been the referent of choice for all discussions and debates on the subject of sanctuaries. Holding aloft another state in this way hardly broke the archetypal mould. There have been many exemplars to choose from over the years: Somalia, to be sure, but also Iraq, the Philippines, and others. The irony of McChrystal's remarks was that they relied on their own set of bumper sticker truths. This suggests also, in part, some incoherence of the public debate on sanctuaries – though incoherence is, perhaps, the least of its problems.

There is a robust literature on militant sanctuaries, but its pages tile the mosaic of international security unevenly. Sanctuary is, at once, the most important form of support a state can provide to armed surrogates (Byman 2005: 65–6; see also Becker 2006), a prerogative of the intervening humanitarian enterprise designed to shelter civilians in war (McQueen 2005; see also Lischer 2006), and an adapted form of strategic depth – a protected base area – from which guerrilla movements spring forth to do battle with their Goliaths (Brynen 1990). It is, too, an electric realm of data diodes and digital death (Stenersen 2008; Gray and Head 2009), catalytic architectures infused with social meaning

(Sorkin 2008), and sacred sites that metabolize human violence and divine will (Fair and Ganguly 2008; Hassner 2008, 2009). It is, above all, an occult geography that competes in the imagination with the fate of truths preferred by soldiers and statesmen: states are immutable facts of international politics, and sanctuaries are their illegitimate offspring.

This chapter argues that US foreign policy and armed intervention in the post-2001 decade privileged a distorted reading of militant sanctuaries and their significance. Policymakers and practitioners relied on a borrowed lexicon, rife with conceptual metaphors and historical analogies, to frame the problem. Although there is a robust literature on the use of historical and analogical reasoning in political discourse (Khong 1992; Record 2002), there has been very little scholarly attention paid to this particular schema of interpretation. What follows seeks to sketch the rough edges of that gap. It begins with a brief outline of the research problem and the questions it inspires. It briefly reviews major themes in the secondary literature, focusing on tensions between traditionalist and constructivist analyses. It takes specific aim at three issues – militant practices, units and levels of analysis, and social distance – to argue these should be more central in analysis of militant sanctuaries.

The problem

Thanks to the efforts of Martin van Creveld, Mary Kaldor, Thomas X. Hammes, and others, conflict in the post-Cold War era has come to be understood for its protean, improvisational, and networked features – 'new wars' fought between state and non-state actors across traditional political boundaries and through ubiquitous media, amplified in its capacity and reach by advances in communication and information technology (Hoffman 2007). This view found an apotheosis of sorts in the post-2001 period. The complexity of armed conflict had become an article of faith among scholars and practitioners, and a new enemy, Al Qaeda, was the most complex of all. Ambitious of vision even while comparably bereft of capability, its attacks on the World Trade Center towers and on the Pentagon nonetheless precipitated a decade of war. The US and Al Qaeda, it hardly bears emphasizing, both framed their contest in polarizing, existential rhetoric that left little room for thoughtful, nuanced consideration of marginal or liminal phenomena.

The most telling of its disconnects has been spatial. If terrorists organized themselves as distributed networks rather than in paramilitary formations, then surely their requirement for territorial states should have been variable at best. Theologically, Al Qaeda did not purport to wrest control of states (even if some of its members have been little more than dislocated nationalists), but rather to overthrow the system of states and restore the *Ummah*. Strategically, it named specific states as enemies and warned them of its intent to do damage. Operationally, it had to contend with the same facts of states as anyone else: controls and constraints on travel, identity, and the like – even as it worked to bypass them. It was certainly states – in the 1990s, Sudan under Hassan al-Turabi and Afghanistan under the Taliban – that provided it with its most significant operational headquarters (see, e.g., Coll 2004).

But it was at the functional level of scattered individuals and small, dispersed cells that Al Qaeda conducted itself. Despite various disputes about its leadership role, this essentially distributed and tactical character of the organization has not been generally disputed. Yet analysts, I argue, have generally conceptualized militant sanctuaries in dire terms, as problems so magnified in scale and extreme in consequence that only the most aggressive and resource-intensive foreign policy response would do. One of the first essays after 9/11 to put the question to the reading public, published in *The Washington Quarterly*, asked, 'Do terrorist networks need a home?' (Takeyh and Gvosdev 2002). Implicit in such a question is that networks are physically distributed in ways incommensurate with the consolidated nature of territorial states. Yet official denial-of-sanctuary discourses continue to privilege states as sanctuaries for illicit transnational networks.

A personal vignette is worth mentioning here. I was in the Western Balkans in 1997 as a member of the Stabilization Force in Bosnia-Herzegovina, when international affairs were preoccupied with stabilization, democratization, human rights, and prosecuting war crimes suspects. From 2003 to 2009, I served as a civilian advisor and analyst to NATO in Belgium, Bosnia-Herzegovina, Kosovo, and Afghanistan. These were radically different experiences. In the former, my role was that of a simple soldier, bearing close witness to the aftermath of genocide and other large-scale human rights violations. The latter was more physically remote from the human consequences of extremism, though nonetheless fixated on its most intimate details. Let me explain.

Systemic corruption and organized crime had plagued Bosnian reconstruction in the 1990s. It was elevated in importance after 2001, not for its crippling effect on Bosnia's post-war recovery, but for how it positioned Bosnia's resources in a global network of real and imagined Al Qaeda assets (see especially Andreas 2004). Nationalist militants and fugitive Persons Indicted for War Crimes (PIFWCs) remained at large; meanwhile resources were newly expended monitoring small, isolated communities of Wahhabi Muslims and retired Mujahedin fighters. US generals governing in the Western Balkans issued repeated cries that Bosnia was – or could become – a 'terrorist sanctuary'. That the language of these cries was borrowed from wars in Afghanistan and Iraq should not be entirely surprising. What is significant, however, is that in Afghanistan and Iraq, that very language was in itself a complex of borrowed analogies and metaphors.

What changed between 1997 and 2003? The easy answer is 9/11 – or rather, justifications of intervention after 9/11. Carol McQueen's study of safety zones in the 1990s is useful in this respect (2005). Her survey identifies four categories of statutory haven: hospitable, neutral, non-defended, and demilitarized zones. These have five key attributes: first, one party to a conflict may request the establishment of a safety zone, but both parties must consent; second, establishment of a safety zone precludes any military activity within it; third, safety zones are predicated on a civilian protection regime; fourth, there are generally no internal security provisions; and finally, such areas are manageable in scale. In the 1990s, safety zones in Iraq (no-fly zones), Bosnia (UN safe cities, 1994), and Rwanda (the French *zone humanitaire sûre*, 1994), 'most closely resembled the neutralized zones envisioned by Article 15 of the 1949 Geneva Convention IV or the demilitarized zones of Article 60 of the 1977 Geneva Protocol I' (McQueen 2005: 6–8).

The Iraq, Bosnia, and Rwanda cases diverge from earlier forms in five ways. First, they were externally imposed, rather than established by, or on, the consent of the warring parties. Second, civilians in safety zones were not peripheral to armed conflict, but were in fact the principal targets of the violence. Third, because the zones were externally imposed to protect civilians, they were also defended. Fourth, demilitarization and continued military use of the safety zones 'became issues of contention or confusion' (ibid.: 7). Finally, the Iraq, Bosnia, and Rwanda safety zones were much larger in area than their historical antecedents, and larger than the law intended. This made them 'much more difficult to monitor than a hotel or hospital, and much more important strategically to the belligerents' (ibid.). This is a striking observation, equally applicable to humanitarian intervention in the 1990s or to counterterrorism and counterinsurgency after 2001.

To put it another way, occasional attempts to strike terrorists 'at source' in the 1990s were overshadowed by the liberal internationalism of the time, which prioritized the plight of civilians caught in the crossfire or deliberately targeted in various post-Cold War conflicts. During the Clinton administration, statutory havens in Iraq, Bosnia, and Rwanda exceeded manageable scale, and ultimately failed to achieve their aims (ibid.: 7). During the post-9/11 Bush era, tolerance for either diplomatic or territorial middle ground essentially evaporated. The world was thought to be rife with extraterritorial elisions, and the Bush administration took on the herculean task of trying to secure them all.

Such sanctuaries were treated as problems rather than solutions – as vulnerable resources that armed non-state actors would inevitably attempt to exploit for their own gain, for which states must be held to account and made to secure. In post-2001 Bosnia, awkward resort to a borrowed rhetoric positioned the fledgling state as either a failed or rogue entity. This somewhat thoughtlessly imputed criminal intent, motive, capacity, and opportunity. In response to those cries of angst, I have argued that realist claims linking militant sanctuaries to the capacities of states did not hold up in the Bosnian case (Innes 2005). It was only nominally a politically unitary actor, and Bosnia *qua* Bosnia was far too ethnically and jurisdictionally fractured to be actively offering state resources or preventing their exploitation.

The potential for discourse to shape and direct policy, prioritize resource expenditures, and persuade actors to inflict damage is clearly substantial. Locating militant sanctuaries in international politics, moreover, is as much a problem of epistemology as it is of geography. If one is a function of the other – sanctuary as something that occurs within international security – then how security is defined surely governs what forms of sanctuary are relevant. A prominent Bush administration frame for the invasion of Iraq, for example, was that the state that was under Saddam Hussein's control was an important sanctuary in Al Qaeda's global insurgency. Counterinsurgency theorists might argue something similar, looking to the role of neighbouring or regional states such as Jordan, Syria, Saudi Arabia, and slightly further afield as places of refuge or rear base areas for insurgents fighting in Iraq. A more culturally attuned view might consider tensions between the national and transnational identities of militants, and assess their selection of base areas as necessary outcomes of those processes. Another, constructivist view, might similarly seek to understand the significance of the 2006 destruction of the Al Askariya shrine in Baghdad – a sanctuary in its classical, religious sense – and its relationship to the state – a sanctuary in the modern, Westphalian sense.

The secondary literature

The literature on militant sanctuaries reflects the same chronic tension that bedevils theoretical debates on traditionalist and constructivist international relations and international security (see especially Buzan and Hansen 2009). For realists, terrorist sanctuaries have dogmatically territorial implications. They are macro-level problems of states, for which projecting and preserving interests dictates the parameters of debate. Sanctuaries are symptomatic of the perpetual anarchy and disorder characteristic of the political lives of states.

For constructivists, the emotive rather than the rational is what matters. Ideas, beliefs and identities, changeable and fluid, define why and how states do what they do, and give substance, equally, to the conduct of non-state entities. In this sense, militant sanctuaries do not exist independently of the ideas and identities through which they are constituted; places are categorized as safe or exceptional because irrational human beings define them as such through discourse and action.

Underpinning this complexity is an array of metaphors that depict a global contagion of transnational insurgents and the viral spread of their ideas through social media and web technologies. Both Afghanistan and Iraq have since 2001 been labelled 'sources' of terrorism, a distinct category of historical phenomenon (Roberts 2005). Intervention in both cases, however, was also justified in large part based on the 'unprecedented' nature of threats alleged to emanate from them.

The significance of this apparent contradiction requires further study. The militancy associated with each case could not be both epiphenomenal *and* symptomatic of wider contagion unless they were, in fact, the first of their kind, in purely analytical or metahistorical terms – akin to the first observed incidence in a disease outbreak (Daniel 2009). The model extends, interestingly, to notions of containment, wherein striking terrorists is akin to disease management practices; reverse-engineering pandemics to identify their first observable incidence, thereby understanding the subsequent trajectory of contagion (e.g., Salehyan 2008; Kilcullen 2009: 35–8). Much of the literature suggests cross-border rebel groups and ether-bound subversives internationalize conflict, consolidate ungoverned territories into proto-states that threaten the *status quo*, and wage a disembodied war of ideas.

Practices and places

In keeping with the overarching themes of this volume, this chapter focuses on *practices* as well as *places*. This is, in part, a response to a literature that has dealt principally with militant sanctuaries as relatively static material resources understood for their defensive, protective qualities. This is a relatively uncontested aspect of the literature, derived from a literal reading of etymology and history. Most English-language discussions of sanctuary refer first to its Latin root, *sanctus*. They infer from this classical allusion a genealogy that begins with biblical protections, sacred cities and other holy sites, and ends with the sovereign entitlements of Westphalian states and their citizens (see other chapters in this volume; also Hancock and Mitchell 2007: 4–12).

Such discussions, however, do two things. First, they fail to reconcile the uneven and conflicting historical trajectory of this original meaning, wherein states, now, still have to contend with retrograde examples of sanctuary-seeking and granting behaviours by non-state actors (see especially Lippert 2006). The state, in other words, is not the only form that sanctuary can take. Second, they elide more recent genealogical extensions, for *sanctus* is also the root of 'sanction'. Whether used as a noun or verb, 'sanction' is a contronym, a term with two opposite meanings (Innes 2008: 261; also Innes 2007: 15). In its negative sense, a 'sanction' is a consequence or a penalty, a punishment levied for violations of proscribed behaviour. In its positive sense, it is a permission or endorsement. In international law and security, sanctions are a well-worn subject of debate, generally understood among economists, jurists, political scientists, and others as sticks in the diplomatic toolbox. Stripped to its essentials, the fact of sanctioning – of permitting or prohibiting action – can be viewed as either an act or a process, but ultimately it concentrates the mind on the ascription of quality to a thing – how a location comes to be understood for its imputed value or meaning.

The 'thing', in this sense, is secondary – a by-product of the perceptions, behaviours, and processes associated with it. Reconciling the two – sanctions and sanctuaries – requires a careful reappraisal of their respective intellectual content. These are not incommensurate domains. Nor are they limited to the more obvious, realist dimensions of international relations that one might expect. They are more closely connected than previously acknowledged, and analytical progress will require greater engagement through social constructivism and its variants (Buzan and Hansen 2009: 36–8).

To put it another way, much of the secondary literature and official discourse on sanctuaries limits itself to relatively literal readings of state failure, proto-states that jeopardize the Westphalian status quo, and regions perceived to be 'black holes', 'ungoverned', 'ungovernable', 'under-governed', or variations on these analytical themes (Stanislawski 2008). This forces awkward constraints: by failing to consider a fuller range of referent objects; by fixating on static, measurable entities; and by failing to explore the cognitive and cultural schema that shape why and how sanctuary is understood, by whom, for what reasons, at any given point in time. Tapping into this broader array of analytical options opens the subject to both wider and deeper scrutiny. A fixation on sanctuary practices as dynamic exemplars of political behaviour does not, however, preclude consideration of its material dimensions. Quite the opposite – it allows for more meaningful and holistic study of a thorny, sometimes convoluted problem.

Units of analysis

Traditional international relations, in its preoccupation with states, is poorly equipped to deal with the complexities of militant sanctuaries. I suggest four units of analysis as a starting point for moving past the statist chokehold on the subject.

The first is the post-2001 decade, roughly bracketed at its inception by the Al Qaeda attacks of 11 September 2001 and at its terminus by the killing of Osama bin Laden in Pakistan. The former is non-controversial. 11 September 2001 was a watershed in recent history, setting in motion two phenomena of consequence for this chapter: a deluge of discursive effort, followed by a remarkably disproportionate train of events (Mueller 2005). The latter is a slightly more arbitrary benchmark. For years, bin Laden was deemed both symbolically central and operationally irrelevant (or *vice versa*) to events unfolding in Afghanistan, Iraq, and elsewhere. His death at the hands of US commandos in an Abbottabad safehouse in May 2011 is thus of mixed significance.

Other dates and events certainly warrant as much attention. The end of the Bush administration in 2008, for example, would make for convenient periodization, but it would offer a false – or at least presumptive – reading of the significance of sanctuary practices. Certainly the new Obama administration did not bring with it any significant changes, extending rather than truncating patterns of foreign policy and intervention set in motion under Bush. Bin Laden's death, at least, punctuates – with a harsh, glottal stop – the debate on where and how he hid from US authorities.

The second unit of analysis for this project is discourse – specifically, the boundaries and substance of post-9/11 security discourse and the framing processes within it. There is, granted, a tension in how each of these is understood and how they relate to each other. For some, discourse is about tapestries of meaning embedded in texts; for others, it is about a wider realm of communicative practices. The same arguments have been made about framing, conflating it with discourse more generally (Autesserre 2009), an approach that, in my view, fails to reconcile and make best use of discourse analysis and frame analysis as distinct but complementary approaches to political communication. My understanding of this is fairly straightforward, derived from Weldes, Laffey, Gusterson, and Duvall, who assert that it is 'misleading to associate notions of culture, or discourse, or of codes of intelligibility with the "merely linguistic" … discourses are composed of linguistic and [material] practices, both of which are indispensable to the production of worlds and of insecurity' (1999: 16).

Discourse is thus contextual. It establishes the ideational boundaries of social meaning. It is a category of practices that includes framing. Framing is a practice bounded and informed by discourse. Since Erving Goffman's *Frame Analysis* (1974), there has been a deluge of scholarly publication on the subject (Goffman 1974; Benford and Snow 2000). Goffman defined frames as 'schemata of interpretation … seen as rendering what would otherwise be a meaningless aspect of the scene into something that is meaningful'. The organization of such schemata varies. 'Some are neatly presentable as a system of entities, postulates, and rules,' Goffman writes, while 'others – indeed, most others – appear to have no apparent articulated shape, providing only a lore of understanding, an approach, a perspective' (1974: 21). I adhere to the classical meaning of frame analysis found in the sociological literature, particularly as it was originally set out by Goffman and more recently in a much-cited article by Robert Benford and David A. Snow (2000).

The third unit of analysis, militant sanctuaries, is perhaps the most difficult to accurately define. Its meaning has been contested by state and non-state actors; there is also a rich intellectual tradition of sanctuary that spans cultures, geographies, and historical periods. It should come as no surprise, then, that such a foundational yet complex aspect of the human experience is so frequently framed using terms that resonate across cultures, contexts, and fields of inquiry. In this it is much like terrorism, which has 'often been understood metaphorically,' in part because it is 'refractory to a broadly accepted definition' (Kruglanski *et al.* 2008: 98). The challenge is that scholarly treatments of militant sanctuaries have not generally questioned their own epistemological presuppositions. Nor have they progressed much beyond the view of sanctuaries as static physical locations, fixed in time and space and divorced from the human context that gives such places highly variable and elastic meaning.

The fourth unit of analysis in this project consists of those very entities – states, organizations, and individuals alike, who at one time or another have been caught up in what US Senator John McCain once referred to as a game of 'whack-a-mole' – one of many memorable turns of phrase used to describe the furtive cat-and-mouse dynamics of counterterrorism and counterinsurgency (Safire 2006). There is obviously a distinction to be made between *units* and *levels* of analysis. The state must remain central to any discussion of militant sanctuary practices, not least because it is the dominant referent in international relations, history, and law. Why it must remain so warrants additional explanation and requires considerable sensitivity.

Wars fought with large contingents of military force deployed across international borders were central to the post-2001 decade, the asymmetry of post-Cold War conflicts notwithstanding. The US, motivated by various considerations, deployed its military resources to Afghanistan first, and, second to Iraq. It has remained embroiled in various forms of violence, in contest with a number of actor types, under complex and ambiguous conditions – all marrow in the bones of post-Cold War conflict analysis. Problems of action and agency are often either elided or amplified in the sanctuary literature, and it is at this juncture of state and non-state violence that such fundamental issues acutely present themselves most acutely. Indeed, as Stathys Kalyvas notes, the disconnect between identities and actions at various levels of organization (elite/central vs. local/mass), in turn challenge 'prevailing assumptions about the locus of agency in civil wars' (2003: 475–6).

Social distance

One of the more prominent characteristics of militant sanctuaries and sanctuary practices has been relative proximity to (or, alternately, distance from) the battlefield. Al Qaeda propaganda referred very early on to 'near enemies' and 'far enemies'. US and allied views on sanctuary-seeking behaviour, as earlier sections of this chapter allude, are, for all their awkwardness, explicit about this as well. Sanctuary discourses and practices are thus inherently spatial or 'locative', to borrow from pop culture. They refer to physical locations, but more importantly they require navigation of relative spaces between opposing parties – seeking to locate actors in relation to one another.

Over the past decade, sanctuary-seeking actors – those who rely on it for survival, and those who would seek to deny it to them – have all grappled with problems of social distance, at once attempting to bridge and swell cultural, linguistic, religious, even civilizational differences. Indeed, preoccupation with social distance is a significant but underexplored facet of the sanctuary literature – the preoccupation with knowing and understanding hidden, unreachable, and mysterious enemy locations cannot help but speak to this.

More literal readings of sanctuary as place and territory have attempted various statistical measures (e.g., Salehyan 2008). They are problematic in two ways: first, they rely on narrow, sometimes idiosyncratic, and almost always material definitions of sanctuary; and, second, they are derived at the expense of deeper explorations of the human condition. Quantitative measures are of course useful, but can often lack context and depth afforded by closer scrutiny of qualitative sources. In this we are fortunate for the plethora of material now available to students of the subject. Personal memoirs (e.g., Bush 2010; Rumsfeld 2011), war diaries, and blogs too numerous to count have proliferated in the past decade. Such primary sources are essential to understanding Washington's post-9/11 sanctuary discourse, which was articulated in different ways by various organs of government.

These sources contributing to a narrative context might help explain why and how militant sanctuary practices were framed as they were – a counter of sorts to the official script on terrorist sanctuaries. One episode in particular, the remarkably public feud between former White House speechwriters Michael J. Gerson and Matthew Scully, is worth noting here. In 2007, lead speechwriter Gerson, a Bush aide from 1999 until his resignation in 2006, published *Heroic Conservatism* (2007), a memoir of his time in the White House. In an advance review published in the September 2007 issue of *The Atlantic Monthly*, Scully excoriated the book, accusing Gerson (noted for his Christian evangelical commitments) of self-aggrandizement, romanticization, and outright fabrication. For Scully, intellectual claim-staking over presidential speech of the era was unseemly: speechwriters, he wrote, belong 'off to the side, where even the best there ever was … was always content to stay' (Scully 2007).

The Gerson–Scully affair, in other words, represented a serious attack on the framing process. 'Speechwriting is a job with many privileges,' Scully concluded, 'but also its own rules, temptations, and demands of conscience, obvious and nonnegotiable' (ibid.). For scholars, the episode provides a unique and useful window into the inner workings of White House framing processes, courtesy of those most directly involved in crafting the presidential rhetoric that immediately followed 9/11. While there are limitations to the use of memoirs as credible sources of verifiable historical facts, they can be extremely useful for understanding the beliefs and perceptions of their authors – and in turn, the cognitive schema that informs their framing strategies.

For all their weaknesses as historical documents, memoirs function as important barometers of social alienation and social distance in war. Military sources are particularly valuable in this regard (e.g., Mansoor 2009; Gallagher 2010). They have been published in various formats, and innovations in publishing and social media technology have enabled their authors to convey their observations to much wider readerships than previously possible. Other hybrid texts, such as Thomas M. Mowle's edited volume *Hope Is Not a Plan: The War in Iraq from Inside the Green Zone* (2007) and David Kilcullen's influential *The Accidental Guerrilla: How to Win Small Wars in the Midst of a Big One* (2009), are part memoir and part scholarly analysis. What these sources provide are self-aware insights into the social and cultural disconnects that separated interveners from host populations and their environments. This preoccupation eventually blossomed into an institutionalized campaign to overcome the limits of knowing in conflict-affected areas. Such efforts, I argue, were sometimes overblown, naively preoccupied with the alleged mysteries of alien cultures and mystified unknowns of the ways of clandestine actors.

Locating terrorists 'at source' (i.e., in their sanctuaries) and associated framing processes, in this sense, are essentially efforts at overcoming social distance. Examples of this abound in the primary sources, nowhere more evident than in narratives – there are many – anchored to particular locations in Iraq and

Afghanistan. Accounts by journalists and writers have been especially penetrating. Two in particular, Dexter Filkins' *The Forever War* (2008) and Rajiv Chandrasekaran's *Imperial Life in the Emerald City* (2006), are emblematic of pervasive American self-criticism that arose amid the counterinsurgency muddles of Iraq and Afghanistan.

Filkins, reporting from Iraq for the *New York Times* from 2003 to 2006, and Chandrasekaran, the *Washington Post*'s Baghdad bureau chief from April 2003 to October 2004, provide radically different views of the limits of knowing in fragile environments. Filkins' acutely personal account relates his chronically dissociative state and repeated efforts to overcome moral and psychological numbness, achieved primarily by breaking free of the physical confines of the *New York Times*' bunkered Baghdad staff house (Mnookin 2008). Chandrasekaran, by contrast, plays the dispassionate, omniscient observer. His chronicle of life inside Baghdad's hermetic Green Zone paints a surreal tableau of blinkered reality amid the chaos of occupation and insurgency.

Conclusion

My argument has been that US security policy after 2001 hitched itself to distorted readings of militant sanctuaries and their significance. I argue that policymakers and practitioners framed the problem using a borrowed lexicon rife with metaphor and analogy. Unpacking the sources of those ideas and images is the stuff of a larger project; here, I suggest three points. Understanding sanctuaries requires a closer look at the dynamism of practices rather than the static limitations of fixed places. It should involve closer scrutiny of a complex of issues, rather than assuming them to be simple, one-dimensional problems. It should involve significant self-questioning and exploration of epistemological issues before making uncritical assumptions about the nature of sanctuary. Thus, sanctuary practices, units of analysis, and social distance conspire to limit what can be known of these issues – though only if we let them, as my brief notes here suggest.

Acknowledgements

Significant portions of this chapter have been presented, at various times and in various forms, in seminars and papers at the University of Leeds, King's College London, University College London, the London School of Economics, and the Peace Research Institute Oslo. It has benefitted immensely from discussions with colleagues and students, though the standard provisos apply about my own responsibility for any errors of fact or interpretation. Special thanks also to the editors of this volume for their patient editing and thoughtful suggestions.

References

Andreas, P. (2004) 'The Clandestine Political Economy of War and Peace in Bosnia', *International Studies Quarterly*, 48: 29–51.

Autesserre, S. (2009) 'Hobbes and the Congo: Frames, Local Violence and International Intervention', *International Organization*, 63(2): 249–80.
Becker, T. (2006) *Terrorism and the State: Rethinking the Rules of State Responsibility*, New York: Hart Publishing.
Benford, R.D. and Snow, D.A. (2000) 'Framing Processes and Social Movements: An Overview and Assessment', *Annual Review of Sociology*, 26: 611–39.
Brynen, R. (1990) *Sanctuary and Survival: The Palestinians in Lebanon*, Boulder, CO: Westview Press.
Bush, G.W. (2010) *Decision Points*, New York: Crown Publishing.
Buzan, B. and Hansen, L. (2009) *The Evolution of International Security Studies*, Cambridge: Cambridge University Press.
Byman, D. (2005) *Deadly Connections: States that Sponsor Terrorism*, New York: Cambridge University Press.
Chandrasekaran, R. (2006) *Imperial Life in the Emerald City: Inside Baghdad's Green Zone*, London: Bloomsbury Publishing.
Coll, S. (2004) *Ghost Wars: The Secret History of the CIA, Afghanistan, and Bin Laden, from the Soviet Invasion to September 10, 2001*, New York: Penguin Books.
Cooper, H. and Sanger, D.E. (2010) 'Obama Says Afghan Policy Won't Change After Dismissal', *The New York Times*, 23 June.
Daniel, T.M. (2009) 'Wade Hampton Frost and the Index Case Concept', *International Journal of Tuberculosis and Lung Disease*, 13(11): 1345–6.
Fair, C.C. and Ganguly, S. (eds) (2008) *Treading on Hallowed Grounds: Counterinsurgency Operations in Sacred Spaces*, New York: Oxford University Press.
Filkins, D. (2008) *The Forever War*, New York: Random House, Inc.
Gallagher, M. (2010) *Kaboom: Embracing the Suck in a Savage Little War*, New York: Da Capo Press.
Gerson, M.J. (2007) *Heroic Conservatism: Why Republicans Need to Embrace America's Ideals (And Why They Deserve to Fail If They Don't)*, New York: HarperOne.
Goffman, E. (1974) *Frame Analysis: An Essay on the Organization of Experience*, New York: Harper and Row.
Gray, D.H. and Head, A. (2009) 'The Importance of the Internet to the Post-Modern Terrorist and its Role as a Form of Safe Haven', *European Journal of Scientific Research*, 25(3): 396–404.
Hancock, L. and Mitchell, C. (2007) *Zones of Peace*, Quicksilver Drive, VA: Kumarian Press.
Hassner, R.E. (2008) 'At the Horns of the Altar: Counterinsurgency and the Religious Roots of the Sanctuary Practice', *Civil Wars*, 10(1): 22–39.
——(2009) *War on Sacred Grounds*, Ithaca, NY: Cornell University Press.
Hoffman, F. (2007) *Conflict in the 21st Century: The Rise of Hybrid Wars*, Arlington, VA: Potomac Institute for Policy Studies.
Innes, M.A. (2005) 'Terrorist Sanctuaries and Bosnia-Herzegovina: Challenging Conventional Assumptions', *Studies in Conflict and Terrorism*, 28(4): 295–305.
——(2007) *Denial of Sanctuary: Understanding Terrorist Safe Havens*, Westport, CT: Praeger.
——(2008) 'Deconstructing Political Orthodoxies on Insurgent and Terrorist Sanctuaries', *Studies in Conflict and Terrorism*, 31(3): 251–67.
Kalyvas, S. (2003) 'The Ontology of Political Violence: Action and Identity in Civil Wars', *Perspectives on Politics*, 1(3): 475–6.
Khong, Y.F. (1992) *Analogies at War: Korea, Munich, Dien Bien Phu, and the Vietnam Decisions of 1965*, Princeton, NJ: Princeton University Press.

Kilcullen, D. (2009) *The Accidental Guerrilla: Fighting Small Wars in the Midst of a Big One*, New York: Oxford University Press.

Kruglanski, A.W. et al. (2008) 'What Should This Fight Be Called? Metaphors of Counterterrorism and Their Implications', *Psychological Science in the Public Interest*, 8(3): 98.

Lippert, R.K. (2006) *Sanctuary, Sovereignty, Sacrifice: Canadian Sanctuary Incidents, Power, and Law*, Vancouver: University of British Columbia Press.

Lischer, S.K. (2006) *Dangerous Sanctuaries: Refugee Camps, Civil War, and the Dilemmas of Humanitarian Aid*, Ithaca, NY: Cornell University Press.

Mansoor, P.R. (2009) *Baghdad at Sunrise: A Brigade Commander's War in Iraq*, New Haven, CT: Yale University Press.

McChrystal, S. (2009) 'Address', International Institute of Strategic Studies, London, 2 October. Available at: http://www.iiss.org/recent-key-addresses/general-stanley-mcchrystal-address/ .

McQueen, C. (2005) *Humanitarian Intervention and Safety Zones: Iraq, Bosnia and Rwanda*, New York: Palgrave Macmillan.

Mnookin, S. (2008) '*The New York Times*' Lonely War', *Vanity Fair* (December). Available at: http://www.vanityfair.com/politics/features/2008/12/nytimes200812.print (accessed July 2011).

Mowle, T.M. (ed.) (2007) *Hope Is Not a Plan: The War in Iraq from Inside the Green Zone*, Westport, CT: Praeger.

Mueller, J. (2005) 'Six Rather Unusual Propositions about Terrorism', *Terrorism and Political Violence*, 17: 487–505.

Record, J. (2002) *Making War, Thinking History: Munich, Vietnam, and Presidential Use of Force from Korea to Kosovo*, Annapolis, MD: US Naval Institute Press.

Roberts, A. (2005) 'The "War on Terror" in Historical Perspective', *Survival*, 47(2): 101–30.

Rumsfeld, D. (2011) *Known and Unknown: A Memoir*, New York: Sentinel HC.

Safire, W. (2006) 'Whack-a-Mole', *The New York Times*, 29 October. Available at: http://www.nytimes.com/2006/10/29/magazine/29wwln_safire.html (accessed 14 July 2011).

Salehyan, I. (2008) 'No Shelter Here: Rebel Sanctuaries and International Conflict', *Journal of Politics*, 70(1): 54–66.

Scully, M. (2007) 'Present at the Creation', *The Atlantic Monthly*, September. Available at: http://www.theatlantic.com/doc/200709/michael-gerson.

Sorkin, M. (ed.) (2008) *Indefensible Space: The Architecture of the National Insecurity State*, New York: Routledge.

Stanislawski, B.H. (ed.) (2008) 'FORUM: Para-States, Quasi-States, and Black Spots: Perhaps Not States, But Not "Ungoverned Territories" Either', *International Studies Review*, 10: 366–96.

Stenersen, A. (2008) 'The Internet: A Virtual Training Camp?', *Terrorism and Political Violence*, 20: 215–33.

Takeyh, R. and Gvosdev, N. (2002) 'Do Terrorist Networks Need a Home?', *The Washington Quarterly*, 25(3): 97–108.

Weldes, J., Laffey, M., Gusterson, H., and Duvall, R. (1999) *Cultures of Insecurity: States, Communities and the Production of Danger*, Minnesota: University of Minnesota Press.

Index

abjuration 48
abjuration oath 20
abstraction: violence of 185
accompaniment: radical 8, 113, 114, 115
accuracy: chronological 152, 153
Act of Eric 121
activism 46, 77, 109; and faith 101
activists 80, 101; Central American 74; divided 181; educating 115; immigrant 80, 81; religious 109; solidarity 67; transnational circulation 86
adaptation: attempted 107; creative 63; strategic 114–15
advocacy 85, 183, 186, 207, 236–41, 238; cross-border 234, 240; inspiring 92
advocates 170–71
Agamben, G. 7, 43, 48, 54, 61
agency 6, 49, 198, 253
agent network 64
Aghai, N. 125
Agnos, A. 211, 212
Al Qaeda 246–47
Alsike monastery 129–30
Alviola, S. 137
American Baptist Churches v. Thornburgh 82–83
amnesty 128
analogies 246
Arab Spring 39
Arellano, E. 93
Arendt, H. 49
asylum: church 128, 137–40, 143–45; justifying 184; politics of 194; protective 166; restrictions 135; rhythm of 197; right to 135, 156; symbolic 144; time politics 197, 201, 202; uniqueness of 157
asylum claims 83, 149, 150, 169; Canada 235; Germany 135, 136; reviewing 150, 175, 182; Scandinavia 131; supporting 238; United Kingdom 63; United States 112
asylum compromise 136
asylum demand 233, 234
asylum policies *see* refugee policies
asylum shopping 142
asylum system 52; appeals 53, 184; broken 36, 98; Canada 163–66; credibility 152; detention 143; European harmonization 136; experiences of 198; fairness of 38; frustrations 199; Germany 135–37, 142–43; limitations of 160; mistakes 142, 150–51, 168, 182; reforms 164–66; romanticizing 164; speed of process 197; United Kingdom 29–30; United States 82–83, *see also* refugee determination system; refugee policies
asylum-seekers: as agents 198; Bangladeshi 124; concept 58; entry 142; illegitimate 43; Kosovan Albanian 126, 127; legitimate 43, 59; living conditions 143; as passive recipients 198; refused 31, 36, 165; rejected 121; worthiness of 52, *see also* refugees
authority: challenging 185; defying 205; limiting 178, 185; moral 213, 223; resistance to 176, 186; temporal dimensions 198, *see also* power

Basic Law (Germany) 135, 149, 156–57
Battle Abbey 15
Beckett, T. 31
belonging 51, 58; hierarchies 57; national 96
Berkeley (California, USA) 46, 219, 223
bias 168
The Bible 30, 221

Bin Laden, Osama 251
biopolitics 61
Blaikie, D. 7
border: control 165, 234, 242; crossing 236, 237, 240; enforcement 86, 234; fuzzy 58; militarized 162; re-conceptualizing 241; re-defining 64; reclaimed 242; security 137
Border Protection, Anti-Terrorism, and Illegal Immigration Control Act (USA) 110
Bosnia-Herzegovina 247, 248
boundary: as connection point 241; international 232
Britt, H. 207–8
Britton 20–21
bureaucracy 153, 168, 234
bureaucratic culture 165
busy: keeping 201

Calais 57, 60; C-SUR agreement 60
camp 48–50, 50, 61; squatter 60
Canada 44–45, 162–74, 183–85; Immigration and Refugee Board 163, 168, 182; Montreal 182–83; Ontario Sanctuary Coalition 10, 168–73; Quebec selection certificate 182; Safe Third Country Agreement 242; sanctuary justifications 35–37
capitulation 233
caring 35–36, 154
cases 148, 173; reviewing 175
Central American Resource Center 78, 79
Centro de Refugiados Centroamericanos (CRECEN) 78, 79
Chandrasekaran, R. 255
chaos 245, 251
Charlemagne 20
children 53, 97, 129, 130; refugee 129, 130, 131
Christian duty 31
church asylum 128, 137–40, 143–45, *see also* asylum
church congregations 143–45, 166; educating 208; leaders 122; network 209, 216
churches 39, 107; arrest in 132; attitude change 129; Brorson church 123; Catholic Church 176–85; Christian 5; collaboration 241; confessional conflict 25; as holy territory 121, 125–27; internal debate 132–33; Lutheran Church 121, 122, 125; mobilizing 79; negotiating 184; Nordic 9; position of 140; rotating church sanctuary 150, 154; as sanctuaries 121–33; and state 123–24, 126, 132, 171, 177, 185; state church 127, 128
citizen-participants 94, 200
citizens 186; urban 200; worthy 194
citizenship: act of 58; boundaries 67; categories 66; hierarchies 57; as participation 200; questioning 66; right of 51; transforming 62
city: border 234, 242; as political space 233; position within 200; right to 10, 192, 200–201; services 206, 210, 212, 214, 225
civil disobedience 5, 34, 39, 113, 171–72; critique of 176; Debré law 67; refugee-hiders 130–31; and sovereignty 180
civil initiative 10, 47, 171–72, 173, 235
civil society 85, 184
civilians 248
coalition culture 10
collaboration 86; cross-border 139, 240–41
De Colores (Spanish-language song) 105
Commission on Social Justice, Latin American Task Force 206
Common European Asylum System 136–37
community: activist 101; cross-border 241; faith 5, 101; host 159, 186; imagined 101–2; local 159–60; political 50, 51; refugee participation 35; religious 102, 110
compassion 10, 143, 149, 154–57, 160, 167
conflict 159; with authority 141–43; church-state 177
conscience 35, 39, 145, 172; freedom of 141
conscientious objector 222
consciousness-raising 80, 81
consequences: unintended 74, 82, 88
conspiracy 224
Constantine, Emperor 20
constructivism 249
containment 249–50
coping 199
Coral Sea (USS) 221
corruption 247
counterinsurgency 249, 252
counterterrorism 252
countries: safe 136
Coutin, S.B. 8, 74
credibility 149; in intimate sphere 153–54; socially constructed 151–53

crime 3, 22, 224; confession of 20–21; encouraging 17, 24; organized 247
criminal jurisprudence 22–26
criminals 6, 19; fugitive 15, 110
criminology 17
crisis 96, 97; sanctuary 177
Crisóstomo, F. 93
critique: positive 60–63
cruelty 18
cultural change 192
cultural events 193
culture 152; religious 171
Cunningham, H. 10
customs 19, 131; universal 158
Czajka, A. 7

Danish Social Democrats 124
Darling, J. 10
debate 195; public 122, 124, 126, 127–28, 133, 144, 176
decision 107, 109, 116
decision-making 179
Decretum Gratiani 22
democracy 10; liberal 178–79; republican 179–80; strong 179
democratic deficit 179
Denmark 123–26
Department of Homeland Security (USA) 112
deportation 83, 112; challenging 138, 141, 149, 170; escaping 139, 150, 177; policies 8; practices 142; preventing 9; risks of 96, 142, 167; separating families 99; threat of 158; unethical 167; withdrawn 125, 167
deportation orders 169
deportation process 30
desperation 163
detention 142; conditions of 143; mass 228
deterrence 23, 24; and sovereignty 6
Detroit Sanctuary Coalition 237
Detroit/Windsor Refugee Coalition 11, 232, 237, 241
disappearance 97, 239
discernment process 208
discourse: anti-crime 226; anti-immigrant 226; counter-discourse 92; dominant 195; liberal 183, 186; locative 253; official 184–85; performative role 101; political 246; power of 248; on refugees 43; republican 183, 186; security 251; spatial 253; state 7, 52; testimonial 59
discourse analysis 252

discrimination 142; police 213; racial 65, 66
disease 249
disobedience 179, *see also* civil disobedience
dispersal 197, 247; politics 195
disruption 114, 191, 196
disruptive acts 191, 196
Dobyn, J. 21
dramatization 237–38
droit du sol (right of the soil) 181
Dublin II Regulations (European Union) 142
Durgun, S. 163, 165, 173

echoes 29, 31, 34–35, 37
economic crisis 176
economic liberalism 177
economic readjustment 84
education 208; activist 115; community 206, 208, 237; parishioner 210; peace 155; war 207
Église Saint-Bernard 180–82
Église Saint-Jean de la Croix 182–83
El Salvador 75–76; remittances 84
empathy 80
empowerment 201
encounters 148; everyday 193, 196–97; human 143; personal 154
enemy 246, 253
entry: country of 142; legal 242
ethnography 148
European Convention of Human Rights 142
European Union (EU) 136–37; Dublin II Regulations 142–43
exception 61, 66, 185; space of 50; state of 48
exclusion 4, 194
execution 21
exile: penitent 21
exposure 3, 122, 124
expulsion 65
Extended Voluntary Departure 82

faith 7; and activism 101, 109; as call to action 101–2; and community 101; in daily life 144; as justification 30–31, 37–38, 95, *see also* religion
families 53; hidden 166–67, 169; mixed-status 113; separation of 97–98, 99
family unity 100
family values 97

Farabundo Martin National Liberation Front 76, 77
fieldwork 74
Filkin, D. 255
Finland 124–26
Finnish Ecumenical Council 125
flexibility 109, 115, 116
foreign policy: contesting 238; critique 95; USA 76, 78, 94, 235, 246
forgery 15
forgetting 199
formalization 109
fortress 137
Foucault, M. 61
frame analysis 252
framing 75, 80–81, 88; process 251, 254
France 25–26, 180–82, 183–85; humanitarianism 58–60, *see also* Sangatte
freedom 178
Freedom House 232
freemen 23
Frontex 137

geography 232, 242
German Ecumenical Committee on Church Asylum 138–40
Germany 135–45; Basic Law 135, 149, 156–57; church asylum 140; church sanctuary movement 148–60; sanctuary movement 9
Gerson, M.J. 254
Giuliani, R. 227
God 37
governance: sanctuary 11; strong 18; tensions in 223, 227
government: art of 206; cooperation within 228; defying 28; disobeying 172; municipal 11, 205, 212–16, 223, 227, 228; trust in 214
government officials 170, 210, 211
grandma cases 125
Greece 143
guests 128, 132, 158, 194; and hosts 196, 202; indebted 201
guilt 16

hardship 83, 84
helplessness 49
Henry II, King 20
Henry VIII, King 25
hiding 98, 129, 166–67, 169
historical watershed 251
history 108

Holt, A. 128
hope 197
hospitality 10, 158–60; *abamenya* (vagabond/stranger) 158–59; culture of 10, 193–95; guilt of 160; and privilege 191, 202; relations of 192; right of 160
hosting 96, 196, 202
housing 162
Van Der Hout, M. 210
human dignity 141
human rights 29, 141, 157–58, 185; family unity 100; freedom of conscience 141; freedom of religion 141; freedom of speech 222; international community of 59; international obligations 31; violations 96, 179
Human Rights Commission (San Francisco) 212–13
humanitarian aid 33, 107, 111
Humanitarian and Compassionate Review proceeding 167
humanitarian crisis 96
humanitarian imaginary 236
humanitarianism 7, 58, 59, 131
humanity 100
hunger strike 180, 182
Huntington, S. 98

identity 114, 116; fluid 159; framing 80–81; militant 249; pretend 163; refugee 80, 81, 88
ignorance 170
Illegal Immigration Reform and Immigrant Responsibility Act (USA) 82
immigrants *see* migrants
immigration control 184–85
immigration enforcement 111, 112, 210, 224, 225, 226, 234
immigration limbo 163
Immigration and Naturalization Service (USA) 205, 210, 225; co-operation with 226, 227; and police 212, 216
immigration policy 107; challenging 176; reforms 164–66
Immigration Reform and Control Act (USA) 225
Immigration and Refugee Board (Canada) 163, 168, 182
impunity 16, 22–23
incidents 45, 177
individuals 178
infighting 78–79
information-sharing 138
inhabitants 201; rights of 213

Innes, M. 11
insurgents 249
integration 124
intercession 121
international relations 249, 251
interrogation 153
intimate sphere 153–54, 154, 160
invisibility 3, 173; strategic 74, 75
Iraq 248
Islam 38
isolation 197
Italy 143

journalists 255
Just, W. 9
justice 8, 221; advancing 18; claims to 196; natural 29; summary 21; zeal for 24
justifications 28–39, 141–43; Canada 35–37; contemporary 7; ethical 127, 128; faith-based 30–31, 38, 95, 98; humanitarian 126; immigrant rights 8; themes 29; UK 29–31; USA 32–35

killing: accidental 220–21; forced 222
kingship 18–20
knowledge 255; migration 63–64

law: application of 184, 185; asylum 82; challenging 34, 183; criminal 20; divine 17; English common 20–22; exceptions to 185; federal 221, 223; higher 98; human rights 100; humanitarian clause 61; immigration 34, 82–84, 220, 224; immoral 172; international 5, 34, 142, 172, 224; medieval 16; natural 5; refugee 205, 224; rule of 18, 141, 145, 172, 184, 205; and sovereignty 179; unjust 34, 47, 98; upholding 235; violating 98, 224
law enforcement 18
law firms 85
Laws of Edward the Confessor 19
lawyers 85; negligent 168
leadership: moral 39
learning 140; from refugees 143; mutual 209
Lefebvre, H. 192, 200
legal framework 239, 240, 242
legal status 3, 163; blindness to 206, 215–16, 228; mixed 113; precarious 233; secure 236, 239
legality 5, 29, 98, 113–14, 141; debate about 47–48; optics of 238, 240; perceptions of 240; prioritizing 240; respecting 184
legalization 111, 112
legitimacy 74, 80, 81, 131, 141–43
Leis Willelme 19
liberal internationalism 248
liberalism 178–79, 183, 186
liberties: ecclesiastical 23; individual 178
life: bare 7, 50; everyday 200; power over 61; rhythm of 200; saving 33, 38, 126
living conditions 143
lobbying 237, 238
Loga, J. 9

McChrystal, Gen. S. 245
Mahony, R. 99
Mancina, P. 11
Médecins du Monde 59
Médecins Sans Frontières 59
media 94, 102, 122, 224, 239; bias 29; new sanctuary movement 97
metaphors 246, 249
Michels, D. 7
migrants: citizens as 67; distinguishing 87; economic 59, 82, 176; fraudulent 185; irregular 57, 67, 177; Latino 76; needs 111; resident 107; undocumented 32, 93, 97, 99, 110, 112
migration: autonomy of 58, 62; risks 87; root causes 87, 89, 211
military intervention 76, 77, 246, 247
Moakley-Deconcini legislation (USA) 82
mobility 159, 177
mobilization 79, 88
Montreal 182–83
moral imperative 33, 35, 39, 47, 51, 99
moral outrage 29–30
moral reflection 208
moral standard 212
murder 23, 34, 96

narrative 45, 151, 254; personal 93–94; undocumented migrants 99, *see also* stories
narrative mode 148
nation: tolerant 195
naturalization 107
negotiation 184, 233, 242
neighbours 35–36, 99, 121; duty towards 125; loving 144
network 196–97; action 206–7; building 197; communication 63; congregational 209, 216; political 207;

sanctuary 45, 140; social 86; transnational 247
new sanctuary movement 2; defining sanctuary 115, 116; goals 44; history 107; identity 108–9; launch 92; as legacy 8; media coverage 97; National Convening 105; newspaper reports 32–33; origins 95–96; rhetoric 96–98
New York City 226–27
newness: liability of 109, 116
newspapers 28
Nicaraguan Adjustment and Central American Relief Act (United States) 84
non-governmental organizations (NGOs) 59, 86
Nordic countries 123–31
norms 121
Northern California Sanctuary Churches 209
Norway 126–29
nostalgia 105
nuisance 25

obedience 176
occupation 64, 65
Occupy Wall Street 39
Oda, H. 9
Ontario Sanctuary Coalition 10, 168–73
organizational change 109
others 80, 100; pain of 154–55; and self 149, 155
Overground Railroad 235
overground routes 11

pain 154–55; sensitivity to 156; sharing 156
Paris 180–82
participation 179, 200; preventing 198
particularity 89, 186
les passeurs (people-smugglers) 64
passivity 75, 197
Patsias, C. 10
people-smugglers (*les passeurs*) 64
Perla, H. 8, 74
personal experience 154, 156, 211
police: border police 63; changing behaviour 215–16; in churches 1323; cooperation with 126; discrimination by 66, 213; and Federal Bureau of Investigation 227–28; and immigration 212; and immigration status 228; raids 65, 100, 130, 181, 213, 225; riot police 63; trust in 213–14; violence by 137
policy-making 179
political acts 62

political beings 51
political context 108, 109, 116
political divisions 181
political obligation 176, 178–80
political persecution 144, 151, 156
political traditions 177
politicians: sanctuary 211
depoliticisation 43, 53, 123, 194
power: challenging 175–76; ecclesiastical 16; kingly 20; North-South imbalance 181; rationalities of 193–94; royal 16; state 50, 175–76, *see also* authority
practices 250–51, 255; locative 253; mediated 94; spatial 253
prayer 101
priestly duty 121
privilege 191; challenging 202; and hospitality 10, 191, 202; patterns of 196; reinforcing 201
prosecution 22
protection 30, 141; personal 159
protesters 57
protests 65
public sanctuary 169–70, 205, 208
publicity 124, 139
publicity stunt 102
punishment 23; evading 25
Pyykkönen, M. 9

Quebec selection certificate 182

racial profiling 225, 228
realism 249
recidivism 19
recipients 198; suitable 52; vulnerable 43
recognition 164
recruitment 115
Red Cross 57, 59, 60, 63
Refugee Act (1980) (USA) 32, 34
refugee determination hearing 9, 142
refugee determination system 52, 166, 167, 183–84, 236, *see also* asylum system
refugee policy 5, 144, 236; contesting 237, 238; critics 166, *see also* asylum system
refugee-hider 130–31
refugees: agency 49; as bare life 49; celebrating 195; Central American 32, 36, 73–89, 223–24, 225; children 129, 130, 131; Chilean 182; community of 155; as contributors to society 30, 194; deserving 53; distinguishing 87; dominant discourse 43; encounters with

143; framing 75, 88; as fraudulent 185; genuine 183; Guatemalan 205, 208, 235; as guests 128, 132; hidden 129, 166–67, 169; identifying with 155; identity 80–81, 88; illegitimate 154; as innocent victims 53, 81, 88; Iraqi 123; learning from 143; legal definition 80; as non-citizens 51; as political beings 51, 62, 81; Salvadoran 76, 205, 208, 235; stories 148, 149–51; strategic 81; threatened 158; unrecognized 158; unreturnable 129, *see also* asylum-seekers
refuges: city of 38, 46, 209, 220–21, 225, 233; negotiated 233
regret 24
regularization 181
relationships 155–56; cross-border 241; face-to-face 159; fluid 160
religion 100, 116; freedom of 141; history 221; and state 132, *see also* faith
religious associations 101
religious duty 95, 125
religious organizations 60, 219
remittances 84
removal notices 167
repetition 201
representation 93
repression: compassionate 61
republicanism 179–80, 186
research 213
residence 51, 84
resistance 50, 176, 202; acts of 3; opportunity for 4; sanctuary as 4; and waiting 198
resourcefulness 64
resources 250
reventia loci (inviolability of holy territory) 121
rhetoric 92, 95–96; anti-immigration 98; anti-terrorist 227; religious 98
Ridgley, J. 11
rights: asylum 135, 156; citizens' 49; civil 225, 228; deprivation of 159; foreigners' 149; immigrant 8, 82, 85, 87, 92, 110; individual 157, 178; mobility 177; respecting 178; right to have 49, 51, 52, 196; sanctuary 29, 48, 50; sovereign 51; unconditional 66; unique 157; violations 179, *see also* human rights
Romero House 162, 166, 168–69
Romero, O. 162
routine 201, 234
Rwanda 248

safe haven 3, 7, 227; statutory 247–48
safe houses 162
safe third countries 136
Safe Third Country Agreement (Canada-US) 242
safety 35, 233, 241; reframing 241–42
Sammon, Fr. P. 212, 214
San Francisco 11, 205, 224–26; Board of Supervisors 207
San Francisco Catholic Archdiocese's Catholic Social Service 206–9
San Francisco Sanctuary Covenant 208–9, 210
sanctuary movement: Canada 235–36; Central American 44, 75–81; church 148–60; criminalizing 224; faith-based 219; German 9; grassroots 11; heterogeneity of 46; historical context 75–76; history 94–95; international exchange 139; legacies 8, 73, 82–86, 105; limitations 195; organizational structure 140; San Francisco 206–9; transnational 73, 76–81; USA 8, 32, 75–81, 206–16, 223–24, *see also* new sanctuary movement
Sangatte 7, 57; routes through 63–64
sans-papiers (without papers) 7, 64–66
screening 52, 165
scripture 99, 221
Scully, M. 254
security: defining 249; international 245; national 112, 180, 227, 228; post-9/11 attack 251
security agenda 227–28
security policies 58
self 149, 155
self-criticism 255
self-expression 151
self-transformation 62
senescence: liability of 109, 116
Sensenbrenner Bill (USA) 99, 110
SHARE Foundation 86
Sheffield 10, 192–95
Shoemaker, K. 6
slavery 100
slaves 23
smuggling 63, 64, 224
social movement 173; age 116; faith-based 44, 228; strategy 107, 108–10; tactics 108–10; USA 2
social movement organizations 109
social movement theory 88
social services 85
soldiers: deserters 36; war resisters 221

solidarity 64–66, 238; act of 123; groups 8, 237; international 232; philosophy 7; practices of 197; sanctuary as 5
sovereignty 4; challenging 185; and civil disobedience 180; and deterrence 6; disrupting 50, 51; expression of 48; and foreigners' rights 149; infringing 17; and law 179; loss of 179; pockets of 186; popular 179, 180; questioning 156–58; reinforcing 7; relocating 172; resisting 127; territorial 43, 45, 50; undermining 132
space: alternative 241–42; apolitical 50; border-spanning 240; of exception 50; holy 125, 127, 128, 131–32; political 50; redefined 233; sacred 36, 45, 171; safe 80; urban 200
speech: freedom of 223
spiritual sanctuary 96
Squire, V. 10
state: capacity 248; care of nation 61; challenging 183; and church 123–24, 126, 132, 171, 177, 185; conflict with 141; discourse 7, 52; failure 251; inclusionary systems 3; international action 249; opposing 133; and people 51; power 50, 175–76; and religion 132; system 246; transcending 59; violence 75; within a state 172
status 194; official 192–93, *see also* legal status
Stenvaag, H. 9
stereotypes 30, 154
Stop Our Ship 221
stories: questioning 183; refugee 94, 148, 149–51; undocumented immigrants 97, 99, *see also* narrative
storytelling 153; public 93
strangers 99, 155; protecting 144; responsibility to 30, 37
strategy 107, 108–10; political 219; sanctuary as 168–69; spatial 234
suffering 38, 154
superstition 17
survival 78
Sweden 129–31
symbolic sanctuary 125, 170–72
sympathy 53; moral 63
synagogues 107

tactics 108–9, 114
temporality 152, 197

Temporary Protected Status 4, 83
terrorism 252; September 11th attack 227, 251; War on Terror 227
terrorists 246; locating 254
testimony 59, 78, 207, 211; refugee 80, 94
Third World Resource Centre 237
time: importance (Germany) 152; politics 197, 201, 202
torture 96, 142, 151; state 34
transformation 5, 43
transportation 98
trust 213
truths: bumper-sticker 245
Turkey 149
typologies (sanctuary) 44–48, 54

uncertainty 198, 199
Underground Railroad 98, 111, 162, 235; overground terminus 164
United Kingdom (UK): asylum claims 63; sanctuary justifications 29–31; Sheffield 10, 192–95
United Nations Convention Relating to the Status of Refugees 142
United States of America (USA): asylum claims 112; asylum system 82–83; Berkeley (California) 46, 219, 223; Department of Homeland Security 112; Detroit Sanctuary Coalition 237; Detroit/Windsor Refugee Coalition 11, 232, 237, 241; foreign policy 76, 78, 94, 235, 246; Illegal Immigration Reform and Immigrant Responsibility Act 82; immigration law 82–84, 112; Immigration Reform and Control Act 225; justifications 32–35; Moakley-Deconcini legislation 82; New York City 226–27; Northern California Sanctuary Churches 209; Occupy Wall Street 39; Refugee Act (1980) 32, 34; Safe Third Country Agreement 242; sanctuary movement 8, 32, 75–81, 206–16, 223–24; sanctuary practices 7–9, 45; self-criticism 255; Sensenbrenner Bill (USA) 99, 110; social movement 2; violence by 253; Windsor Central American Refugee Network 237, *see also* Immigration and Naturalization Service (USA); San Francisco
urban collectives 191
urban context 193

Le Vacher, R. 21
victims: contact with 80; innocent 53, 81, 88
Vietnam War 221, 222
violence 18, 227; of abstraction 185; against asylum-seekers 136; by police 137; by United States 253; fleeing 107; state 75; targets of 248
visibility 3, 6, 159, 234, 239, 242
voices: hearing 29–37; immigrant 94
volunteering 191, 193, 199; and everyday life 200

Wagner, F.W. 156–57
waiting 192, 197–200; and resistance 198; routines of 201
Walker, N. 207–8, 211
war 159, 207, 253; complex 246; illegal 223; Iraq War 36; resisters 36, 221, 222; witnessing 211
War on Terror 227
Ward, D. 211
William, the Conqueror 15, 18–19
Williams, N. 10
Windsor Central American Refugee Network 237
witness 96
women 22, 53, 124, 125
work: right to 198
workers: migrant 32
worthiness 194

Young, J. 11
Yukich, G. 8